Sexualities in the Works
of Joss Whedon

ALSO OF INTEREST FROM MCFARLAND

*Blood Relations: Chosen Families
in* Buffy the Vampire Slayer *and* Angel
Jes Battis, 2005

The Aesthetics of Culture in Buffy the Vampire Slayer
Matthew Pateman, 2006

*The Existential Joss Whedon: Evil and Human Freedom
in* Buffy the Vampire Slayer, Angel, Firefly *and* Serenity
J. Michael Richardson and J. Douglas Rabb, 2007

Faith and Choice in the Works of Joss Whedon
K. Dale Koontz, 2008

The Truth of Buffy: *Essays on Fiction Illuminating Reality*
Edited by Emily Dial-Driver, Sally Emmons-Featherston,
Jim Ford and Carolyn Anne Taylor, 2008

*Buffy Goes Dark: Essays on the Final Two Seasons
of* Buffy the Vampire Slayer *on Television*
Edited by Lynne Y. Edwards, Elizabeth L. Rambo
and James B. South, 2009

Buffy and Angel Conquer the Internet: Essays on Online Fandom
Edited by Mary Kirby-Diaz, 2009

Buffy Meets the Academy: Essays on the Episodes and Scripts as Texts
Edited by Kevin K. Durand, 2009

Sexual Rhetoric in the Works of Joss Whedon: New Essays
Edited by Erin B. Waggoner, 2010

Buffy in the Classroom: Essays on Teaching with the Vampire Slayer
Edited by Jodie A. Kreider and Meghan K. Winchell, 2010

The Literary Angel: *Essays on Influences
and Traditions Reflected in the Joss Whedon Series*
Edited by AmiJo Comeford and Tamy Burnett, 2010

Cult Telefantasy Series: A Critical Analysis of The Prisoner,
Twin Peaks, The X-Files, Buffy the Vampire Slayer, Lost,
Heroes, Doctor Who *and* Star Trek
Sue Short, 2011

Power and Control in the Television Worlds of Joss Whedon
Sherry Ginn, 2012

Buffy and the Heroine's Journey: Vampire Slayer as Feminine Chosen One
Valerie Estelle Frankel, 2012

*Joss Whedon and Religion: Essays on an Angry Atheist's
Explorations of the Sacred*
Edited by Anthony R. Mills, John W. Morehead and J. Ryan Parker, 2013

The Comics of Joss Whedon: Critical Essays
Edited by Valerie Estelle Frankel, 2015

*Joss Whedon as Shakespearean Moralist: Narrative Ethics
of the Bard and the Buffyverse*
J. Douglas Rabb and J. Michael Richardson, 2015

At Home in the Whedonverse: Essays on Domestic Place, Space and Life
Edited by Juliette C. Kitchens, 2017

Joss Whedon and Race: Critical Essays
Edited by Mary Ellen Iatropoulos and Lowery A. Woodall III, 2017

WORLDS OF WHEDON SERIES

Joss Whedon Versus the Corporation:
Big Business Critiqued in the Films and Television Programs.
Erin Giannini. 2017

Joss Whedon's Big Damn Movie: Essays on Serenity.
Edited by Frederick Blichert. 2018

The Whedonverse Catalog:
A Complete Guide to Works in All Media.
Don Macnaughtan. 2018

Joss Whedon, Anarchist?
A Unified Theory of the Films and Television Series.
James Rocha and Mona Rocha. 2019

Sexualties in the Works of Joss Whedon.
Lewis Call. 2020

Sexualities in the Works of Joss Whedon

Lewis Call

Foreword by Mary Ellen Iatropoulos

Worlds of Whedon
Series Editor Sherry Ginn

McFarland & Company, Inc., Publishers
Jefferson, North Carolina

This book has undergone peer review.

Library of Congress Cataloguing-in-Publication Data

Names: Call, Lewis, author.
Title: Sexualities in the works of Joss Whedon / Lewis Call ; foreword by Mary Ellen Iatropoulos.
Description: Jefferson : McFarland & Company, Inc., Publishers, 2020. | Series: Worlds of Whedon | Includes bibliographical references and index.
Identifiers: LCCN 2020015009 | ISBN 9781476675060 (paperback) ♾
ISBN 9781476639956 (ebook)
Subjects: LCSH: Whedon, Joss, 1964–Criticism and interpretation. | Sex on television. | Sex in motion pictures. | Sexual minorities on television. | Sexual minorities in motion pictures. | Sex role on television. | Sex role in motion pictures.
Classification: LCC PN1992.4.W49 C35 2020 | DDC 791.45/75093538—dc23
LC record available at https://lccn.loc.gov/2020015009

British Library cataloguing data are available

ISBN (print) 978-1-4766-7506-0
ISBN (ebook) 978-1-4766-3995-6

© 2020 Lewis Call. All rights reserved

No part of this book may be reproduced or transmitted in any form or by any means, electronic or mechanical, including photocopying or recording, or by any information storage and retrieval system, without permission in writing from the publisher.

Front Cover: Spike (James Marsters) and Buffy (Sarah Michelle Gellar) negotiate their DS relationship in *Buffy the Vampire Slayer*, 2001 (UPN/Photofest)

Printed in the United States of America

McFarland & Company, Inc., Publishers
Box 611, Jefferson, North Carolina 28640
www.mcfarlandpub.com

For Kate and Rory
"Slayers, every one of us"

Acknowledgments

Small portions of this book appeared previously, in substantially different form, in *Slayage: The Journal of Whedon Studies* and in *Marvel's Black Widow from Spy to Superhero: Essays on an Avenger with a Very Specific Skill Set* (McFarland, 2017). I thank Rhonda Wilcox and McFarland for permission to reprint revised versions of this material.

Over the past decade, I have presented various bits and pieces of this book at Slayage: The Biennial Conference on the Whedonverses and in "The Works of Joss Whedon" area at the Southwest Popular and American Culture Association Conference. I have benefited tremendously from the conversations I've had with other conference attendees, and I thank them for discussing, debating, critiquing, chatting, eating, drinking, laughing, crying, singing, doing tai chi, and hanging out in airports with me.

I thank Cal Poly and the members of the College of Liberal Arts Professional Leave Committee for granting me a sabbatical leave in the fall of 2018, which gave me time to finish the manuscript.

Most of all, I thank Michelle for spending countless hours watching all things Whedonesque with me, holding my hand during the sad and scary bits, and giving me the inspiration to do this work.

Contents

Acknowledgments	viii
Foreword by Mary Ellen Iatropoulos	1
Preface: "Kinky Business"	5
Introduction: "Love Dares You"	9
One. "It's About Power": The Rise of the Whedonesque Dominant Woman, or Whedomme	39
Two. "Love Keeps Her in the Air": Radical Sexual Pluralism Aboard Firefly *Serenity*	61
Three. "The Breakable Ones": Disabled Sexualities in Joss Whedon's Superhero Narratives	87
Four. "Majestic Creature of Legend": Human/Animal Hybridity and Zoophilia in the Buffyverse	112
Five. "The Hammer Is My Penis": Queer and Heteronormative Sexualities in *Dr. Horrible's Sing-Along Blog*	135
Six. "They Want to See Us Punished": Subverting the Sexual Tropes of the Slasher Film in *The Cabin in the Woods*	156
Seven. "To Bind Me, or Undo Me": Dominance and Submission in Joss Whedon's *Much Ado About Nothing*	178
Afterword: Reconsidering Whedonversal Sexualities in the #MeToo Era	203
Chapter Notes	207
Bibliography	211
Index	227

Foreword
by Mary Ellen Iatropoulos

I first met Lewis Call when I interrupted his conference presentation in February of 2009, in Albuquerque, New Mexico. It happened during the final session of the final day of that year's Southwest/Texas Popular Culture Association conference. My then-boyfriend (and, happily, now-husband) and I had just come from outside of the Hyatt Regency, posing for pictures with the sidewalk statues just beyond the hotel's northwestern entrance. At some point, we realized we had lost track of time. We were already late to the last session! We'd been looking forward to attending a specific panel, too, one called "Maturity and Sexuality in the Whedonverses," so we decided to make a run for it. We sprinted inside and up the gold-carpeted stairs, looking for the room called Fiesta 4. Once found, we tried to enter quietly, but of course, since a presentation was underway, the room was silent except for the speaker. Just opening the door was embarrassingly loud. Everyone's heads whipped around towards us, made all the more mortifying by the fact that this was my very first conference. Throughout the three-day conference, I'd been awash with anxiety over my inexperience with the etiquette, yet there I was, daring to crash into a session, panting and sweating from the sprint. I had blown it for sure.

The presenter, however, remained unfazed. We slunk guiltily to some open seats in the back, and he continued laying out his ideas. He spoke of how heteronormativity operates in *Buffy the Vampire Slayer*, and how the show offers several visions of alternative sexualities that portray the alternative sexualities in a positive light. Within moments, we were spellbound. This presenter had a uniquely engaging manner: friendly and knowledgeable, with something of a scientist's certainty in reading data to arrive at plausible conclusions. He persuasively argued his points, but he wasn't argumentative, maintaining a cordial but purposeful tone, like a guide walking the audience through the woods of his thinking. And yet, that description seems almost too wholesome, because the topics he discussed were, themselves, what certain parts of society would consider scandalous, things like female orgasms and zoophilia. With every point he made about "slaying the heteronormative," you could see the subversive twinkle in his eye.

Once the presenter began discussing Centaur-Dawn, I knew we would wind up being friends. He flipped to a slide featuring an image from the Dark Horse *BTVS* Season Eight comics, specifically the cover of "Time of Your Life: Part Three." Readers of the comic may recall this oil-painting-esque portrait of Dawn as a centaur, in which she stretches provocatively and looks the reader straight in the eye, long strands of hair barely covering her nipples serving to accentuate her voluptuous human nudity from the waist up. I knew the cover well, as now-husband and I had talked about Centaur-Dawn in detail when we were reading the Season Eight comics. The topic of sexy centaurs in science fiction has been fair game for conversation ever since we both read John Varley's *Titan* series when we started dating. The second book in the series, *Wizard*, features horse-human hybrids who coexist and interact with humans, so when it came up in the *Buffy* comics, we couldn't help but start comparing/contrasting the two narratives.

And sure enough, the presenter soon flipped to another image, a panel sequence featuring Xander standing near Centaur-Dawn as she wrings out her hair. The presenter described how the image of a sexualized horse-human hybrid challenges heteronormativity, how Xander's obvious confusion and shame at finding Dawn sexy in horse-form hits all the harder because we, the readers, may be feeling confusion or shame while gazing at a sexy centaur, too. As if on cue, the presenter then said, "I mean, I haven't seen centaurs depicted in such a strongly sexualized manner since John Varley!" Now-husband and I gasped with delight at the reference, and the presenter nodded in our direction, recognizing shared fandom. "Right?"

The presenter, of course, was Lewis Call, a brilliant scholar whom I am now proud to call my friend. While he may or may not recall that day the same way I do, I love revisiting the Albuquerque memory in the context of writing this foreword, because this magnificent book you now hold in your hands includes an in-depth discussion of Centaur-Dawn. Ten years have passed since that conference, and throughout that time Lewis has mapped the relationships between sex, power, and ethics via expression of alternative sexualities all across the Whedonverses, turning his critical eye to *Dollhouse*, then to Black Widow, then to Beatrice and Benedick. *Sexualities in the Works of Joss Whedon* compiles years of research and similarly stimulating conference presentations into a comprehensive and cohesive piece, creating an authoritative text that will inform Whedon Studies for years to come. Because while Lewis' academic analyses are astute and his arguments compelling, the greatest pleasure of this book lies in just that: pleasure. It feels good to revisit and re-examine the sexiest parts of the lives of the characters we love. This book shows us (perhaps "uncloset" would be a better term) deep, rich layers of meaning behind those scenes that move us, the quotes which stick in our brains. Revisiting them through the lens of this book, we experience them anew as the sexy, sexy stories they are.

Yet pleasure is not the only reason why this book is an engaging and important read. An equally compelling (though far less pleasant) reason for this book's importance is that we, as a society, desperately need more thoughtful, reflective discussion of the relationship between sex, power, and ethics in general, let alone discussion with such succinct and accessible language as is Lewis' calling card. For better and for worse, recent times have provided multiple examples of how the relationship between sex, power, and ethics has never been murkier, never been more incendiary, never been more prevalent a guiding force in shaping political reality than it is in our world today. On one hand, America has a president who has spewed such vulgarities about women that I don't even want to repeat them here. On the other, in the wake of #MeToo, entertainment industry tycoons who built their businesses on sexual harassment are finally being brought to justice. The LGBTQIA community is more visible than ever, and yet suicide rates for queer and trans youth continue to be unacceptably high. Even the chief subject of this book, the problematic auteur Joss Whedon himself, has gotten into hot water regarding the question of sex, power, and ethics.

I could go on forever listing examples of how these intersecting issues impact each of us in ways big and small. That's why the pragmatic utility of this book matters as well. Each chapter thoughtfully lays out an in-depth close reading of some aspect(s) of the Whedonverses conducted alongside application of various critical theories, subtly modeling patterns of inquiry and analysis readers can pick up and use to slay the heteronormative elsewhere in their worlds.

Now more than ever we need accessible frameworks for deconstructing, analyzing, and understanding the nuanced dynamics between sex, power, and ethics to support us as we experience and negotiate our roles as fans of fictional worlds and as citizens of the real world. The timely and invaluable *Sexualities in the Works of Joss Whedon* provides the world of Whedon Studies precisely that. I trust it will be as good for you as it was for me.

Mary Ellen Iatropoulos is an award-winning author and educator who has thrice won the Mr. Pointy Award for Best Work in Whedon Studies. She co-edited Joss Whedon and Race: Critical Essays *(McFarland, 2017). She works as director of education for The Art Effect, a nonprofit focussing on student empowerment through visual and media arts, and oversees youth media arts curricula and workforce development programs for thousands of students annually.*

Preface:
"Kinky Business"

The American screenwriter, director, producer, composer, librettist, and comic book writer Joss Whedon (b. 1964) creates films, shows, musicals, and comics that show a strong commitment not only to gender equality, but also to sexual equality. Ever since *Buffy the Vampire Slayer* debuted on television in 1997, Whedon's works have encouraged their audiences to love whomever and however they wish. For two decades, these works have consistently conveyed the message that the shape of someone's sexuality should be determined by the form of their desire, not by the arbitrary conventions of our frequently heteronormative society.

Whedon and his co-creators have done a great deal to promote various non-normative sexualities. Whedon's worlds (sometimes called "Whedonverses") have provided particularly powerful positive portrayals of lesbian, gay, and queer sexualities; this is especially true of the world depicted in the *Buffy* and *Angel* shows and comics (sometimes called the "Buffyverse"). Although bisexuality and transgender sexuality have been less visible, that has begun to change in more recent works like *Runaways* and *Dollhouse*. The Whedonverses also offer sympathetic representations of such controversial sexual practices as BDSM, fetishism, and sex work. Whedon's works support the sexuality of disabled people. These works even sanction certain forms of intergenerational desire, incestuous desire, and zoophilia, while carefully discouraging unethical expressions of those dangerous but very human desires. The Whedonverses advocate a philosophy of sexuality that is provocative, yet surprisingly simple and ultimately compelling. That philosophy holds that all consensual, desired sexualities are ethical and should therefore be celebrated, while sexualities that lack consent or desire must be resisted.

The Whedonverses' sympathetic representations of non-normative sexualities are revolutionary. They have had a profound impact on American popular culture, and on the society that consumes that culture. Some queer people have found that the sexualities of Whedon's fictional characters helped them come to terms with their own sexuality. Some have been able to come out of the closet because of Whedon's works (see, for example, Lavery and Burkhead 75). Ever since Buffy Summers emerged as an icon of third wave "girlie" feminism in the late 1990s (Baumgardner and Richards 135), a great deal has been written about the ways in which Whedon's works have empowered girls and women. Much less has been written about how Whedon's works have empowered queers, non-normative straights, and anyone else whose sexuality fails, in some way, to conform to arbitrary cultural norms—which is to say, almost everyone. That is why I wrote this book.

I first encountered the works of Joss Whedon in the early 2000s, when my best friend, Professor Kurt Depner of New Mexico State University, told me that I absolutely had to watch a show called *Buffy the Vampire Slayer*. I replied, approximately, "you have got to be kidding." I later learned that Joss Whedon had chosen the name Buffy—had insisted on it, actually—precisely to show that a tiny blonde woman with a ridiculous name could turn out to be the strongest person in the world, and to prove that a show bearing this ludicrous name could have important things to say. Despite my reservations, I watched *Buffy*. I loved *Buffy*. I developed a healthy addiction to *Buffy*. I binge watched it with my wife Michelle when she was on bedrest, pregnant with Kate, one of the kids to whom this book is dedicated. At around four in the morning, when Buffy and her friends suddenly burst into song in "Once More with Feeling" (6.7), we thought we were hallucinating, but in a good way. When we ran out of *Buffy*, we turned to Whedon's other works, and found in them the same love of story and structure, the same commitment to character, the same witty dialogue, the same progressive portrayals of gender and sexuality. I became a Whedon fan. I watched all his shows, went to all his movies, read all his comic books. Though I didn't know it at the time, I was doing primary source research, making my initial pass through the archive of sources that would one day form the foundation of this book.

I soon realized that I wanted to become that unique hybrid creature of the postmodern age, the scholar/fan. Luckily, I'm an intellectual and cultural historian, so this is not as outrageous as it might seem. I knew I wanted to write about sexuality. What fascinated me most about *Buffy* was the show's bold, honest, innovative representations of alternative sexualities, especially dominance and submission (DS), and very especially the DS relationship that Buffy and Spike developed in *Buffy*'s sixth season. "Sounds like kinky business to me," as Anya (a dominant straight woman) said to Andrew (a closeted gay man) in "Storyteller" (*Buffy* 7.16). I wrote a paper about it. I nervously submitted it to *Slayage: The Online International Journal of Buffy Studies* (as it was then called). To my surprise and delight, they published it. To my astonishment and even greater delight, it won the 2007 "short" Mr. Pointy award. I had spoken about sexuality in the Buffyverse, and someone had heard me.

I realized that I had not only found a lot of great TV shows to watch and the most enjoyable research field I had ever encountered, though that would have been plenty. I had found a community. I dove in, headfirst. Since 2009, I have presented almost every year in "The Works of Joss Whedon" area at the Southwest Popular and American Culture Association conference. Since 2012, I have presented every other year at the biennial Slayage Conference on the Whedonverses. At the 2014 Slayage conference at Sacramento State University, I was honored to share the Mr. Pointy paper award with Stephanie Graves, whose brilliant critique of gender representation in *The Avengers* was the perfect counterpoint to my reading of Black Widow as a sexually dominant woman. At the 2016 Slayage conference at Kingston University, I extended my reading to include Black Widow's DS relationship with Bruce Banner/Hulk. I grouped the Widow with other dominant women like *Firefly*'s Zoë, *Dollhouse*'s Echo, and *Agents of S.H.I.E.L.D.*'s Melinda May. When I proposed to call these Whedonesque dominant women "Whedommes," my proposal was met with what I hope and believe to be the good kind of laughter: Whedon Studies, as it is now called, is all about doing serious scholarly work and having fun while you do it. Everyone was "shocked, shocked!" when, at the 2018 Slayage conference at the University of North Alabama, I read Beatrice and Benedick from Whedon's *Much Ado About Nothing* as a DS relationship. My fellow Whedonists know where my obsessions lie. They will have heard many of the arguments in this book before, though I hope these arguments are more nuanced now, for I have benefited tremendously from my colleagues' comments and critiques. Any remaining errors or outlandish interpretations are, of course, my own.

This book covers representations of sexualities across all the genres and media that Whedon has called his home. I believe that generic diversity is a vital aspect of Whedon's work, and that his multiple media are part of his message. The stories that he tells about the myriad forms of human sexual love need to be told in every popular genre and medium, so that every audience can hear them. I discuss Whedon's TV shows, especially *Buffy* and *Firefly*, at length. I analyze his comic books, especially *Buffy* and *X-Men*, but also *Firefly* and *Dr. Horrible*. I look at his horror film (*The Cabin in the Woods*), his superhero films (*The Avengers* and *Avengers: Age of Ultron*), and his cinematic adaptation of Shakespearean comedy (*Much Ado About Nothing*). I investigate his experiment with the form of the film musical (*Dr. Horrible's Sing-Along Blog*). This book does not contain substantial discussions of *Angel* or *Dollhouse*. That is not because I regard these shows as unimportant—quite the contrary—but rather because I have already said what I wanted to say, about BDSM in *Angel* and consensual sexual play-slavery in *Dollhouse*, in my previous book, *BDSM in American Science Fiction and Fantasy* (Call, BDSM Chapters Six and Seven).

I am certainly not the first to recognize the importance of the Whedonverses' representations of sexuality. I am indebted to those who came before me, upon whose work this book intends to build. I stand on the shoulders of—not giants, but rather, perhaps unsurprisingly, powerful women who are often of less than average height. The first significant book-length work on sexuality in the Whedonverses was Lorna Jowett's *Sex and the Slayer*, published in 2005 by Joss Whedon's alma mater, Wesleyan. This early work looked exclusively at *Buffy*, and while it offered crucial insights into *Buffy*'s queer destabilization of sexual binaries, it focused more on gender in the Buffyverse, which was still an under-researched area at that time. In 2010, McFarland published *Sexual Rhetoric in the Works of Joss Whedon* (ed. Erin B. Waggoner), which broadened the discussion to include Whedon's other works. This multi-author collection brought many important voices into the conversation, including those of Hèléne Frohard-Dourlent, Alyson Buckman, Patricia Pender, Don Tresca, and Tamy Burnett. More recently, the 2017 special issue of *Slayage: The Journal of Whedon Studies* on "Queering the Whedonverses," guest edited by Jowett and Frohard-Dourlent, added significant discussion of queer representations in a variety of Whedon's texts, including some of the newest ones.

Sexualities in the Works of Joss Whedon differs from these earlier works in three principal ways. First, I consider the broad arc of Whedon's two-decade career, from the beginning of *Buffy*'s first season in 1997 through the conclusion of its twelfth (comic book) season in 2018. Second, I discuss each unique sexuality in more depth and detail than is possible in a single essay. Third, and perhaps most significantly, I look not only at the better-known queer sexualities of the LGBTQ+ spectrum, but also at lesser-known non-normative sexualities such as BDSM, fetishism, disabled sexuality, sex work, and intergenerational sexuality. Those who practice these minority sexualities still struggle to gain even the limited recognition and respect that the LGBTQ+ community has, after tremendous struggle, finally achieved. It is my sincere hope that members of these most marginalized sexual minorities may gain some hope and pride from Joss Whedon's sympathetic portrayals of their practices, and from this book's analysis of those depictions.

Introduction:
"Love Dares You"

This book is a history of the sexualities that have flourished in the fictional worlds that Joss Whedon and his many collaborators have created. Whedon's works offer important, realistic, empathetic depictions of non-normative sexual desires, practices, and lifestyles. The groundbreaking *Buffy the Vampire Slayer* (1997–2003) gave American network television its longest lesbian relationship (Warn), its longest lesbian kiss (Lavery 180), and its first lesbian sex scene (Frost).[1] Whedon's works also offer progressive representations of disabled sexuality, sex work, intergenerational sexuality, BDSM, and various forms of fetishism. These works represent non-normative sexualities in ways that offer substantial psychological benefits to audience members who practice those sexualities. For example, Collier et al. found that *Buffy*'s depictions of lesbianism gave lesbian viewers increased self esteem, more positive perceptions of their sexualities, and support for the development of healthy lesbian identities (597–598).

Sexualities in the Works of Joss Whedon argues that since *Buffy* debuted on American television in 1997, Joss Whedon's works have generally promoted a diverse, inclusive, and pluralist sexual culture. This culture is founded upon a system of sexual ethics which derives from the three interrelated principles of consent, desire, and trust. In the Whedonverses, sex is considered ethical if and only if all participants consent actively to it, genuinely desire it, and trust one another to do it responsibly. Representations of sexualities in the Whedonverses are, for the most part, feminist. Whedon's works promote women's sexual agency. Thus, *The Cabin in the Woods* critiques the slasher film's practice of punishing young women who exercise such agency, while *Dr. Horrible* shows that when men try to make a woman's sexual choices for her, the result is disastrous.

My historical analysis shows that the Whedonverses' representations of queer sexualities become more inclusive and more explicit over time. Lesbianism came first, in the groundbreaking relationship between Willow

(Alyson Hannigan) and Tara (Amber Benson) in *Buffy* seasons 4–6, then in the more sexualized relationship between Willow and Kennedy (Iyari Limon) in seasons 7–8, then in the highly sexualized relationship between Willow and the demon sorceress Aluwyn in seasons 8–10 (see, for example, Whedon and Moline). Gay male sexuality was almost entirely subtextual in the televised Buffyverse, although there was a good deal of homoeroticism between Angel (David Boreanaz) and Spike (James Marsters) on *Buffy* and *Angel*. The first significant out gay man in the Whedonverses was *Buffy* season nine's Billy the Vampire Slayer (Espenson, Greenberg, and Moline, 2012). The second was Andrew; when Andrew finally came out to the Scoobies in 2015, they accepted his gayness as part of their sexual culture (Gage, Brendon, and Levens; Call, "Find What Warmth" ¶ 17). Bisexuality has remained mostly invisible in the Whedonverses; although characters like Buffy and Willow have sex with both men and women, bisexuality is not presented as an option for them. Transgender sexuality has also been mostly invisible. However, Whedon's *Runaways* comics (2007–2008) do include a trans relationship, and on *Dollhouse* (2009–2010), minds could be imprinted onto bodies without regard to gender, which permitted a few brief expressions of transgender sexuality. Whedon's works do not represent all queer sexualities equally, but the ones that are shown are generally portrayed in affirming ways.

However, these representations are hardly perfect; the Whedonverses can sometimes be heteronormative and even homophobic. This was particularly true on the *Buffy* show, which was produced in an American network television culture that refused to show even something as innocuous as a kiss between two lesbians in a stable, monogamous, mostly de-sexualized relationship (Lavery and Burkhead 11). *Buffy* directs a good deal of homophobia towards the closeted Andrew (Tom Lenk) (Greenwood ¶ 17). Much of this comes from Andrew himself, who performs the stereotype of the closeted, homophobic gay man (Pender 122). The vast majority of intimate relationships in the Buffyverse are heterosexual. Characters typically assume that this is the natural order of things; in other words, they propagate heteronormativity. *Buffy* and Whedon's other works do privilege non-normative dominance/submission (DS) relationships, but almost all of these are straight relationships. An interesting exception is Xander's homoerotic DS relationship with Dracula, which develops extensively in *Buffy*'s season ten; this relationship is presented as consensual and mutually satisfying (Call, "Find What Warmth" ¶ 18–20).

In the Whedonverses, representations of non-normative sexuality that fall outside the LGBTQ+ spectrum are genuinely innovative, authentically unique, and frequently empowering. The Buffyverse has always shown sympathy for zoophilic desire, by demonstrating that humans can love werewolves like Oz (Seth Green), or centaurs like Dawn in *Buffy* season eight (Whedon and Moline). Whedon's superhero narratives suggest that heroes who experience their superpowers as physical impairments can have successful sexual relationships, as Kitty Pryde does with Peter Rasputin, Scott Summers does with Emma Frost, and Bruce Banner does with Natasha Romanoff. *Firefly* legitimizes fetishism via Jayne's (Adam Baldwin) love of guns and Kaylee's (Jewel Staite) love of engines. Both *Firefly* and *Dollhouse* suggest that while sex work can sometimes be exploitative, it can also be consensual, ethical, and rewarding. Whedon's comics support sexual relationships in which the partners' ages differ by up to a decade (Kitty/Peter, Xander/Dawn).

Throughout this book, whenever I speak of the works of Joss Whedon, I mean the works of Whedon and his many creative collaborators. Whedon puts his personal stamp on everything he works on, so it is tempting to treat him as an *auteur* (Lavery 25). Yet as David Kociemba and Mary Ellen Iatropoulos point out, Whedon Studies problematizes auteurism, for the veneration of a single author masks the feedback loops of collaborative creation (43–44). As David Lavery notes, Whedon works in inherently collaborative media like TV, film, and comics, so his creative achievements are not solely his own, and he is unfailingly magnanimous in his praise of those who work with him (139–140). Any discussion of Whedon's works must therefore also be a discussion of his co-creators.

Foremost among Whedon's collaborators are the following highly creative individuals, all of whom have made significant contributions to the Whedonverses' portrayals of sexualities. Feminist writer/producer Marti Noxon joined *Buffy* in the show's second season, wrote several key episodes about werewolf sexuality, became showrunner in season six, and initiated the Buffy/Spike relationship. Writer/producer Jane Espenson is a major advocate for the LGBTQ+ community. She wrote the *Buffy* episode that hinted most strongly at Andrew's gay sexuality ("Storyteller" 7.16), and the *Firefly* episode that established most clearly the power that Inara (Morena Baccarin) holds as a sex worker ("Shindig" 1.6). Drew Goddard wrote the *Angel* episode that most strongly highlights the homoerotics of Angel/Spike ("The Girl in Question" 5.20) and the *Buffy* comics that feature Buffy's same-gender liaison with Satsu (Goddard and Jeanty). Goddard co-wrote (with Whedon) and directed *The Cabin in the Woods*. Whedon's brother Jed and Jed's wife Maurissa Tancharoen co-wrote (with Joss and Zack Whedon) *Dr. Horrible*'s critique of modern masculine sexualities. Jed Whedon and Tancharoen later served as showrunners for *Agents of S.H.I.E.L.D.* Joss Whedon's brother Zack wrote important *Dr. Horrible* and *Firefly* comics. Actor Nathan Fillion played a terrifying misogynist preacher on *Buffy*, a likeable dominant man (rare in the Whedonverses) on *Firefly*, and the hegemonically masculine Captain Hammer in *Dr. Horrible*. Fran Kranz played *Dollhouse*'s ethically challenged programmer Topher, *Cabin*'s heroic stoner Marty, and *Much Ado*'s jealous lover Claudio. Scarlett Johansson made Natasha Romanoff into a dominant woman in *Avengers* and *Age of Ultron* and continues to perform the character in that same spirit even in films not made by Whedon. For example, in *The Winter Soldier* (Anthony Russo and Joe Russo 2014), Johansson uses Natasha's playful, flirtatious dominance to establish the character's political and professional authority with respect to Captain America (Chris Evans), a very masculine character whose authority is unquestioned in every other context. This testifies to the broader influence Whedon has had on representations of sexuality.

"All of Sexuality Is a Spectrum": The Queer Feminist Pluralism of the Whedonverses

The Whedonverses reflect the culture of sexual pluralism that sex radicals such as the cultural anthropologist Gayle Rubin and the transgender activist Pat Califia have been fighting for since the 1980s. In the early '80s, Rubin famously argued that "modern Western societies appraise sex acts according to a hierarchical system of sexual value" which privileges a "Charmed Circle" of heterosexual, marital, monogamous, reproductive, and non-commercial sex as natural and normal ("Thinking Sex" 279–281). At the opposite end of the sexual hierarchy stands the "Outer Limits" of marginalized, devalued, and prohibited practices such as homosexual, unmarried, promiscuous, non-procreative, commercial, sadomasochistic, fetishistic, and intergenerational sex (Rubin, "Thinking Sex" 281). As an alternative to this sex hierarchy, Rubin called for a "pluralistic sexual ethics," a "concept of benign sexual variation," and a "democratic morality" that would judge sexualities "by the way partners treat one another, the level of mutual consideration, the presence or absence of coercion, and the quantity and quality of the pleasures they provide" ("Thinking Sex" 283). In short, Rubin sketched out a philosophy of sexual ethics based on the triple principles of consent, desire, and trust. Rubin recognized that "smaller, more stigmatized" sexual communities such as sadomasochists were especially vulnerable to persecution ("Leather Menace" 195). Rubin's fellow sex radical Pat Califia called for a "broad coalition" of people who share "a common identity as *sadomasochists*" ("Personal View" 271). Califia also argued that sadomasochists should reach out to members of other stigmatized sexual minorities ("Personal View" 251). By the late '80s, the broad coalition of sexual minorities which Rubin and Califia envisioned had materialized. Lynda Hart points out that as alternative sexualities came under fire from the New Right during the '80s, this assault "enabled a certain (often uneasy) coalition among these disparate groups" (38).

The "sex wars" which raged within the American feminist community throughout the 1980s provided sexual minorities with another powerful incentive for coalition-building. During the sex wars, cultural feminists argued that sadomasochism (SM), pornography, and prostitution were inherently patriarchal and oppressive, while sex radicals argued that such alternative sexual practices could be feminist and liberating. By the late '90s, the sex wars had largely "burnt themselves out" (Highleyman, "Playing with Paradox" 165). The feminist community had become more willing to accept SM and other non-normative sexualities. In 1997, just as *Buffy* was making its television debut, Liz Highleyman noted that "a more pluralistic philosophy that embraces a wider range of acceptable sexual choices for women has become the norm among feminists" ("Playing with Paradox" 165). The Buffyverse reflects the victory of the sex radicals' position, notably through Buffy's relationship with Spike. As Dee Amy-Chinn notes, the sadomasochistic Buffy/Spike relationship clearly occupies Gayle Rubin's outer limits ("Bitch" 321–322). Yet the relationship features mutual consent, desire, and trust.[2] Spike and Buffy love each other, trust one another, and provide each other with more and better sexual pleasure than either of them experience with any of their other lovers.

The Whedonverses represent a queer model of sexuality that builds upon Rubin's sexual pluralism. "I think all of sexuality is a spectrum," Whedon said in 2006, "and to say that there's the one thing and the other is to oversimplify" (Lavery and Burkhead 140). Whedon rejects the binary logic of a system which assigns sexual identities solely according to the gender of one's object choice (of which there are assumed to be only two). His position is thus fundamentally queer. Queer theory emerged in the 1980s, with a recognition that although the identity-based movements that emerged in the wake of the 1969 Stonewall rebellion gave American gays and lesbians active communities which effectively promoted an important civil rights agenda, these identity-specific communities risked becoming isolated from a larger political movement. Queer activists recognized, as Pat (now Patrick) Califia observed in 2000, that one's political allies do not have to be people who share one's identity (*Speaking Sex* 180). Califia hoped that the "heir of identity politics" could "form a chain of alliances" strong enough to withstand a social hostility towards alternative sexualities that did, sadly, outlast the twentieth century (*Speaking Sex* 78). Throughout the 1990s, queer theory effectively challenged heteronormativity; i.e., the assumption that heterosexuality was natural, normal, and desirable. Queer theorist Michael Warner rejected "a minoritizing logic of toleration … in favor of a more thorough resistance to regimes of the normal" (16). No longer content merely to advocate for the interests of individual minority sexualities, queers now waged war against the very concept of sexual normality. Queer theory confronted a heteronormative American culture with "its worst nightmare, a queer planet" (Warner 16). In the late '90s, America got to see what such a planet might look like, for the Buffyverse is just such a world. The later Whedonverses are just as queer as *Buffy*'s world, though in different ways. As Don Tresca argues, "normative sexuality is not an option; the fabric of the Whedonverse rejects it" ("Paraphilia" 146).

Queer encompasses *all* non-normative sexualities, which makes queer a majority minority: since almost everyone deviates from sexual normativity in some way, practically anyone could claim the label. Eve Kosofsky Sedgwick suggests that all it takes to make the description "queer" true is the impulse to use it in the first person (*Tendencies* 9). This raises the important possibility of the straight queer, a non-normative heterosexual with an affinity for queer people. Joss Whedon and many of his co-creators can reasonably be viewed as straight queers. They identify *with* queers, if not *as* queers. They fight against homophobia, and they work hard to promote a maximally inclusive sexual culture. "I'm super-gay," Whedon declared in a 2006 interview (Lavery and Burkhead 139). By this he seems to mean not that he has same-gender relationships, but rather that he is attracted to gay culture and aesthetics. Jane Espenson says that "gay rights is a cause close to my heart and it shows up in my writing a lot" (Broverman). Espenson has been so successful at promoting sexual diversity that although she is straight, *The Advocate*'s Jacob Anderson-Minshall named her "an honorary lesbian," a title she loves. Marti Noxon, the daughter of two lesbian mothers (Mangels), scripted some of *Buffy*'s most important queer moments, including the episode where Willow comes out as gay ("New Moon Rising" 4.19).

Although Whedon considers himself a feminist, his relationship to feminism is a matter of some controversy. Renee St. Louis and Miriam Riggs argue that despite its "alleged feminist 'mission statement'" about female empowerment, *Buffy* mainly portrays women with idealized body types who are nonessential, ignorant, and incapable of fighting the forces of evil (¶ 2 and 6). This critique has merit; by giving Buffy (Sarah Michelle Gellar) superpowers, Whedon made the human women who surround her look relatively powerless, though that changes in later seasons, when women like Willow, Anya, and Dawn develop powers of their own. On the other hand, Lauren Schultz views Whedon as "a dedicated feminist auteur whose belief in gender equality consistently and productively informs even his works that feminists find most problematic," such as *Dollhouse* (357). The question of Whedon's purported feminism cannot and need not be settled. For the purposes of my analysis, it is enough to make the hopefully uncontroversial claim that strong feminist themes appear in all of his major works. However, it is also important to note that the Whedon Studies community is reconsidering those themes in light of the argument that Whedon's former wife Kai Cole has made: that Whedon's alleged marital infidelity and gaslighting are incompatible with the feminist ideals he professes (see Afterword).

Whedon has cited his mother, "radical feminist" Lee Stearns, as "an extraordinary inspiration" (quoted in Pascale 30). The second wave feminism that Whedon learned from Stearns (and as an unofficial gender studies minor at Wesleyan) was about achieving political and economic equality for women. Whedon's work does contain strong second wave elements. For example, three of *Firefly*'s women characters pursue occupations usually coded masculine, yet this is presented as normal, and all three enjoy equal relationships with the male crew (Amy-Chinn, "Whore" 177–178). Yet for all its second wave influences, Whedon's work belongs more properly to the third wave. Patricia Pender argues that *Buffy* reconfigures, and sometimes challenges, "the ideals of U.S. second-wave feminism for a wide third-wave audience" (2).

A central component of third wave feminism was its impulse to reclaim sexuality as a source of power and agency for women. This pro-sex perspective was an especially important component of the American "girlie" feminism that became popular during the decade of *Buffy*'s birth. In their 2000 *Manifesta*, Jennifer Baumgardner and Amy Richards used "girlie" to denote an "intersection of culture and feminism" which had been reclaiming "tabooed symbols of women's feminine enculturation," such as makeup and fashion, throughout the '90s (136). They explicitly listed *Buffy* in their catalog of girlie cultural artifacts (135). Girlie feminism encouraged young women to be sexually assertive or even aggressive (Baumgardner and Richards 138). For girlies, it was just as oppressive to be denied the right to wear a miniskirt as it was to be forced to wear one (Baumgardner and Richards 140). The miniskirts that Buffy favored in season one proclaimed her affiliation with girlie feminism. Girlie culture returned the favor, proudly claiming *Buffy* as its own. The important girlie feminist magazine BUST introduced a "Buffy Watch" column, all about girl power (Byers 174). Buffy and her fellow girlies taught '90s U.S. television audiences that an assertive female sexuality was perfectly compatible with feminism. Irene Karras views Buffy as a "prototypical girly feminist activist ... combining sexuality with real efforts to make the world a better and safer place for both men and women." Vampire Slayer Faith (Eliza Dushku) famously described herself and Buffy as "hot chicks with superpowers" ("End of Days" 7.21). Yet as Pender notes, it is really Buffy who "provides the compound pleasures of both the hot chick and her superpowers" (52). *Buffy* also showed that superpowers are not a prerequisite for hotness, and Buffy is not the only woman on the show who models an assertive sexuality. Indeed, as Tamy Burnett argues, Anya (Emma Caulfield) is the character who most effectively celebrates and encourages direct expression of women's sexual desires ("Anya" 134).

"None of Us Are Ever Gonna Have a Happy, Normal Relationship": The Buffyverse's "Polymorphously Perverse Subtext" and Text

Buffy's sympathetic portrayals of non-normative sexualities appeared mainly in the show's subtext and in fan fictions during the early seasons; they became more textual and more explicit in later seasons (Call, *BDSM* Chapter Six). The restrictions of American network television initially limited the show to "gestures of deviance" (Larbalestier 211). But as Esther Saxey points out, this created a unique opportunity for fans sympathetic to non-normative sex to recognize the subtle signs of such sex, which in turn offered audiences a deeper ratification of alternative sexualities (203–204). In a post to The Bronze (an early online discussion board for *Buffy* fans), Whedon acknowledged that the Buffyverse "lends itself to polymorphously perverse subtext" (quoted in Saxey 208). By invoking Freud's concept of polymorphous perversity, Whedon authorized fans to search *Buffy* enthusiastically for signs of all consensual sexualities, no matter how unorthodox, marginalized, or stigmatized.

Early seasons of *Buffy* provided refreshingly honest representations of adolescent sexuality, including intergenerational sexuality. Most of the main characters have their first sexual experiences in the early seasons. Tragically, after Buffy has sex for the first time, her partner Angel loses his soul and becomes evil. Burnett argues that this is a problematically conservative narrative move: Buffy is punished for having sex, which implies that teen sex is wrong ("Anya" 123). Yet it is not uncommon for a young woman (including at least one *Buffy* viewer) to have an experience similar to Buffy's: she has sex and her partner stops calling her (Lavery and Burkhead 8, 58). Early *Buffy* also offered innovative depictions of relationships between adolescents and older partners. Don Tresca points out that although Whedon's works present pedophilia as monstrous, adult desire for adolescents is almost normalized; such desire receives no judgment from writers or audiences ("Runaways" 138). The clearest example of this is Buffy and Angel. When their relationship begins, Buffy is not quite 17, and Angel is over 240 (Cocca ¶ 10). Yet the show endorses this radically intergenerational relationship between an adolescent girl and a *much* older man. Since Angel is immortal, one of the most common concerns regarding intergenerational relationships—the older partner's limited life expectancy—doesn't apply. Since Buffy's under eighteen when she dates Angel and Angel knows it, their sexual relationship would count as statutory rape under California law. But as Carolyn Cocca notes, Buffy is only a year underage; she is mature for her age and is not necessarily more vulnerable just because she is younger and female (¶ 14 and 16). Tresca agrees, arguing that Buffy is not victimized by Angel ("Paraphilia" 148). Buffy is clearly capable of making informed sexual choices. The audience is likely to read the relationship as consensual and legitimate rather than abusive. Thus, *Buffy* encourages its audience to recognize the possibility of a healthy and ethical intergenerational relationship, even though such relationships occupy the furthest reaches of Gayle Rubin's outer limits.

Early seasons of *Buffy* also explore zoophilia, or sexual desire of humans for non-human animals. As Ananya Mukherjea argues, "representations of animals and animality in *Buffy* serve as indicators of, or ways to explore, the development of selfhood with respect to gender, sexuality, individual agency, and humanity" (55). Tresca notes that the "animals" with which humans have sexual relationships in the Buffyverse are not true animals; they are partly human creatures such as werewolves, and they have the ability to consent to sex, just as a human would ("Paraphilia" 155–156). The Buffyverse's representations of zoophilia are thus metaphorical, yet they are no less important for that. *Buffy* suggests that werewolves are wolves all the time; one can therefore argue, as Tresca does, that when Willow has sex with Oz, she is "engaging very much in a form of zoophilia" ("Paraphilia" 156). And Willow is not punished for having sex with Oz (Pascale 142); *Buffy* refuses to condemn zoophilia. Chapter Four of this book examines representations of zoophilia in the Buffyverse, including Willow/Oz and the sexuality that Xander shares with Dawn in the later (comic book) seasons, when Dawn takes on a number of inhuman forms, including animal forms like the centaur. I argue that the animality of the Buffyverse's hybrids profoundly informs their sexualities and those of their partners. These zoophilic relationships succeed when and because humans embrace their partners' animal natures. The Buffyverse's zoophilic relationships will not and should not convince audiences that real-life zoophilic *practices* are ethical. But they do show that zoophilia is a legitimate form of *desire*.

The most influential representation of sexuality on *Buffy* was certainly the show's portrayal of lesbianism. As Susan Driver notes, Willow was the most complex lesbian girl character on American TV in the late 90s (62). Willow's relationship with Tara mainstreamed lesbianism in important ways. Queer viewers, especially girls, appreciated a lesbian relationship that was usually uneventful (Driver 75). Following Buffy's second death at the end of season five, Willow and Tara act as surrogate moms to Dawn, further normalizing their relationship and placing it in a domestic context (Ford 98). Yet for some scholars, this normalization of lesbianism is dangerous. Lorna Jowett notes that their quasi-parental relationship with Dawn de-eroticizes their own relationship (51). Driver points out, however, that while the light, gentle sexuality of Willow and Tara might seem conservative, queer teens value it highly (76). Queer fans were justifiably outraged when Tara died and

Willow became evil at the end of season six. This propagated the infamous "Dead-Evil Lesbian Cliché" (Wilts 41). Whedon admitted that given the underrepresentation of lesbians on television, these complaints were legitimate (Mangels). Yet although representations of lesbianism on *Buffy* were sometimes clichéd and potentially damaging, lesbian fans felt that *any* representation of lesbianism was preferable to invisibility (Collier et al. 598). Lesbian fans were able to extrapolate affirming, validating, and empowering messages even from negative depictions (Collier et al. 598). Some young queer fans told *Buffy*'s creators that they were able to come out because of Willow and Tara (Lavery and Burkhead 75).

The relationship that Willow developed with Kennedy in season seven offered audiences an important image of an authentically sexual lesbian relationship (Jowett 59). Willow and Kennedy gave American network TV its first lesbian sex scene (in "Touched" 7.20). This scene was intercut with several heterosexual sex scenes (Faith/Wood and Anya/Xander, plus a non-sexual but very erotic Buffy/Spike). This suggests that lesbian sex is equivalent to straight sex (Beirne). Yet while Willow may finally have discovered the joys of lesbian sex, lesbian *culture* remained invisible at the show's conclusion. All three of *Buffy*'s lesbians—why are there only three?—are femmes. Alissa Wilts points out that all three could pass as straight (42, 53). Willow and Kennedy remained an isolated island of lipstick lesbianism, with no broader community around them (Wilts 54).

Although *Buffy* contains almost no explicit representations of gay male sexuality, the show is rife with male homoeroticism. The vampires Angel and Spike are formally straight but signify as gay in important respects. Alyson Buckman observes that the Angel-Buffy-Spike triangle features clear male homoeroticism ("Triangulated Desire" 74). The spinoff series *Angel* (1999–2004) continued to emit the signifiers of gay male sexuality on behalf of its title character. On his own show, Angel is regularly positioned as a homoerotic object (McCracken 117). The subtextual homoeroticism between Angel and Spike becomes increasingly textual in *Angel* season five. Spike as much as admits that the two have had sex at least once during their long relationship ("Power Play" *Angel* 5.21). Indeed, *Angel* encourages homoerotic readings of every relationship (McCracken 138). But it is the figure of Lorne (Andy Hallett), the flamboyant demon owner of the Caritas karaoke bar, that gives *Angel* its strongest representation of gay sexuality. As Stan Beeler argues, Lorne exemplifies the strategy of using camp humor to force mainstream culture to tolerate images of gay men (89).

Unfortunately, *Buffy* perpetuates the bisexual erasure that is all too common in the real world. Em McAvan notes that Willow could easily have been imagined as bisexual (¶ 2), but neither she nor *Buffy* ever did so. Although *Buffy* often disrupted or destabilized binary concepts of gender and sexuality (Jowett 6), Willow always understood her own sexuality in terms of the polarized heterosexual/homosexual binary (Burnett, "Anya" 129). In season five, Willow emphatically described herself as "gay now" ("Triangle" 5.11), implying that she believes she has made a permanent transition from straight to gay in a sexual economy which she understands as binary. The show's writers apparently thought that making Willow bisexual would have made her relationship with Tara seem less authentic (Liddell ¶ 23; Moorman 113). As usual, fans took matters into their own hands, reimagining and reclaiming Willow as bisexual (Moorman 111).[3]

Buffy also began an important conversation about disabled sexuality, notably through Xander. As Katherine Whaley notes, disability in the Buffyverse is relative: since Xander is an ordinary human surrounded by people with superpowers, he is effectively disabled (¶ 3–4). Xander becomes physically impaired when he is blinded in one eye in "Dirty Girls" (7.18). However, he's not disabled by this. Disability theory's social model suggests that people with impairments are disabled by the ableist society that surrounds them (Shakespeare, Gillespie-Sells, and Davies 2). For the most part, Xander's friends try not to disable him (Iatropolos). Thus he can still take action, date, and lead (Iatropolos).[4] *Angel* offered a more in-depth exploration of disability, particularly through the character of Lindsey McDonald (Christian Kane), the morally ambiguous lawyer who works for the evil law firm Wolfram and Hart. After Angel cuts off Lindsey's hand, Wolfram and Hart provides him a transplant, which unfortunately gives him "evil hand issues" ("Dead End" *Angel* 2.18). In *Angel* season five, Spike also experiences hand amputation and reattachment. Discussion of *Angel*'s disability arcs figured prominently in the 2012 Slayage Conference on the Whedonverses at the University of British Columbia in Vancouver. In her keynote, Tamy Burnett argued that hands are powerful symbols of agency, and that the loss of agency that comes with hand amputation is analogous to castration ("Evil Hand Issues"). Here impairment produces a loss of sexual agency, as it often does in real life. In an essay that won the conference's Mr. Pointy paper award, Mary Ellen Iatropolos argued that the narrative arcs of *Buffy*'s Xander, *Angel*'s Lindsey, and *Dollhouse*'s Bennett Halverson (Summer Glau) show that characters have the ability to choose how they negotiate disabling situations, and that positive paths are open to them (Iatropolos; Comeford et al. 39). Iatropolos showed that in the Whedonverses, characters with physical impairments are often surrounded by supportive friends, who help them find the path to self-acceptance. I would add that characters with impairments can still be sexual beings, as Xander is with Dawn in the later seasons of *Buffy*, as Lindsey is with Eve (Sarah Thompson) in *Angel* season five, or as Bennett could have been with Topher.

Despite the excellent work of Whaley, Burnett, and Iatropolos, disability remains an under-researched area in Whedon Studies, and very little work has been done on representations of disabled sexuality in the Whedonverses. In Chapter Three of this book, I aim to correct that by examining the disabled sexualities of the superheroes Kitty Pryde, Scott Summers, Bruce Banner, and Natasha Romanoff. I argue that Kitty and her lover Peter develop a sexuality compatible with Kitty's impairment, and that as they do so, they provide one of American pop culture's rarest representations: a healthy, happy, satisfying sexual relationship between a disabled woman and an able-bodied man. I argue that Emma Frost teaches her lover Scott to control his impairment without ever suggesting that he can or should be cured, thus allowing Scott to manage his disability successfully. And I argue that Natasha teaches Bruce to let her manage his disability by controlling his impairment. Furthermore, by disclosing the fact that she herself is impaired by sterility and disabled by society's marginalization of the sterile woman, Natasha establishes the possibility of a healthy, satisfying non-reproductive sexual relationship with Bruce. Tragically, his internalization of his disabled status prevents him from pursuing this possibility.

The later seasons of *Buffy* and *Angel* also offer important images of consensual sexual dominance and submission, and the shows' representations are generally quite positive. Jenny Alexander was the first scholar to notice how sexual power was configured in the Buffyverse, and to recognize the ethical significance of that configuration. She noted in 2004 that on *Buffy*, male sexual dominance only appears in historical flashbacks (¶ 18). In the show's narrative present, *Buffy*'s "queer and feminist sensibilities" ensure that women dominate, while men are dominated (¶ 9).[5] By far the most important female-dominant DS relationship in the Buffyverse is Buffy/Spike. As Dee Amy-Chinn notes, Buffy is clearly in control, which makes this different from her previous relationships ("Bitch" 320). Buffy and Spike legitimize female dominance and male submission and encourage the audience to consider these positions ethically viable. What's more, the Buffy/Spike relationship establishes a close alliance between straight female dominance and queer sexualities. As McCracken argues, female dominance of the kind that Buffy enjoys over the submissive Spike is not heteronormative (127).

Yet the Buffy/Spike relationship has always been controversial. Early criticism often read it as destructive (e.g., Hibbs 57). A common early critical narrative held that it was an abusive relationship (Larbalestier 195). More recently, Wendy Fall has suggested that the sympathetic Spike and his apologists may inadvertently promote rape culture. Certainly, there are times when the relationship contains abusive elements, especially before Spike regains his soul in season seven. Spike is frequently deceitful. Although he loves Buffy, he also enjoys hurting her. While their relationship is generally consensual, he did sexually assault her once. But this led to a long, four-season break in their sexual relationship. Buffy did not take Spike back until he had shown that he could consistently be respectful and consensual with her. I therefore argue that although it was once tainted with abuse, the Buffy/Spike relationship evolved into a healthy and loving one. Vivien Burr calls the relationship "loveless" (51). However, I disagree: season seven confirms that Spike genuinely loves Buffy, and the comic book seasons confirm that she loves him. Buffy/Spike is probably Spike's healthiest relationship, and in many ways, it is Buffy's. This relationship initiated the Whedonversal paradigm of the successful female-dominant/male-submissive relationship.

Chapter One of this book investigates Whedon's dominant women ("Whedommes") and their male submissives. I focus on Buffy and Spike, and Natasha Romanoff and Bruce Banner from *Avengers* and *Age of Ultron*. I use Jacques Lacan's influential psychoanalytic model of human experience, which holds that there are three fundamental orders of human reality: an unrepresentable Real, an Imaginary realm of image and emotion, and a Symbolic world of language, culture, and law. Lacanian developmental theory suggests that a child moves out of the Real, first into the Imaginary via an imagistic relationship with the mother, then into the Symbolic via a linguistic (and Oedipal) relationship with the father. This is generally considered to be a one-way trip. Whedon's dominant women, however, can take their submissive partners back through the Imaginary and into the Real. I argue that the Whedommes control their partners' movement through the three realms, that this control allows unusual kinds of movement, and that the Whedommes use this power for the benefit of their submissives. Buffy uses it to bring Spike back into the Symbolic after he gains his soul and loses his mind. Natasha uses it every time she deploys her unique disciplinary technique, the lullaby, to take the Hulk of the Real back through the Imaginary and into the Symbolic, where he becomes Bruce. She also uses an anti-lullaby to push Bruce out of the Symbolic and make Hulk Real. She always invokes whatever Lacanian order would be best for Bruce/Hulk and for the Avengers. Both Natasha and Buffy use their dominance to provide their submissive partners opportunities for heroism, therapy, and sexual satisfaction. Bruce and Spike consent to this, desire it, and trust their partners to do it right. These Lacanian DS relationships thus serve as a cornerstone of the Whedonversal system of sexual ethics.

"That Was Real": Psychoanalytic Media Theory and the Interpretation of Whedonversal Sexualities

My use of Lacanian theory as a way to understand the Whedonverses' representations of DS is an example of this book's main methodology: psychoanalytic criticism which uses the concepts of Lacanian analysis as critical tools to decode and critique pop culture's portrayals of sexuality. I acknowledge that psychoanalysis is only one among many approaches to the study of human psychology. I make no claims regarding the veracity or clinical efficacy of psychoanalysis. However, I do believe that psychoanalysis is an effective instrument for analyzing cultural representations of sexuality. Psychoanalysis includes a comprehensive account of the ways in which sexuality and culture inform one another, from Freud's discussion of the cultural superego (*Civilization* 106–110) to Horkheimer and Adorno's critique of the effects of repression on mass culture (120–167). I share Mary Ann Doane's conviction that psychoanalysis is "a particularly appropriate methodology for deciphering the psychical operations of the cinema," and that psychoanalysis is especially useful for understanding "the cinema as the realm of fantasy and desire," the forces that constitute sexuality (7). I extend the feminist psychoanalytic film criticism that Doane has developed (along with Laura Mulvey, Kaja Silverman, Barbara Creed, and others), by applying it to other visual media such as television and comic books. As Slavoj Žižek says of Mulvey and Silverman, I am not a Lacanian, but rather someone who engages with Lacan, appropriating some of his concepts "as the best description of the universe of patriarchal domination," while challenging Lacan's uncritical acceptance of that universe (Žižek, *Real Tears* 2). The application of Lacanian concepts to the Whedonverses shows that those universes may be less patriarchal and more feminist than our world, as I will demonstrate by applying those concepts to the Buffy/Spike relationship. The Whedonverses model a culture of gender and sexuality towards which we may aspire.

Psychoanalytic film theory of the 1970s associated film with the Lacanian Imaginary. Jean-Louis Baudry's influential "apparatus" theory suggested that the cinematic apparatus of camera, projector, screen, etc., permitted the Imaginary to fill in the gap in the spectating subject by encouraging the audience to identify with the point of view of the camera itself (294–295). Following Baudry, Christian Metz argued that the cinema's visual and auditory perceptual elements involve the audience in the Imaginary more than other media can do (42–45). This early Theory (capitalized by its critics) came under fire in the 1990s. "Post-Theory" critics like Noël Carroll claimed that psychoanalytic film theory lacked an empirical basis (66). Two main alternatives to psychoanalysis emerged: a cognitive approach which focused on the "cognitive and perceptual processes of spectators" (Carroll 48), and a Deleuzian philosophical approach which emphasized the affective, bodily experience of film spectatorship (Shaviro, *Cinematic Body* viii; Tyrer 7). These alternatives show that just as there are many approaches to psychology, there are many different methods of media criticism. Cognitivism demonstrates that it is possible to do criticism that is informed by psychological theory, without relying on psychoanalytic concepts. However, Lacanian criticism remains relevant and useful today; its defenders have successfully answered the cognitivist and Deleuzian critiques. Early twenty-first-century Lacanian film theorists like Todd McGowan argue that 1970s film theory focused too much on Lacan's early theory of the mirror stage, and thus placed undue emphasize on the Imaginary (McGowan 1; McGowan and Kunkle xiii). Just as Lacan called for a return to Freud, contemporary theorists like McGowan and Žižek have called for a return to Lacan, especially the later Lacan (McGowan 5, Žižek *Real Tears* 2).[6]

The recent call for a return to Lacan is also a call for a return to the Real, and Žižek is the film theorist who has most effectively made these calls. Following the later Lacan, Žižek analyzes the Real as a "black hole" whose space is filled with a fantasy through which "*we learn how to desire*" (*Looking Awry* viii, 6, emphasis in original). For Žižek, the Real, not the Imaginary, is the "screen of fantasy" on which fantasies, including sexual ones, play themselves out (*Enjoy Your Symptom!* 220). Following Žižek, McGowan and Kunkle argue that early twenty-first-century film is radical because it can involve its audience in an encounter with the Real (xviii). I extend this argument to other contemporary visual media like television and comics. Thus, for example, when the Gentlemen silence the Symbolic by taking speech from Sunnydale in "Hush" (*Buffy* 4.10), *Buffy* performs "a radical release of the Real," and it is in the silent Real that Buffy and Riley learn how to desire as they share their first kiss (Call, "Buffy the Post-Anarchist Vampire Slayer" 188).[7] McGowan and Kunkle argue that film theory should focus less on spectatorship (the central concern of early theory), and return to an interpretation and analysis of film texts which would elaborate the contours of the cinematic Real and show how contemporary film enacts the Lacanian concepts of trauma, *jouissance*, fantasy, and desire (xix–xxvii). My approach is similar to theirs, though I believe that visual media can stage encounters with the Imaginary and the Symbolic as well as the Real: while early and later psychoanalytic media theories focus on different Lacanian registers, they are essentially compatible.

I argue that the Lacanian concept of desire provides an accurate account of the ways in which Whedon's fictional characters experience their desires and thus their sexualities. To the extent that audiences recognize something of their own desires in Whedon's representations—for these representations can still serve as the mirror of the Imaginary, as well as the site of encounters with the Real—Whedon's works may help audiences come to grips with their own sexualities. For Lacanians, desire is constituted and sustained by a fundamental lack (Lacan, *Encore* 6). Desire's principal goal is to perpetuate itself rather than gaining satisfaction (McGowan 9). There is, as McGowan points out, therefore something fundamentally masochistic about desire (9). This describes Spike's desire for Buffy. Looking back on their relationship in season seven, Spike says that he has come to redefine the words pain and suffering since he fell in love with Buffy ("Never Leave Me" 7.9). He's right where he wants to be when he says it—in bondage, courtesy of Buffy—and his new definition of pain and suffering is desire. As McGowan argues, desire is drawn to "the point at which power is entirely lacking" (10). This is the essence of Spike's submissive desire. He seeks the point at which his power vanishes, and Buffy's dominance over him becomes total. The submissive Spike shows the radical potential of Lacan's theory, which authorizes all desires, no matter how unorthodox or queer. Lacan claims that his brand of psychoanalysis has "restored full civil rights to perversion" (*Ethics* 194). He famously asserts that the only thing of which one can be guilty is "giving ground relative to one's desire" (*Ethics* 321). This invites audience members who see their own desires reflected in the desires of the gays, lesbians, dominants, submissives, fetishists and other "perverts" who inhabit the Whedonverses to pursue those desires without guilt, as long as they do so within the bounds of consent.

Lacan's name for the unattainable object of desire is *objet petit a*. This impossible object sustains desire through a lack of satisfaction (Lacan, *Encore* 6). It is an empty form filled by fantasy (Žižek, *Looking Awry* 133). *Objet a* is central to male sexuality; for men, Lacan argues, "the whole realization of the sexual relationship leads to fantasy" (*Encore* 86). Thus, the initial manifestation of Spike's desire for Buffy involves not Buffy herself but rather the lifelike Buffy robot, a material realization of Spike's fantasy of Buffy. The Buffybot shows that television can be eroticized through the same mechanism that McGowan ascribes to cinema: by showing the form of *objet petit a* (16). *Objet a* is not to be confused with the Lacanian phallus; indeed, it is "the exact opposite of the phallic master-signifier" (Žižek, *Real Tears* 65). Unlike *objet a*, the phallus is "a signifier for symbolic knowledge, power, and privilege" (Silverman, *Acoustic Mirror* 26). The phallus signifies the sexual power that Buffy holds over Spike, and her elusive knowledge of that power.

Because the true object of desire can never be attained, Lacan repeatedly insists that the (hetero)sexual relationship is impossible (see, for example, *Encore* 9). For Lacan, relations between men and women "are not working out," and yet thanks to a number of linguistic prohibitions, the sexual relationship "works out anyway" (*Encore* 32–33).[8] Žižek interprets the impossibility of the sexual relationship to mean that such a relationship can exist only in the frame of fantasy (*Looking Awry* 168). For Žižek, the (hetero)sexual relationship can work only if man's and woman's fantasies overlap (*Real Tears* 88). This is why Buffy and Spike's relationship does eventually work—but only when Buffy's fantasy of Spike as someone who can help her return to the Symbolic from the lost Real she calls Heaven overlaps with his fantasy of her as the Slayer who transforms death into love. For Lacan, love makes up for the impossible sexual relationship (*Encore* 45). Thus, the love that Buffy and

Spike share exceeds the desire they experience and extends beyond the limits of their sexual relationship, reaching to the end of season twelve.

If the *objet a* can't be attained and the sexual relationship is impossible, for Lacan there is nonetheless a special kind of enjoyment, *jouissance*, that is available to desiring subjects. *Jouissance* is an enjoyment of the Real; it radically disrupts the Symbolic. Lacan's initial formulation understands *jouissance* as Sadistic. He cites Sade's law of *jouissance*: "lend me the part of your body that will give me a moment of satisfaction and, if you care to, use for your own pleasure that part of my body which appeals to you" (Sade quoted in Lacan, *Ethics* 202). Lacan notes that "any reasonable being" would have trouble accepting this maxim and the consent it assumes (*Écrits* 648). But when it comes to sex, beings are not reasonable. The fact that Lacan recognizes the possibility of a consensual *jouissance*, however unreasonable, suggests that *jouissance* can be sadomasochistic rather than simply sadistic. And indeed, Lacan clarifies that *jouissance* modifies the Sadean experience, for it "depends on an echo that it sets off in the Other" (*Écrits* 651). Lacan ascribes to women a *jouissance* on the basis of which they "possess men" (*Encore* 73). This female *jouissance* underwrites Buffy's dominant possession of the submissive Spike. The nature of their relationship is clear by season five, when Spike is ruthlessly tortured by Glory but refuses to reveal that Dawn is the Key. Buffy visits the grievously wounded Spike in the guise of his fantasy of her, the Buffybot. When Spike discovers her ruse, Buffy declares that the bot "wasn't even real" ("Intervention" 5.18). Rather, the bot was Spike's desperate attempt to fill the void of the Real with sexual fantasy. Buffy continues: "what you did, for me and Dawn ... that was real." The masochistic enjoyment that Spike derives from embracing Glory's torture in the service of his submission to Buffy is a radical *jouissance*, an enjoyment of the Real. It is the kind of enjoyment the subject suffers (McGowan 10), and Buffy suffers from it, too. Buffy breaks down in tears when she confesses to Tara that she's "using" Spike ("Dead Things" 6.13): although she is only following the law of *jouissance* (as is Spike), she can't accept her "use" of Spike as ethical. She attempts to renounce her enjoyment of Spike, but as Žižek observes, the renunciation of enjoyment actually produces masochistic enjoyment (*Enjoy Your Symptom!* 22).

The imperative of *jouissance* is Enjoy!, but Lacan correlates this with castration (*Encore* 7). In the Lacanian model, *jouissance* depends upon the "part objects" (Lacan, *Ethics* 202), including the gaze and the voice (Lacan, *Encore* 126), and the loss of these part objects is experienced as castration (Silverman, *Acoustic Mirror* 7). Here is where feminist theory engages most effectively with psychoanalytic film theory. Laura Mulvey's highly influential 1975 essay "Visual Pleasure and Narrative Cinema" argues that film "depends on the image of the castrated women" for order and meaning (14). For Mulvey, cinema's castrated women are "displayed for the gaze and enjoyment of men," yet they simultaneously invoke male castration anxiety (22). Mulvey argues that the male viewer can respond either with a scopophilia that turns women into a fetish object, or with a sadistic voyeurism that punishes the castrated woman (and, not incidentally, serves the sadistic needs of narrative) (22). Kaja Silverman reminds us that the castration which cinema may activate is not literal, but rather the symbolic castration that comes from the traumatic separation from the Real and entry into the Symbolic (*Acoustic Mirror* 1, 9). In the Lacanian model, castration is an issue for both sexes, not just for men (Lacan, *Écrits* 463). As Barbara Creed notes with respect to horror, cinema represents both men and women "as castrated and as agents of castration" (*Monstrous-Feminine* 152).

The Buffyverse stages many encounters with castration; probably the clearest example is Spike's behavioral modification chip, which prevents him from attacking humans. The chip was installed by the Initiative under the direction of a castrating woman, Dr. Maggie Walsh, who also tried to castrate Riley by foreclosing his sexual relationship with Buffy. The show explicitly connects the chip to castration when Spike has "trouble performing" and can't bite Willow ("Pangs" 4.8). Silverman argues that like its images, cinema's sounds serve to conceal male castration (*Acoustic Mirror* 41). More recently, Žižek has argued that cinematic sound can reverse the usual condition, in which the Real is a hole in the Symbolic: sound can form an "'aquarium' of the real surrounding isolated islands of the symbolic" (*Looking Awry* 40). When Spike sings "Rest in Peace" in "Once More with Feeling" (6.7), the lyrics express his Symbolic desire to be dominated by Buffy, while the music and his gestures point to his Real *jouissance*. Buffy and Spike begin their sexual relationship almost immediately thereafter, once they learn that Spike isn't castrated with respect to Buffy: she doesn't activate his chip. Buffy helps Spike overcome his castration and the anxiety it brings. Together they are able to confront their mutual traumatic separation from the Real, share desire and love within the Imaginary, and learn to endure the Symbolic.

"The Dolls Hold All the Cards": Sex Work, Bisexuality, Transgender Sexuality, DS and Other Desires on Firefly *and* Dollhouse

Whedon's beloved space western *Firefly* (2002–2003) introduced several innovative representations of sexuality. Andrew Aberdein argues that the Companion Inara implements Pat Califia's utopian call for a spiritual form of sex work performed by independent, highly educated workers (65). Yet as Amy-Chinn points out, Inara's agency is undermined by the strict regulatory regime to which the Companions are subjected ("Whore" 175). Inara also represents a very traditional form of femininity "that firmly endorses the link between romantic love and sexual monogamy" (Amy-Chinn, "Whore" 181). Despite her repeated objections, Mal continues to call her a "whore." As Amy-Chinn notes, this is not only insulting but performative ("Whore" 184): the word makes her into the thing it names. In this context it is significant that Inara only begins her sexual relationship with Mal in Zack Whedon's *Leaves on the Wind* comics (2014), after she has lost her Companion's license. This suggests that Inara has accepted Mal's conservative definition of sex work, and that she, like him, views such work as incompatible with the monogamous, romantic sexual relationship which represents the surprisingly strict limit of her erotic imagination.

Recent scholarship has shown that Inara also embodies a troubling representation of bisexuality. Meredith and Sutherland point out that although Inara does choose her clients, she chooses men far more frequently than women; because she is a sex worker, it's not clear that her (very) occasional choice of women indicates that she is bisexual (¶ 24; see also Liddell ¶ 45). Inara's ambiguous sexuality thus contributes to bisexual erasure. Even worse, the crew are allowed to fetishize Inara's "bisexuality," if that's what it is (Liddell ¶ 48), and this encourages the audience to do the same. Jayne provides a caricatured version of a straight man's response to the thought of two women having sex: "I'll be in my bunk" ("War Stories" 1.9). His crude comment reduces Inara's "bisexuality" to a masturbatory fantasy.

Although *Firefly*'s fraught portrayals of sex work and bisexuality have received a good deal of scholarly attention, the show, film, and comics also include positive depictions of several other important sexualities, and these have not been widely studied. Chapter Two of this book considers *Firefly*'s unexplored sexualities. I argue that Zoë provides another good example of a Whedomme, while her husband Wash models a healthy male sexual submission. *Firefly* authorizes male fetishism by repeatedly allowing Jayne's gun fetish to save the ship and her crew. The show also endorses female fetishism, for it is Kaylee's fetishistic relationship to machines in general and *Serenity* in particular that keep the ship flying. The story of Simon and River has the structure of a Gothic sibling incest narrative. Like its Gothic forebears, this narrative creates the possibility for incestuous desire to develop at the subtextual level, while carefully prohibiting any textual expression or consummation of this desire (if indeed it exists). River has a sensual connection with the universe itself; her formless desire indicates that with *Firefly*, the polymorphously perverse subtext that Whedon identified in *Buffy* has become textual. Meanwhile, the celibate Shepherd Book refuses to act on his sexual desire.

Dollhouse amplified the concerns about representations of sex work that scholars had expressed regarding *Firefly*. *Dollhouse*'s mindless "actives" are imprinted with temporary personalities and sent out on missions which are frequently sexual in nature. *Dollhouse* seemed anti-feminist in its presentation of prostitution's victims as disposable objects (Schultz 360). The show left Joss Whedon open to the charge that he was glamorizing human trafficking (Pascale 312). Whedon did what he could to deflect criticism, notably by hiring women showrunners: Sarah Fain and Mere Smith in season one, and Michele Faszekas and Tara Butters in season two (Lavery 128). But to a large extent, *Dollhouse*'s troubling portrayal of sex work was beyond Whedon's control. Whedon had originally envisioned the show as a critical *commentary* on sex trafficking (Pascale 313). But Fox objected to *any* depictions of prostitution; therefore, as Whedon says, "we had to sort of gloss over it or joke about it, and it became kind of offensive" (quoted in Pascale 314).

The show also features disturbing representations of child abuse. Samira Nadkarni argues that in their unimprinted "wiped states," the emotionally immature dolls are analogous to children, that such childlike dolls are incapable of giving or refusing consent, and that any sexual relationship between a regular human and an unimprinted doll is therefore necessarily abusive (¶ 2, 9). The main example of such abuse occurs when Sierra (Dichen Lachman) is raped by her handler. Nadkarni's argument is persuasive with respect to unimprinted dolls, but sexual relations with imprinted dolls have a different ethical status. Imprinted dolls are almost always emotionally mature and can generally defend themselves. Their personalities are typically dominant. "We don't send the actives to be submissives," says Dr. Saunders (Amy Acker) ("A Spy in the House of Love," 1.9). Importantly, the latter part of the show's narrative suggests that imprinted dolls might be able to evolve to the point where they could give sexual consent. As Nadkarni notes, Echo becomes increasingly self-aware in the second season, and "appears to reach a stage at which she is capable of making choices," though those choices are constrained by her circumstances (¶ 22).

Dollhouse's troubling depictions of sex work and child abuse are balanced by a surprisingly positive portrayal of consensual BDSM. Echo, imprinted as a professional dominatrix, explains BDSM to her handler Boyd, and to the audience. "It's about trust. Handing yourself over fully and completely to another human being. There's nothing more beautiful than letting go like that" ("A Spy in the House of Love" 1.9). Here Echo articulates the major pillars of the Whedonverses' system of sexual ethics: consent, desire, trust. This image of "leather Echo" appears in the season two credits, further reinforcing the message (Call, *BDSM* 185). It is unfortunate that the show's (too) obvious sex trafficking allegory obscured its subtler allegorical vision of a play-slavery which real-world BDSM communities generally consider to be extreme yet ethical (Call, *BDSM* 192). As in real-world play-slavery relationships, *Dollhouse*'s "slaves" actually have tremendous power: "the dolls hold all the cards" ("A Love Supreme" 2.8). As Schultz argues, the dolls take steps to regain control of their bodies and rediscover their identities, which are closely tied to their sexualities (368). As the dolls gain agency and identity, they show that consensual play-slavery is potentially ethical (Call, *BDSM* 187).

Dollhouse also represents an important transgender moment in the Whedonverses. In Jane Espenson's "Belle Chose" (2.3), the doll Victor (Enver Gjokaj) is imprinted as Kiki, "a constructed female personality in a male body" (Boulware ¶ 3). Lillian DeRitter notes that Victor is unapologetically female as Kiki, and that most of his imprints actually lack traditional markers of masculinity (199–200). This suggests that Victor is the show's most transgender character (and that Enver Gjokaj is its best actor). By the end of the series, Echo has also become transgender. She adds the personality of her dead lover Paul (Tahmoh Penikett) to her group mind. Julie Hawk argues that this "queers her relationship with Paul by allowing deeper penetration than is possible for any human subject" (¶ 19). I would add that the specific form of this queer relationship is transgender. Not only is Echo "penetrated" by Paul (as she might have been if they had consummated their desire in their cisgender bodies). Paul has become part of her. When the mind of her male lover takes up residence in Echo's female body, Echo attains a non-binary gender identity. As Paul interacts with Echo's female personas, they perform a transgender sexuality.

"It's about trust." Echo (Eliza Dushku), imprinted as a dominatrix, explains the ethics of BDSM. *Dollhouse* (2009). Mutant Enemy/20th Century-Fox Television.

"You Have to Not Be Stupid About Gays": Queer and Non-Normative Sexualities in Whedon's Comic Books

As Kociemba and Iatropolos argue, there are "specific formal distinctions between television and comics" that change the way stories are told across media (40). Building on that argument, I claim that these differences make comics the more powerful form. In almost every case, the formal elements of comics are more versatile than those of television. Panel composition is more flexible than the director's frame, page layout is more powerful than television editing, comic book coloring is more versatile than television lighting, and the interplay between word balloons, thought balloons, and text captions is more fluid than the interaction between spoken dialogue and voice-overs on television. In comics, Whedon and his co-creators could let their imaginations run wild (Lavery and Burkhead 144). Most importantly for the purposes of this book, comics enable representations of sexuality that are far more diverse and more radical than those which can appear on American television. As Kociemba and Iatropolos argue with respect to *Buffy*, "the shift to the comics medium freed the story from the more restrictive sexuality representation regime of network television" (38). Whedon's comics offer more committed representations of sexualities than did his shows (Greenwood ¶ 35). Sexualities that were only implicit on TV become explicit in Whedon's comics. And the comics portray queer and non-normative sexualities that were entirely absent from the shows. These sexualities are generally depicted as desirable, consensual, and ethical.[9]

Whedon's *Astonishing X-Men* (2004–2008) moved DS and disabled sexuality into the mainstream. Whedon wrote the Emma Frost character as a Whedomme, and John Cassady drew her as one. Emma's midriff-baring white bustier, tight white pants, and thick boots emphasize her sexual agency, while her white cape codes her power as superheroic. Whedon wrote team leader Scott Summers as a submissive partner for Emma, and gave Emma the role that Jean Grey had played for many years: the powerful telepath who becomes Scott's lover and helps him manage his disability, as I discuss in Chapter Three.[10] Whedon has said that no character in comics means more to him than Kitty Pryde (quoted in Lavery 154).[11] In the Chris Claremont/John Byrne X-Men comics of the 1980s, Kitty dated Peter Rasputin, the taciturn Russian X-Man known as Colossus. However, Marvel's editorial staff ended the relationship due to the characters' (relatively small) age difference (Morris 128). But Buffy/Angel had shown that Whedon had no qualms about representing a relationship between a teenaged girl and an older man. In *Astonishing*, Whedon presented Kitty as sexually mature, and allowed her to consummate her relationship with Peter. Claremont had imagined that Kitty might have trouble controlling her power to "phase" through solid matter (see, for example, Claremont and Byrne, "Days of Future Past," *Uncanny X-Men* #141–142), but he hadn't considered how this impairment might impact her sexuality. Whedon did, and I analyze his Kitty/Peter story as a narrative of disabled sexuality in Chapter Three.

Whedon wrote a six-issue arc of Marvel's *Runaways* comics in 2007–2008; the most delightful surprise about his *Runaways* is that it portrays a healthy, happy transgender relationship. The humanoid alien Karolina identifies as female and "gay" (for Whedonversal lesbians have a strange aversion to naming themselves as such). Karolina's lover is the shapeshifting alien Skrull Xavin. Xavin's gender presentation alternates between male and female, and Karolina is only attracted to Xavin's female form.[12] The powerful desire that Karolina feels for Xavin's female self validates Xavin's gender identity and enables an important representation of a loving sexual relationship between a lesbian and a trans woman. In our world, such relationships are sometimes controversial even among queers (especially among "trans-exclusive radical feminist" lesbians or TERFs), so Whedon does the trans community an important service by providing a positive picture of such a relationship. The Whedonverses' first queer relationship began in 1999, when Willow and Tara joined hands to combine their magic power and protect themselves from the Gentlemen in "Hush" (*Buffy* 4.10). A decade later, Whedon had become comfortable with more sexualized images of queer women combining their powers in this way. During the climactic final battle scene in Whedon's *Runaways*, Karolina places her hand on Xavin's female breast so the two women can mesh their energy shields and save everyone from an explosion (#30). The otherworldly power that this alien lesbian shares with this alien trans woman stands as a powerful metaphor for the strength of their queer transgender relationship. This representation is a real step forward for the Whedonverses, in which transgender sexuality had previously been invisible.

Buffy season eight through twelve comics continued the narrative that the show began, while offering representations of queer sexualities that are far broader and more inclusive than those that appeared on television. As Lisa Gomez argues, Billy, the first male Slayer, provides a realistic and honest portrayal of a young gay man that avoids sexual objectification (29). As such, Billy represents a landmark in the Buffyverse's portrayal of gay sexuality. The comics' representations of lesbianism and bisexuality are unfortunately conservative in some respects, however. Lesbian characters are often portrayed in clichéd terms. As Gomez argues, Satsu's lesbianism seems to define her entire character (27). Although Buffy has sex with Satsu twice (Goddard and Jeanty), bisexuality is never considered as a possible (indeed, likely) explanation for the fact that Buffy is attracted to, and enjoys sex with, both men and women. Buffy is presented as "heteroflexible" rather than bisexual (Forhard-Dourlent 42). Jennifer DeRoss argues convincingly that this is "yet another example of bi-erasure, which is a problem throughout the Buffyverse" (58). However, the comics do contain one thoughtful, positive portrayal of a lesbian relationship: Willow and the snake-bodied demon sorceress Aluwyn. The comics present this as an intricate, complex DS relationship, one in which Willow is

Clockwise from top: Spike and Buffy (a submissive male vampire and a dominant female Slayer), Xander and Dawn (a human man with a visual impairment and a woman who is also a "key" of mystical energy), Giles and Olivia (the mind of a middle-aged man trapped in the adolescent version of his body, and a woman who finds this horrifying), Willow and Aluwyn (a human witch and a demon sorceress with the body of a snake). None of these relationships are anything like normative, and the Buffyverse portrays them all with sympathy. Art by Rebekah Isaacs with Dan Jackson. *Buffy the Vampire Slayer* season ten (2015). Dark Horse Comics/Twentieth Century–Fox Film Corporation.

uncharacteristically submissive (Call, "Find What Warmth" ¶ 6–9). Here Aluwyn is the Whedomme. *Buffy* comics also continue to validate the most marginalized of all sexualities, intergenerational desire. Although Xander is only a few years older than Dawn, other characters perceive their relationship as intergenerational, yet their friends admire this relationship nonetheless (Whedon and Jeanty, "Turbulence"). Xander and Dawn remain together until the end of the series; by season twelve, they have a child. In season ten, Giles is transformed into an adolescent version of himself. Teen Giles tries to pursue a relationship with his old flame Olivia; this, too, falls within the horizons of ethical sexuality in the Buffyverse (Call, "Find What Warmth" ¶ 22–24).

"The Status Is Not Quo": Subverting Tropes of Masculine and Feminine Sexuality in Dr. Horrible *and* Cabin in the Woods

Whedon has a lifelong love of musicals; not content to limit himself to film, television, and comics, he has dreamed of working in musical theater. "I'd ... like to explore making a musical motion picture," he remarked in 2005 (quoted in Lavery 204). Two years later, he had an unexpected opportunity to realize this dream. In 2007, the Writer's Guild of America went on strike, forcing Whedon to stop work on *Dollhouse* (Pascale 291). Unwilling to sit idle, Whedon and his family created a short, three act musical film about the origin of an aspiring supervillain: *Dr. Horrible's Sing-Along Blog*. As Kendra Preston Leonard argues, by transplanting the trope of the superhero into the "primarily gay aesthetic" of musical theater, *Dr. Horrible* challenged contemporary American standards of masculinity (208). Chapter Five of this book investigates that challenge. I use R.W. Connell's influential sociological model of masculinity as a lens through which to view the characters of *Dr. Horrible*. I argue that Captain Hammer (Nathan Fillion) embodies hegemonic masculinity, a form of masculinity that is based on the subordination of women and gay men. Dr. Horrible (Neil Patrick Harris) embodies a masculinity that is sometimes subordinate to Hammer's hegemonic masculinity but is also frequently complicit with it. Horrible and Hammer engage in a vicious and ultimately deadly competition for the sexual affections of a young woman named Penny (Felicia Day), who embodies a compliant femininity organized around the accommodation of male desires. This competition reveals the homoerotic heart of heteronormative masculinity, a theme that has long fascinated Whedon. Following Eve Kosofsky Sedgwick, Alyson Buckman notes that Horrible and Hammer develop their sexual desire mainly in relation to one another; the ostensible female object of that desire becomes strangely irrelevant, serving largely as "a means to the construction of masculinity between Hammer and Horrible" (Buckman, "Say it was Horrible" ¶ 19 and 21).

I argue that *Dr. Horrible* articulates scathing critiques of contemporary American heterosexuality, and of the toxic homosocial masculinities which underwrite that sexuality. I also argue that the musical presents queer aesthetics and sexualities as desirable alternatives. A potent queer masculinity haunts the bankrupt heterosexualities of Horrible and Hammer. I locate *Dr. Horrible* within the histories and formal structures of the two surprisingly compatible and distinctly queer genres that it occupies: the American film musical and the superhero story. Like the male rivals of both film musicals and superhero stories, Horrible and Hammer find themselves on a relationship trajectory which runs from the homosocial to the homoerotic, and perhaps even to the homosexual. Their relationship with one another and their failed heterosexual relationships with Penny point to a crisis of heteronormativity. That crisis clears the way for a queer planet. On such a planet, women and non-normative men would be respected as people, and everyone would be able to pursue and express their sexualities as they saw fit. This is the utopian possibility that lies hidden within the tragedy of *Dr. Horrible*.

The Drew Goddard/Joss Whedon film *The Cabin in the Woods* (2012) effectively critiques the conservative sexual politics of that sub-genre of American horror known as the slasher film. In her landmark study of the slasher genre *Men, Women, and Chainsaws*, Carol Clover argues that killing young people "who seek or engage in unauthorized sex" is "a generic imperative of the slasher film" (34). The killer murders the most sexually active teens first. His last target, whom Clover famously dubs the Final Girl, is a masculinized, sexually reluctant young woman whose relative sexual innocence authorizes her to defeat or escape the killer and survive the film (Clover 35–41). Thus, slasher films present teen sex as a capital crime, while brutally punishing young women who dare to exercise sexual agency.

In Chapter Six, I analyze *Cabin*'s successful subversion of slasher sexuality. *Cabin* fulfills its generic imperative by killing the sexually active Jules (Anna Hutchison) and Curt (Chris Hemsworth) first. But it simultaneously challenges that imperative by showing that their assertive sexuality is the result of psychological and chemical manipulation (Parrish ¶ 14). This narrative device serves as an alibi for Jules' active female sexuality, and for Curt's masculine sexual aggression. The intellectual Holden (Jesse Williams) is sexually cautious, yet *Cabin* kills him anyway, which highlights the arbitrary nature of the slasher's generic conventions. Having recently concluded an illicit affair with her married professor, Dana (Kristen Connolly) is perhaps the most sexually transgressive character in the film, yet Goddard and Whedon assign her the position of Final Girl nonetheless. As Jaclyn Parrish notes, they also add a Final Boy (¶ 15). However, *Cabin*'s Marty (Fran Kranz) defies all expectations regarding the Final Boy's role in the slasher's structure. While the formal logic of the slasher holds that his marijuana-fueled hedonism should doom him to an early death, he survives to the end of the film.

In Chapter Six, I argue that *Cabin* simultaneously performs and subverts the basic psychosexual drama of the slasher film. *Cabin* critiques the sadistic male gaze and castration anxieties that drive the genre. The film locates itself in the sub-genre of the self-aware "meta-slasher" via an effective formal mechanism. Middle-aged male technicians Hadley (Bradley Whitford) and Sitterson (Richard Jenkins) orchestrate the teenagers' doom on behalf of unseen elder gods. The real-life audience watches Hadley and Sitterson watching the teens suffer. This forces viewers to confront their complicity with the film's horrors. The patriarchal technicians perform the slasher's standard intergenerational conflict, visiting their castration anxiety on the teens by deploying the slashing violence of *Cabin*'s monsters. Yet neither the techs nor the real-life audience gain scopophilic pleasure from watching women punished for being women, and young people for being young. Instead, *Cabin* offers the feminist pleasures of Dana's independent female gaze and active female sexuality (Williams, "Woman Looks" 34; Halberstam 156). By simultaneously performing and subverting the sexual archetypes of the slasher film in these ways, *Cabin* opens up a space for a more progressive type of horror film, one which celebrates youthful sexuality and female sexual agency.

"You're Not a Threat to Me": Female Dominance and Male Submission in The Avengers, Age of Ultron *and* Much Ado

In 2012, superhero fans rejoiced at the release of *The Avengers*, written and directed by Joss Whedon. The film was a critical and financial success, receiving a 92 percent critic rating on the review aggregator Rotten Tomatoes and earning over $1.5 billion worldwide, making it the highest-grossing superhero film ever at the time of its release. Although Marvel Studios originally envisioned the Avengers as an exclusively male superhero team, Whedon insisted on including one Whedomme: Natasha Romanoff, the Black Widow. Whedon's representations of Black Widow avoided the hypersexualization that is so common in portrayals of female superheroes. As Stephanie Graves argues, Natasha "isn't sexualized, apart from the way she sexualizes herself." Her sexualized persona is a conscious, deliberate performance. In its refusal to objectify its female hero, *Avengers* is consistent with Whedon's previous work. In its insistence that a woman has the right to wield her sexuality as she sees fit, for her own benefit and that of her allies, the film represents a continuation of *Buffy*'s third wave girlie feminism.

Joss Whedon directing Scarlett Johansson's performance of Black Widow on the set of *Marvel's The Avengers* (2012). Marvel Studios/Paramount Pictures.

Whedon's Black Widow subverts the superhero genre's stereotypical representations of female sexuality. The dominant Widow lets herself appear to be a helpless victim of sadistic Russian mobsters and of Loki (Tom Hiddleston), when in fact she is in full control (Kociemba 132). Nor is her dominance limited to her foes. David Kociemba points out that her fight with Hawkeye (Jeremy Renner) demonstrates the sexual tension in their friendship (141), and she is clearly the dominant partner in this sexualized friendship. The film's narrative inverts the "damsel in distress" trope that is all too common in superhero stories, for it is Hawkeye who needs rescuing (from Loki's mind control), and it is the dominant Black Widow who rescues him.

Whedon's *Avengers: Age of Ultron* (2015) gave Natasha Romanoff the opportunity to express her dominant sexuality through a consensual relationship with Bruce Banner. As Kociemba notes, the film reverses the gender dynamic that typically obtains in the superhero film, since it is Natasha who actively pursues the reluctant Bruce, even as her alter ego (Black Widow) pursues his (Hulk) (145). *Ultron* reveals that Black Widow was forcibly sterilized by the Russian state. This storyline was widely denounced by critics who believed that it articulates a conservative sexual politics which measures a woman's worth by her reproductive ability (e.g., Stewart; Woerner and Trendacosta). Yet Bruce is far more concerned about his inability to have children than Natasha is about hers (Kociemba 145): again, the usual gender and sexual roles are reversed here.

Ultron laid the groundwork for a non-reproductive, female-dominant DS relationship between Natasha and Bruce. The centerpiece of this relationship is the "lullaby," a technique of discipline that Black Widow deploys to soothe the savage Hulk and make him revert to Bruce Banner. Kociemba makes a strong case that the lullaby is feminist; he views it as "a potentially progressive turn on the otherwise retrograde trope of the Beauty and the Beast, as skill rather than blind love is the woman's solution to masculine aggression run amok" (145). In Chapter One, I treat Natasha/Bruce as a paradigmatic example of a Whedominant/submissive relationship that meets the psychological and emotional needs of both partners. In Chapter Three, I consider the relationship from a Disability Studies perspective. Here I argue that although their mutual impairments (especially their sterility) may preclude a typical heteronormative relationship based on penetrative sex and potential reproduction, these impairments need not prevent Natasha and Bruce from developing a healthy and satisfying non-normative sexual relationship.

In addition to his love of superhero stories, horror films, and Broadway musicals, the eclectic Whedon has always loved Shakespeare. After completing principal photography for *The Avengers*, Whedon directed a film version of *Much Ado About Nothing*. Whedon's *Much Ado* was released in 2013, earning generally positive reviews (an 85 percent critic rating on Rotten Tomatoes) and modest financial success; the film grossed over $5 million globally. The film was successful for three reasons. The first was Whedon's choice of source material. *Much Ado* was Shakespeare's most modern play, and it features his most modern heroine: Beatrice, brilliantly realized by Amy Acker. Acker's Beatrice is, as Rhonda Wilcox has it, a "smart, sexual wom[a]n presented with respect and understanding" ("Swords"). Second, Whedon strategically deleted dialogue from Shakespeare's text, removing lines that restricted women's power or sexual agency to produce a more feminist version of *Much Ado*. Third, Whedon skillfully used every element of *mise-en-scène*, including set design, props, scene composition, shot blocking, and framing to give women characters more power, and to show that men could find such power attractive. The result is a film which effectively implements the representational project that Whedon has been pursuing since he created the dominant Buffy and surrounded her with submissive men and male vampires.

In Chapter Seven, I argue that Whedon's film transforms the Beatrice/Benedick relationship from Shakespeare's "battle of the sexes" (Lavery 166) into the kind of female-dominant DS relationship that characterizes Whedon's entire *oeuvre*. Acker's Beatrice is strongly dominant, while Alexis Denisof's Benedick is thoroughly submissive, and happy to be so. Jillian Morgese performs Hero in a way that works against the stereotypical submissiveness that the character usually exhibits (Wilcox, "Swords"). In a reversal of Black Widow's strategy, Morgese's Hero tempers submission with tactical dominance. This allows her to establish an equitable relationship with Claudio (Fran Kranz), something that eluded previous Heroes. By making Conrade (Riki Lindhome) into a woman, Whedon creates an opportunity to critique both her unreflective submission to Don John (Sean Maher), and Don John's exploitative male dominance. Conrade is, however, dominant with everyone *except* Don John, which suggests that absent the seductive allure of her lover's unethical dominance, Conrade could have become a Whedomme.

For over two decades, Whedon's works have given their audiences a vision of sexuality that is diverse, inclusive, innovative, and above all, honest. Ironically, Whedon's fantastic worlds provide the clearest possible reflection of our world's human sexualities. All of these worlds, fictional and real, have sometimes struggled with homophobia, a bit less now than in the past. All have perpetrated bisexual and transgender erasure, and all have begun to learn how not to do that. All of them began heteronormative, and gradually became more queer. And all of these worlds have slowly started to realize that such diverse sexualities as BDSM, fetishism, sex work, intergenerational sexuality and disabled sexuality properly belong not in Gayle Rubin's outer limits of despised, marginalized sexualities, but in a charmed circle whose boundaries must be increased to encompass all consensual, desired sexualities. In the Whedonverses, ethical beings are free to love each other however they wish, provided they abide by the triple law of consent, desire, and trust. The more progressive elements of our culture, including especially queers and sexual minorities of all kinds, aspire to the kind of pluralist sexual culture that the Whedonverses represent. For over twenty years, the Whedonverses have mirrored and supported a culture of sexuality that privileges no kind of sex as normal, and prohibits no consensual, desired sex as perverse. The real-world culture of sexual diversity and the Whedonesque cultural artifacts that reflect and encourage it have a powerful symbiotic relationship. This book is a history of that intimate symbiosis.

One

"It's About Power"

The Rise of the Whedonesque Dominant Woman, or Whedomme

From *Buffy* through *Age of Ultron*, Joss Whedon's works portray sexual dominance and submission (DS) as healthy and beneficial. Buffy herself provides a handy abstract for Whedon's *oeuvre* at the beginning of season seven: "It's about power. Who's got it. Who knows how to use it" ("Lessons" 7.1). The dominant and submissive characters of the Whedonverses know how to use power, for their own benefit and for the benefit of their partners. Whedon's vision of DS is not utopian, and his works do not suggest that DS can guarantee psychological health or successful relationships. However, Whedon's corpus does contain a clear and consistent argument for the *potential* advantages of DS.

Whedon's characters often derive the same sorts of benefits from DS that real-world dominants and submissives enjoy. Real-world DS can lead to "increased trust, bonding, and connection" (Ortmann and Sprott 97).[1] Like their real-life counterparts, Whedon's dominants and submissives find that the emotional bond they share is "perhaps the single most important element in the power exchange" (Brame, Brame, and Jacobs 77). In the real world, some dominants "like to control their submissive's behavior with a goal towards improving his life" (Easton and Hardy 169), and Whedonesque dominants are no different. Buffy's dominance helps Spike make the long journey from villain to champion, while Black Widow's dominance disciplines the dangerously chaotic Hulk and allows him to become an effective superhero. In real-world DS cultures, the submissive is often someone who has "weighty responsibilities" in the non-sexual areas of their life; by yielding responsibility to their dominant partner in the context of DS play, these submissives gain an important respite from their "worldly obligations" (Brame, Brame, and Jacobs 74). On *Firefly*, Wash gains some relief from the responsibility of flying *Serenity* and her crew safely through the unforgiving void of space by submitting sexually to Zoë, while Scott Summers can temporarily escape from the burden of being the X-Men's team leader by submitting to Emma Frost (Call, "'That Weird, Unbearable Delight'" ¶ 25–40). Real-world submissives do not lose social or professional power when they submit to their dominants; indeed, they often find the act of submitting on their own terms to be "a profoundly empowering experience" (Brame, Brame, and Jacobs 54). Similarly, by submitting to Natasha Romanoff, Bruce Banner gives her the responsibility for controlling his transformations to and from Hulk, which allows him to be a more effective scientist and a better Avenger. His submission actually increases his professional power in both his scientific and superheroic careers.

In Whedon's works, DS is usually configured as female dominant.[2] The Whedonverses are full of dominant women, including *Buffy*'s Anya, *Firefly*'s Inara, *Dollhouse*'s Echo, and many more. *Agents of S.H.I.E.L.D* features a dominant woman with superpowers (Daisy, played by Chloe Bennet), and one without (May, played by Ming-Na Wen). In 2016 Whedon declared that "everything I write is about power and helplessness and somebody being helpless. Their journey to power is the narrative that sustains me" (Reyes). In Whedon's works, it is most often women who undertake this journey to power. These Whedonesque dominant women or "Whedommes" are consistently presented as powerful, independent, and desirable. Whedon's male characters recognize the benefits of female dominance. Whedon's works are full of men who find happiness and satisfaction by submitting to women more powerful than they are. Spike is only happy when Buffy dominates him. Xander is the same way with Anya. On *Agents of S.H.I.E.L.D*, Lincoln (Luke Mitchell) submits to Daisy, and everybody submits to May. Scott Summers can't even function unless Emma Frost is dominating him. Bruce Banner is like Scott but moreso: the only way he can hope to live his life as anything other than a giant green ball of Hulkish rage is by submitting wholeheartedly to the dominant Natasha Romanoff.

This chapter considers two of the Whedonverses' major female-dominant DS relationships: Buffy/Spike and Natasha/Bruce. These relationships developed in different media and at different moments in Whedon's career. Buffy/Spike began on television in 2001 and continued in comics through 2018. The cinematic Natasha/Bruce relationship began in 2015. Natasha's death in *Avengers: Endgame* (Anthony Russo and Joe Russo 2019) presumably precludes any future relationship between her and Bruce (though one can never be sure of that, since superheroes frequently come back from the dead). In both of these relationships, female-dominant DS provides each partner with self-confidence, agency, and personal happiness. In each case, such DS enables the successful management of mental disorder, including the madness that Spike experiences after regaining his soul and Bruce Banner's dangerous inability to control the rage that makes him Hulk. The Whedonverses thus present dominance and submission as an important part of a healthy and gratifying disabled sexuality (see Chapter Three).

"It's Always the Staff": Female Sexual Dominance as a Challenge to Patriarchal Power

In the real world, people who practice DS and the other components of BDSM often find that these practices can provide an effective challenge to patriarchal power. Research has shown that BDSM can lead to an increased awareness of gender hierarchies (Bauer, "Playgrounds" 182). In the 1980s, some feminist critics argued that BDSM was "firmly rooted in patriarchal sexual ideology," hence inherently antithetical to feminism (Linden et al. 4). However, more recent research has found no evidence that practitioners of BDSM are anti-feminist (Cross and Matheson 146). Indeed, in the early twenty-first century, there is a large overlap between the BDSM and feminist communities (Bauer, *Intimacies* 44). Some BDSM participants believe that their practices can reveal and subvert "gendered power imbalances" (Simula and Sumerau 454). Many participants understand their practices as "deliberately, consciously antithetical to ... patriarchal heterosexuality" (Taylor and Ussher 302). Women participants, in particular, often regard their practices as "parodying" traditional, oppressive sexual relations (Taylor and Ussher 303).

Dominant women often find their sexual dominance empowering. Health educator and professional dominant Liz Highleyman argues that for many real-life women, "exercising sexual power has allowed them to overcome, at least temporarily, the subordinate social and sexual position of women in this society" ("Playing with Paradox" 169). Importantly, Highleyman doesn't overstate the feminist potential of female dominance; here she acknowledges that while a sexually dominant woman may be able to subvert some aspects of patriarchal power, such subversion is likely only temporary. Highleyman maintains that "erotic dominance may provide the taste of power and agency that enables a woman to empower herself in other areas" ("Playing with Paradox" 169). Some dominant women find that their sexual dominance helps them achieve professional success. In the Buffyverse, a dominant Buffy makes a better Slayer, because she is better prepared to resist the patriarchal power that has haunted the Slayer line since three ancient Shadow Men made the first Slayer by imbuing a girl with dark magic against her will ("Get it Done" 7.15). Unlike that first Slayer, the dominant Buffy can seize the phallic staff that symbolizes the Shadow Men's patriarchal authority. "It's always the staff," Buffy muses. Buffy's concept of power is Lacanian. She intuitively understands that the phallus is a signifier of power that can be wielded by women as well as men. By asserting agency on behalf of Slayers and other women, Buffy challenges the shadowy, non-consensual phallic dominance of patriarchy.

Female dominance can help restore some balance to the structure of gendered power relations, and a dominant woman can use her sexual power to promote a broader feminist agenda. However, the effectiveness of such an agenda will be limited if it continues to rely on the gendered categories of power that it purports to subvert. In a patriarchal culture, power is often coded as male, and many forms of power are available to women only on the condition that they become more masculine. If a woman can only become dominant by invoking a sexual power that remains coded as masculine, she will not have attained an authentic *female* dominance. However, Buffy and other girlie feminists show that it is possible to code power as feminine. Professional dominants, also known as pro dommes or dominatrices, provide a good real-world example of this possibility. As Highleyman argues, the pro domme is "the quintessential embodiment of the combination of power and femininity" ("My Life as a Dom" 79). In her study of professional dominatrices, sociologist Danielle J. Lindemann found that pro dommes "destabilize the established gender/power hierarchy by assuming the role of the dominant female in the erotic dyad" (173). By taking the conventionally masculine dominant position in erotic relations while maintaining a feminine gender presentation, dominatrices call into question the broader elements of male social and political dominance that male sexual dominance often symbolizes and sometimes sanctions.

Although female dominance can empower women in important ways, its real radical potential lies in its ability to subvert patriarchal gender roles altogether (Newmahr 118). In her study of an early twenty-first-century American BDSM community, ethnographer Staci Newmahr found that BDSM does not "simply invert the gender enactments of patriarchal narratives" (116). To do so would be to perpetuate patriarchy's unequal power structure under a feminist guise. Since male and female dominance convey equal status in BDSM communities (Newmahr 117), these communities actually promote a radical gender equality. Most importantly, Newmahr found that female dominance defies gender expectations and troubles the binary concept of gender itself (Newmahr 117). Male submission carries a similar radical potential. Male submissives claim "a desire that does not align with traditional expectations regarding masculinity" (Yost and Hunter 254), which may subvert hegemonic masculinity. On the other hand, male submission can be "framed as an example of strength, self control, and resilience," thus reinforcing "hegemonic gender beliefs" (Simula and Sumerau 465). But this simply shows the complexity of BDSM, which has, as Simula and Sumerau argue, the potential to both "resist and reproduce hegemonic gender frames" (458).

The destabilization of conventional gender roles that BDSM facilitates provides a way to address some of the concerns that feminist psychoanalytic media theory has raised about the political implications of female dominance. Laura Mulvey warns that the reversal of traditional sex roles may simply reproduce the male-dominant conventions of narrative cinema (120). Visual media that promote a simplistic, unexamined female dominance may actually contribute to hierarchical gender relations. Mulvey also warns that visual media can promote "a fetishistic male fantasy about fascinating, phallic women" (120). It would be easy for submissive men like Spike and Bruce to fetishize the phallic power of women like Buffy and Natasha. Luckily, as Mulvey notes, the "role reversal of the socially demanded 'masculine' and 'feminine' positions as 'active' and 'passive'" which is characteristic of female dominance and male submission can easily lead to the collapse of "masculinity masquerading as phallic power" (137). As hegemonic masculinity collapses, it may take the phallic power of both men and women with it. This could create the opportunity to develop a new, oppositional masculinity that might refuse the temptation to fetishize phallic power. This anti-phallic submissive masculinity could facilitate an egalitarian sharing of power between men and women, dominants and submissives. This possibility corresponds to the power sharing experiences of real-world BDSM participants. Real-world DS involves a consensual "sharing of power" in which the submissive lends power to the dominant (Easton and Hardy 10). Real-world submissives have a good deal of power and a high degree of control over BDSM play (Ortmann and Sprott 16; Taylor and Ussher 299). Indeed, since they typically control the limits of this play, submissives arguably have more power than dominants.

The masochistic desire of a male submissive like Spike is crucial here. Kaja Silverman argues that the male masochist "exhibits his castration for all to see" (*Male Subjectivity* 206), as Spike does when his chip strips him of the power of violence. Silverman suggests that "the male masochist magnifies the losses and divisions upon which cultural identity is based ... in short, he radiates a negativity inimical to the social order" (*Male Subjectivity* 206). A submissive male masochist like Spike amplifies the symbolic castration which is, in the psychoanalytic model, characterized by the loss of the Real and the entry into the cultural order. He also points to a way beyond this castration. By emphasizing the loss that underwrites the Symbolic order, the submissive masochist shows that this order is unsustainable. This permits a return to the order that ensures the Symbolic will always remain incomplete: the Real.

In Lacanian theory, the human child becomes a subject by gradually leaving the Real, developing first an Imaginary relationship with the mother, then a Symbolic relationship with the father (and with culture in general) via the Oedipal law that Lacan calls the Name-of-the-Father (Grosz 73–74). Lacan postulates that the young child develops an ego during the "mirror phase," when they identify with a reflective image or imago (*Écrits* 75–76).

The imago is an Imaginary image of another person, someone close to the child; the child often creates an imago of the mother (Lacan, *Écrits* 93). The Mother is the child's Other (Lacan, *Écrits* 688). The child identifies with the (m)other's image, which captivates the child's Self (Lacan, *Écrits* 147). The young subject develops an erotic relationship with this "image that alienates him from himself"; this is where the ego originates (Lacan, *Écrits* 92). The superego develops later, during the Oedipal phase, via the symbolic function of the Name-of-the-Father.

Although the Real and the Imaginary always remain an important part of subjective reality, people don't generally return to those realms once they enter the Symbolic. Whedon's dominant women, however, can bring a submissive subject back through the Imaginary and into the Real. Black Widow does this in *Ultron* when she causes Bruce to transform into Hulk. Bruce occupies an intellectual culture which is very much a part of the Symbolic. Towards the end of the film, Black Widow brings him back into the Imaginary via one of that realm's most powerful gestures: a wordless, tactile kiss. She then pushes him into the Real (literally, by shoving him into a pit in order to force him to transform into Hulk). Here Natasha demonstrates one of the greatest powers of the Whedomme: the ability to offer a Whedonesque submissive some respite from the tyranny of culture, an escape from the Symbolic, if only a temporary one. Whedon's submissive males can also help their dominant partners move through the three Lacanian orders. They do this via the act of submission itself, as when Spike's submission to Buffy helps her return to the Symbolic following her resurrection in season six.

Whedonesque DS relationships not only satisfy the erotic needs of all participants; they also provide an effective form of psychotherapy. Some real-life BDSM practitioners use their play as a way to heal past trauma (Newmahr 95). Similarly, Terry Spaise views Buffy's DS relationship with Spike as a "therapeutic exercise" that helps her "re-embrace life" (761). But here we must be careful. Meg Barker et al. point out that when we describe BDSM as therapeutic we run the risk of pathologizing it all over again, by implying that BDSM is only for the sick, the mentally ill, the disabled (205). More recently, Danielle Lindemann has warned that "by reconstituting pathology as cure, [DS] participants ... run the risk of creating an even stronger link between sexual deviation and medicalization" (151). Yet Lindemann also acknowledges that the discourse of DS as therapy not only legitimizes these historically taboo practices, but actually posits them as beneficial, transforming the pathologized into the prescribed (135–136). For real-world dominants and submissives, as for their Whedonesque counterparts, this is clearly a healthy and affirming transformation. Of course, people practice DS for a variety of reasons that have nothing to do with the need for therapy. These reasons include, most obviously, sexual gratification and fun. But as long as we keep this diversity of purpose and meaning in mind, it is reasonable to list psychotherapy among the potential benefits of DS. It is particularly important to do so as we consider how submissives and dominants help each other move freely through the three Lacanian orders.

"The Slayer Ain't No One's": Buffy's Female Dominance and Spike's Male Submission

The first major Whedonesque DS relationship developed between Buffy and Spike. This relationship was implicit in *Buffy* seasons two through five and became explicit in season six. It thrilled some season six viewers and terrified others. Small wonder: as Cori Mathis points out, in the divisive season six, showrunner Marti Noxon "deftly explores the fears and concerns that come with young adulthood, particularly through Buffy's exploration of non-normative sexuality with Spike" (¶ 8). The relationship continued to develop canonically in *Buffy* comic books, and extra-canonically in "Spuffy" slash fiction. Indeed, as Milly Williamson argues, Spuffy greatly expanded the boundaries of slash fiction by adding "monster-human" pairings to slash's subject matter, and by contributing extensively to the "hurt/comfort" subgenre so central to slash (303, 305). Spuffy also blurred the boundaries between canon and fan fiction. Jane Espenson has referred to *Buffy*'s sixth season *as* fan fiction (Penny 58), while Joss Whedon describes himself as "a Buffy/Spike shipper" (Tharpe).

At the end of season five, Buffy dies and (we learn later) enters the Real of Heaven. At the beginning of season six, Willow resurrects her. Buffy claws her way out of her grave, leaving the Real and moving traumatically into the Imaginary ("Bargaining, Part Two" 6.2). Buffy enters the Lacanian mirror stage in a literal way when she encounters her perfect reflection, the Buffybot, only to see the alienating other of her mirror self torn to pieces, again literally, as the demon biker gang dismembers the Buffybot. Buffy's traumatic re-entry into the Symbolic consists of a single agonized "no" as she watches her other self die. She will only be able to return fully to the Symbolic, via the Imaginary, with Spike's help. On some level she knows this, which is why Spike is the only person to whom she can reveal the secret that she has lost her heavenly Real. As for Spike, he intuitively understands that the only thing that could bring Buffy completely back into the Symbolic is a DS relationship. He explicitly offers Buffy such a relationship, with himself in the submissive position, in the celebrated musical episode "Once More, With Feeling" (6.7). Here *Buffy* takes advantage of the musical's formal power to show emotion through song (Barry Grant 2). In "Rest in Peace," Spike sings that he is willing to be Buffy's slave. Then he falls to his knees, confirming in Imaginary gesture what he has just expressed in song: that his desire for Buffy has taken the form of a powerful submission. The decision to place himself in the submissive posture shows us something important about Spike: consent matters to him. Indeed, as Dee Amy-Chinn points out, sexual consent is crucial to Spike ("Bitch" 323). Spike has created a situation in which Buffy may either see her desire through or turn her back on it. It might appear that Spike's decision to force Buffy's hand is coercive, but in fact he is only revealing to her the choice which her own desire has already forced upon her: "kinks or vanilla," as Faith said casually in season three ("Consequences" 3.15), but this time for real, as a life choice. Spike's song is also performative. By requiring Buffy's consent before he proceeds, Spike models the values of modern BDSM communities.

Buffy opens her song "Something to Sing About" by singing about how everyone plays their part in the show of life. The long black leather coat she wears at the beginning of the number signifies dominance. Here Buffy seems to be playing the dominant part, or at least thinking about it. But she quickly sheds the coat and the part and starts singing about how she wants to be an ordinary woman. Perhaps she fears that if she embraced her dominance over Spike, she couldn't be like everyone else. Finally, she reveals the source of her misery: her friends unwittingly tore her out of Heaven. She nearly dances herself to death; only Spike's intervention saves her. He grabs Buffy by the shoulders, stops her dancing, and sings to her that she must live in order to recover from the trauma of her resurrection. Spike and Buffy are framed almost exactly as they were in his crypt, when he sang about being Buffy's slave: Whedon shoots over Buffy's left shoulder, to show Spike singing these important truths to her. The only difference is that Spike is on his feet rather than his knees in "Something to Sing About." He has switched briefly to the dominant role that Buffy seems to have rejected, but only to try to convince her that she should embrace living. Spike's adoring gaze suggests that he means "living" to include some kind of relationship with him. The framing evokes Spike's earlier submission in "Rest in Peace" in a way that suggests he has in mind a DS relationship. Spike is now offering Buffy an intimate, two-person Imaginary relationship, something to heal the trauma of a mirror stage that consisted solely of watching her robot-self die. Buffy recognizes that she needs what Spike is offering, and she accepts. The musical concludes in the Imaginary realm, with a confirmation that Buffy and Spike's negotiations have succeeded: a passionate kiss, their first.

Only an outbreak of magical amnesia ("Tabula Rasa" 6.8) can keep Buffy and Spike from moving into the sexual phase of their DS relationship immediately; they do so two episodes later, in "Smashed" (6.9). Buffy initiates sex with Spike and participates enthusiastically. This lends credibility to Angie Burns' argument: although Buffy sometimes describes the relationship in terms that suggest Spike is the dominant partner, this construction is at odds with the way in which their physical sex acts are portrayed (¶ 9). Yet as Rhonda Wilcox notes, Buffy and Spike do not actually have sex until they know that he can hurt her (*Why Buffy Matters* 89). It is important to remember here that Spike is a switch—that is, he has the ability to switch back and forth between the dominant and submissive roles. Indeed, as Dee Amy-Chinn has observed, Spike is an accomplished switch ("Bitch" 316). Spike's submission contains the possibility of dominance, and that possibility enables his submission. Spike thus reflects the basic erotic orientation of the Whedonverses, and the values of contemporary American BDSM communities. He represents an egalitarian sexuality in which relations of dominance and submission are always reversible. He shows that a flexible, switchable DS has the potential to subvert gender binaries and hierarchies.

The Buffy/Spike relationship continues to grow more intense. "He's not getting any gentler," Buffy observes ("As You Were" 6.15). Buffy tries to end the relationship (6.15), but Spike has a hard time accepting that decision. He becomes increasingly unstable and obsessive. In the highly disturbing episode "Seeing Red" (6.19), Spike attempts to rape Buffy. What is most striking about the rape scene is how profoundly different it is from Buffy and Spike's initial sex scene in "Smashed," and from all their subsequent consensual scenes. Those scenes mainly operated at the levels of the Imaginary and the Real; they relied upon image and sound. The consensual scenes were filmed erotically, with sexy music and low lighting. By way of contrast, as Wilcox notes, the lighting in the rape scene is bright, cold, and grim (*Why Buffy Matters* 35). Showrunner Marti Noxon decided to use no music in it at all because, as scriptwriter Steven S. De Knight says, "we wanted it not to have any fantasy element, to be nasty and violent" (quoted in Kaveney, "Writing the Vampire Slayer" 127). By stripping away the fantasy that covers over the void of the Real, *Buffy* reveals the traumatic kernel that ensures the Symbolic is always already crippled (Žižek, *Looking Awry* 33).

Spike's attempted rape is one of the most clearly wrong things that happens in the entire series. By filming it in such a uniquely disconcerting way, *Buffy*'s creators were able to show, discreetly, that what Buffy and Spike had done before was *not* wrong. The heavy audio-visual distinctions between this rape and the previous scenes of consensual BDSM create an ethical space in which the audience can condemn the former while embracing the latter. The rape scene foregrounds the Symbolic, by emphasizing the language of consent. After Spike first puts his hands on Buffy in this scene, Buffy says "no" three times. She says "stop" no fewer than five times. The episode's title, "Seeing Red," evokes BDSM's most common safeword, "red." "Red" means "stop right now." Spike's problem, ironically, is that he does *not* see red in this episode. When Spike ignores Buffy's safeword, the Symbolic collapses and the Real returns traumatically. Worst of all, play becomes rape. By highlighting the vital distinction between the two, "Seeing Red" actually endorses the ethical philosophy of real-world BDSM.

Wendy Fall warns that *Buffy*'s refusal to let Buffy speak about the trauma she experienced when Spike tried to rape her may contribute to contemporary rape culture (69, 78). This is a valid concern. However, it is also important to recognize that the consensual DS that Buffy shares with Spike helps her to heal from a different trauma, namely the trauma of her second death and subsequent resurrection. Absent the consensual DS that she shares with Spike prior to the attempted rape, it's hard to see how Buffy could ever have recovered from the experience of being forcibly removed from a peaceful afterlife and thrust back into a harsh and violent world. Not only does she recover; her DS relationship with Spike helps her learn how to live in the Symbolic again. Buffy does feel guilty about her relationship with Spike. Just before they have sex for the first time, Spike claims that Buffy came back from the dead "wrong," a little less human, and that's why he can hurt her despite his chip ("Smashed" 6.9). Buffy internalizes this idea, which quickly becomes an alibi for her desire for Spike, a way to alleviate the guilt she feels for having that desire. She asks Tara to check the resurrection spell to see if she came back wrong ("Dead Things" 6.13). Tara assures her that she didn't, that there's nothing wrong with her. But Buffy insists that there must be, because if there isn't, then she can't understand why she lets Spike "do those things" to her. She can only comprehend the DS she shares with Spike as a wrongness. She asks Tara, the most out queer person in the Buffyverse, to keep her perverse desire for Spike secret, because she couldn't take how her friends would look at her if they knew. Buffy's fear is motivated not only by her recognition that her friends will reject her choice of partners, but also by her fear that they won't understand (as she herself doesn't) the *jouissance* she shares with Spike. She has the same anxiety about coming out to her friends that real-life BDSM participants have (Ortmann and Sprott 90), so she keeps her DS relationship in the closet. It's only in the season ten comics that Buffy finally learns to let go of this fear, embrace the DS sexuality that she shares with Spike, and enjoy the Real things they do together without guilt. In the end, Buffy is ethical in the Lacanian sense: she doesn't give ground on her desire.

Although "Seeing Red" marks the *temporary* end of Buffy and Spike's *sexual* relationship, it is by no means the end of their DS relationship. The rape was empty of ethics and erotics, and Spike knows it. He is so dismayed by what he has done that he goes to Africa and tortures a soul into himself. Like Angel's soul, Spike's is the *objet petit a*, the unattainable object of desire whose endless pursuit the subject experiences as suffering. "All it does is burn," says Spike ("Beneath You" 7.2). Stacey Abbott notes that the rapist Spike is only one of the multiple Spikes who emerge in the show's last two seasons. One of these Spikes is indeed "a monster intent on embracing his monstrousness," but there is also the ensouled Spike, the mad Spike, the tormented Spike, Spike the friend, Spike the champion, and (most importantly for my analysis) Spike the lover (Abbott 334–335). The mad Spike is trapped in the traumatic Real; his hold on language is tenuous at best. Much of season seven concerns Buffy's attempts to bring Spike out of madness and back into the Symbolic. Naturally, she uses the power of the Whedomme to achieve this, gently drawing Spike into an intimate Imaginary relationship. As Wilcox notes, "by the sixth season, it is generally accepted that Spike actually loves Buffy" (*Why Buffy Matters* 86). And by the seventh season, she has begun to love him. In season seven, Spike and the Scoobies believe that Spike might be killing again, so he agrees to be restrained for everyone's safety. This bondage is consensual, but it is practical rather than erotic. Yet the care that Buffy gives Spike while he is enchained is deeply erotic. Buffy gently washes the blood from his wounded face. She is very much the loving Mistress here. She is also operating within the maternal Imaginary, which is where Buffy must work if she wants to return Spike to sanity and the Symbolic. Spike's attempted rape was profoundly wrong, but he has done everything in his power to make amends, and Buffy has begun to forgive him. She knows that he is not responsible for his current violence (since he's being controlled by the First), so she can be tender with him, even intimate.

This new intimacy culminates in the amazing love scene in "Touched" (7.20). The night before an apocalypse is traditionally a very sexual time in the Buffyverse, but this beautiful montage of intercut sex scenes takes that tradition to new heights. Xander and Anya have sex one last time. Faith and Robin Wood (D. B. Woodside) have steamy interracial sex. Willow and Kennedy have pierced-tongue lesbian sex, a first for American network television (Frost). Meanwhile, Buffy is sleeping peacefully, fully clothed, in Spike's arms. The Buffy/Spike scene is not at all sexual, but it is stunningly erotic. Indeed, it has the feeling of the time beyond the BDSM scene, the "after care" time. Buffy feels safe with Spike once again. Just as she cared for him when he was chained up in her basement, he spends the night looking after her. Having brought Spike back into the Symbolic, Buffy now trusts him enough to switch to the submissive role and join him once more in the Imaginary. The night that Buffy and Spike spend together in the Imaginary at the "end of days" is crucially important to both of them. Spike calls it the best night of his life, and when he asks Buffy if she was there with him, she assures him that she was, and speaks of the strength he gave her ("End of Days" 7.21). Justine Larbalestier claims that Buffy and Spike's relationship "can't work," and that Buffy's night of having Spike hold her is simply "masochistic" (in, one presumes, a bad way) (216–217). But I argue that the relationship *does* work. It gives them both what they need. What Buffy needed before going off to save the world was a night when she could be vulnerable, submissive, and safe. Spike needed to be caring, protective, and gently dominant. So they did what they've always done. They switched into the necessary power configuration and satisfied their mutual needs.

Buffy renews her sexual relationship with Spike in "Love Dares You," a season ten comic book story written by Christos Gage and Nicholas Brendon, with art by Megan Levens. Levens draws a dominant Buffy initiating a kiss with Spike (10.11). In the first panel, she puts her hand on his shoulder. In the second, she closes her eyes, leans in, and pulls Spike towards her by the lapel of his coat. The final half-page panel bleeds to the edges of the page.[3] Standing in a silent graveyard of the Real, the two lovers kiss their way into the Imaginary. Surprisingly, Spike retreats into the Symbolic and resists the possibility of renewing his relationship with Buffy (10.12). He questions her commitment, accusing her of always wanting what she can't have. He suggests, cruelly, that after a month she might get bored with him and develop a sudden desire for Andrew (a gay man), Willow (a woman), or Giles (a man old enough to be her father). Spike can imagine every sort of non-normative relationship *except* the DS relationship that Buffy is actually offering. If she wants what she can't have, he doesn't seem to want what he *can* have. Perhaps he's scared of the risk he would run by submitting to her now, after so long. But he soon overcomes this fear. After a big demon battle during which, not incidentally, Andrew comes out as gay, Spike confronts his own fears. Buffy makes an impassioned speech about how much Spike means to her and offers him real friendship. But Spike is now done with the Symbolic: "Pretty speech, Slayer. Every word you said is true and right. Just one problem." And here Spike utters the sentence that makes the Symbolic eat itself and give way to the sexual Imaginary: "I'm in love with you." They spend the last third of the page gazing adoringly at each other. In the panel that occupies the top half of the next page, Levens draws Spike kissing Buffy passionately as he slams open the door to the apartment he shares with Xander. Buffy kicks the door closed and slams Spike against the wall so hard that the impact sends Xander's action figures tumbling off their shelf. Although Buffy and Spike do not destroy the building as they did in "Smashed," they definitely move it. Their relationship is presented as a more mature version of the one they shared in season six. Buffy tells Willow that Spike "*does* make me happy. He really cares about me. I like who I am when I'm with him. I like who we are together" (10.13).

Spike becomes fully comfortable in his submissive role. When Dawn tells Spike that Buffy is his girlfriend now, artist Rebekah Isaacs draws a close-up of a contemplative Spike who replies "the Slayer ain't no one's, little bit. If she was … wouldn't be her" (Gage and Isaacs, "Old Demons" 10.16). Spike understands that he cannot possess Buffy, though she may well be able to possess him. The characters do not comment on it (for it is a thing of the Imaginary, not the Symbolic), but Spike wears a small lock on a chain around his neck. This features prominently in the aptly named story "Taking Ownership," wherein Buffy considers, and rejects, the idea of breaking up with Spike (Gage and Isaacs, "Taking Ownership" 10.28). In the Anglo-American DS subculture, Spike's lock and chain would be known as a collar, and it would signify that he is the submissive partner in a committed, long-term DS relationship. This is how season ten ends. Another kiss firmly establishes Buffy's dominance. Buffy is smartly dressed in a skirt and jacket; she is about to dominate the initial session of the newly constituted magic council (Gage and Isaacs, "Own It" 10.30). With a single finger under Spike's chin, she turns his head towards hers and kisses him deeply. Willow watches joyfully, happy that her friend has finally found the sexuality that is right for her.

Buffy and Spike continue their sexual relationship through season eleven. They formally end that relationship prior to season twelve, but this certainly does not mean that their DS relationship is over, any more than the previous four-season pause in their sexual activity did. Spike is still a Scoobie in good standing. He is still one of Buffy's staunchest and most powerful allies. And she is still the dominant partner in their relationship, as she almost always is. The key to understanding Buffy and Spike's DS relationship is to recognize that not only do they love each other, *each of them loves the person they are when they're with the other*. Buffy said as much to Willow (Gage, Brendon, and Levens 10.13). Buffy loves the powerful, dominant woman that Spike helps her to be. Spike loves the submissive undead man that Buffy helps him to be. The great strength of their relationship comes from their ability to help each other return to the Lacanian mirror stage whenever they need to do so. In the mirror stage, the lovers reflect the best versions of their partners, the ones that those partners most want to be.

At the end of season twelve, Buffy and Spike reaffirm their commitment to this profound project of cooperative self-creation. Spike and Buffy share their final hug of the series (Gage, Whedon and Jeanty 12.4). "I'm my best around you," Spike declares. "All of you [Scoobies] … but especially you [Buffy]. Nothing's ever going to change that." This ensouled vampire recognizes that submitting to Buffy will always make him the best possible version of himself. And Buffy knows that she is the best of all possible Buffies when she's dominating Spike. "That goes both ways, William Pratt," she assures him. Her rare use of Spike's human name indicates that Buffy accepts him fully as a person. It also suggests that what she has always loved, and will always love, is his submissive side: the sensitive William more than the aggressive Spike. *Buffy* ends with Buffy in the company of Spike and Angel, the two submissive male vampires who have helped her become the mature dominant woman she is today. Perhaps some day they will be able to explore the female-dominant, polyamorous threesome that they all clearly long for, but that has so far appeared only in Buffy's Imaginary sex fantasy (Whedon and

Jeanty, "Long Way Home" 8.3), and has only been named by Harmony (Gage and Isaacs, "Day Off" 10.10). Meanwhile, viewers and readers may continue to enjoy the pleasures of the female-dominant sexuality that Buffy has modeled for the past two decades. The persistence of patriarchy ensures that many women and men in the audience would not have considered dominance and submission as a sexuality for themselves—until Buffy and Spike showed them the possibility.

"We Just Play": Natasha Romanoff's Female Dominance and Bruce Banner's Male Submission

Joss Whedon's Black Widow is the very archetype of the Whedonesque dominant woman. She first appears in *The Avengers* tied to a chair, apparently helpless as the Russian gang boss Luchkov (Jerzy Skolimowski) interrogates her. The *mise-en-scène* encourages the audience to read this encounter as male dominant. The camera frames Luchkov as he plays with his collection of torture instruments. The dialogue in the first part of the scene emphasizes Luchkov's supposed dominance and Black Widow's apparent submission.

"The famous Black Widow," Natasha Romanoff (Scarlett Johansson), feigning submission in order to dominate the Russian gang. *Marvel's The Avengers* (2012). Marvel Studios/Paramount Pictures.

Luchkov mocks what he perceives as the Widow's feminine weakness: "The famous Black Widow, and she turns out to be simply another pretty face." The Widow cleverly performs the weakness that Luchkov has ascribed to her: "Do you really think I'm pretty?" By revealing his baseless assumptions about her weakness, Luchkov has actually revealed *his* weakness. The Widow takes full advantage of that weakness. When she receives her phone summons from Coulson (Clark Gregg), she immediately switches to the dominant role. She escapes her bondage and gives the Russian gang a thorough thrashing. She wraps a chain around Luchkov's leg and leaves him dangling in the air. Whedon points out that this scene is his career in a microcosm: the "helpless" female who turns out to be stronger than anyone around her (Whedon, "Commentary" on *Marvel's The Avengers*).

Black Widow also switches from submission to dominance during her interrogation of Loki (Tom Hiddleston). This is Whedon's favorite scene from *The Avengers*; he loves the power struggle (Whedon, "Commentary" on *Marvel's The Avengers*). The Widow appears to offer Loki her submission. "You're a monster," she says, her voice quivering. This foreshadows *Age of Ultron*'s debates about who is, and who is not, a monster. Loki replies, "No, you brought the monster." The moment Loki gives her the information she wants, she switches to the dominant role. She turns to face Loki, calm, centered, steady. "So. Banner. That's your play." She immediately undermines Loki's (illusory) dominance, simply by revoking her (equally illusory) submission. "Thank you for your cooperation," she says smoothly. Once again, she has used submission tactically, in the service of her dominance. This scene shows how easily she can switch from the submissive role to the dominant one. It also demonstrates the malleability of gender roles, and of audience perceptions of those roles, as Masani McGee observes (¶ 26). Like Buffy, the generally dominant but flexible Black Widow shows that the real power of female dominance lies in its ability to detach gender from the structure of power relations altogether.

The Widow tries to dominate Bruce Banner in *The Avengers*, so he will not transform into the Hulk. She fails, probably because at this point in the narrative, she hasn't yet developed the DS relationship with Hulk/Banner that will enable her to perform the "lullaby" in *Age of Ultron*. The enraged Hulk chases her through the corridors of the Helicarrier. This scene reads like an attempted sexual assault. As Daniel Snyder observes, Hulk is "the perfect embodiment of the unchecked male rage that so often victimizes women." Black Widow is afraid of this rage, as anyone would be, but she is never a helpless victim. She manages to protect herself from an assailant far more physically powerful than she is. The fact that the Widow survives an attempted assault by Hulk in *The Avengers* gives a special significance to the DS relationship that develops between the two characters in *Ultron*. That relationship gives the Widow the power she needs to protect herself against any future Hulkish aggression.

Like *The Avengers*, Whedon's *Age of Ultron* focuses on Black Widow's dominance. In *The Avengers*, her dominance was subtle. But in *Age of Ultron*, Natasha Romanoff comes out of the closet as a dominant woman. She openly dominates Bruce. Natasha and Bruce develop an affectionate, beneficial, female-dominant relationship which meets the erotic, emotional, and practical needs of both partners. Some feminists have criticized the representation of Black Widow in *Ultron*. Shaun Huston views Natasha's reaction to her forced sterilization and her somewhat awkward attempts to develop a relationship with Bruce as evidence that *Ultron* takes "a strong turn towards conventional gender roles." I argue, however, that both of these elements may reasonably be read as feminist, provided that we take the crucial step of reading Natasha as a dominant woman, and her relationship with Bruce as a non-reproductive relationship of erotic dominance and submission. Non-procreative sex occupies Gayle Rubin's outer limits of sexuality ("Thinking Sex" 281), yet Natasha is eager to seek such sex with Bruce. By pursuing her relationship with Bruce despite her sterility, she challenges the ableist culture that would define her as disabled based on her inability to have children. Her *reaction* to her sterilization is empowering. She deals with it in a way that reflects her dominant personality, rejecting a powerful set of cultural values and substituting her own. The only problem is that her chosen partner, Bruce Banner, is unable to overcome the reprosexual value system that defines both him and Natasha as disabled (see Chapter Three). Tragically, their relationship is impossible in the Lacanian sense: his reprosexual fantasy of her is incompatible with her fantasy of him as a submissive man who could be happy without children.

Absent his commitment to reprosexuality, Bruce could participate in a non-normative, female-dominant relationship with Natasha. A psychoanalytic reading can explain how he might benefit from such a relationship. Hulk is a manifestation of the id's darkest drive, the death drive, which is represented by "the instinct of destruction" (Freud, "Ego and Id" 42): Hulk smash! Bruce, on the other hand, represents the superego. He constantly struggles to keep the violent impulses of the Hulk in check. When he fails, he feels the essential manifestation of the superego: guilt (Freud, "Ego and Id" 53). The more Bruce tries to control Hulk's rage, the guiltier he feels, and the more his ego is threatened (Freud, "Ego and Id" 54). The character's fragile ego is located precisely at the nexus of Bruce Banner and the Hulk. This ego is thus even more thoroughly split than that of a typical human subject. A Lacanian reading is indicated. Bruce/Hulk's ego derives from his alienating identification with the reflection of himself that he sees in the imago he has created, the image of Black Widow. Bruce wants what everyone wants: to see his desire reflected back onto him by the object of that desire. As Lacan says, desire is desire for the Other's desire (*Écrits* 723).

In Lacanian terms, the primal, pre-linguistic Hulk occupies the Real, which is the world of objects that can be smashed. Black Widow controls his entry into the Imaginary. The fact that the Widow does this with a "lullaby" casts her relationship with him in maternal terms. This makes sense, since Lacan's Imaginary order is the site of two-person relationships, "usually identified with the pre–Oedipal mother-child relationship" (Grosz 46). The Widow also controls Hulk's entry into the Symbolic order, where, as Bruce, he gains language and culture. This is remarkable, because in the Lacanian model, it is the *father* who brings the child into the Symbolic. But the Hulk has no father. Or, since he was created by gamma radiation, maybe the universe is his father. Or, since Banner conducted the gamma radiation experiment, maybe he's his own father. In any case, it is Natasha Romanoff who holds the father's power in this scenario. She functions as a kind of "maternal superego," which Slavoj Žižek defines as "an agency that perturbs and hinders the rule of the Name-of-the-Father" (*Looking Awry* 97). In Žižek's Lacanian model, the maternal superego haunts fatherless men; it blocks the "normal" sexual relationship (Žižek, *Looking Awry* 99). In this case, that blockage creates a space for a DS relationship. This relationship gives Black Widow a power which exceeds that of the Lacanian father. The Widow doesn't just bring Hulk into the Symbolic; she decides which of Lacan's three orders he will occupy, and when. Her psychological dominance over him is total. Both Bruce and Hulk clearly desire her dominance, for dominance is the form of *her* desire.

Ultron's most controversial reveal is the fact that Natasha Romanoff was forcibly sterilized by the Russian state. The foreclosure of the Widow's reproductive options makes room for her Imaginary maternal relationship with Hulk and permits Natasha to Imagine a DS relationship with Bruce. Whedon shot some footage for *Ultron*'s farmhouse scene that didn't make it into the final film. In this deleted footage, Natasha tries even harder to get Bruce to run away with her. "We keep moving," she suggests. "And we don't play 'circle of life.' We just play." The existence of this deleted scene suggests that at certain points in the scripting, filming, and editing process, Whedon considered creating a version of *Ultron* in which Natasha explicitly contrasts a vanilla reproductive sexuality with BDSM play.

Her relationship with Bruce allows Natasha to transform the dominance that she used non-consensually against the villains Luchkov and Loki in *The Avengers* into something consensual, erotic, and loving. Krystal Clark and Tara Bennett lament that "not only does the film put her in an unnecessary romance but they actually make her a damsel in distress." I argue, however, that the relationship *is* necessary, in that it allows the couple to explore the potential benefits of dominance and submission, something they both need.

And I agree with Scarlett Johansson's assessment of the character she plays: "I love that she's never a damsel in distress," says Johansson (quoted in Surrell 70). *Age of Ultron* rejects the damsel in distress trope just as thoroughly as *The Avengers* did. Captured by Ultron, Black Widow cobbles together a transmitter to alert her teammates to her location. When Bruce arrives to rescue her, she refuses. "I'm here to get you to safety," Bruce declares. "Job's not finished," she replies. Far from throwing away her agency by pursuing a relationship with Bruce, Natasha uses that relationship to lay claim to an extremely *powerful* type of agency: that of the dominant woman. Mark Ruffalo understands that his character's relationship with Johansson's does not compromise the Widow's agency or diminish her strength. "I don't think it makes her any weaker," he says. "If anything, Black Widow is much stronger than Banner. She protects him" (quoted in Carolyn Cox).

She does this especially through the mechanism of the lullaby, her unique method of pacifying the Hulk. The lullaby is the centerpiece of her DS relationship with Hulk/Bruce. Bruce is justifiably terrified of his uncontrollable Hulkish powers. He therefore makes the rational, ethical decision to grant Natasha control over his body and its powers, just as Spike submits to Buffy when he fears he can't control his own violence. Like Buffy, Natasha uses her power responsibly, to meet her partner's needs. The relationship meets her needs, too; like Buffy, Natasha "needs some monster in her man" ("Into the Woods" *Buffy* 5.10). Indeed, as Alyssa Rosenberg argues, Natasha "would rather bring out her lover's dark side than contain it." Black Widow does not merely tolerate the Hulk's darkness, rage, and monstrosity. She desires it, needs it, and seeks it out (via the "anti-lullaby").

The Widow first performs the lullaby after *Ultron*'s opening battle scene. The lullaby begins with a ritualistic phrase: "Hey, big guy. Sun's gettin' real low." Once upon a time, sunset heralded the subversion of the Symbolic and the return of the Real, as in "Hush" (*Buffy* 4.10), when the Imaginary Riley of Buffy's dream said, "if I kiss you, it'll make the sun go down," just before the Gentlemen took speech away from Sunnydale. Now sunset has the opposite significance: the Symbolic beckons. The Widow will make Hulk speak (as Buffy made the Primal Slayer speak in "Restless" 4.22). Hulk will enter the Symbolic, but at the cost of the freedom he enjoyed in the Real. The Hulk has developed a strong desire for Black Widow's maternal aspect within the realm of the Imaginary, but the lullaby prohibits that quasi-incestuous desire. Here the ritual phrase "hey, big guy" functions as the Name-of-the-Father. The Symbolic father is, after all, the ultimate big guy. Hulk will now try (and fail) to reconcile his desire for the Widow with the inescapable mandate of the father's Law, which places inexorable restrictions on that desire. But the Widow offers him another option.

The next phase of the lullaby is visual and tactile rather than linguistic;

this phase operates at the level of the Imaginary rather than the Symbolic. The Widow offers Hulk pouty lips, bedroom eyes, and gentle touches along his fingers, hand, and upper arm. She is deploying a form of physical discipline which is designed to create a particular emotional state in her submissive. The only difference between this and a real-life DS scene is that the evidence of the dominant's success is more obvious here. Natasha turns her head and allows herself a half-smile when she sees that the lullaby has succeeded. This is the smile of a Whedomme who has just performed a successful act of dominance. As Hulk reverts to Banner, he enters the Symbolic, but he does so via the Imaginary. Black Widow has ensured that he retains the ability to leave the Symbolic, re-enter the Imaginary, and return to the Real.

Critics argue that the lullaby infantilizes Hulk and points the Widow towards a problematic maternalism. For Woerner and Trendacosta, the film's message is "Black Widow don't be sad—you have a baby Hulk." But I argue that the infantilization of the Hulk and the corresponding maternalization of the Widow are the precise *purposes* of the lullaby. The lullaby allows Black Widow and Hulk to Imagine a mother-child relationship that is prior to the Symbolic. Such a relationship could free the Hulk from the father's Law, for the Widow has the awesome power to give the Name-of-the-Father, and the even more awesome power to take it away.

This reversion to a pre–Oedipal, Imaginary mother-child relationship takes a form that is well known in the BDSM community. Widow's infantilization of Hulk looks like "age play," a form of DS play in which the submissive partner pretends to be a child. As David Ortmann and Richard Sprott point out, since "our culture organizes power along the dimension of age in some very pervasive ways," it makes sense that people in the DS community might organize their play along that same dimension (106). It is particularly understandable that Black Widow and Hulk would play in this way. As Ortmann and Sprott note, age play is the domain of deep shame, dark secrets, and extraordinary fantasies (111), all of which Banner/Hulk has in great abundance. The age play that Widow and Hulk pursue takes the specific form of "adult baby play," a form of roleplaying in which the submissive partner takes on the role of a baby (usually male), while the dominant partner acts as a parent (usually the mother). As Mistress Lorelei Powers observes, "by totally accepting her submissive's helplessness," the mother in a baby play scenario "gives him what he needs—and herself all the power and satisfaction of mothering" (121). Baby play gives Hulk a respite from the overwhelming responsibilities of the superego, a means of escape from the Symbolic realm where Bruce must always reside. The Widow enjoys the power that this play gives her over Hulk.

Crucially, the film also models the "anti-lullaby," Black Widow's method for turning Bruce into Hulk. Bruce is understandably reluctant to go through this process. "You're not gonna turn green?" Natasha demands. "I've got a compelling reason not to lose my cool," Bruce replies. The Oedipal logic pushes him to keep his Hulk-self permanently disciplined, to accept the Law and abide in the Symbolic forever. But Natasha won't let that happen. "I adore you," she says. Her powerful desire quickly leaves the realm of language and enters the Imaginary. Her adoring gaze reflects Bruce's desire, allowing him to revert to Lacan's mirror stage and return to the Imaginary. As he goes through the mirror stage in reverse, he will be able to re-enter the Real as Hulk and give Ultron a sound smashing. The two lovers share a passionate Imaginary kiss. As their lips part, Natasha pushes Bruce into a pit, forcing him to transform into Hulk, sending him back into the Real. "But I need the other guy," she explains, to herself and to the audience. "Let's finish the job," Black Widow concludes. Once again, she has used her dominance to create a particular emotional state in her submissive—in this case, rage. And once again, she has used DS in the service of her mission. She has invoked the powerful death drive of a fully enraged Hulk, in order to deploy that drive against Ultron.

One could argue that by forcing Bruce to become Hulk, Black Widow has violated her submissive's consent and betrayed his trust. Such a betrayal could explain why Hulk leaves at the end of the film. However, I argue that Black Widow's anti-lullaby should not be interpreted as a betrayal. What we know of the power exchange between Natasha and Bruce suggests that the decision to make Bruce into Hulk is probably within the scope of the Widow's authority, since Bruce seems to have consented to let Natasha control his transformations. Natasha knows that Bruce has a deep desire to do the right thing. Like the best dominants, the Widow orders her submissive to take actions which she believes will allow him to become his authentic self, even if he is reluctant to pursue those actions. "Now go be a hero," she orders. Here she authorizes an important type of ego-formation. She presents the possibility of a superhero self that will include both Bruce Banner and the Hulk. She allows him to Imagine himself at the cusp of monster and man, of id and superego. This strategy also allows the Widow to pursue authenticity herself. Darren Franich suggests that "there's an angle where Black Widow loves Bruce Banner *because*, not despite, the Hulk." I argue that this is precisely the angle the film pursues. If we read this as a DS relationship rather than a more conventional vanilla one, then we can see that the Widow loves not only Bruce but also Hulk. She particularly loves the power she holds over both.

Towards the end of the film, the Widow tries twice to give Hulk a lullaby. Both attempts fail, but through no fault of the Widow's. She's wounded during the first attempt, which interrupts the lullaby but gives Hulk the chance to play the role of the concerned submissive, caring for his injured dominant. The second attempt fails because the physical distance between Widow and

Hulk prevents her from deploying the lullaby's tactile component. But these unsettling interrupted lullabies actually highlight the power of the Black Widow. They emphasize the fact that under typical circumstances, the dominant Widow has total control over the submissive Hulk.

Taika Waititi's *Thor: Ragnarok* (2017) confirms that the lullaby is a crucial component of the DS relationship that Natasha and Bruce share. Although Waititi's interpretation of the lullaby differs slightly from Whedon's, *Ragnarok*'s version is compatible with *Ultron*'s in every major respect. *Ragnarok* confirms that the lullaby depends upon the specific power dynamic that exists between Natasha and Bruce. *Ragnarok* drives this point home with great comedic effect when Thor (Chris Hemsworth) attempts to give Hulk a lullaby in the arena. Thor recites the ritual phrase: "Hey, big guy … the sun's gettin' real low." Thor raises his open hand and offers it to Hulk. Hulk's face softens. In a side shot framed exactly like the first lullaby in *Ultron*, Thor and Hulk reach their hands towards each other. Here Waititi encourages the audience to believe that Thor's lullaby might be as successful as Black Widow's, which it closely resembles. "That's it," murmurs Thor. "Sun's going down." Thor's fingers touch Hulk's palm as Thor tries to deploy the tactile element that Black Widow used so effectively. Hulk gazes down at Thor's hand. Thor smiles, believing that his lullaby is working. And Hulk grabs Thor and bashes him back and forth into the arena floor like a ragdoll, precisely as he did to Loki in *The Avengers*. The sudden invocation of Hulk's violently antagonistic relationship with Loki immediately subverts the visual connection between Thor's attempted lullaby and Black Widow's successful one. It becomes painfully obvious (especially to Thor!) that Thor does not possess the power of the lullaby. Nor should he possess this power, if Widow/Hulk is indeed a DS relationship, as I have been arguing. Hulk has granted the power of the lullaby exclusively to the Widow, as part of his consensual submission to her. Thor's attempt to take the Widow's place as Hulk's dominant is not only ludicrous, but unethical.

Luckily, Thor learns from his mistake. When Hulk boards the Quinnjet and starts smashing everything, Thor has the presence of mind to bring up the video recording of Black Widow's last transmission to Hulk. There is sorrow and love on Hulk's face as he reaches, teary-eyed, for the disembodied image of Black Widow. This strengthens the suggestion, already present in *Ultron*, that Black Widow has a DS relationship with Hulk as well as Bruce. Hulk screams, punches himself in the face, and slams into bulkheads. "No Banner!" he shouts. Hulk is now openly hostile to Bruce; id is at war with superego. But Hulk is unable to resist Black Widow's virtual siren song. While Whedon's version of the lullaby appeared to require a tactile component, Waititi's version suggests that the tactile element may facilitate the lullaby but is not essential to its success. Perhaps Hulk's urge to revert to human form is especially strong in *Ragnarok* since he has been Hulk for an unusually long time. In that case, it may be that the lullaby doesn't need the tactile component if it is merely enabling a transformation that Hulk already wants to undertake. In any event, *Ragnarok* makes one thing quite clear: the lullaby belongs to Black Widow. It is a unique aspect of the powerful DS dynamic that exists between her and the Hulk. It cannot be deployed by anyone else (certainly not Thor), but Hulk's dominant can deploy it even when the two are on different planets, light years apart, for hers is the potent power of the Whedomme.

The Whedommes and their submissives share the power to move freely between Lacan's three orders, not according to the rigid dictates of maternal reflection or paternal Law, but rather according to the will of their trusted partners. The Whedommes give their submissives everything they need: sexual satisfaction, self confidence, mental health, the chance to be heroic, and most of all, love. The submissives give their dominant partners all of those things, plus one more: the opportunity to develop a kind of female sexual agency that may be effectively deployed against patriarchy. This potent agency, together with the promise of a more egalitarian world that it brings, are suitably generous gifts for the women whom these submissive men adore.

Two

"Love Keeps Her in the Air"
Radical Sexual Pluralism Aboard Firefly Serenity

Joss Whedon's acclaimed space western *Firefly* (2002–2003) tells the tale of the nine unique individuals who live aboard the spaceship *Serenity*. Their story continues in the 2005 feature film *Serenity* (written and directed by Whedon), and in Dark Horse's *Serenity* comics (2005–2016).[1] Whedon originally conceived *Firefly* as a story "about nine people looking into the blackness of space and seeing nine different things" (Brioux). Those nine people also experience nine different forms of sexual desire. Captain Malcolm Reynolds (Nathan Fillion) provides something that is rare and valuable in the Whedonverses: a positive representation of male dominance. His first officer, Zoë, models female dominance; Zoë's husband Wash models the male submission that complements his wife's dominance. The Companion Inara is a high class, high status sex worker; ironically, she desires a monogamous relationship with Mal. The story of the Tam siblings has the structure of a Gothic sibling incest narrative; the subtext of this story hints that Simon may desire his sister River, who has a polymorphously perverse sensual connection with the entire universe. Jayne has a fetishistic desire for weapons, especially his favorite gun, Vera. The ship's mechanic, Kaylee, models female fetishism: she desires machines, especially *Serenity* herself. The celibate cleric Shepherd Book refuses to partake in sexual pleasure at all.

Firefly offers generally positive portrayals of these diverse desires. The show authorizes Mal's dominance, provided that he respects the boundaries of consent and honors the limits of other people's relationships. When he violates these limits—notably by interfering with the DS relationship that Zoë and Wash share—the narrative punishes him. Mal serves as an important exception to the Whedonverses' general preference for male submission. He protects the Whedonversal system of sexual ethics from the rigid, restrictive, and ethically unsustainable position that men must *always* be submissive. Zoë's female dominance is presented as consensual and empowering, which is consistent with her status as a Whedomme. The show portrays Wash's eager submission to Zoë as the healthy counterpart to her dominance. Significantly, Zoë and Wash (Alan Tudyk) are the only married couple on the ship, and their marriage is depicted as a happy one. Representations of successful marriages are notably rare on American network television, while portrayals of happy female dominant/male submissive marriages are almost unheard of outside the Whedonverses.

The figure of Inara offers a qualified endorsement of sex work, but with several important caveats. As a legal, registered Companion, Inara manages her own business, chooses her clients, and has almost total control over her working conditions. Ironically, Inara is initially far more successful in her paid sexual relationships than in the personal relationship she hopes to cultivate with Mal. This has two important cognitive effects on the audience. First, it suggests, counterintuitively but convincingly, that under certain conditions sex work can actually be *more* satisfying than unpaid sexual relationships. This encourages viewers to take sex work seriously and to regard it as a potentially legitimate form of sexual activity. Second, *Firefly* consistently shows Inara being dishonest with Mal. This encourages the audience to privilege honesty in all sexual relationships. The show thus advances the important argument that Whedon's works have always made: that honesty is a necessary precondition for any successful relationship, especially sexual ones.

It is only in Zack Whedon's *Leaves on the Wind* comics—which take place after the *Firefly* show and *Serenity* film—that Inara and Mal finally manage to establish an honest and successful sexual relationship. At this late point in the narrative, Inara is no longer working as a Companion. This implies that her dishonesty was being driven, to some extent, by her sex work. It also suggests that while *Firefly*'s model of Companionship mitigates many of the problems of real-world sex work, the jealousy that a sex worker's personal partner may feel towards her clients has not been overcome. Thus, the show, film, and comics maintain a troubling equation between sex work, emotional dishonesty, and jealousy. The narrative also suggests, in all three of its media, that Mal and Inara's relationship had to be deferred to give them time to develop a relationship style that could account for the fact that they are both sexually dominant.

Dr. Simon Tam is a manifestation of the bourgeois brother-hero who was a common figure in the Gothic literary tradition. Like his literary forebears, Simon stands allied with his sister and tries to rescue her from the institutional prisons that patriarchy creates for young women (DiPlacidi Chapter Two). Like the Gothic narratives to which it alludes, *Firefly* implies that Simon may feel an incestuous desire for his sister, without explicitly saying so. As in the Gothic novel, Simon's possible incestuous desire is sanctioned by the siblings' relatively equal power, by the brother's determination to defend and protect his sister even at great personal cost to himself, by his inability to realize any incestuous desire he may feel, and by his eventual selection of a suitably exogamous sexual partner, i.e., Kaylee (DiPlacidi Chapter Two). The quasi–Gothic narrative of the Tam siblings makes it clear that incestuous desire, if it does exist, may operate *only* on the level of desire. Like its generic forebears, *Firefly* effectively forecloses the possibility of actual sibling incest.

River Tam's desire is diffused throughout the entire physical universe (known on *Firefly* as "the 'verse"); River (Summer Glau) has an intimate sensory connection with every object around her, and every object has potential erotic meaning for her. In psychoanalytic terms, River is polymorphously perverse. The Freudian model understands polymorphous perversity as an early stage in childhood development; it represents an "immature" sexuality which should, according to Freudian psychoanalysis, be left behind as the child matures towards a "normal" genital sexuality (Freud, *Three Essays* 57, 73). But River never matures in this way. Instead, she learns to cherish her unique sensory experiences and to eroticize them. By the end of the film *Serenity*, River and her crewmates have realized that River's sensuality provides vital benefits to the crew. Her acute sensory awareness gives her a strong natural aptitude for flying; she serves as *Serenity*'s primary pilot after Wash's death. By representing River's polymorphous perversity as socially useful, *Firefly* offers an interesting and important alternative to the Freudian understanding of childhood and early adult development. River's sexuality lacks both fixed sexual object and definite sexual aim. A Freudian would diagnose her with a serious case of arrested development. Yet she becomes a healthy, well adjusted, valued member of the crew.

Jayne and Kaylee offer positive representations of male and female fetishism respectively. This provides another useful alternative to the Freudian model. For Freud, fetishism represents a deviation of sexual object: the sexual desire that would "normally" be directed towards a human partner is instead directed towards a fetish object. Freudian psychoanalysis (though not Lacanian analysis) understands fetishism as an "unproductive" sexuality, for it does not generally serve as the basis for reprosexual relationships. Yet *Firefly* presents fetishism as vital to the crew's success, and even to their survival. Jayne is a gun fetishist. On several occasions, his fetish for firearms saves the crew from almost certain doom. Kaylee's fetishism is even more vital to the crew's health and safety, for Kaylee is a machine fetishist whose love for *Serenity* keeps the ship flying in situations that no other mechanic could handle. At the end of the *Serenity* film, Mal reviews the thesis of the show, film, and comics: "Love keeps her in the air when she oughta fall down, tells you she's hurting 'fore she keens. Makes her a home." It is largely Kaylee's love that does these things.

Shepherd Book (Ron Glass) is a celibate holy man. He certainly experiences sexual desire, which he understands as temptation. But he chooses not to act on that desire. When he first meets Kaylee, he tells her that he never married ("Serenity" 1.11), which implies that he could have been sexually active if he so desired. Instead, he chose to live as an ascetic. Shepherd Book is the ship's moral center. In a crew of criminals, misfits, and fugitives, the moral voice of this minister carries significant weight. The show uses Book's moral authority to endorse his celibacy. In this way, *Firefly* encourages its audience to accept a sexual asceticism which might otherwise be regarded as archaic and prudish. Book does not, however, impose his celibacy on others. Instead, he models the acceptance of sexual diversity which is the core of *Firefly*'s system of sexual ethics.

Tolerance is the central feature of *Serenity*'s sexual culture. The characters embody a wide variety of potentially incompatible sexual identities. These identities are motivated by forms of desire so radically different from one another that these desires might seem mutually unintelligible. The narrative gives the characters ample opportunity to judge and condemn one another's sexualities. Yet they almost never do so. As Heather M. Porter argues, "*Firefly* shows an idealized world with regards to sex; even the most puritanical characters do not judge others for their sexual choices" (99). *Firefly* thus offers its audience an important model of a pluralist sexual culture. The culture that *Firefly* imagines accepts any consensual sexuality, no matter how rare or unorthodox. This culture achieves the Lacanian dream of restoring full civil rights to the perversions.

Firefly was an artifact of the millennium; as such, it occupied a cultural environment which was very supportive of sexual pluralism. By the 1990s, the AIDS epidemic had inspired queer activists to build a "coalitional politics" based on "affinity rather than essence" (Jagose 94). The coalition that formed to combat AIDS in the early 90s included "not only lesbians and gay men but also bisexuals, transsexuals, [and] sex workers" (Jagose 94) ranging from high-class Inara-like call girls to brothel workers like the ones *Serenity*'s crew meets in the Heart of Gold. The urgent necessity of confronting the AIDS crisis motivated the creation of a pluralist political coalition that included a broad spectrum of gender identities and sexualities (Rubin, "Elegy" 131). By the time *Firefly* took flight on television in 2002, this coalition included fetishists like Jayne and Kaylee, and queer straights like Zoë and Wash. As *Serenity* sails through the outer limits of known space, her crew explore a number of positions within the outer limits of sexuality that Gayle Rubin described in the 1980s. The crew learn to accept and respect the eclectic, eccentric desires of their shipmates. In this way, the crew of *Serenity* realize the vision of a radically pluralist sexual culture which sex radicals and AIDS activists have been promoting since the 1980s.

"Have You Ever Been with a Warrior Woman?" Varieties of Dominance and Submission in the Zoë/Wash/Mal Triad

Like her fellow Whedommes, Zoë is a powerful woman who is comfortable with her power, and this is precisely what attracts Wash to her. By letting the audience see Zoë through Wash's adoring eyes, *Firefly* invites its viewers to embrace Zoë's strength. Interrogated by an Alliance officer, Wash asks a rhetorical question that speaks volumes about the sexual relationship he shares with Zoë: "Have you ever been with a warrior woman?" ("Bushwhacked" 1.2). Wash certainly has. He's "madly in love with a beautiful woman who can kill [him] with her pinky" ("Our Mrs. Reynolds" 1.3). Wash resembles real-world male submissives who are attracted to modern Amazons: muscled, athletic women who confidently express their personal power (Brame, Brame, and Jacobs 464). Zoë fits this description perfectly. Gina Torres, who plays Zoë, would later ask Joss Whedon to consider her for the role of Wonder Woman. "I'm the only damn Amazon you really know," she told Whedon (quoted in Pascale 271). Leigh Adams Wright notes that the main inequality in the Zoë/Wash relationship "is that she's a gorgeous, stacked, battle-hardened warrior and he's an only semimuscular man with an overactive mouth and humorously poor sense of timing" (30). But Wash and Zoë eroticize this inequality. Like real-world Amazon/submissive couples, they find that inequalities in power and physical strength encourage high

Zoë Washburne (Gina Torres). The submissive Wash adores Zoë the Amazon warrior. *Firefly* (2002). Mutant Enemy/20th Century–Fox Television.

levels of trust, and this trust promotes intimacy (Brame, Brame, and Jacobs 472–473).

The Wash/Zoë relationship is similar to a "lifestyle" DS relationship, i.e., one in which "the power dynamic is an ever-present reality in all areas of [the] relationship" (Brame, Brame, and Jacobs 165). David Magill notes that Zoë "dominates their sexual relationship, and she controls their decisions" (78). Lifestyle DS partnerships "resemble traditional marriages" in some ways (Brame, Brame, and Jacobs 165). However, while the husband is often the dominant partner in a traditional marriage, "the lifestyle dominant is as likely to be female as male" (Brame, Brame, and Jacobs 165). Maybe that's why, as Wash says, "not everybody gets me and Zoë at first glance" ("Our Mrs. Reynolds" 1.3).

Unfortunately, Zoë's submission to Mal interferes with Wash's submission to Zoë. Zoë and Mal don't share sexual power, but he still has military power over her. He was her Sergeant during the war. Now he's her Captain. The show establishes this dynamic immediately, early in what was meant to be the pilot episode, when Wash says to Zoë, "Don't forget to call him 'sir.' He likes that" ("Serenity" 1.11). The actual pilot episode, "The Train Job" (1.1), confirms the dynamic. When the two of them are forced to masquerade as newlyweds, Zoë finds that she can't plausibly pretend to be Mal's wife, because she can't break her habit of military submission: "Right. Sir. Honey."

Wash wants his submission to Zoë to be total and all-consuming, but it can't be, because every day he sees Malcolm Reynolds dominating his Amazon warrior. All of this comes to a head in Cheryl Cain's "War Stories" (1.7), when Wash and Mal are captured and tortured by the sadistic gangster Niska. In Niska's torture chamber, the characters can negotiate the terms of their DS relationship in a strikingly explicit and effective way. Michael Fairman, who plays Niska, confirms that when performing the torture scenes, he "was trying to communicate a perverse sexual pleasure" (*Firefly Companion Two* 100). Niska's sexual sadism combines with the generally sadistic *mise-en-scène* of his torture chamber to create an environment where honest conversations about power are possible. Niska likes to quote the work of the tyrant-philosopher Shan Yu, a cross between Sun Tzu and the Marquis de Sade. Shan Yu holds that you must torture a man if you want to meet his true self. Certainly, we meet the true Wash in Niska's torture chamber. Niska's non-consensual sexual sadism contrasts sharply with the consensual DS which is, as Wash is beginning to understand, the basis of his relationship with Zoë. While Wash doesn't enjoy the torture, he does enjoy the truths that it reveals. He suffers a powerful *jouissance* as his submission, which has been mainly implicit until now, gradually becomes conscious. "I'm the one she swore to love, honor and obey!" he declares. Mal doesn't buy it: "She swore to obey?" "Well, no," Wash admits. "But that's my point! You she obeys! She obeys you! There's obeying happening right under my nose!" In this very Whedonesque line, Wash phrases his basic point three different ways. What's at issue here is not any sexual tension between Zoë and Mal (there is none). The problem is the obeying. Wash wants to obey Zoë, but she's busy obeying Mal.

Zoë comes to Niska with a ransom, but he will only give up one of his prisoners. She chooses Wash, without hesitation. Series editor Lisa Lassek identifies this moment as the center of the episode: "that decision being so instantaneous is something that tells you so much about their marriage.... It shows that the relationship between Zoë and her husband is so different to the relationship between Zoë and Mal" (*Firefly Companion Two* 99). The precise difference is located in the power configurations which inform these relationships. Forced to choose between her submissive and the man who dominates her, Zoë makes the only choice available to an ethical dominant: she protects her submissive.

Things change for the triad after this. Wash and Zoë plan a brave but foolish "one-man/one-woman assault" on Niska's skyplex. This emphasizes the equality that exists between Zoë and Wash, as well as their commitment to the third partner in their triad, Mal. In the event, the rest of the crew help; their daring assault is successful, and they rescue Mal. Safe aboard *Serenity*, Mal tries to "get all this burning sexual tension out in the open" by offering to have sex with Zoë. "It's a difficult mission," he says to Zoë, "but you and I have to get it on." Gina Torres provides a pitch-perfect deadpan response, entirely devoid of sexual desire. "I understand. We have no choice. Take me, sir. Take me hard." Jayne finds this "downright unsettlin.'" Here Zoë acknowledges that the only power Mal will ever have over her is the military kind. The more intimate, sexual kind of power is something she only shares with Wash. Nancy Holder argues that "because she was presented as submissive, she is 'excused' from responsibility for any perception that she belongs to anyone but Wash" (147). By reading Wash/Zoë as a DS relationship, I arrive at a somewhat different conclusion. On my reading, Zoë is not presented as submissive here. Zoë doesn't belong to Wash; he belongs to her. And that kind of belonging, based as it is on consensual, reciprocal dominance and submission, is the source of a surprising equality. By the end of "War Stories," Mal has learned to respect the lifestyle DS which provides the foundation for Zoë and Wash's marriage. Wash has learned that the military dominance and submission which Zoë and Mal share is no threat to the sexual DS which Wash shares with his warrior wife.

Wash will take orders from Mal on the bridge and from Zoë in their bunk, but the system only works if both his captain and his wife listen to Wash, for he is a submissive, not a doormat. In the *Better Days* comics, Wash objects strongly to Zoë's plan to use herself as bait to rescue Mal from the

Alliance (Whedon, Matthews, and Conrad, *Better Days* #3). By now Zoë feels comfortable asserting her dominance over Wash. "In case you hadn't noticed, I'm the direct sort of person, dear." But she suspects that Wash still feels the jealousy he felt in "War Stories." Will Conrad draws a tight close up of Zoë, which shows that she is tense and suspicious as she tells Wash that what she hopes to get is "The captain. Or is that the part you don't like?" But Zoë has underestimated her submissive husband. When Zoë tries to claim that this is her mess to deal with, Wash disagrees: "No... *We. We* have to deal with this. I think that's all I'm meaning to say." This is enough to prompt Zoë to make a rare declaration of her feelings for Wash: "I do love you sometimes—." This love is built on a solid foundation of sexual dominance and submission.

"All of You": Inara and Mal's Dominance/ Dominance Relationship

Mal is a dominant who is attracted to other dominants; until Inara finally teaches him, in the *Serenity* comics, how two dominants can share sexual power, a relationship involving Mal remains a Lacanian impossibility. Such a relationship would require Mal and a dominant woman to replace their fantasies of dominating a submissive partner with overlapping fantasies of mutual dominance. While the 'verse contains several dominant women who are capable of this, Mal initially is not. He assumes that a relationship with any of these women would require him to submit, which he fears. His potential relationship with Saffron (Christina Hendricks) is a good example. Nancy Holder argues persuasively that "Mal equated succumbing to Saffron's sexual invitations as a loss of power, with which he is preoccupied" (150). Saffron is capable of switching to the submissive role, though as far as we know, she only does so for deceitful purposes. In this respect, her tactical submission is similar to Black Widow's (see Chapter One). Mal faces a similar problem with Nandi, the madam who runs the whorehouse in "Heart of Gold" (1.12). Actress Melinda Clarke, who plays Nandi, observes that she always seems to get cast as a madam, or a dominatrix, or in science fiction (*Firefly Companion Two* 167). In *Firefly*, she manages all three simultaneously. Remarkably, Mal is able to consummate his relationship with the dominant Nandi. But she is killed, much too conveniently, the next day. Without really considering the possibility of a relationship between two dominants, Brett Matthews' "Heart of Gold" concludes that such a relationship is fundamentally unsustainable.

No such relationship would appear in the *Firefly* 'verse until a decade after the show's cancellation, although the show heavily foreshadowed Mal's future relationship with Inara: every major *Firefly* character *except* Mal and

Inara recognized their desire for one another and viewed them as potential sexual partners. But Mal and Inara are initially too similar, and so they are unable to serve as each other's Other. The dominant desire they reflect back upon one another is identical. To pursue that desire would be an act of narcissism. The other problem is Inara's dishonesty. She is initially incapable of admitting that she desires Mal, either to herself or to him. Not only is Inara guilty, in Lacanian terms, of giving ground on her desire; she can't even acknowledge that this desire exists. This is consistent with the general ethics of the Whedonverses, which hold that deceit regarding desire is the ultimate bane of all sexual relations.

Firefly suggests that such deceit is, at least in part, an effect of Inara's chosen profession. Andrew Aberdein is being kind when he says that *Firefly*'s writers "never provide definitive proof that the traditional association of prostitution and deceit has been broken in the 'verse" (71). Indeed, this association seems stronger than ever in the future that *Firefly* imagines. Inara is a very specific kind of sex worker. As Aberdein has shown, she closely resembles the ancient Greek hetaeras, a "professional elite" of "sole proprietors" with a high degree of agency and autonomy (65). But Aberdein also notes that "the positive interpretations of the hetaera and the Companion may be illusions"; it may be that "prostitution is inherently shameful, since inextricably linked to deceit" (75). Inara is unable to overcome the deceit which, *Firefly* implies, lies at the heart of her profession. This prevents the show from offering a truly progressive representation of sex work.

Inara lets the truth slip in an intimate encounter with her one female client, the nameless Councillor ("War Stories" 1.7). "One cannot always be one's self in the company of men," Inara admits. The Councillor changes "not always" to "never," and Inara does not disagree. Dee Amy-Chinn recognizes what this implies: "that all of Inara's encounters with her male clients involve a 'performance' of femininity at odds with Inara's true self" ("Whore" 180). Thus, as Amy-Chinn argues, the show's representation of Inara "completely fails to embody any of the possibilities that a valorisation of whoredom might open up" ("Whore" 175). I join Amy-Chinn in suggesting that the televised version of Inara represents a missed opportunity. Frustratingly, the show's creators used the character to consider possible solutions to all the problems of prostitution—except for the most important problem, dishonesty.

When we finally learn the true shape of Inara's desire, we find that what Inara really wants is a very traditional relationship with Mal. Amy-Chinn notes that "in her desire for a love-based, heterosexual, monogamous relationship with Mal," Inara ironically falls within Gayle Rubin's charmed circle ("Whore" 181). Inara's desire is a caricature of monogamous sexuality: unconscious, unnegotiated, and deeply informed by jealousy. But this "straw man" version of monogamous desire is simplistic, and ultimately ineffective. Inara's desire is the only one which the show openly condemns: through her tearful breakdown after Mal beds Nandi in "Heart of Gold" (1.12), and through the inevitable conclusion of that episode, when Inara tells Mal she's leaving *Serenity*. Morena Baccarin, who plays Inara, identifies this as the first moment of honesty between Inara and Mal (*Firefly Companion Two* 181). But it is too little, too late. Inara and Mal could have modeled an ethical form of polyamorous desire. Instead, their characters degenerated into a bundle of stereotypes, which *Firefly* used to teach its audience a lesson they'd already learned.

In Zack Whedon's *Leaves on the Wind* comics (2014), Inara and Mal finally enter into the relationship that their dishonesty and jealousy precluded for so long (Zack Whedon and Jeanty, *Leaves*). One of the first things that Whedon reveals about Inara is that she has been "decommissioned": she has lost her Companion's license. Apparently, Mal never did find a way to reconcile his sexual interest in Inara with the disgust he felt at her sex work. The source of that disgust remains unclear. Mal certainly isn't religious or moralistic, so it's likely simple jealousy. Conveniently, Mal was able to begin his relationship with Inara without ever confronting that jealousy, since she no longer practices the work that she still won't let Mal call "whoring." Like the show, the comics miss the opportunity to present a personal sexual relationship that is compatible with sex work.

Still, the comics present Inara and Mal's relationship as reasonably successful. Two crucial factors enable this success. First, Mal and Inara have finally achieved a hard-won interpersonal honesty; they can now reveal how they truly feel about one another. Just as importantly, they've found a power dynamic that allows them both to remain dominant. In the first issue of *Leaves*, Inara strips naked and climbs on top of Mal, reminding him, as she did moments earlier, that "we need money. We need food" (Zack Whedon and Jeanty, *Leaves* #1). "I don't much care for having a conversation twice," Mal replies. Artist Georges Jeanty frames a tight shot of Inara's gorgeous face. She has perfect confidence in her own sexual power, and she is no longer shy about using that power on Mal. "Then shut up," Inara says simply. The next panel pushes the limits of comic book propriety. A full-width, full-bleed panel shows Inara and Mal, both naked, kissing and making love. But now Mal is on top, physically and, Jeanty's drawing implies, psychologically. Inara and Mal dominate one another easily and comfortably here. Clearly, they are *both* on top, and their newfound DD relationship seems to satisfy them both. Importantly, this relationship also provides a solution to the Whedonverses' erasure of male dominance. Mal and Inara give comic readers a valuable model of a non-exploitative, egalitarian relationship that includes male sexual dominance.

Two. "Love Keeps Her in the Air" 71

Inara and Mal negotiate their dominant/dominant sexual relationship, with and without words. Script by Zack Whedon. Art by Georges Jeanty and Karl Story. *Serenity: Leaves on the Wind* (2014). Dark Horse Comics/Twentieth Century–Fox Film Corporation.

The relationship works out particularly well for Mal. His sexual relationship with Inara means that he can confide in her, in a way that he never could with Zoë. When Mal asks Inara what she wants, she replies "you. All of you" (Zack Whedon and Jeanty, *Leaves* #3). This is what she has always wanted, but now she can be refreshingly honest about her desire. Inara is as gorgeous as ever, but now also maternal in a full-bleed corner panel that shows her feeding Zoë's baby Emma from a bottle. Inara assures Mal that "you don't have to be Captain Reynolds with me," as he does with everyone else on the ship, especially Zoë. Here Inara draws a compelling contrast between the military-style power that Mal shares with Zoë and the sexual power that he now shares with Inara. "I don't want you to be," Inara continues. "You can tell me if you think we're in trouble." Inara is strong enough to handle the truth. By placing baby Emma in Inara's arms as she shows Mal her strength, Zack Whedon and Georges Jeanty hint that Mal and Inara could even parent children together. In fact, this kind of parental domesticity is now available to the whole crew, who tend to experience it as couples.

"Everything I Have Is Right Here": Gothic Sibling Incest Narrative and Polymorphous Perversity in the Simon/River Story

The influential historian of sexuality Michel Foucault identifies the family as the site of an important interchange between an ancient system of alliance based on marriage, kinship, and property transmission, and a modern system of sexuality (106–108). This permits Foucault to declare, in his typical provocative way, that modern "sexuality is 'incestuous' from the start" (108–109). For Foucault, this is particularly true of the modern social class that is most preoccupied with questions of family alliance and property preservation: the bourgeoisie. *Firefly*'s Tam family is clearly represented as bourgeois, and Foucault argues that the modern bourgeois family contains "a perpetual incitement to incest" (129). Foucault argues that in the late nineteenth century (which is the period of history that *Firefly* represents), "at a time when incest was being hunted out as a conduct, psychoanalysis was busy revealing it as a desire and alleviating—for those who suffered from the desire—the severity which repressed it" (130). On this account, Simon Tam (Sean Maher) looks like an analysand: if he feels desire for his sister, such desire could never be fulfilled, yet his psychological wellbeing could depend upon decreasing the repression of that desire. This impossible, unfulfillable desire operates at what Foucault calls the level of discourse. In the nineteenth century, it appeared in Romantic and Gothic literary discourses; in the late twentieth and early twenty-first centuries, it manifested in the discourse of science fiction.

While Gothic literature typically viewed sexual desire of a parent for a child as abusive due to the considerable inherent differences in age and power between the two, this literary tradition understood relationships between siblings to be "grounded on a more even distribution of power," and thus somewhat less susceptible to abuse (DiPlacidi 85). River was sixteen years old when Simon rescued her from the Alliance lab. She would thus be above the age of consent in most Western countries and American states today, and certainly in the nineteenth-century American West that *Firefly*'s 'verse represents. In nineteenth-century American culture as in the British culture from which it descended, siblings "became a focus for intense attachment" (Davidoff 202). In this culture of intensely affectionate sibling relationships, sibling incest was often represented "not as a perversion or accidental inversion of the normal sibling relation, but as an extension and intensification of it" (Richardson 554).

Modern Romantic literature idealized incestuous sibling *desire*, while consistently warning against its fulfillment. As Alan Richardson argues, "for Romantic writers, sibling attachment fuses with sexual desire to constitute an idealized erotic love, yet death disrupts or closely follows upon the consummation of that love" (555). The paradigmatic example of Romantic sibling love can be found in Viktor von Frankenstein's feelings for his "more than sister" Elizabeth (Richardson 556). If we accept Brian Aldiss' claim that *Frankenstein* is the first real work of science fiction (Aldiss Chapter 1), then representations of sibling incest have been part of the SF tradition since the beginning. The incestuous desire of brothers for sisters would remain a major concern of SF through the twentieth century, notably in *Star Wars*, which was an important inspiration for *Firefly*. Luke Skywalker's desire for Leia—whom he does not initially recognize as his sister—reads like a modern literary narrative of unwitting sibling incest.

It is in the Gothic tradition, to which *Frankenstein* also belongs, that the subversive potential of sibling desire really becomes clear. Jenny DiPlacidi observes that Gothic writers present sibling incest as positive and even ideal (22, 89).[2] DiPlacidi's insightful analysis reveals how "Gothic authors deploy the generic convention of incest" to critique both heteronormativity and patriarchy (23). The story of Simon and River Tam features all the major generic components of a typical Gothic sibling incest narrative. The brother is not presented as a threat to his sister; instead, he is shown as "an equal sufferer under patriarchal power" (DiPlacidi 85). Brief flashbacks in "Safe" (1.7) show Simon chafing under the tyrannical authority of his father in the stifling, quasi–Victorian Tam household. Like the typical literary Gothic brother, Simon is not "complicit with male tyranny" because "his position in the family is aligned with the sister's as equally fearful of paternal threats" (DiPlacidi 104). The Gothic novel conflates the brother with the hero, changing the brother into a kind of "ideal spouse with whom the heroine escapes the patriarchal castle" (DiPlacidi 106). The flashback scenes in "Safe" show how Simon became the archetypal Gothic brother-hero. The Tam parents refuse to rescue River from the Alliance "Academy," leaving Simon to do so. Young and reckless, Simon squanders a very promising medical career to save his sister. The passion which drives Simon clearly exceeds the bounds of normal brotherly love. His parents find his behavior odd, and yet they are not entirely mystified by it. His mother tells him, knowingly, that "nothing is going to keep you two apart for long." This strange combination of confusion and understanding is exactly what one might expect to find in a family which harbors incestuous desire.

In this representation of late nineteenth-century Anglo-American bourgeois culture, incestuous desire remains below the threshold of discourse, but only just. For this reason, we should not expect explicit textual statements of incestuous desire from the Tam family and should look instead for subtextual signs of such desire. In nineteenth-century Gothic narratives, the incestuous desire of one sibling for another was often "expressed as hidden subtext" (DiPlacidi 85). There is every reason to expect that the story of the Tams, which follows the formal and generic conventions of the Gothic novel so closely, would follow this one as well. The desperate heroism that Simon exhibits when he rescues his sister from the patriarchal castle's stand-in, the Alliance Academy, may be a subtextual sign of forbidden desire. Like Gothic siblings, Simon and River share an intense bond that makes them "dangerous and potentially destructive to patriarchal society" (DiPlacidi 86). "It's love, in point of fact," the Operative (Chiwetel Ejiofor) notes as he reviews video of the Tam siblings' daring escape (*Serenity*)—a love which eventually deals crippling damage to the 'verse's larger patriarchal society, as the Tams help reveal the Miranda scandal.

After their escape, Simon and River move from the dangerous space of the Alliance Academy to the relatively safe space of *Serenity*. Simon smuggles River aboard in a crate, in suspended animation. When Mal discovers her, he immediately assumes that River is Simon's sex slave. As Alyson Buckman notes, the high-angle full shot that Whedon uses in this scene matches Mal's point of view, validates his male gaze, and relegates River to the role of object ("Much Madness" 42). Since Whedon's camera privileges Mal's viewpoint, the audience is encouraged to read the Simon/River relationship as a sexual one. When Mal and the rest of the crew learn that River is Simon's sister, they immediately reconceptualize the relationship as a non-sexual sibling relationship. But the initial framing of River as a sex object for Simon leaves traces in the narrative. The audience will not necessarily forget the possibility that Simon may harbor an incestuous desire for River. This possibility could perhaps be repressed, but if so, it would eventually return—just as a repressed desire might return when the forces of cultural repression are weakened, as they are in the "present tense" of "Safe," when Simon and River are kidnapped by hill folk. Here River feels guilty, because Simon gave up everything he had for her. Simon says "Mei mei [Little sister].... Everything I have is right here." Simon is surprisingly comfortable with the situation. He has suddenly found himself alone with River, outside the boundaries of civilization, living among hill folk who appear to have a limited breeding population and, one imagines, liberal attitudes towards sibling incest.

An incestuous desire for his sister would explain Simon's agonizing inability to connect with Kaylee. It would explain his constant self-sabotage, his malapropisms, and his shocking rudeness. Simon almost manages to be honest with Kaylee when they visit the freak show at the space bazaar ("The Message" 1.14). Standing in front of a floating cow fetus, Simon explains to Kaylee that "every other girl I know is either married, professional or closely related to me, so you are more or less literally the only girl in the world." The simplest explanation for Simon's bizarre and insulting statement is that the only thing preventing him from expressing a desire for River is the incest taboo, which he groups with the taboos against adultery, and against personal relationships with sex workers, that make Zoë and Inara unavailable to him. The incest taboo ensures that River could only ever be an *objet petit a* for Simon—the unattainable object of a prohibited desire. This suggests that what he really feels for her is *jouissance*, which he naturally experiences as suffering. Incestuous longing is, in a sense, the perfect form of desire. By definition, it can never be satisfied, and so it exhibits the self-sustaining, unfulfillable, masochistic elements which the Lacanian model takes to be characteristic of desire in general.

In sharp contrast to its sympathetic treatment of possible incestuous sibling desire, *Firefly* consistently presents actual sibling incest as barbaric. In a deleted scene from "Our Mrs. Reynolds" (1.3), River asks Shepherd Book to marry her and Simon. Simon protests, but perhaps too much: River's request may have touched a nerve. "No, River, mei-mei, of course I love you too, but we can't be married." Simon tells Book that River is "really crazy"; she kicks him in the shin. So Simon changes his characterization of sibling incest from "crazy" to the more flexible category of uncivilized. "I don't mean crazy—that's just not something brothers and sisters do. I mean on some planets, but only pretty bad ones." Rather than ruling sibling incest completely out of bounds, Simon relegates it to "bad" planets. This implies that although sibling incest is uncivilized, it may be tolerated in places where the bounds of civilization are loose, as they are among the hill folk. River stuffs a pillow under her shirt to feign pregnancy. "Now we have to be married. I'm in the family way." This leaves Simon speechless. River has named the unnamable desire. She is only able to do this because her mental illness provides an alibi for her, just as it did for the Victorian madwomen of Gothic fiction. When River invokes forbidden incestuous desire, it seems playful and harmless. Her mental instability means that the crew need not take the content of her speech seriously.

Like the *Firefly* show, *Serenity* comics authorize the possibility of incestuous *desire*, while foreclosing the possibility of actual incest. Simon's fantasy in *Better Days* shows him and River, standing side by side in crisp white lab coats, smiling as they do medical research together (Zack Whedon and Jeanty, *Leaves* #2). Physical intimacy will always be forbidden to the Tam siblings, but Simon can imagine an intellectual intimacy with his sister. Like the show, the comics read actual incest as primitive, something that could only happen in the least civilized parts of the 'verse. Jayne tries to impress the resistance leader Bea by invoking the memory of "Jaynestown" (1.4): "there's some worlds where I'm revered as a hero" (Zack Whedon and Jeanty, *Leaves* #2). Bea immediately equates reverence for Jayne with sibling incest, rejecting both as barbaric: "Same worlds where siblings marry, I'm guessing."

Like the Romantic and Gothic heroes who came before him, Simon makes the brother's journey away from forbidden sibling love, towards a proper exogamous marriage. Simon's relationship with Kaylee gives him what he could never get from River: sex, domestic bliss, and the prospect of family. When they finally manage to get together, Simon and Kaylee have a very active sex life—"couple of rabbits, those two," says Zoë (Zack Whedon and Jeanty, *Leaves* #1). Simon and Kaylee frequently act as surrogate parents to Zoë's infant daughter Emma. This positions their relationship as potentially reproductive. Kaylee takes on maternal responsibilities; Simon holds her gently and looks on with interest as she feeds Emma from a bottle (Zack Whedon and Jeanty, *Leaves* #2). Simon makes dinner for Kaylee, showing that he's comfortable living a domestic life with her (Roberson and Jeanty, *No Power* #1). After River uses her superhuman aerial acrobatics to save Emma from falling, Kaylee calls River a hero. "River does have her moments, doesn't she?" Simon muses as he chops vegetables. Kaylee quickly shifts the conversation to the domestic relationship that she and Simon are now building. "I'm just glad that *your* talents include cooking, because I am starving." Kaylee still fears that Simon is just "making do" with her, but she underestimates the value of what she gives him. Thanks to Kaylee, Simon and River can remain safely within the bounds of a socially sanctioned, non-sexual sibling relationship. Kaylee precludes the incestuous crime that would surely destroy Simon and River if it ever occurred. As forbidden desire gives way to exogamous domesticity, the Romantic and Gothic conventions that inform the story of the Tam siblings permit Simon a happy ending.

As for River, she is the ultimate sensualist. As Lyle Zynda suggests, River derives a "sensual joy" from her acute awareness of tactile sensations (91). River's extreme sensuality is a byproduct of the brain surgery which Alliance scientists performed upon her.[3] When Simon and River have to don space suits and hide outside the ship in "Bushwhacked" (1.2), Simon is terrified, but River is radiant. She delights at the sight of the bright stars against the blackness of space. Her smile speaks of sensual ecstasy. "Let's go again!" she cries when they return to *Serenity*, sounding very much like a child who has just experienced some exciting new sensation for the first time. *Firefly*'s pluralist sexual culture endorses River's polymorphous perversity, i.e., her ability to take erotic delight from any sensory experience. This places *Firefly*'s open system of sexual values in opposition to the more restrictive value system of Freudian psychoanalysis. Freud understood psychological and sexual maturity as a reaction-formation *against* the polymorphously perverse eroticism of childhood (Freud, *Three Essays* 105). In the Freudian model, it is the struggle to overcome polymorphous perversity which supposedly allows people to become mature individuals. But River models a new way to grow up, one that may be less traumatic than Freud's. River comes into her own not by giving up polymorphous perversity, but by embracing it. River becomes a whole person by learning to love the sensual satisfaction that she takes in every experience. Without this delight, her total sensory experience makes her nothing more than a cold-blooded killing machine. After witnessing one of River's periodic outbursts of extreme violence, Kaylee says, "not nobody can shoot like that that's a person" ("Objects in Space" 1.10).

The value of River's polymorphous perversity becomes clear in "Objects in Space." River sees Wash and Zoë kissing on the bridge. Then River *feels* Wash and Zoë, directly and intimately. When the bounty hunter Jubal Early (Richard Brooks) boards the ship, River conducts an elaborate ruse to convince Early that she has somehow become *Serenity*. Her ruse is effective because it has an element of truth to it. River may not be the ship, but she has immediate and total sensory access to *Serenity* and every person and object aboard her. She feels everything that happens on the ship and finds joy in those feelings. River is able to use her sensuality to defeat the bounty hunter, save her friends, and earn her rightful place among *Serenity*'s crew.

The comic book form permits representations of River's polymorphous perversity that would scarcely be possible on television. River's fantasy is by far the strangest of those expressed in *Better Days*. Will Conrad draws River in a fantastic fairy tale world, wearing a long purple gown, surrounded by fairies, dragons, balloons, and a small yellow submarine (Whedon, Matthews, and Conrad, *Better Days* #2). She is holding hands with a giant fish in a pale blue tuxedo. The comics continue to emphasize River's extreme sensory sensitivity. Although River is not sexually active herself (in any conventional sense), she is especially attuned to sensations of sex. In a sign of Zoë's growing understanding of DS, Zoë sacrifices military-style discipline for the sake of sexual dominance: she climbs on top of Wash and has sex with him at *Serenity*'s helm (Whedon, Matthews and Conrad, *Those Left Behind* #2). When River comes onto the bridge, she declares, with her usual bluntness, "it stinks like sex in here."

Zoë's pregnancy provides a healthy focus for River's polymorphous sensuality, while also giving her a safe space to explore her fascination with human reproduction. River rests her head on Zoë's swollen belly. "I can hear everything, all at once," River announces. "I can hear the whole 'verse" (Whedon and Jeanty, *Leaves* #1). Rather than drawing Zoë's belly, Georges Jeanty draws River's reality: half a dozen planets and moons, a spiral galaxy, a field of stars. Zoë's unborn baby enhances River's sensory access to the 'verse. River looks over Simon's shoulder as he delivers the baby. Always direct, she provides a succinct statement of her feelings: "this is very exciting." River knows, without being told, that Zoë needs hospitalization after a difficult delivery. Since she's now *Serenity*'s pilot, it's River's job to get Zoë to the hospital ship as quickly as possible. It seems strangely proper that River channels Zoë's dead husband as she executes the kind of hard burn that Wash would certainly have performed in this situation. River recites Wash's last words as she flies: "I am a leaf on the wind. Watch how I soar."

"We Still Talking About Machines?": Jayne's Firearm Fetishism and Kaylee's Machine Fetishism

Jayne Cobb's firearm fetishism fits the pattern first identified by nineteenth-century sexologists like Richard von Krafft-Ebing and early twentieth-century psychoanalysts like Freud. It also reveals the limitations of these early theoretical models. Krafft-Ebing associated fetishism with masturbation (175). Jayne is certainly an enthusiastic masturbator, as indicated by his iconic line, "I'll be in my bunk" ("War Stories" 1.7). Krafft-Ebing argued that in the absence of the fetish object, the fetishist would find coitus to be either impossible or forced and unsatisfying (172). While Jayne may not need his guns in order to have sex, his most satisfying sexual experience involves a sex worker and a small arsenal of firearms ("Heart of Gold" 1.12). Freud associated fetishism with castration anxiety. According to Freud, fetishism happens when a little boy refuses to give up the illusion that his mother has a penis, out of fear of losing his own penis. The boy then seizes upon a fetish object as a substitute for the lost mother-penis (Freud, "Fetishism" 152–153). Jayne often seems to feel that his penis is at risk. When River reminds him that "Jayne is a girl's name," he replies defensively "well, Jayne ain't a girl" ("Trash" 1.13). From a Freudian perspective, Jayne's favorite gun, Vera, makes a perfect fetish object. Vera is a very phallic object, yet she is also a very feminine phallus: Jayne gives her a woman's name and speaks to her as if she were a woman.

The Freudian model of fetishism is, at best, incomplete. As Valerie Steele argues, "the fetish may well be a substitute for the mother's penis, but that is not *all* it is" (18). Twentieth-century psychiatrist Arthur Epstein suggests that "the fetish object may be related to fundamental levels of aesthetic appreciation" (148). Jayne definitely has a strong aesthetic appreciation for Vera, a "Callahan fullbore autolock, customized trigger and double cartridge thorough-gage" ("Our Mrs. Reynolds" 1.3). He considers Vera "the best damn gun made by man." Epstein also associates fetishism with "the strong human interest in external objects, stemming from tool-use" (148). Jayne does view his guns as practical tools, which he uses to defend *Serenity* and her crew.

Firefly not only tolerates Jayne's fetishism, but celebrates it. Visual Effects Supervisor Loni Peristere points out that although *Serenity* herself doesn't have any guns, "when she's in a pickle, she always has Jayne and Vera" (123). Indeed, *Serenity*'s best defense is neither Jayne nor Vera, but rather the relationship between the two. Jayne and Vera save *Serenity* from the chop shop.

They don space suits so that Vera will have enough oxygen to fire at the electric breakers and shut down the ship trap ("Our Mrs. Reynolds" 1.3). "You see, Vera?" Jayne says as he takes aim. "You dress yourself up, then you get taken out somewhere fun." Here Jayne performs heterosexual courtship rituals with Vera, a sure sign that he sees her as a sexual fetish object. The show endorses Jayne's firearm fetish again in "Heart of Gold" (1.12). Jayne prepares for the inevitable siege of the bordello by showing his favorite guns to a whore called Helen (Heather Black). He then invites Helen into his relationship with the guns. "These here are my favorites, and you're to keep 'em coming 'til there ain't no more to be had. I shoot, I run out, you just hand me the next biggest and so on. Is there an understanding here?" Helen answers with a simple "Yes." Negotiations complete, Jayne and Helen "get to work." She mounts him with an enthusiasm which exceeds her job description. When the siege arrives, Jayne, Helen, and the guns make a crucial contribution to the defense of the bordello.

Here and elsewhere, Jayne represents one of the Western genre's major archetypes: a man who uses gun violence to defend peaceful people against violent outlaws. Richard Slotkin describes this figure in *Gunfighter Nation*. Joss Whedon studied with Slotkin at Wesleyan; "Heart of Gold" scripter Brett Matthews, another Wesleyan alumnus, may also have known Slotkin's work. The "good man with a gun," most famously exemplified in *Shane* (George Steeves 1953), is a man whose gun violence is redeemed by his willingness to use that violence to defend the "liberties of the people" (Slotkin 396). In this case, Jayne defends the freedom of another stock Western character type, the one for which the brothel is named: the whore with a heart of gold. Of course, Jayne's benevolence is unreliable. He frequently uses violence to serve his own self-interest. Yet even when his violence is self-serving, Jayne is sometimes perceived as a "good outlaw" who robs from the rich and gives to the poor (Slotkin 294). This is precisely how the Mudders describe him when they sing "Hero of Canton, the Ballad of Jayne Cobb" ("Jaynestown" 1.4).

Jayne's fetishistic desire becomes more explicit in the *Serenity* comics, and he becomes more comfortable openly expressing his love for Vera. Jayne takes up a sniper position when Zoë and Wash meet the Alliance officers who are holding Mal (Whedon, Matthews, and Conrad, *Better Days* #3). Sighting through his rifle scope, Jayne asks, "Now, when the purple-bellies gettin' here? Because I'm developing a cramp in a mighty personal place." It's unlikely that Jayne's "cramp" is coincidental. His guns give him erections. His desire to make his guns do what they were built to do is a sexual desire. Audiences may well find Jayne's sexualized desire to commit gun violence disturbing, but again, that desire is sanctioned by Jayne's eagerness to deploy this violence to protect his crewmates.

In *Leaves on the Wind*, Jayne tries to use his gun fetish to initiate a sexual relationship with Bea. This encounter shows that, contrary to what most readers surely expect, Jayne is capable of experiencing feelings for a human woman who is not a sex worker. He can even articulate those feelings, as long as he is able to describe them according to the logic of his fetish. Bea resists Jayne's unwanted attentions by pulling a pistol and pointing it directly between his eyes (Zack Whedon and Jeanty, *Leaves* #2). Suddenly Jayne only has eyes for the gun. Staring cross-eyed at the pistol's barrel, Jayne asks "is that a Strickland forty-four twelve?" As Bea stomps off, Jayne says, to her backside, "that's a helluva nice weapon." Bea's rejection has simply refocused Jayne's desire: suddenly Bea's most attractive feature, for Jayne, is her taste in weapons. Ironically, Jayne makes a fetish of the means by which Bea enforces her consent. In a strange way, Bea's sexual agency has now become part of Jayne's fetish. This leaves Jayne in a bizarre but viable ethical position: his fetish for Bea's phallus requires him to respect her wishes.

Jayne tries to spark Bea's interest by emphasizing his proficiency with firearms. "You got me on your side. I'm sure you met smarter but I know you never met no one can shoot like me. That ain't nothing" (Zack Whedon and Jeanty, *Leaves* #3). Bea remains uninterested, and Jayne retreats to his bunk, where Vera no doubt awaits. He mutters to himself "Stupid, Jayne. What's she care if you're expert at killin' folks? Gorram moron." There may be occasions when Jayne's shooting expertise makes him sexually desirable, as it did during the siege of the Heart of Gold. This is not one of those times. The comics do not judge Jayne's firearm fetish, but they do suggest that if Jayne can *only* express his desire in terms of guns and shooting, he may want for human sexual companionship.

In the end, however, *Leaves* provides a fairly unambiguous endorsement of Jayne's fetish. When the crew break into the Academy lab to rescue the other girls who were tortured there with River, they confront a seemingly impenetrable wall. Jayne steps forward, confident that his beloved can save the day once more. "Vera's got this," he declares (Zack Whedon and Jeanty, *Leaves* #4). Vera promptly blows a hole in the wall. Jayne is injured in the raid, but he protests when Mal excludes him from the team that will rescue Zoë from the Alliance prison camp. "I can still shoot," Jayne insists. Once again, Jayne has become Slotkin's "good man with a gun." By authorizing Jayne's gun violence in this way, *Firefly* endorses male fetishism and simultaneously honors the generic conventions on the American western.

Ship's mechanic Kaylee Frye provides an effective representation of female fetishism. While early theorists like Krafft-Ebing and Freud believed that female fetishism was extremely rare, recent research has revealed that this is not the case (Gamman and Makinen 98). The female fetishist challenges the common stereotype that women are sexually passive. Gamman and Makinen argue that women can be "active practitioners of fetishism"

(89). This interpretation views women as sexual agents, rather than passive objects of male fetishism. Reading fetishism as a practice that is common among both women and men contributes to an argument for sexual diversity (Gamman and Makinen 3). To be truly inclusive, *Firefly*'s coalition of minority sexualities must include both male and female fetishists. Female fetishism has its own unique forms. For women, food "can become a fetish object" (Gamman and Makinen 8). Kaylee fetishizes a rare fresh strawberry in *Firefly*'s original pilot episode, "Serenity" (1.11). As she bites into the strawberry, Kaylee appears to experience an orgasm of sensual delight. For Joss Whedon, this is the most important scene in the episode (Pascale 213). The strawberry scene establishes Kaylee as a fully sensual being. As she considers her desire for Simon, Kaylee says that she just wants to "take a bite out of him" ("Safe" 1.7), as she did to the strawberry.

Kaylee's strongest fetish is for machines. Like any fetishist, Kaylee sees the object of her desire as something much more than an inanimate object. Machines are like people to Kaylee. "Machines just got workin's, and they talk to me," she says ("Serenity" 1.11). Kaylee is especially fond of engines. David Gerrold argues that "Kaylee's relationship with starship engines borders on the carnal" (184), but I wish to go further: the relationship *is* carnal. Kaylee's true love is *Serenity* herself. She always leaps to her lover's defense, as when the Alliance officer calls *Serenity* a "junker" ("Bushwhacked" 1.2). Kaylee won't even let her prospective human lover speak ill of *Serenity*. When Simon calls *Serenity* "luh-suh" ("garbage"), she calls him "mean" ("Safe" 1.7).

The flashback scene in "Out of Gas" (1.5) reveals that Kaylee first came on board *Serenity* for a sexual liaison with Bester (Dax Griffin), the clueless slacker that Mal had hired to be the ship's first mechanic. But that liaison happened—as it had to happen—in the engine room, which is the true nexus of Kaylee's desire. Even Bester gets it: "She likes engines. They make her hot." When Mal fires the incompetent Bester and offers Kaylee the job, she is more than happy to bid her erstwhile lover farewell, for he was never more than a means to an end. He brought her to the place where her desire could finally take its true form and find its true object: the beating heart of *Serenity* herself. From here on, Kaylee's sexual identity is that of *mechanic*. When *Serenity* executes a successful "Crazy Ivan" maneuver, Kaylee strokes her hull and says "that's my girl... That's my good girl" ("Serenity" 1.11). She treats *Serenity* precisely as she would treat a human lover. In "Out of Gas," an explosion severely damages the ship and knocks Zoë unconscious. The concern which Kaylee shows for *Serenity* mirrors the concern Wash shows for Zoë. "She ain't movin'," Kaylee laments. She's looking at Zoë but talking about *Serenity*. "*Serenity*'s not movin'." Her concern for her injured lover is tempered by anxiety over her lover's failure to communicate about the problem. "Usually she lets me know when something's wrong." Here and elsewhere, *Serenity* appears as the show's tenth major character, and it's clear that she has an erotic relationship with her mechanic. Since *Serenity* (like all ships) is female, this relationship represents an interesting form of same-gender desire.

Louise Kaplan argues that female fetishism "entails a masquerade or impersonation of femininity" (249). Kaylee performs this type of masquerade in Jane Espenson's "Shindig" (1.6). In a desperate attempt to appear more feminine, Kaylee temporarily abandons her masculine mechanic's persona. She covets an elaborate, frilly pink dress with a huge hoop skirt. "What're you gonna do in that rig?" Mal demands. "Bounce around the engine room?" Mal recognizes that the dress is at odds with Kaylee's soft butch gender presentation. But he has to buy the dress for her, so she can accompany him to the fancy ball where he's planning to arrange some "exciting new crime." Kaylee is entirely out of her element at the ball. Cruel aristocratic girls mock her working-class mannerisms and store-bought dress. But Kaylee rescues herself by abandoning her ill-conceived feminine masquerade and embracing her masculine machine fetish. She deploys an elaborate technical discourse about spaceships and their engines. Kaylee finds a receptive audience of adoring aristocratic men. These men hang on her every word; when one of them tries to interrupt her, another man silences him so that Kaylee can continue her oration about spaceship technology. "Let her talk. The lady's talking." Kaylee's machine fetish ends up dominating the party's cultural discourse.

Serenity comics depict Kaylee's machine fetish in explicit detail. The fantasy scene in *Better Days* provides a particularly effective formal mechanism for this (Whedon, Matthews, and Conrad, *Better Days* #2). Sitting in a hot tub with the other women of *Serenity* while microscopic machines manicure her fingernails, Kaylee describes what she would do if she were filthy rich. She articulates a machine fetish fantasy with Electra overtones. "First I'd put together a little shop for my Daddy and me. Decent inventory—and all the latest tech stuff from the glossies that ain't on the market yet, you know? Not much more to it. Mostly the machines, getting to work 'em proper, you know?" Kaylee can imagine herself happy with nothing more than the company of her father and a few good machines. But she is an adult, and she has worked through her Electra situation, transferring her desire from her father to a more suitable object. Will Conrad provides a striking image of Simon taking Kaylee from behind. "Really get 'em hummin'," Kaylee concludes, in a voice-over against the image of her and Simon in the sweaty throes of ecstasy. Kaylee makes an easy connection between the mechanical and human objects of her desire. Though the characters can't see Kaylee's fantasy as the readers can, Zoë recognizes this connection. "We still talking about machines?" Zoë asks. Kaylee has revealed more than she meant to: "Leave me be," she fumes.

Kaylee's fetishistic fondness for machines aligns her with women who use electric vibrators to achieve sexual satisfaction. Kaylee uses electric sex toys for this purpose, although she regards them as inferior to men. In the film *Serenity*, she informs her crewmates that it's been "goin' on a year now I ain't had nothin' twixt my nethers weren't run on batteries!" Kaylee's choice of human sexual partners is especially interesting in this context. In the late nineteenth and early twentieth centuries, the electromechanical vibrator was considered a medical device, not a sex toy. Physicians used the vibrator to induce orgasm in their female patients, as a treatment for hysteria (Maines 11). It's not surprising, then, that Kaylee would choose a skilled physician like Simon Tam to be her lover. Kaylee and Simon finally have sex at the very end of *Serenity*. Naturally, the lovers embrace in Kaylee's engine room. They begin by working on the engines; this is foreplay for Kaylee. Both partners are half-naked and covered in engine grease. Kaylee prefers this to lingerie. Simon does, too: we already know that he thinks Kaylee is especially pretty when she's covered with grease ("Jaynestown" 1.4). By accepting and cherishing Kaylee's machine-mediated desire, Simon makes it possible for the two of them to develop a successful sexual relationship, while also promoting sexual pluralism aboard *Serenity*.

The ultimate endorsement of Kaylee's machine fetishism appears in *Leaves on the Wind*, when *Serenity* is boarded once again by the bounty hunter Jubal Early. Kaylee relives one of the most disturbing moments in the *Firefly* series: the scene in "Objects in Space" (1.10) where Early

Kaylee's mighty wrench. Kaylee's fetish for tools and machines, especially spaceship engines, is the love that keeps *Serenity* flying. Art by Dan Dos Santos. *Serenity: Leaves on the Wind* (2014). Dark Horse Comics/Twentieth Century–Fox Film Corporation.

ties her up and threatens to rape her. But this time Kaylee is in charge, and Early is helpless. Having incapacitated most of the crew, Early remembers that "there was one more" (Zack Whedon and Jeanty, *Leaves* #3). His eyes go wide as Kaylee, speaking from off panel, identifies herself and names her desire with two simple words: "the mechanic." She then knocks Early unconscious with a giant wrench. This wrench becomes absurdly huge in Dan Dos Santos' cover for issue four: a highly sexualized image of Kaylee, bruised and grease stained, brandishing a wrench that's almost as long as she is tall. Early awakes to find himself bound to a chair (Zack Whedon and Jeanty, *Leaves* #3). Kaylee stands over him, performing the role that he played in "Objects in Space." "What's the worst you ever been hurt, Jubal?" she asks. She empties a large bag of tools on the deck. "I ain't special like River," she says as she goes through the pliers, wrenches, and screwdrivers. "But I am good with tools." Kaylee is uncharacteristically menacing as she threatens Early with a pair of pliers while she recites the lines he once said to her. "You mess with us, your body is forfeit. It's just a body to me, Jubal. And I can find all unseemly manner of uses for it. Just gimme a gorram reason." The pliers click shut, scant centimeters from Jubal's eye. "Hope you brought a change of shorts, big guy," Kaylee concludes with a grin.

The cruelty that she shows Early in this scene may seem out of character for *Serenity*'s gentlest crew member. But Kaylee is the survivor of a vicious sexual assault, and she has been given a unique opportunity to take her revenge on the man who assaulted her and save her crew in the process. In that context, her actions make perfect sense. Her fetishistic love for tools gives her revenge fantasy the perfect form, for it allows her to show Early, herself, and the reader the incredible power that Kaylee draws from tools and machines of every kind. By the end of *Leaves*, Kaylee is back where she belongs: in the engine room with Simon (Zack Whedon and Jeanty, *Leaves* #6). When Mal orders her to "fire up the engines," his intercom message echoes through a seemingly empty engine room. Suddenly Kaylee appears and acknowledges Mal's order, even as Simon's hand reaches up from the deck to pull away the blanket that Kaylee clutches against her naked body. She has already fired up the engines, in her own uniquely fetishistic way.

"I Just Direct My Energy Elsewhere": Book's Clerical Celibacy

In a pluralist sexual culture which endorses a wide spectrum of active sexualities, Shepherd Book's celibacy is, in some ways, the most radical sexuality. Book's celibacy is motivated by his religious faith, which is a necessary condition for his celibate practice. Book clearly experiences sexual desire. In

Better Days, he shocks the crew by describing a highly sexualized fantasy of what he would do with massive wealth (Whedon, Matthews, and Conrad, *Better Days* #2). Will Conrad draws Book in an enormous chair, smoking a cigar in front of a table full of cash, playing cards, booze, cocaine, and a pistol. A buxom, brown haired young woman wearing a purple bustier, panties, and fishnets sits on his lap, reaching her hand under his robe to caress his bare chest. A young blonde in a matching corset stands by Book's side, caressing his huge chair, ready to assist her colleague. The women are probably sex workers, but definitely not Companions. Of course, this is pure fantasy. "Kidding," says Book as Kaylee, Jayne, Wash, and Zoë stare at him, shocked and silent. "Reckon I'd give it to the abbey." Book's joke works because his very specific fantasy, which includes every conceivable instrument of sin, is inherently absurd, especially when his crewmates imagine the ascetic Shepherd fulfilling that fantasy. But the very specificity of his fantasy suggests that it contains a kernel of truth. Book *can* conjure himself as the man who could revel in unrestrained, loveless lust with two women young enough to be his granddaughters. Naturally, he would never act on this desire, but the desire is real, and it humanizes Book. Without this desire, his celibacy would be meaningless. His asceticism is only possible if he has desires that he can deny. Book's sexuality is thus characterized by the kind of desire that a Lacanian would find perfect: a desire whose form renders its fulfillment structurally impossible. Lacan says that "desire disappears under pleasure's sway" (*Écrits* 652), but since Book has foresworn sexual pleasure, his desire need never vanish. In place of the pleasure he has renounced, Book enjoys the masochistic *jouissance* of the ascetic.

As holy men have done for thousands of years, Book deliberately and methodically channels his unfulfilled sexual desire into his religious devotion. In the language of psychoanalysis, he sublimates. Jayne finds this process fascinating; trying to understand, he pushes Book to distinguish celibacy from castration. "I mean, you still got the urge, right? They don't cut it off or nothing..." ("Objects in Space" 1.10). Jayne's castration anxiety is apparently so extreme that he is even capable of experiencing this anxiety on behalf of another man. This suggests that Jayne's firearm fetish may be driven, at least partly, by his need to defend himself against fear of castration. Book finds Jayne's second-hand castration anxiety amusing, for Book experiences his celibacy as the opposite of castrating: for him, it is empowering. "No, I'm more or less intact," he replies. "I just direct my energy elsewhere." Predictably, Jayne proves incapable of comprehending sublimation. He assumes that Book is simply referring to a change in his sexual aim. "You mean like masterbatin'?" Jayne guesses. Book dodges this question completely by turning it around on Jayne: "I hope you're not thinking of taking orders yourself..." But it seems clear that Book does not mean masturbation. Like many men who turn to celibacy for religious reasons, Book could well be tempted to masturbate. But his religious devotion drives him to deny himself all sexual pleasure. Book's celibacy thus represents what Freud called aim inhibited love. Indeed, Book represents this love in its most classical form, for aim inhibited love is the love of the holy man. It is the love of those who displace "what they mainly value from being loved on to loving," directing their love "not to single objects but to all men alike" (Freud, *Civilization* 56). Freud gives St. Francis of Assisi as the classic example.

Firefly takes pains to normalize Book's clerical celibacy, and to present sexual abstinence as a viable lifestyle choice. Occasionally, the show even presents abstinence as a moral imperative. Mal is normally quick to criticize Shepherds and their moralistic preaching; he thinks that men of God make people feel guilty and judged ("Safe" 1.7). Yet when Book tells Mal that he will burn in the special hell if he takes sexual advantage of Saffron (whom Book believes to be underage), Mal has absolutely no response ("Our Mrs. Reynolds" 1.3). "The *special* hell," Book repeats, and again Mal is silent. Mal's silence gives Book's pro-abstinence position discursive priority, by ensuring that Book's endorsement of abstinence has no rhetorical rival.

By the time Chris Roberson's *No Power in the 'Verse* comics appeared in 2016, the form and nature of *Serenity*'s sexual relationships were well established. Georges Jeanty nicely captures *Serenity*'s sexual culture in a wordless four panel sequence that shows how the crew spend their nights (Roberson and Jeanty, *No Power* #1). Jayne is in his bunk, cleaning his beloved Vera. River watches, amazed and delighted, as Zoë puts baby Emma to bed. While their relationship is not at all sexual, River clearly takes vicarious sensory pleasure from Zoë's experience of motherhood. In this capacity, River serves as a kind of surrogate Wash, and the only strange thing about her performance of this role is how natural it seems. Meanwhile, sleeping Simon spoons Kaylee, while Inara sleeps peacefully on Mal's naked chest. Everyone is where they need to be. They're all happy, or at least on their way to becoming so. Most importantly, each of them wants their crewmates to achieve happiness. The ship is finally free of jealousy and resentment. The crew have finally found *Serenity*.

Three

"The Breakable Ones"
Disabled Sexualities in Joss Whedon's Superhero Narratives

Joss Whedon's superhero stories reject American pop culture's discredited stereotypes to provide fair, realistic portrayals of disabled sexuality. While pop culture often presents disabled people as sexually innocent and passive, Whedon's narratives treat people with disabilities as mature, active sexual agents who are just as capable of making sexual choices as their able-bodied peers. While pop culture has a particularly strong tendency to deny disabled women sexual agency, Whedon's disabled superwomen have at least as much sexual agency as his disabled supermen. Whedon effectively uses the superhero genre to address disabled people's anxieties about loss of bodily control, and the related but more intimate anxiety about how this loss might preclude a satisfying sexuality. Many of Whedon's superheroes experience their powers as physical impairments. Yet all of these heroes have the potential to develop successful sexual relationships, and most of them negotiate such relationships. Whedon's superhero stories also reject the heteronormative eugenic logic which values only those sexualities that might lead to procreation. These stories illustrate the central insight of disability theory's social model: that individuals might suffer from physical impairments, but it is ableist society that disables those individuals (Shakespeare, Gillespie-Sells, and Davies 2). Whedon's heroes may be impaired by their uncontrollable superpowers, but they are only disabled when their teammates or society at large uses those impairments as an excuse to marginalize them. For example, Bruce Banner's impairment is the Hulk, but his disability is his unquestioning acceptance of ableist culture's assumption that his Hulkish impairment precludes a meaningful sexual relationship with Natasha Romanoff.

Whedon's stories of disabled superheroes clearly show that disability requires a broader concept of sexuality, and an expansion of the definition of sex. Disability theorist Tobin Siebers argues that there exists a sexual culture for disabled people. This culture rejects the numerous unexamined rules and restrictions by which ableist society denies the possibility of an authentic disabled sexuality. Disability theory's more inclusive model of human sexuality shows that disabled people can have healthy, happy sexual relationships, but only if they do so on their own terms, and not on the terms of the society that disables them. As Siebers argues, people with disabilities have already "begun to explore an alternative sexual culture based on the artfulness of disability" (148). This new sexual culture features "different conceptions of the erotic body, new sexual temporalities, and a variety of gender and sexed identities" (Siebers 148). In order to accommodate a sexual culture for disabled people, ableist society needs to change its thinking about sexuality substantially, and ableism is notoriously resistant to such changes.

Disabled sexual culture recognizes "the continuum of sexual practices—of which penetrative sex is only a part—and a greater willingness to embrace diversity, experimentation and … alternative techniques" (Shakespeare, Gillespie-Sells, and Davies 99). Such a culture encourages eroticization of body parts beyond the traditional erogenous zones (Siebers 149). Disabled sexuality challenges normative sexuality's understanding of sex as "a performance with a beginning, middle, and end" (Siebers 150), and the normative assumption of sexual simultaneity (i.e., the idea that all partners can, should, or must have sex simultaneously) (O'Toole 213). Unlike normative, ableist sex, disabled sex does not require or expect that all partners should climax (O'Toole 213). Indeed, for disabled people, sex "may not conclude with an orgasm" at all (Siebers 151). In this regard, the goals of disabled sexual culture are quite compatible with those of sex therapy, which promotes intimacy rather than orgasm.

A disabled sexual culture makes it possible "to imagine the sexual benefit of a given impairment, to claim and celebrate it as a sexual advantage" (Siebers 143). A reconceptualization of sexuality along disability-positive lines offers clear and important political benefits. As Abby Wilkerson argues, the creation of new sexual pleasures enables a powerful counter-discourse which can challenge the shame and judgment that normative culture imposes on disabled sexuality ("Sex Radicalism" 52). This recognition of the need for new political discourses about disabled sexuality confirms disability's status as the organizing principle for a specific sexual minority, comparable in form and structure to the various LGBTQ+ communities. Tobin Siebers argues compellingly that, although people with disabilities usually do not regard themselves in this way, they nonetheless do "constitute a significant sexual minority" (136). The needs and desires of this minority are frequently different from those of the majority, and sometimes radically so. In this regard, Robert McRuer's "crip theory" makes clear the intimate relationship between disabled and queer sexualities. McRuer argues that the compulsory heterosexuality that characterizes heteronormative culture is intertwined with the compulsory able-bodiedness that characterizes ableist culture (*Crip*

Theory 31). As McRuer emphasizes, compulsory able-bodiedness could be challenged or even eliminated by implementing the pluralist culture of "benign sexual variation" that Gayle Rubin called for back in the 1980s (McRuer, "Disabling Sex" 109). McRuer believes that the creation of overlapping queer and disabled theoretical spaces can challenge "heterosexual, able-bodied hegemony" (*Crip Theory* 19). This suggests the possibility of a productive alliance between queer and disabled sexualities, an alliance that could effectively resist the multiple forms of oppression that all of these sexualities face. Here McRuer's crip theory finds itself allied with Siebers's disability theory, for Siebers argues that recognizing the status of disabled people "as sexual citizens will advance the cause of other sexually oppressed groups" (136).

Whedon's superhero stories show what a sexual culture for disabled people might look like. In Whedon's *Astonishing X-Men*, Kitty Pryde learns that her inability to control her mutant phasing power need not preclude a successful sexual relationship with her fellow X-Man Peter Rasputin (Colossus). However, Kitty's impairment does require the two lovers to develop a new understanding of sexuality, one that is flexible and innovative enough to account for the fact that Kitty's occasional involuntary intangibility sometimes makes physical contact impossible. X-Man Scott Summers (Cyclops) usually needs a medical prosthesis to control the destructive red beams that his eyes constantly emit. Scott shows the limits of the medical model of disability, which regards the impaired individual's body as defective (Siebers 54). The medical model holds that an impaired person's body is simply broken, and that only medical science can fix it. But Scott learns that the telepathic discipline he receives from his dominant lover Emma Frost can give him what high-tech medicine cannot: a way to accept his impairment, come to terms with it, and incorporate it into a satisfying sexual relationship. Similarly, Bruce Banner learns that the discipline he receives from the dominant Natasha Romanoff allows him to manage the impairment he calls Hulk. But his unthinking commitment to an ableist reprosexuality gives this superhero story a tragic ending. Though Natasha works hard to show him how they could share a sexuality compatible with their mutual reproductive impairment, he is too disabled to see this, and must remain alone. The tragic story of Bruce and Natasha is Whedon's critique of an ableist culture that views reproductive ability as a prerequisite for sexual happiness.

"Everything Is So Fragile": A Sexual Culture for Disabled Superheroes

As numerous disability theorists have pointed out, contemporary American cultural representations of disability rely heavily on unrealistic stereotypes.

Representations of disabled sexuality are particularly caricatured, unrealistic, and exclusionary. Disabled people are typically portrayed as being uninterested in sex, incapable of having sex, or both (McRuer, "Disabling Sex" 107). This is partly due to the fact that disabled people are often infantilized; like children, they are presumed to be asexual (Shakespeare, Gillespie-Sells, and Davies 10). This denies disabled people sexual agency. Since they are presumed to be sexually passive, they are often thought to have no need for such agency. Since women are also frequently thought to be sexually passive, the assumption that disabled women will be passive is particularly strong (Oliver 72). As Robert McRuer argues, twenty-first century cultural representations may no longer present the disabled as figures of absolute deviance, yet they "are still visually and narratively subordinated" (*Crip Theory* 18).

Although pop culture works hard to marginalize disability, this culture ironically depends upon the very disability that it seeks to exclude. As David T. Mitchell and Sharon L. Snyder argue, disability pervades narrative, both as a feature of characterization and as a metaphoric device (*Narrative Prosthesis* 47). Pop culture's consistent efforts to marginalize, exclude, ignore, and/or caricature disability constitute a narrative impairment. Just as a disabled person might employ a prosthetic device to function within an ableist society, pop culture resorts to prostheses as a way to manage its impairment. Mitchell and Snyder call "this perpetual discursive dependence upon disability *narrative prosthesis*" (*Narrative Prosthesis* 47, emphasis in original). Disability functions "as a crutch upon which literary narratives lean for their representational power" (Mitchell and Snyder, *Narrative Prosthesis* 49). This explains pop culture's "love/hate" relationship with disability: our cultural narratives desperately need the disability which they so soundly reject. This is especially true of superhero narratives. As José Alaniz argues, the superhero genre comes into existence via an "always-erased though always-implied disabled/dying/dead body" (25). This is a perfect example of narrative prosthesis in action: superhero narratives are *enabled* by the *disabled*.

The function of disability is particularly important in stories about the X-Men, the team of mutant superheroes to which Kitty Pryde and Scott Summers belong. As Alaniz notes, "*X-Men* has earned a reputation as the preeminent disability allegory in superhero comics" (134). Like real-world disabled people (Shakespeare, Gillespie-Sells, and Davies 74), fictional mutants often find themselves unable to control their bodies. As Scott Bukatman points out, the fear, anxiety, and disgust that mutant superheroes feel towards their own bodies is driven by the uncontrollability of their superpowers, such as the optic blasts that shoot out of Scott's eyes, whether he wants them to or not (66–67). Ableist culture assumes that mutants would not make suitable sexual partners. As Alaniz argues, *X-Men* comics have been promoting this attitude since Stan Lee and Jack Kirby created the team in the 1960s, particularly through the figure of Professor Xavier, a wheelchair user (125). Like most fictional characters with obvious physical impairments, Xavier has usually been portrayed as sexually passive or asexual (Alaniz 124). Whedon's *Astonishing X-Men*, however, presents mutants with obvious impairments (such as Scott) and less obvious ones (like Kitty) as sexually active. Joss Whedon and artist John Cassady grant these mutants far more sexual agency than previous creative teams have done.

The film medium's representations of disability are typically just as limited and marginalizing as those of comics. As Martin Norden argues, the American movie industry seldom presents physically disabled people as sexual beings (315). Norden notes that American film often uses physical disability to suggest emotional disability (5). Emotional disability can also trigger physical disability, as when Bruce Banner's uncontrollable rage causes him to transform physically into the monstrous Hulk. Lennard Davis shows how Lacanian analysis can explain (and critique) the connection between emotional or psychological disability and disabled bodies. In the Lacanian model, the child experiences their body as fragmented (Davis 138). The child constructs a self by identifying with an image of a unified body during the mirror phase (Davis 139). Davis argues that this identification is a kind of "armor" which the child deploys against the fragmentary body (139). Expanding upon Davis' Lacanian theory, Margrit Shildrick interprets adult sexuality as "a nostalgia for the fragmented, incomplete body" (95). For Shildrick, the Lacanian problematic becomes most disruptive in the place "where disability intersects with sexuality" (94). On this interpretation, Bruce Banner's incessant rage represents a constant threat to the unity of his body. Bruce's transformation into the Hulk can be read as a failure of the psychological armor which protects him from bodily fragmentation, a fragmentation that he secretly desires. His sexual desire for Natasha Romanoff represents a nostalgic wish to be fragmented. But since the fragmentation of Bruce's body would unleash the monstrous Hulk, this desire must be repressed at all costs. This explains Bruce's consistent refusal to act upon what is very clearly a mutual, reciprocal desire.

The Hulk is a good example of one of Hollywood's stock disability stereotypes, which Norden describes as "violence-prone beasts just asking to be destroyed" (3). Kitty Pryde represents another of these stereotypes, the "sweet young thing" whose goodness and innocence justify an end to the isolation which would otherwise inevitably characterize the life of a fictional disabled person (Norden 3). And Scott Summers is an example of what Norden calls the "Techno Marvel," a disabled person who manages his disability with a science fictional prosthesis (in this case, the ruby quartz visor) (Norden 293). Snyder and Mitchell make the important point that a few films actually challenge these stereotypical depictions of disability; interestingly, they list Bryan Singer's *X-Men* (2000) and *X-Men 2* (2003) among these ("Body Genres"

Bruce Banner (Mark Ruffalo) and Tony Stark (Robert Downey, Jr.), two male scientists who attempt to create life without the help of women, much as Viktor von Frankenstein did. *Avengers: Age of Ultron* (2015). Marvel Studios/Walt Disney Pictures.

192). As Snyder and Mitchell note, disability is a core element of these cinematic stories about mutant superheroes, and these films "dramatize a canny awareness about a social model of disability," i.e., a recognition that disability is produced not by physical impairment itself, but rather by the way that society interprets and constructs such impairment ("Body Genres" 192). Whedon and Cassady take advantage of the representational opening that Singer's *X-Men* films provided. *Astonishing X-Men* continues the project of Singer's films in the comics medium, challenging stereotypes and dramatizing the social model of disability.

The most damaging representation of disability in American cinema is driven by one of the modern world's most dangerous sciences: eugenics, a scientific project which proposed to eliminate disability from human existence through selective breeding. As Angela Smith has shown, eugenic representations are particularly prevalent in the horror genre. One of the central tenets of eugenics is the idea that "biological defects render … certain people 'unfit' for reproduction" (Smith 9). Horror cinema represents this idea by suggesting that when monsters have sex or try to reproduce, the result is inevitably disastrous. This eugenic concern about the dangers of monstrous reproduction is central to the narrative of Whedon's *Age of Ultron*. Ultron himself is the monstrous child of two male scientists, Bruce Banner and Tony Stark. These men may suffer from the "womb envy" that Whedon views as a major source of patriarchal culture's misogyny and violence against women (Whedon, "Let's Watch"). Bruce and Tony use mad science in an attempt to create life without the help of women, much as Viktor von Frankenstein did, and with similarly disastrous results. Bruce is horrified when he sees that the "child" he created with Tony is a genocidal monster. Bruce's horror reflects his anxiety about his reproductive disability. Later, Bruce rejects the prospect of a sexual relationship with Natasha on the grounds that he can't have children. But Natasha rejects his rejection, discloses her own sterility, and offers the possibility of a mutually satisfying non-reproductive sexual relationship which would obviate the concerns of eugenics.

"That Weird, Unbearable Delight": The Disabled Sexuality of Kitty Pryde and Peter Rasputin

Whedon and Cassady's *Astonishing X-Men* comics affirm the sexuality of disabled people through the relationship between Kitty and Peter. When Kitty experiences involuntary intangibility, her mutant phasing power becomes an impairment. Perhaps it is no coincidence that Kitty Pryde chose Peter Rasputin to be her lover. Peter is quite literally a man of steel. His mutant power allows him to transform his body into living, organic metal. If anyone could provide Kitty with the tactile sensation she seems to crave—indeed, if anyone could succeed in touching her *at all*—surely it is Kitty's solid steel lover, Peter. As Kitty and Peter work together to devise a sexuality compatible with Kitty's impairment, they model a mutually satisfying sexual relationship between a disabled woman and an able-bodied man. Since popular culture rarely represents such relationships at all, and almost never represents them as potentially successful, this representation holds considerable potential for disabled people and disability theorists.

Kitty challenges the infantilization of the disabled, and the related assumption that disabled people are asexual. As a young, female "X-Girl," Kitty always projected an aura of sexual innocence. Her fellow X-Men generally saw Kitty as passive and asexual, as did comic book fans until *Astonishing*. But Whedon's Kitty Pryde is an active sexual agent. Lack of bodily control leads many real-world disabled people to dissociate from their bodies (Shakespeare, Gillespie-Sells, and Davies 74). Kitty represents this dissociation in a radical way: when she loses control of her body, it *ceases to exist* until she regains that control. In order to become a sexual being, Kitty must develop a new understanding of both embodiment and sexuality. Margrit Shildrick suggests that the coming together of bodies "is encompassed within an implicit anxiety about the loss of self-definition," and that this anxiety "is at its most acute where the body of the other already breaches normative standards of embodiment" (84). Kitty and Peter illustrate this breach. They radicalize what always happens during (good) sex: the dissolution of the boundary between self and other.[1] Their sexuality is based upon the premise that Kitty *will* lose her self-definition. Kitty and Peter confront their mutual anxiety about that loss together, as lovers. Since Kitty's radical incorporeality completely breaches all normative standards of embodiment, their eventual triumph over anxiety is nothing short of heroic.

Kitty and Peter are clearly sexual beings, but ableist culture has one remaining ploy at its disposal. If Kitty and Peter share an undeniable sexual love, that love can still be rejected as perverse. When ableist culture cannot deny the sexuality of disabled people, that culture assumes that this sexuality must be deviant (Shakespeare, Gillespie-Sells, and Davies 10). As Shildrick observes, the two characteristic responses to disabled sexuality are to silence that sexuality, or to focus fetishistically on disabled bodies *as* sexual (96). But when Joss Whedon writes Kitty and Peter, these characters do not allow either of those responses. Kitty and Peter share a sexuality which most certainly speaks; indeed, it speaks to the maximum extent possible in a superhero comic book marketed mainly to American teens. But Whedon does not fetishize these bodies. The easiest way to argue that such fetishization is occurring would probably be to read Kitty/Peter as an amputee/devotee relationship. Real-life amputation devotees desire women whose limbs have been amputated. When Kitty phases, she is essentially experiencing a full-body amputation. Like the women amputees whom devotees desire (Solvang 58), Kitty is young and beautiful, made different only by her disability. If Peter wanted Kitty *because* of her disability, then like real-life devotees, he might help achieve pride for the disabled body (Solvang 62), but he would otherwise continue to promote the hegemonic standards of the heterosexual male gaze (Solvang 58; see also Shakespeare, Gillespie-Sells, and Davies 124–125). But Peter does not desire Kitty because of her disability. Nor does he desire her *despite* that disability. Instead, he simply accepts Kitty's periodic incorporeality as a natural part of the woman he loves. Peter's desire for Kitty includes, but does not fetishize, her intangibility.

Kitty and Peter are sexually different from other people, but this difference occurs within the framework of a healthy, loving relationship which is, in most other ways, surprisingly conventional. While this may limit the radical potential of the Kitty/Peter relationship, it also creates an important mainstreaming effect. Readers are offered the opportunity to accept a radically different disabled sexuality as part of a relationship which can otherwise be read as "normal." This representation contributes to a destigmatization of disability, while simultaneously avoiding the temptation to stereotype or fetishize the difference of disability.

Kitty and Peter had a pre-existing romantic relationship, but they never actually managed to consummate that relationship until Whedon's *Astonishing X-Men*. This was partly due to the restrictions on the representation of sexuality that the Comics Code Authority imposed on Marvel Comics until Marvel quit the Authority in 2001. And it was partly due to the fact that Peter was dead, until Whedon brought him back. In a wordless scene in *Astonishing* #4, Kitty discovers that her long-lost lover is alive. The bad guys who have been holding Peter open fire. The bullets pass harmlessly through Kitty's intangible body and bounce harmlessly off Peter's solid steel form. Peter then charges through Kitty's body, to confront his captors. And Kitty reaches up to touch her heart, which has just been pierced not by love's arrow, but by her lover's body itself.

The freshly resurrected Peter Rasputin is understandably confused about many things. (Think season six Buffy.) His confusion has a strong impact on Kitty. She wants to resume their

Intangible Kitty Pryde phases through her solid steel lover, Peter Rasputin. Kitty and Peter devise a healthy and satisfying disabled sexuality that accommodates Kitty's impairment, involuntary intangibility. Art by John Cassady. *Astonishing X-Men* (2005). Marvel.

relationship, but fears that she's crowding Peter. He assures her that she is not crowding him "nearly enough" (#11). John Cassady makes frequent and effective use of full-width panels; here he uses such a panel to show Kitty's face as Peter says these last two words, so readers have a full view of her wide-eyed astonishment. The next time we see the couple alone together, they're cuddling under a tree. Colorist Laura Martin uses a brilliant palette of oranges and yellows to give the scene a lush, vibrant look. "So what do you think?" Kitty asks. "Does this qualify as 'crowding' you?" (#13). "It is what I would call a good start," Peter replies, smiling. "And uh ... what would you call a good finish?" Kitty inquires awkwardly. This is where Kitty first hints at the idea that her impairment has implications for her sexuality. The phrase "good finish" is a clear reference to male orgasm, comparable to the "happy ending" of sex work. Kitty may already suspect that her impairment could make it difficult to give Peter the "good finish" she so clearly wants to give him. Peter's response is equally awkward: "Uh, I'm not sure I—." Like many real-world partners of disabled people, Peter doesn't actually know how sex with Kitty should conclude.

The scene is interrupted by the arrival of Kitty's dead father, and readers learn that they've been watching Kitty's nightmare, which Emma has prompted telepathically. But the fact that this is all a dream in no way undermines its status as valid data on Kitty's fears. Since Emma presumably drew the raw material for this nightmare from Kitty's unconscious, the dream provides the best possible evidence of Kitty's anxiety about having sex with Peter. Her nightmare of disabled sex differs from her subsequent experience of *actual* disabled sex in two ways. First, in reality Kitty and Peter are not interrupted by the ghost of her dead father; Kitty's Electra complex remains unconscious. And the real Peter, unsurprisingly, turns out to be far more understanding than his dream doppelgänger. Kitty awakens from her nightmare to find herself in the real Peter's arms. His first thought, as always, is for her safety: "Are you all right?" Smiling, she nestles in his huge arms and replies: "Gettin' better already."

Peter and Kitty attempt to negotiate their reborn relationship with spoken language (#13). Naturally, these efforts end in spectacular failure. Whedon's works consistently argue that sex can only be negotiated in the Imaginary and consummated in the Real; the Symbolic is no place for sex. (Think Buffy and Riley at the end of "Hush," *Buffy* 4.10.) Kitty threatens to go through Peter's body, as he went through hers previously. He expects to get yelled at some more, and so stands around, as Kitty says, "like a big dumb big guy." Finally, they abandon their futile efforts at Symbolic spoken communication, and suddenly everything *works*. Cassady spends a full wordless page on their kiss. He shows the two lovers embracing from the side, then from behind Peter's head. He provides a tight close-up of the lovers staring adoringly into one another's eyes. The final panel on the page shows Emma walking by in the hallway outside Peter's room. As the architect of Kitty's recent nightmare, Emma is, in some sense, midwife to the disabled sex which follows this kiss.

Peter and Kitty have sex for the first time. Meanwhile, an unsuspecting mutant student is watching television on the lower floor of the X-Men's mansion headquarters. Suddenly Kitty's naked body falls *through the floor*! (#14) Kitty races back upstairs to Peter. When she reaches the bedroom, a wide-eyed Peter deploys his go-to question: "Are you all right?" "Oh my God!" Kitty gasps. "I phased!" Peter is an unstoppable Colossus of care. He insists that he must ascertain Kitty's mental and physical health before pursuing any other topic of conversation. "Are you all right?" he repeats, gazing deep into Kitty's eyes. "Are *you*?" she replies. Kitty's question is a manifestation of her anxiety about disabled sex.

It seems likely that Kitty phased before Peter reached orgasm, but he seems unconcerned about this. Peter appears to understand sex therapy's insight that intimacy is more important than orgasm. "It was strange," he admits. He does not say that it was scary, grotesque, or horrible. It was strange, but then sex is always strange the first time. First sexual experiences are "rarely wonderful or fulfilling," especially for disabled people (Shakespeare, Gillespie-Sells, and Davies 101). Kitty continues to obsess about her impairment, and about how that impairment impacts her sexuality. "I can't believe I phased just then! That's never…" If Kitty is being honest here, the word "never" suggests that her impairment does not interfere with masturbation, but only with great sex. Here Kitty stumbles upon an effective cure for the guilt that derives from her (mis)perception that she can't please Peter. If it truly takes a superior orgasm to activate Kitty's phasing power, then her bout of involuntary intangibility is grounds for celebration, not guilt. "It was totally your fault," she concludes. "I like to think so, yes," Peter agrees. Peter has immediately understood that he should take pride in his ability to activate Kitty's impairment. The bedroom door closes, separating the audience from the delighted lovers. Kitty giggles through the door: "Tee hee." She has every reason to be happy. She and Peter have just proven that her impairment does not preclude a satisfying sexual relationship. What's more, they've shown that Kitty's impairment can be a fundamental *part* of their sexuality. Like real-life disabled/non-disabled couples, Kitty and Peter are able to share desire, pleasure, and love, despite the fact that the disabled partner's impairment makes her difficult to touch. Peter and Kitty learn to go beyond penetrative sex, and indeed beyond physical contact of any kind. In this way, they encourage their audience to develop a broader understanding of sexual love.

Peter and Kitty travel to the alien Breakworld, where they make love again. Whedon and Cassady spend two pages on the negotiations which precede Peter and Kitty's second sexual encounter (#21). Peter is "so confused ... so tired." The top third of the next page features Peter wide-eyed in the background. Kitty stands naked in the foreground, facing Peter, her back to the reader. The remainder of the page consists of three full-width panels, all tight close-ups: Kitty's bedroom eyes, blue-eyed Peter saying, "now I am *more* confused," and finally Kitty looking down, smiling, powerful, triumphant, as Peter concludes, "but somehow not as tired." Already Peter has learned not just to accept the confusing strangeness of sex with Kitty, but to cherish that strangeness. He understands that a successful sexual relationship with his disabled lover must be based, in part, upon that strangeness.

The out-of-panel sex which follows these negotiations appears to have been highly satisfying for both partners. Kitty and Peter lie in bed together, big smiles on their faces (#22). Kitty is on top of Peter in this panel. Like many real-world disabled people (Shakespeare, Gillespie-Sells, and Davies 97), Kitty seems to have rejected the missionary position which ableist culture privileges. Kitty has apparently remained substantial long enough for both her and Peter to reach orgasm. She is now prepared to answer his important questions: why so soon? So suddenly?

Peter's questions allow Kitty to articulate the central thesis of Whedon and Cassady's *Astonishing X-Men*: "Everything is so fragile.... If happy comes along—that weird, unbearable delight that's actual happy—I think you have to grab it while you can. You take what you can get, 'cause it's here, and then..."[2] Clearly, the happiness that an intangible woman shares with her solid steel boyfriend is both weird and unbearable. Yet Whedon's Kitty Pryde insists that people have not only the right but the responsibility to seek such happiness. The audience may be reminded here of Dracula's exhortation to "find what warmth you can" as Buffy had sex with Satsu for the second time in *Buffy* season eight comics (Goddard and Jeanty 8.15), which date from the same time period as *Astonishing*.

Kitty and Peter build a sexual relationship which unites her intangible body with his metal body. This turns out to be good news not only for the triumphant lovers, but also for the Earth itself. The narrative of *Astonishing*'s final story arc, "Gone," hinges on Kitty's ability to phase through the weird alien metal of the Breakworld. Kitty initially finds this difficult and painful. She must phase herself and Peter through the strange skyscrapers of the Breakworld when their spaceship crashes. Kitty protests: "The metal—like Ord's ship, it's... I can't..." (#20) Peter gazes upon Kitty's sweating, straining face. His own face is silent, stoic, steel. He turns to put himself between Kitty and the ground. When Kitty inadvertently solidifies, they crash into a window and through a floor, coming to rest stunned but unharmed. Here Kitty's phasing power and Peter's metalizing power combine very effectively; indeed, theirs is one of the few power combinations which could have landed them safely. This scene emphasizes the interdependence of their intangibility and metalization.

The Breakworlders fire a massive, planet-smashing bullet at the Earth. When Kitty phases through the bullet, the alien metal provokes an existential angst. Kitty is surrounded by blackness (#24). "Nothing," she says telepathically to Emma. "I've gone more… than a mile…" A close-up shows Kitty sweating, eyes closed. "This metal…" she moans. Kitty struggles to phase the deadly bullet through the Earth. "Come on…" she growls. "I can't be that weak." (*Giant-Size* #1) The point, of course, is that she is the opposite of weak; she is, in fact, the strongest member of the team. This is consistent with Whedon's overall interpretation of the Kitty Pryde character. That character served as the inspiration for Willow Rosenberg, another tiny, courageous Jewish girl of immense, sometimes uncontrollable power (Kaveney, *Superheroes!* 210).

As Kitty speeds towards Earth inside the alien bullet, she learns the form of her own strength. She tries to explain it telepathically. "I don't feel weak, Emma. I feel … sick." Crucially, she has learned not to interpret the effects of the Breakworld metal as evidence of weakness. She continues: "Not pain, not … just like it got in me. Like I'm meshed to this metal. It wants me here." Kitty speaks of her physical relationship with the metal in strangely intimate terms. This is also the first time she speaks of the metal's desire. If the Breakworld metal got in her and if it wants her to be inside it, then this metal sounds much like a lover. Unsurprisingly, this is the moment when Kitty associates the Breakworld metal with her metal lover, albeit initially in negative terms: "I'm in the cage I freed Peter from." If Kitty can associate the weird alien metal with the metal man she loves so much, then she may be able to reciprocate the Breakworld metal's desire and save the earth. Having learned to love a metal man, she's now ready to consummate her relationship with the Breakworld metal. "Disappointed, Ms. Frost?" she asks Emma. "Astonished, Ms. Pryde," Emma replies. If even Emma can say this of Kitty, then Kitty is truly the most astonishing of the Astonishing X-Men.

"The Source of All Your Extraordinary Self-Doubt": The Disabled Sexuality of Scott Summers and Emma Frost

Scott and Emma both understand that mutant "superpowers" often turn out to be physical impairments, and they both emphasize that it is important for mutants to learn how to control these impairments. The narrative of *Astonishing X-Men* begins with Emma lecturing on this topic to an audience of young mutant students. "Control of your powers, the safety of those around you, is of paramount importance," Emma declares (#1). A few pages later,

Scott develops Emma's argument further. "The perception is that we're freaks, or worse. That we're Magnetos waiting to happen." Scott's use of the word "freaks" suggests that mutants have much in common with the circus freaks whose disabilities were made into public spectacles in the late nineteenth and early twentieth centuries (Garland-Thompson). Scott also recognizes that his own personal disability makes it hard for him to gain the trust of ordinary humans. "Me.... I can lead a team. But I haven't looked anybody in the eye since I was fifteen." John Cassady draws a tight shot of Scott's ruby quartz visor as he says that last sentence; image and words combine to suggest that Scott's disability carries social consequences that are similar to those of blindness.

Emma and Scott recognize that no matter how hard they work to promote tolerance and acceptance of mutants among ordinary humans, human society will always have a powerful desire to eliminate mutants altogether. *Astonishing* develops a "cure narrative" which suggests that it may be possible to turn mutants into normal humans. Emma confronts the inventor of the cure, Dr. Kavita Rao. Emma calls Dr. Rao's ethical credentials into question by invoking the name of the ethically conflicted director of the Manhattan Project. "Nothing but noble intentions, yes. You're a veritable Oppenheimer. What's next? Eliminating the gay gene?" (#5). Here Emma connects the mutant "cure" to the long and troubled history of eugenics, while simultaneously connecting the deeply fraught eugenic project to the equally disturbing campaign to eliminate queer sexualities. The scene evokes Nazi campaigns to eliminate disabled and homosexual Aryan Germans. "Homosexuality doesn't represent a *threat* to human existence," Dr. Rao counters. "We're clearly watching different televangelists," Emma replies drily. This reminds readers that eugenics promotes the agenda of a heteronormative, ableist culture that regards both queerness and disability as threats to humanity.

Emma and Scott have a relationship of sexual dominance and submission (Call, "'That Weird, Unbearable Delight'" ¶ 25–40); Scott's submission to Emma is motivated largely by his desperate need to control his superpower. Their DS dynamic is subtle at first, but by the end of *Astonishing X-Men*, Emma is able to acknowledge it explicitly: "If I'd known you were such a submissive I'd've gone with an entirely different wardrobe" (#21). Emma remains dominant throughout the telepathic sex fantasy that she constructs for Scott. This fantasy allows Scott to see what the world would look like without his ruby quartz visor (#14). Emma (masquerading as Jean Grey) puts her costume back on; apparently, she and Scott have just had out-of-panel mind-sex. She hugs Scott as he puts his visor back on. "You can let go now," Scott says. "I forgot I was holding you in," replies Jean/Emma. Scott finds this remarkable. "Forgot..." Controlling Scott's impairment is instinctive for a dominant woman like Emma. It is so natural for Emma to maintain this control that she sometimes forgets she is doing so. This is part of the reason that Scott finds Emma irresistible: what is so difficult for him is so easy for her.

Like Kitty, Scott recognizes that his impairment impacts his sexuality. Scott admits that when the visor's on, he can't see blue. His impairment includes a kind of colorblindness. After having visorless mental sex with Jean/Emma, Scott knows that she's "really" a redhead. She finishes the thought for him: "—and a natural redhead, too." Since Emma is impersonating Jean and the whole scene occurs in Scott's mind, words like "really" and "natural" are basically meaningless here. Nonetheless, this exchange reveals that Scott and Emma both view red hair as a sexual fetish, and that they both perceive Scott's inability to see the red hair as a sexual disability.

Scott tries to assure Emma-as-Jean that he has accepted his impairment. "I don't mind the way I see things," says Scott. "I just ... I always have to think about it. About keeping the force from breaking free, from disintegrating these glasses and just blasting. I wonder, if it got out of control ... would it still only come from my eyes?" As this disabled superhero imagines red energy blasts coming out of every orifice in his body, he models a common

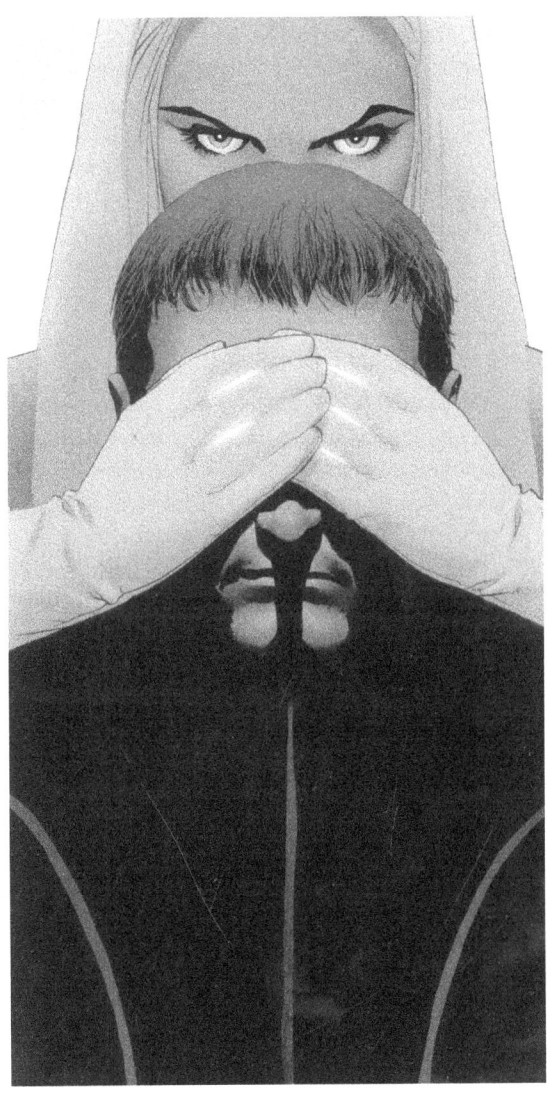

Emma Frost uses telepathic discipline to control Scott Summers' impairment. Without Emma's discipline, Scott needs a medical prosthesis, the ruby quartz visor, to control his powerful eye beams. Art by John Cassady. *Astonishing X-Men* (2005). Marvel.

fear of real-world disabled people: a total loss of bodily control. Scott gazes through the visor into the green eyes of Jean/Emma and says, "I just want you to know, I understand about power that has to be controlled." Scott clearly wants his lover to control his superpower, which he experiences as a disability. Once he turned to Jean for this control. Now he gets it from Emma. It always comes from a powerful telepath. Chris Claremont's Jean Grey was an important prototype of the dominant telepathic woman; Whedon's Emma Frost is the Whedonesque version.

Emma takes Scott on a tour of his most painful memories. She shows him the experiences that constructed his disabled identity. Scott sees his younger self in dialogue with Professor Xavier. Cassady draws the two men in silhouette. Their impairments are emphasized: Xavier's wheelchair is clearly visible, while colorist Laura Martin adds a touch of red to the silhouette of young Scott's face. Xavier, the experienced wheelchair user, acts as a mentor to the disabled boy. "You're a very special person, Scott," says Xavier. "You don't know it yet, but you are." Discourses of disability often draw upon the language of specialness, e.g., special education or special needs. Xavier uses that language as he tries to encourage young Scott to redefine his impairment as a positive power. But Emma gives Scott the hard truth about Xavier's motivations. She reveals the reason for Xavier's seemingly inexplicable choice to name this severely impaired boy team leader: "Potentially the most powerful team on earth and Xavier gave you the top position ... out of pity." When ableist society shows charity to the disabled, such charity is often motivated by pity. A person with a disability will find it especially devastating if this pity comes from another disabled person. The implication—that one stands at the bottom of a hierarchy of disabilities—is intolerable.

Emma finally reveals the source of Scott's psychological problems. She takes Scott to the Bug Room, a mindscape of horrific giant insects introduced by Grant Morrison. Cassady lays out a two-page spread of long, wedge-shaped horizontal panels. Most of these are colored red; they are clearly meant to represent Scott's uncontrollable eye beams. Scott can now be honest about his fears. "I'll fail you," he tells Emma. "I can't control it." Interestingly, he fears his inability to control his impairment not because he worries about failing the X-Men or mutantkind in general, but rather because he's afraid of failing his sexual partner. "Control what, dear?" Emma replies. "Your power? It's your great setback, isn't it? The source of all your extraordinary self-doubt." She then takes Scott through the gaping, dripping belly-maw of a giant bug, to reveal what she calls "the *real* truth." Young Scott sits in a hospital bed, his eyes bandaged: here he models blindness more clearly than ever. "The world is a terrifying place for some children," Emma explains—disabled ones, for example. "That lack of control, that fear of abandon." Grown-up Scott watches child-Scott deciding not to try to control his power, choosing to let it disable him. Emma kisses Scott's cheek as a single tear rolls down from beneath his visor. "You can let go now," Emma says, and colorist Laura Martin fades to a full-width panel of pure blue. Blue is the opposite of red, so the blue panel means that Scott's red eye beams are now totally disciplined. The Imaginary blue bar also marks Scott's exit from the Symbolic. In voice-over, Emma explains that Scott's decision not to try to control his power was "too shameful to remember," so Scott "let it eat [his] life up instead." In the world of the X-Men as in our world, the refusal to participate in ableist culture carries a massive stigma, and that stigma generates tremendous shame. This revelation sends Scott into the Real, rendering him completely catatonic. His impairment becomes, briefly, total.

Surprisingly, this total impairment is presented not as a disability, but as a liberation. "You're free, my love. You're free," Emma declares in voice-over against Scott's mindless, drooling body. Here Whedon executes an interesting narrative reversal. Up to this point, Scott's disability has been defined by his inability to control his power. Now his disability is suddenly redefined as the *loss* of his power. This creates the conditions that will eventually allow Scott to reclaim his power *as* a power. Scott finally regains consciousness in issue 18. He is powerless in the sense that he has no eye beams, but powerful in every other way. "Still can't access my powers, but otherwise I'm fine for now," Scott declares. He now has the opportunity to enjoy the power that able-bodied people take for granted: the power to live without stigma and shame.

Recognizing that his powerlessness makes him expendable, Scott volunteers for a suicide mission to buy time for the rest of the team to escape the Breakworlders. "If anything happens, I'm the most… I'm the one with no powers," he observes (#22). Emma is in close telepathic contact with Scott as he appears to die in the vacuum of space. "He's going," says the silhouette of Emma's face. Cassady then draws Emma's face fully lit, eyes half closed, lips parted, as she says "I'm so close…" Her appearance and her language suggest, strangely, that she is approaching orgasm. The next panel features a similar drawing of Scott's face, his eyes half closed as he succumbs to the vacuum. Here Whedon and Cassady suggest a connection between Scott's (illusionary) death and the "little death" of orgasm. While the dominant Emma experiences the "death" of her powerless lover as orgasm, the submissive Scott experiences his powerlessness as castration. Captured and tortured by Powerlord Kruun, a tearful Scott laments his inability to resist: "If I … had my powers…" (#23).

Scott's eye beams are the narrative prosthesis that drives his story. His achievement of full control over those beams marks the climax of this story. Whedon, Cassady, and Martin emphasize this by spending four full pages on Scott's first fully controlled optic blast, the one that sends Powerlord Kruun into unconsciousness. The scene features three diagonal panels of ruby red, followed by six vertical panels of the same. The final panel shows the ruby red of Scott's eye beams reflected in Emma's blue eyes. This reminds readers that Scott's newfound ability to control or release his power at will originates with Emma. Scott stands triumphant over Kruun, visorless, eye beams ready but held in check, perfectly disciplined. He issues Professor Xavier's classic telepathic summons: "To me, my X-Men." At last Scott *is* team leader, without doubt or reservation, all because of Emma. His fellow X-Men now recognize that Scott is incomplete without his powers. "It's good to see you," says Hank. "All of you" (#24). But Scott understands that he will never truly be free of the prospect of impairment. "Don't get used to it," he says in profile, his eyes shadowed.

At the end of the series, Scott surrenders control to Emma once again (*Giant-Size* #1). Emma has been crying. "Your eyes are red," Scott notes. "Look who's talking," Emma replies, reminding Scott that he is, and always will be, impaired. "I love you," he says. She gazes through the ruby quartz as she installs his visor, embracing the sign of his disability. "I love you too," she replies. Scott's impairment is an important part of what Emma loves about him. As Scott and Emma embrace, a voice-over repeats Kitty's words of disabled wisdom: "Everything is so fragile." The voice-over suggests that if Kitty and Peter were able to find "actual happy" by embracing the fragility of a disabled sexuality, Scott and Emma can do the same.

"Still Think You're the Only Monster on the Team?": The Disabled Sexuality of Bruce Banner and Natasha Romanoff

Bruce Banner and those around him consistently treat the Hulk as an impairment. Like real-world disabled people and fictional disabled mutants, Bruce experiences feelings of fear, anxiety, shame, and disgust around his impairment. He wrings his hands nervously as he discusses it with Natasha during their first meeting. He is so ashamed of it that he can't speak about it directly. Rather than granting his monstrous alter ego a name, he refers to him as "the other guy." Bruce says that when he's the other guy, he's "exposed, like a nerve. It's a nightmare." Real-world ableist society subjects people with visible impairments to just this sort of nightmarish exposure. Towards the end of *The Avengers*, Bruce reveals that although his physical impairment is intermittent, the emotional impairment that is both the cause and the effect of Hulk is constant: "That's my secret, Captain. I'm always angry."

Most of Bruce's anxieties are about becoming Hulk, but the real social and psychological consequences of his disability appear when Hulk becomes Bruce. After falling from the helicarrier, Bruce wakes up, naked and disoriented, in an empty warehouse. A security guard (Harry Dean Stanton) is watching him. Like many real-world disabilities (Siebers 143–147), Bruce's disability denies him the possibility of privacy and makes it difficult to maintain dignity. After confirming that Bruce is not an alien, the guard says, "well then, son, you've got a condition." This is a profoundly disabling statement. It shows how society creates the disabled "condition" that the guard ascribes to Bruce and imposes that condition on impaired individuals. We may assume that this working-class security guard lacks the formal medical training that would qualify him to make a diagnosis, yet he feels perfectly entitled to do so. The guard represents the values of an ableist culture. Within such a culture, he is eligible to render a judgment of disability, for disability is precisely the average person's perception of impairment.

From the moment that Natasha meets Bruce, she tries to help him manage his disability. She points out that Bruce has gone more than a year without "an incident." Her use of the ambiguous word "incident" indicates that she shares (or at least respects) his reluctance to speak directly about Hulk. "I don't think you wanna break that streak," she concludes. Later, when Bruce's anxiety increases aboard the helicarrier, Natasha asks him to think about removing himself from the stressful environment. "Huh," Bruce replies. "I was in Calcutta." Bruce implies that he was living in isolation until Natasha showed up. This is the place where *The Avengers* departs from Martin Norden's "cinema of isolation." In *The Avengers*, Bruce's story arc begins when his isolation *ends*. Rather than representing him as fundamentally isolated, as a Hollywood film would typically do, *The Avengers* portrays him as a disabled character who is escaping isolation with the help of his potential sexual partner. Thus, *The Avengers* challenges at least two major stereotypes about disability: that the disabled must always remain isolated, and that they can't have sexual relationships.

Earlier in the film, Tony Stark tries to express solidarity with Bruce by suggesting that he, Stark, is disabled too. When Stark points out that he is kept alive by a medical prosthesis (his arc reactor), Bruce insists that his situation is different, and he has a point. As Masani McGee argues, "for all of his power, The Hulk is more disabled than Stark; his inability to control his body separates him from his fellow heroes" (¶ 13). Speaking to Natasha, Bruce shows nostalgia for his lost isolation. "I was good… until you dragged me back into this freak show!" Bruce views the Avengers like Scott views the X-Men: as a public performance of freakish disability, such as one might find in an early American circus (Garland-Thompson). Bruce rejects the idea that he can or should associate with other "freaks." He has clearly internalized the logic of isolation, which separates the disabled from one another and treats each instance of disability as a separate, individual case. But in a film whose overarching narrative purpose is to *assemble* the Avengers, the audience will likely understand that Bruce's self-imposed isolation is unsustainable.

Natasha gets her first opportunity to help Bruce with disability management when the brainwashed Hawkeye attacks the helicarrier. Pinned down under rubble, Natasha radios Nick Fury: "We're OK." Then, turning to Bruce, she makes it a question: "We're OK, right?" At this point, they are both lying prone, face down on the deck of the helicarrier. Natasha's able-bodied super-competence usually contrasts sharply with Bruce's disability. However, in this scene, she is temporarily disabled, her mobility impaired by the rubble that pins her down. Although female superheroes are often sexualized, Whedon does so rarely, and always deliberately. Here the camera focuses on Scarlett Johansson's shapely posterior: though temporarily disabled, Natasha is still sexually desirable. As she struggles against her impairment, she encourages Bruce to do the same. "Bruce, you gotta fight it. We're gonna be OK. I swear on my life I will get you out of this. You will walk away." She chooses her words poorly here. "Your life?" Bruce replies, and begins to transform into Hulk. Natasha's life is the kind of life that Bruce desperately craves, but thinks he can never have: a free, active life whose impairments are limited and temporary. By contrasting her active life with Bruce's disabled existence, Natasha inadvertently contributes to his transformation. A tight close-up on Bruce's eyes shows that he is still human, just barely. He gazes back at Natasha, pleading silently for her help. Whedon then cuts to a close-up of Natasha looking back at him. "Bruce?" she says, but Bruce is gone. Now there is only Hulk.

By the time the *Age of Ultron* arrives, Natasha has learned how to meet Bruce's most pressing need, which is to manage his disability by regulating his impairment. She accomplishes this via the lullaby. When she performs the first lullaby in *Ultron*, it's clear that Hulk wants to participate. He snarls and shakes his head, as if to shake off Natasha's influence, but he puts up only token resistance. He comes to her, already docile even before the lullaby really begins. This is a sign that Hulk craves Natasha's discipline as much as Bruce does. The satisfied half-smile that Natasha shows when she sees Hulk transforming back into Bruce is certainly that of a successful Whedomme (see Chapter One), but it is also that of a woman who has just given her disabled partner the care he needs in the wake of his chronic impairment's latest flare-up.

Back on the Quinnjet, Natasha offers Bruce encouragement, and shows some justifiable pride in her disability management skills: "Hey, the lullaby worked better than ever." Natasha asks how long it will be before Bruce trusts her. He replies, "It's not you I don't trust." What he really doesn't trust is his desire for her. He fears (with some reason) that he will be unable to control that desire, and that this will impede his ability to control his impairment. He

Three. "The Breakable Ones" 107

is forced to confront this fear when Ultron attacks the party at Stark Tower. Bruce and Natasha dive behind the bar. He lands on top of her; though fully clothed, they are otherwise in the missionary position that ableist culture defines as "sex." Bruce immediately apologizes, but not for landing on top of her in a sexual position (which she clearly wants, as she has been hinting with ever diminishing subtlety). Rather, he apologizes because he knows that if they follow the penetrative agenda of ableist sexuality, he will lose the precious control she has helped him achieve. Maintaining that control is more important than sex, and so the would-be lovers immediately substitute DS for penetrative sexuality. "Don't turn green," she commands. "I won't," he assures her submissively.

Natasha does not fetishize Bruce's impairment, but it is part of what attracts her to him. "Fact is he's not like anybody I've ever known," she tells him during the party, speaking in the third person to let him keep some distance from the desire that clearly terrifies him. She can only be speaking of his impairment, which is what defines his uniqueness. Surrounded by men who embody conventional kinds of courage, she prefers the courage of a disabled man who fights not to overcome his disability, which would be a stereotype and an impossibility, but to manage it to the point where he can integrate it into a fulfilling life. Both this courage and its sympathetic representation are exceptional in American cinema.

Ultron reveals an important motivation for Natasha's attraction to this disabled man. Although she is generally portrayed as able-bodied—even hyper-able—her Black Widow training has given her a crucial invisible disability. Whedon introduces Natasha's disability slowly, in the flashbacks that Scarlett Witch (Elizabeth Olsen) induces. Natasha watches her young self and other girls undergo relentless ballerina training. "You'll break them," Natasha says to Red Room headmistress Madame B (Julie Delpy). "Only the breakable ones," the headmistress replies. "You're made of metal." Remarkably, Madame B suggests that Natasha is like Peter Rasputin: a woman of steel, and not a breakable disabled person like Kitty Pryde, Scott Summers, or Bruce Banner. "We'll celebrate after the graduation ceremony," says Madame B. Whedon offers a glimpse of what the audience will later learn was Natasha's sterilization surgery. "The ceremony is necessary," the headmistress insists—here the ballerinas place their hands submissively behind their backs—"for you to take your place in the world." Teary-eyed, the adult Natasha realizes, "I have no place in the world." "Exactly," agrees Madame B. The disabled have no place in ableist society.

In one of the film's most disturbing shots, we see Natasha strapped down to a gurney, on her way to be sterilized involuntarily, rolling past girls who have no mouths. Natasha and her sterilized sisters have been effectively silenced. They may not speak about their reproductive impairment. Though she experienced this impairment in her distant past, the trauma that Natasha suffers from it disables her in the present. She spends some time catatonic, much as Scott did after Emma forced him to confront the truth of his disability. Natasha shows uncharacteristic fragility as the Avengers arrive at Clint Barton's farmhouse. She leans on Clint as they approach the house. The first thing Natasha sees is Clint's pregnant wife, Laura (Linda Cardellini), and the two Barton children, who greet her as an honorary aunt. It appears that Natasha has developed a surrogate familial relationship with the Barton children.

In a pivotal scene set in one of the farmhouse's bedrooms, Natasha comes out about her disability, both to Bruce and to the audience. The conversation is structured like a queer coming out: it is difficult and painful, but also potentially empowering, and ultimately necessary. As Shakespeare, Gillespie-Sells, and Davies suggest, disabled people can benefit from publicly affirming their sexual difference by coming out in this way (50). The scene begins with Natasha on the bed in her bathrobe. A flashback shows both her sterilization surgery and the Hulk's rage; this aligns the impairments of the two characters and suggests that they are indeed compatible. Bruce tells her he has to leave; his instinct is still to run from his impairment, even though he knows that this is impossible. Natasha offers to leave with him. He admits that even if he leaves, he has nowhere to go. "Where in the world am I not a threat?" But Natasha doesn't fear his impairment. "You're not a threat to me," she declares. She is actually the perfect potential partner for him. With her by his side, he could keep the Hulk in check, remain Bruce, and build a life. But he's still afraid, and his fear takes the form of the eugenic terror that has haunted American cinema's "Jeckyll and Hyde" films for a century (Smith 144–145). "There's no future with me," he declares. "I can't ever ... I can't have this." He gestures at the trappings of domesticity. "Kids. Do the math. I physically can't." Although he usually understands his impairment as primarily emotional, here he emphasizes its physical aspect. It is *physical* impairment that precludes reproduction, as it has always done, ever since cinema first began to represent eugenic anxieties in the early twentieth century.

Here *Ultron* makes one of its most radical moves. It rejects the flawed premise at the heart of eugenic sexuality—the notion that a satisfying sexual relationship requires at least the possibility of procreation—in order to promote a far more progressive philosophy that detaches sexuality from reproduction. When Bruce protests that he can't have kids, Natasha replies, "neither can I," and gives a heartbreaking account of the sterilization process. "They have a graduation ceremony. They sterilize you." Here she bats her eyes, a typically alluring gesture rendered tragic by context. The dissonance between her words and her gesture subtly reinforces the message that her desirability is independent from her reproductive ability or lack thereof. "It's efficient," she continues, nodding as if trying to convince herself. "One less thing to worry about. The one thing that might matter more than a mission. Makes everything easier. Even killing." Whedon frames Johansson in profile as she delivers the critical and controversial line: "You still think you're the only monster on the team?" Bruce just stares at her, shocked and speechless. If his failure to meet the reproductive requirements of eugenic culture has made him monstrous, hers has surely done the same to her. If anything, her sterility makes her even more monstrous than him, for as child-bearers, women always bear the brunt of society's eugenic imperatives.

Patriarchal culture, which judges women's worth according to their fertility, calls Natasha monstrous. Indeed, patriarchy makes her internalize that judgment, and *name herself monster*. But *Age of Ultron* critiques patriarchy's eugenic values and offers an alternative. Natasha readily recognizes the possibility of a meaningful, non-reproductive relationship with Bruce. Critics who don't notice Natasha's openness to non-reproductive sexuality often read *Ultron*'s sexual values as patriarchal (see, for example, Woerner and Trendacosta). One exception is Amanda Marcotte, who argues that Natasha's willingness to depart from social expectations of what the good life should look like is "pretty feminist." Unfortunately, Whedon scripted, shot, and edited the farmhouse scene in a way that makes the feminist aspects of Natasha's position hard to see. Her tearful equation of her sterility with monstrosity suggests that she has accepted patriarchal culture's eugenic logic. She tries to resist this logic by pursuing a relationship with Bruce. But Whedon doesn't give Natasha sufficient opportunity to establish this resistance. Natasha is trying to challenge one of patriarchal culture's deepest and most dearly held assumptions: that women must be able to bear children if they are to live meaningful lives. To be effective, such a challenge would require more and better dialogue. Whedon cut the part of the scene in which Natasha makes her strongest case for abandoning reprosexual, eugenic culture ("we don't play circle of life") and embracing a non-reproductive sexuality ("we just play") (see Chapter One). The Natasha/Bruce story, already secondary to *Ultron*'s "main" plot, simply doesn't have room for a thorough critique of reprosexuality. By allowing Natasha's declaration of monstrosity to go unchallenged, Whedon creates a dangerous narrative situation in which the audience could easily assume that the eugenic position is the only possible viewpoint.

Reading this scene in the broader context of the DS relationship that Natasha is trying so hard to build with Bruce reveals, however, that a different point of view is possible. In this context, Natasha appears to be resisting her socially constructed reproductive disability by trying to detach sexuality from reproduction via DS. Bruce's stubborn refusal of Natasha's advances is certainly implausible; he's refusing a sexual relationship with a gorgeous, powerful woman who clearly adores him, simply because he can't have children with her. But Bruce's rejection of Natasha is not only unrealistic; it also indicates that he is part of the patriarchal problem. Bruce has internalized the eugenic values of the patriarchal culture so thoroughly that he is unable even to consider Natasha's desire to resist those values. Even worse, he ascribes those values to her, assuming without cause that she could only be happy in a sexual relationship that included the possibility of children. Though Whedon tried to create a feminist position for Natasha, her ability to articulate that position was ultimately hampered by this male filmmaker's inability to imagine a male character who could accept this female character's challenge to eugenic patriarchy, and perhaps even help her develop that challenge.

Natasha's coming out scene concludes with Bruce still unconvinced of their compatibility, and skeptical of her vision of their future. "So we disappear?" he asks. Later in the film, when Natasha is captured by Ultron and Bruce comes to free her, she turns the tables on him. By now her offer to retire from Avenging and run away sounds better to him. "Our fight is over," he tells her. "So we just disappear?" she replies, echoing and critiquing the words he used earlier. But she is unable to dissuade him from disappearing. After the Battle of Sokovia, Hulk steals a plane and flies off. Natasha tries to give him a lullaby by video phone, but he switches off the video and sits calmly as the plane carries him away. Although he still can't fully control the physical impairment that makes him Hulk, he has learned to manage the *disability* that is Hulk. His disability is the meaning that society places on his impairment: fear, threat, danger. By removing himself from society, he renders that meaning irrelevant, but he also returns himself to the isolation he experienced before he met Natasha. Natasha is understandably shaken: by learning to manage his disability, he has accomplished what she always wanted for him, but he has chosen to do it without her.

At the very end of the film, Natasha confronts Nick Fury and asks if he knew what would happen when he sent her to recruit Bruce. "You never know," Fury replies. "You hope for the best, then make do with what you get." Fury and Natasha shared the same vision: Bruce in a stable sexual relationship with Natasha, his impairment controlled, working with the Avengers as both Bruce and Hulk. They came close to realizing that vision. Whedon makes this vision attractive and gives it narrative priority by letting Natasha and Fury dwell on it at the end of the film, with Bruce absent. Bruce's refusal to buy into this tempting vision gives the film's conclusion its tragic character and shows how hard it is for disabled people to throw off the stigma of disability, even when their friends and partners are eager to help them do so.

Natasha, Bruce, Kitty, and Scott may indeed be "the breakable ones," and their sexual relationships may be "so fragile." But they are no different from anyone else. Everyone is breakable, even the temporarily able-bodied. Every relationship is fragile, none moreso than sexual ones. Whedon's stories of disabled superheroes and the people who love them can serve as an inspiration for real-world disabled people and their partners. These stories show that even the most powerful people may suffer from impairments, and that ableist society will attempt to disable even the most extraordinary impaired individuals. More importantly, these stories show that it is possible to resist society's disabling discourse. Most importantly, they show that people with disabilities need not forgo the joys and delights of sexual love, for no matter how a person is disabled, healthy sexualities and eager, understanding sexual partners are available to them. For real-world disabled people and for their intimate partners, the sexualities of Whedon's disabled superheroes represent the hope of happiness.

Four

"Majestic Creature of Legend"

Human/Animal Hybridity and Zoophilia in the Buffyverse

Since *Buffy*, Joss Whedon's works have explored the ontological and ethical status of nonhuman beings. Whedon's works have consistently portrayed nonhumans as intelligent, emotionally complex ethical agents. The Buffyverse shows a particular fascination for a specific type of nonhuman: the hybrid. These liminal creatures combine aspects of humans and nonhuman animals. The most obvious examples are the werewolves, especially Oz (Seth Green) but also Veruca (Paige Moss), who has a brief sexual relationship with Oz; Bayarmaa, who marries Oz and has a child with him; and Nina Ash (Jenny Mollen), who has a brief relationship with Angel. These wolf-human hybrids combine the courage and pack loyalty of wolves with the love and compassion of humans. Buffy's sister Dawn (Michelle Trachtenberg) is actually a "key" of mystic energy. As if to remind us that her natural form is not human, Dawn takes on a number of nonhuman forms in *Buffy*'s later (comic book) seasons. In season eight, she becomes a centaur. Here she provides a contemporary representation of the classical world's ancient horse-human hybrid. Centaur Dawn combines her human dedication to her family and friends with the nobility and power of the horse. Hybrids like Oz and Dawn combine the best elements of human and nonhuman, while simultaneously calling the very categories of "human" and "animal" into question.

The hybrids are animals who can think and speak and love; by doing all the things that nonhuman animals supposedly can't do, they challenge the separation between human and nonhuman that lies at the heart of Western metaphysics. Most importantly, they challenge the assumption that humans are superior (intellectually, spiritually, and/or morally) to other animals. Sympathetic hybrid characters force human audiences to encounter their own anthropocentrism. Positive portrayals of human/nonhuman hybrids not only encourage human audiences to rethink their relationship with nonhuman animals; they also invite those audiences to consider embracing their own animalistic aspects, rather than rejecting those aspects as modern humans have been culturally conditioned to do.

Ananya Mukherjea has insightfully observed that on *Buffy*, representations of sexuality and animality inform one another through a reciprocal process (54). *Buffy* does this by portraying sexual relations between humans and hybrids, as well as relations between different types of hybrids. These representations call into question one of the most powerful taboos in Western culture: the prohibition against interspecies sex. The ethical philosopher Peter Singer founded both the modern animal rights movement and the interdisciplinary scholarly field of Animal Studies (Boggs 105). Singer has argued convincingly that "the vehemence with which this prohibition continues to be held" is driven by our powerful "desire to differentiate ourselves, erotically and in every other way, from animals" ("Heavy Petting"). Yet in our posthuman world, that differentiation is difficult to achieve.

The hybrid human/nonhuman sexualities of the Buffyverse evoke the real-world sexuality known as zoophilia. Zoophiles claim that their sexuality includes an important emotional attachment to animals that distinguishes it from bestiality (Miletski 6; Beetz, "Bestiality/Zoophilia" 11). They denounce bestiality, which they view as driven by a selfish human quest for self-gratification (Williams and Weinberg 526). Zoophiles attempt to distinguish their relations with animals from abuse by claiming that their zoophilia is informed by a model of nonverbal consent (Beetz, "Bestiality/Zoophilia" 15). The ethical claims of real-world zoophilia remain controversial, and debates about the ethical status of interspecies sex are unlikely to be resolved any time soon. *Buffy* makes no ethical claims regarding real-life zoophilic sex, and neither do I. However, I do claim that the sexualities of the Buffyverse's human/nonhuman hybrids validate zoophilic *desire*, without addressing the question of whether or how such desire could be ethically fulfilled in the real world. In this chapter, I argue that *Buffy*'s representations of zoophilic desire challenge the strict boundaries between humans and nonhuman animals that Western metaphysics works so hard to maintain. I argue that these representations prompt audiences to rethink relationships between humans and other animals in a way that will likely promote greater compassion towards nonhuman animals. And I suggest that these representations encourage audiences to make explicit the conditions under which humans should accept or reject potential sexual partners (e.g., the presence or absence of rational thought, or of speech), rather than relying on the arbitrary criteria of the ill-defined category "species."[1]

This chapter examines the sexualities of two hybrid beings: the werewolf Oz, and the polymorphous hybrid Dawn, especially in her centaur form. The canine and equine forms of animality that these hybrids embody are some of the most common objects of real-world zoophilic affection (Miletski 131). I argue that the animality of these characters defines their sexualities and informs their sexual relationships. Willow loves Oz *because* of his wolf-self, not in spite of it. She also sees a connection between his wolfish aspect and her own sexuality. Xander first takes a serious sexual interest in Dawn when she assumes her centaur form. From that point on, Xander's desire is inversely related to Dawn's humanity: the less human she becomes, the more he wants her. *Buffy*'s narrative implies that these relationships succeed because at least one of the partners draws upon a powerful animal nature, and both partners embrace that nature. These relationships promote the hybridity of all participants, since they include "human interaction with the animal body *and* an animalization of human bodies" (Boggs 101).

For centuries, Western werewolf myths have been preoccupied with the question of werewolf sexuality. Twentieth-century American cinema often used the werewolf as a metaphor for the changes that young men go through in puberty, especially the increased sexual urges of adolescence, which are portrayed as difficult to control; *I Was a Teenage Werewolf* (Gene Fowler, Jr. 1957) and *Teen Wolf* (Rod Daniel 1985) illustrate this trend (Douglas 247–251). Here *Buffy*'s hybrids reverse traditional gender and species roles. Oz is hardly the stereotypical rapacious male werewolf. His greatest fear is that his wolf-self might harm Willow. In his sexual relationship with her, he is the gentlest of lovers. Unlike the cinematic adolescent male werewolf of previous decades, Oz is quite capable of controlling his sexual urges. Oz embodies a unique hybridization of beastly wolf and peaceful human. Willow desires this singular hybridity and the exciting tensions it creates.

In her centaur form, Dawn embodies a multiple human/animal hybridity. The centaur is a hybrid of horse and human that symbolizes the hybridization of rider and mount (Thompson 224). The centaur's hybridity has always been strongly sexual. This is especially true of the classical world's male centaurs, to whom the ancient Greeks attributed the "strong sexual potency of stallions" and a "violent lust" (Lawrence 63). Lustful males "overshadowed" the rarer female centaurs (Lawrence 63). Here again, the Buffyverse departs from traditional representations. *Buffy* comics represent Dawn as feminine, and they show that she has a strong sexual agency. She is generally dominant in her relationship with Xander. Centaur Dawn thus reverses the traditional gendered power configuration of the centaur. By doing so, she opens up a space for a feminist version of the ancient horse/human hybrid. The typical riding relationship may be based on a power exchange in which the horse submits to the rider (Thompson 229–230), but this does not describe Dawn's relationship with Xander. Xander shows the submissive side of riding: "absorbing horse, taking horse into our body" (Game 9). This aspect of riding is usually coded feminine, but not in this case. The double hybridity of submissive male human rider plus dominant female centaur mount blurs boundaries of both gender and species.

The Oz/Willow and Dawn/Xander relationships evoke zoophilia, but these relationships are not truly zoophilic. Unlike actual nonhuman animals, Oz and Dawn possess reason and language. Oz can have sex with another werewolf when in wolf form but can only have sex with Willow when in human form. Xander doesn't actually have sex with centaur Dawn, though he clearly wants to; he models zoophilic desire rather than behavior. My argument is that much like Dawn, these relationships open a gateway to another world, a world beyond anthropocentrism. These zoophilic representations authorize real-world audiences to consider a range of ethical relationships with nonhuman animals that is broader and more diverse than that which anthropocentric culture offers. Audiences need not accept real-world zoophilia's ethical claims, and they certainly need not view sexual encounters between humans and other animals as ethical. But if they can accept the sexualities of fictional human/animal hybrids as ethically legitimate, they may be able to accept real-life zoophilic *desire* as a legitimate form of love, which could allow them to view nonhuman animals as beings worthy of compassion. That would represent a major victory for posthumanists, ethicists, and the increasingly numerous scholars who work under the interdisciplinary rubric of Animal Studies, to which I now turn.

"Witches, Werewolves and Centaurs": Hybridity, Zoosexuality and Ethics

For most of its history, Western metaphysics has worked to create, maintain, and enforce strict boundaries between humans and other animals. These boundaries typically feature an assertion that nonhuman animals lack some attribute that is held to be a crucial constituent of humanity, such as a soul (Christianity), reason (the Enlightenment), or language (structuralism). In the last quarter of the twentieth century, however, ethicists, posthumanists, postmodernists, and others concerned with what Jacques Derrida called "the question of the animal" began to mount a serious assault on this tradition that insists on the radical separation of humans from other animals (and on the alleged superiority of the former). In his groundbreaking 1975 book *Animal Liberation*, Peter Singer coined the term "speciesism" to designate the form of irrational prejudice which allows humans to privilege the interests of their own species over those of other species (6). In her famous 1985 cyborg manifesto, the eminent theorist of hybridity Donna Haraway argued that "nothing really convincingly settles the separation of human and animal" (*Simians* 152). In her 2003 "Companion Species Manifesto," Haraway claimed that "companion species" such as dogs "bring together the human and nonhuman" (96). In 1997, Derrida argued that the figure of "the Animal" represents an egregious overgeneralization whose function is to reinforce the increasingly tenuous boundary between humans and "every living thing that is held not to be man" (400). More recently, Cary Wolfe has pointed out that all the traditional markers of "the human," including both reason and language, "flourish quite reliably beyond the species barrier" (2). At the end of the twentieth century, the humanities began to take an "animal turn" comparable in structure and significance to the well-known "linguistic turn" of the mid-century (Armstrong and Simmons 1). Since this animal turn occurred, the now ironically named category of "the humanities" has broadened to include the sophisticated analyses of nonhuman animals that are flourishing in the new interdisciplinary field of Animal Studies. Thanks to the successful propagation of Animal Studies, it has become increasingly common for scholars to argue, as Matthew Calarco does, that *"the human-animal distinction can no longer and ought no longer to be maintained"* (3, emphasis in original).

In an important chapter from their major work *A Thousand Plateaus* (1980), Gilles Deleuze and Felix Guattari efface the human/animal distinction using a method that is different from, yet no less effective than, Haraway's hybrid theory and Derrida's deconstruction. Deleuze and Guattari identify "becoming-animal" as a crucial variety of the becoming whose primacy their work hopes to establish. Becoming-animal is not playing animal or imitating an animal, and humans do not "really" become animals in the world that *A Thousand Plateaus* imagines (Deleuze and Guattari 238), although that last option is entirely possible in fantasy worlds like the Buffyverse. Becoming-animal moves humans into a zone of radical alterity, a place where the carefully cultivated distinction between human and animal loses coherence. Becoming-animal "always involves a pack" (Deleuze and Guattari 239)—of wolves, for example. Significantly, Deleuze and Guattari suggest that packs are formed of "demonic animals" (241)—just the sorts of animals who inhabit the Buffyverse. Even more significantly, Deleuze and Guattari give the werewolf as one of their main examples (241).

Becoming-animal is intimately connected to sexuality. Indeed, Deleuze and Guattari argue that animality drives sexuality in general. "*Sexuality proceeds by way of ... the becoming-animal of the human*," they declare (279, emphasis in original). Though Deleuze and Guattari are quick to emphasize that sexual becoming-animal doesn't require "bestialism," they are equally quick to acknowledge that such bestialism "may arise" (279). Thus, their theory leaves space for zoophilic desire, if not actual sexual relations between humans and nonhuman animals. Deleuze and Guattari also associate becoming-animal with non-normative sexualities such as masochism (260) and fetishism (259; see also Dekkers 147). All of these sexual becomings-animal—zoophilia, fetishism, masochism—share a common trait: they are non-reproductive.

Becoming-animal inspires "abominable loves" which tend to "prevent procreation ... the demon does not himself have the ability to procreate" (Deleuze and Guattari 246). Although the premodern West feared the monstrous hybrid offspring which interspecies unions were thought to produce (Beirne 318), such unions are now generally thought to be non-procreative (Dekkers 21). Oz and Dawn challenge both the premodern and modern concepts of interspecies sex, for they both eventually have babies who are healthy, happy, and apparently human.

While Animal Studies encourages a sympathetic attitude towards zoophilic desire, it is difficult to interpret actual interspecies sex as ethical. Carol J. Adams has made a strong case for the claim that nonhuman animals cannot possibly consent to sex with humans. In Adams' view, "relationships of unequal power cannot be consensual," and human/nonhuman relationships are always unequal (31). Adams emphasizes the inability of animals to provide verbal consent: "only one of the participants in bestiality can talk; and because of the stigma surrounding bestiality, that party usually remains silent" (30). Building on Adams' critique, Piers Beirne suggests that bestiality should be understood as "interspecies sexual assault" (315). Like Adams, Beirne believes that animals are incapable of saying no (or yes) to sex with humans (Beirne 322).

Adams and Beirne rely upon a liberal, humanist model of consent which privileges human speech. They thus participate (perhaps inadvertently) in an increasingly discredited twentieth-century philosophical tradition which argues for a strict separation between humans and other animals on the grounds that nonhuman animals lack language. Sex is the only area where humans apply standards of linguistic consent to nonhuman animals; we do not require that animals consent verbally to be killed, eaten, or experimented upon. As for the question of power, even Beirne acknowledges that inequalities of power characterize most human sex (321). As Foucault argues, power flows through every social relation, especially sexual ones (94, 103). To reject interspecies sex as unethical on the grounds of inequalities of power would require the rejection of most or all human sex on the same grounds. Peter Singer is quick to denounce meat eating and animal experimentation as cruel and abusive, yet Singer insists that sex with animals is "not always cruel" ("Heavy Petting"). If Singer's rigorous utilitarian ethics finds some interspecies sex permissible, then it seems reasonable to make the much more modest claim that zoophilia represents a legitimate form of human desire, especially if we set aside the more challenging question of whether such desire could be ethically fulfilled.

If zoophilia is a valid form of desire, it can also serve as the basis for a sexual identity. Williams and Weinberg observe that "today's zoophile groups ... often participate in the sexual politics of contemporary erotic minorities, notably constructing and propagating a particular identity for themselves" (531). Of the zoophiles who participated in Hani Miletski's study, 72 percent of men and 63 percent of women view their zoophilia as comparable to a sexual orientation (158). Miletski concludes that there does appear to be such a thing as a sexual orientation towards nonhuman animals that includes feelings of love and affection for animals, sexual fantasies about animals, and sexual attraction towards animals (171). Andrea Beetz agrees; she names this orientation "zoosexuality" ("Bestiality/Zoophilia" 19). Monika Bakke argues that zoosexuality is potentially subversive, since it is "disruptive of the anthropocentric order" and "evokes a totally different concept of ourselves, our bodies, and our relations with other animals" (228). Willow's desire for Oz and Xander's desire for Dawn include elements of zoosexuality.

Historically, cultural representations of interspecies sexuality have generally been positive, though actual cross-species sex has usually carried a strong stigma. Fantasies may seem less threatening than actual acts, and zoophilic desire is much easier to justify than zoophilic behavior. Thus, as Midas Dekkers demonstrates, "down the centuries people have enjoyed scenes of bestiality depicted with great beauty, which in reality would have inspired nothing but revulsion" (152–153). These depictions include, most famously, Leda and the Swan (Zeus), and Europa and the Bull (also Zeus—the myth of Europe was founded on an interspecies sexual act, Bakke 232). The power of zoophilic representations lies in their ability to encourage diverse, innovative, creative attitudes towards human/nonhuman relationships. Although there is always an ethics of representation, cultural images of interspecies sex are usually unencumbered by the ethical problems which continue to trouble real-world zoophilia, particularly around the issue of consent. Here is where the radical potential of zoophilic representations lies. Barbara Creed identifies the horror film's "screen animal" as a figure that collapses "the boundary between 'human' and 'nonhuman,'" creating an "order of the animal" that emphasizes the animal's agency by focusing on its desires and dreams ("What Do Animals Dream Of?" 62–63). Oz and Dawn belong to this order of the animal, for *Buffy* focuses strongly on their animal desires and those of their partners. By doing so, *Buffy* asks its audience to take zoophilia seriously as a form of desire.

"The Wolf Is Inside Me All the Time": Oz and Willow's Werewolf/Witch Sexuality

Werewolves are initially coded masculine in the Buffyverse, although like everything about these mercurial lycanthropes, that changes. *Buffy*'s early werewolf storylines use the "teen wolf" trope to explore adolescent male human sexuality. Willow dates Oz briefly before discovering that he's a werewolf. She complains to Buffy that Oz seems reluctant to pursue a sexual relationship with her. Buffy replies, "I think it's nice that he's not just being an animal" ("Phases" 2.15). Here Buffy assumes that the sexual behavior of young men is comparable to that of nonhuman animals. The Scoobies continue to develop this line of thinking as they discuss the nature of werewolves. Giles declares that the werewolf is "predatory and aggressive." Buffy takes a cheap and essentialist shot at men: "In other words, your typical male." Xander's feeble response—"on behalf of my gender, hey!"—implies that the show accepts Buffy's equation between men and sexual aggression. When Xander claims to be an expert on lycanthropy, Willow emphasizes *his* animal nature, pointing out that he has this knowledge because he was once a hyena. Xander agrees; he plays into the "teen wolf" stereotype by insisting that he knows what it's like "to be taken over by those uncontrollable urges." Oz confirms that lycanthropy stands as a metaphor for the transformations that an adolescent human male must go through. When Willow confronts him about his odd behavior, Oz tells her he's "going through some changes." This is the classic description of both lycanthropy and adolescence.

Yet the characters soon realize that Oz's animal nature offers substantial potential benefits, and that Oz's animality might serve as the foundation for a successful relationship with Willow. When the Scoobies discover that Oz is a werewolf, Buffy is quick to emphasize that she sees Oz as "the loyal type." By focusing on Oz's canine loyalty, Buffy implies that as his attachment to Willow grows, that loyalty will strengthen their relationship. Buffy has classified Oz as a companion animal. She sees him not as a wolf but as a domestic dog, the kind of animal that would make a good partner for a zoophilic woman.

The show transcends the "teen wolf" trope by emphasizing that a young woman like Willow has an animal aspect as powerful as any man's. Willow compares the changes that Oz is going through to her own journey towards maturity: "Don't you think I'm going through a lot?" Willow provides the strongest statement of her own animality as she renegotiates her relationship with Oz. After his wolfish nature has been revealed, Willow assures Oz that she can handle the fact that he's a wolf three days a month: "I mean, three days out of the month I'm not much fun to be around either." Equating her menstruation with animality could be viewed as dehumanizing, but it is only disempowering if the animal is viewed as inferior to the human, which is not Willow's view. While Renee St. Louis and Miriam Riggs view Willow's line as an unfortunate joke about the insanity of pre-menstrual women which disregards Willow's experience of her own body (¶ 18), I believe that the line does take the bodily experiences of an adolescent woman seriously. By explicitly connecting Oz's lycanthropy to her own menstrual cycle, Willow suggests that the process of becoming a sexually mature woman is a process of becoming-animal. This implies that there is nothing scandalous about a sexual relationship between a wolf man and a woman who is herself an animal. "You are quite the human," Oz concludes. By naming Willow human after she has just emphasized her animality, Oz calls attention to the always blurry boundary between humans and other animals.

Buffy's werewolf stories queer the horror genre's tropes of teen sexuality. The show does not allow its audience to make a simplistic equation between werewolves and heterosexual desire. Xander becomes convinced that school bully Larry (Larry Bagby) is a werewolf. Xander confronts Larry in the locker room and assures him that he knows what he's going through (see above re. hyena). But Xander discovers that Larry is not a werewolf—he's gay. Xander experiences a homophobic shock at this revelation. But what's really interesting about this scene is how it queers the figure of the werewolf. By suggesting that being a werewolf is similar to being gay, *Buffy* implies that werewolf/human relationships are in some sense queer—even straight ones like Oz/Willow.

In the early stages of the Willow/Oz relationship, Willow normalizes Oz's lycanthropy, while simultaneously trying to maintain a distinction between Oz's human and wolf selves. Here the show takes a double domestic turn. Willow settles into a domestic routine with Oz, positioning herself as his caretaker. This domesticates Oz, in the sense that it turns him from a wild animal into a tame one. Willow reads Jack London's *Call of the Wild* to the caged Oz wolf, claiming that it "seems to soothe the savage beast" ("Beauty and the Beasts" 3.4). She tells Xander that Oz has "had his two o'clock feeding." By now Willow is closer to attaining a sexual relationship with human Oz, but her relationship with wolf Oz is more like a mother/baby relationship. When Oz escapes his cage and is suspected of killing, Willow invokes the supposed distinction between his human and wolf selves: "Wolf you, not you you!" Oz takes little comfort from this; he surely suspects that the line between wolf and man is not nearly as absolute as Willow wants to believe. But he clearly appreciates her domestic attentions. The Scoobies go off to hunt the killer. "And I'll—go lock myself in the cage," Oz offers. His lack of enthusiasm indicates that he would much prefer for Willow to lock him in the cage. Their relationship has become, among other things, the kind of female-dominant DS relationship that will soon become familiar to *Buffy* viewers. As the dominant partner, Willow is responsible for supervising Oz's monthly bondage.

Oz and Willow continue becoming animal for some time before they actually have sex. Oz's wolf self discovers Willow's infidelity; he follows her scent to find her kissing Xander ("Lover's Walk" 3.8). Oz equates his jealousy with his lycanthropy: "seeing you with Xander—well, I never felt that way before ... when there wasn't a full moon" ("Amends" 3.10). Buffy advises Willow to show Oz that he comes first. And so Willow makes a clumsy attempt

Four. "Majestic Creature of Legend" 121

at seduction. She puts on a sexy red dress, sets candles everywhere, and puts Barry White on the stereo. Oz is understandably mystified. "We could do that thing," Willow suggests. She can't name the "thing," for in the Whedonverses, sex is always alien to the Symbolic. Willow claims, quite unconvincingly, to be ready. To her dismay, Oz says that he's not. If Oz were the undisciplined, hormonal animal that the "teen wolf" stereotype says he is, he would surely jump at this offer. Instead he refuses, telling Willow that he wants to have sex with her when they both need it for the same reason. So they kiss and watch videos instead. By choosing not to have sex, Oz asserts his human agency. He shows that despite his animal aspect (and hers, for that matter), he and Willow are capable of having a fully human relationship, one that does not partake of Western culture's stereotypes about "animalistic" sexuality.

Willow meets the vampire version of herself in "Doppelgängland" (3.16), a Joss Whedon episode that confirms the nature of her DS relationship with Oz. The only significant difference between Willow and her vampire doppelgänger is that vampire Willow is more obviously dominant. Buffy tells Willow that her vampire double is like her in every way "except for you not being a dominatrix. As far as we know." Willow scoffs at Buffy's suggestion. "Oh, right. Me and Oz play 'Mistress of Pain' every night." But this strategy backfires. Buffy and Xander immediately go to a "scary visual place": in fact, they have no trouble imagining Willow dominating Oz.

Oz and Willow finally have sex in "Graduation Day, Part 1" (3.21), written and directed by Whedon. The circumstances emphasize Willow's connection to nonhuman animals. Importantly, Willow and Oz are not alone when they have sex for the first time. They share Willow's bedroom with an animal that was once human: Amy, who was magically transformed into a rat. The scene strongly suggests that Willow's witchcraft is an animal power. Willow asserts that she isn't really a witch because she "can't even turn poor Amy back into a person." Here Willow conflates humanity with personhood, while defining her witchcraft as the ability (or inability) to turn a nonhuman animal into a human. Willow becomes frustrated at Oz's "ironic detachment." "Would it help if I panic?" Oz asks. Surprisingly, Willow says yes, since "panic is a thing people can share in times of crisis." Willow once again complains about her chronic virginity, noting that the impending apocalypse could prevent her from getting to do the "sorts of things you're supposed to get to do after high school." She still can't name these Real, animal "things," for they resist integration into the Symbolic. Finally, Oz switches briefly to the dominant role to give Willow what she clearly wants. He gets up, grabs Willow behind the neck, and kisses her hard. "What are you doing?" Willow asks. "Panicking," Oz replies. Oz and Willow kiss enthusiastically.

After the inevitable commercial break, Whedon's frame centers on Amy the rat, emphasizing the animal nature of the act that Willow and Oz have just performed. Whedon pans over to Willow's sneakers, then to her *Witchcraft* book, then up to her and Oz, smiling, eyes closed, naked in bed. Oz strokes Willow's hair in a gesture of animal affection. "I feel different," Willow declares, as well she should: she has finally embraced her own animal nature and consummated her animal relationship with Oz. "Everything feels different," Oz agrees. Oz has had sex before, but that was when he was still fully human. This is the first time that he's had sex since he became a werewolf, and presumably the first time he's had sex with an animalistic witch. Everything is indeed different.

Tragically, the Willow/Oz relationship falls apart just seven episodes later, in the highly effective Marti Noxon tearjerker "Wild at Heart" (4.6). In a scene that features prominently in the season four credits, Willow and Oz snuggle in bed. They consider having sex. Willow has to get to class, but she says, "definitely tonight." Oz reminds her that this will be impossible, since it's the night before a full moon. By now Willow is comfortable with her lover's animal aspect, but the fact remains that for three nights a month, they can have no physical contact at all. Willow wants to attend a meeting of the campus Wicca group. (Here she will meet her next lover, Tara.) She asks Oz to lock himself up so she can go to the meeting. This signals a failure of their DS dynamic. They can easily go three nights without physical contact if Willow is supervising Oz's lycanthropic bondage; without that, their sexual relationship lacks foundation. Later, when Willow sees Oz and Veruca talking, the attraction between the two werewolves is palpable, and Willow is jealous. Buffy assures her that Oz "isn't the type to stray"; she still sees Oz as a loyal domestic dog. Willow agrees that Oz won't be able to stray as long as he's locked in his cage. But that night, Oz breaks out of his cage and has wild, violent animal sex with werewolf Veruca. They wake up in the forest, human again, naked, covered in scratches.

Veruca is astonished to learn that Oz has a cage. "God, somebody has domesticated the hell out of you," she observes. In Veruca's eyes, Oz has fallen prey to the curse of the companion species. Oz protests that it's his choice, which it is. He repeats the claim that he and Willow have been making throughout their relationship: that he's only a wolf three nights a month. This gives Veruca the opportunity to challenge the human/animal boundary. "Or you're the wolf *all the time*," Veruca replies. "And this human face is just your disguise." Veruca offers to have sex with Oz in human form. She is almost irresistible in her black bra, but Oz manages to refuse. Veruca makes the case for embracing animality. "You're scared. I was, too. But then I accepted it. The animal. It's powerful." Veruca is an effective spokeswoman for animality, but this is the moment when the dangers of her position become evident. She feels sorry for ordinary humans, who don't know what it's like to be as alive and as free as werewolves. Veruca's viewpoint is ultimately unsustainable.

For her, becoming-animal means losing-human, but the Buffyverse favors a union of human and animal that keeps the best of both while becoming something more.

Moments before sunset, Veruca arrives at the open door to Oz's cage. Oz demands that she join him in the cage, for her own safety and that of Sunnydale's residents. But Veruca knows what this means. "You'll be safe," Oz assures her. "Not from you," Veruca points out, fondling the bars of the cage seductively. Nor does she want to be safe from Oz. She continues to tease him, sticking her head into the cage, closing her eyes and drawing a deep breath as she feels the change coming. Suddenly Oz switches to the dominant role, as he did the first time he had sex with Willow, but this time it's an animal dominance. He grabs Veruca's hair, pulls her into the cage, and kisses her hard. In a sign of her submission to Oz, Veruca pulls the cage door closed. Veruca and Oz kiss as they fall to the floor. Their human hands come up, palm to palm. The hands become werewolf hands, then clasp as the scene fades to black. American network television would permit no stronger statement of the principle that human sex is always also animal sex.

Willow arrives the next morning to find the two lovers naked on the floor of the cage. She is naturally shocked, particularly since Oz had assured her the previous day that everything was fine between them: Oz gaslighted her. Veruca confronts Willow later that day, near sunset. When Oz intervenes, Veruca offers to submit to him again. "Come stop me. I like it rough, remember?" As the two werewolves start to transform, Veruca insists on their animality. "You're an animal. Animals kill." At long last, Oz accepts his animal nature. "You're right. We kill." A vicious animal fight follows, and Oz tears Veruca's throat out. The episode concludes with Oz's departure from Sunnydale. As he prepares to leave, Oz admits that "Veruca was right about something. The wolf is inside me all the time. And I don't know where that line is any more." In fact, Oz has never known where the line between human and nonhuman animal should be drawn. He shares this uncertainty with Western metaphysics.

Oz's final appearance on the *Buffy* television show is in "New Moon Rising" (4.19), written (like most werewolf episodes) by Marti Noxon. By now, Tara and Willow are on the verge of beginning a sexual relationship that neither of them has explicitly acknowledged yet. This episode simultaneously marks the formal end of Willow's relationship with Oz and the formal beginning of her relationship with Tara. The juxtaposition of Willow/Oz with Willow/Tara retroactively queers the former, confirming an association between animal sexuality and queer sexuality that the show has been making since Xander confronted Larry in the locker room.

When Oz unexpectedly returns, a conversation between Buffy and Riley emphasizes the ethical validity of Willow's former relationship with Oz.

Riley is incredulous when he learns Oz's true nature. "Oz ... is a werewolf. And Willow was *dating* him?" He didn't think Willow was that kind of girl. "What kind of girl?" Buffy demands. "Into dangerous guys," Riley replies. "Oz is not dangerous," Buffy insists. "Something happened to him that wasn't his fault. God, I never knew you were such a bigot." Buffy rarely uses such strong language; the fact that she does so now indicates that she is committed to defending Oz's personhood. "Woah! Hey! How'd we get to bigot?" Riley protests. The answer is that Riley has made a simplistic equation between nonhumans and monsters, and such cold equations violate the ethics of the Buffyverse. Riley finds it "a little weird to date someone who tries to eat you once a month." But of course, *Buffy*'s moral universe is big enough to include such a sexuality. Before and after Riley, Buffy dated vampires who desired to drink her, and occasionally did so. "Yeah, well, love isn't logical, Riley," Buffy concludes.

Buffy and Willow discuss the complexities of Willow's past (and possible future) relationship with Oz. This conversation gives Willow the opportunity to come out to Buffy as a lesbian. Willow chooses her words carefully, sighs, looks at Buffy, and says "it's complicated ... because of Tara." Buffy is the very apotheosis of heteronormativity. "You mean Tara has a crush on Oz?" Finally, comprehension dawns. Willow asks if Buffy's freaked. Buffy says "no," meaning "yes," and then makes a conscious effort not to be.

Once again, Oz's wolf senses reveal that Willow has been with someone else. He confronts Tara. "You smell like her. She's all over you. Do you know that?" Suddenly, Oz reverts to the "teen wolf" stereotype: he is every inch the jealous, sexually aggressive, "animalistic" young man. He grabs Tara's wrist. "Are you two involved?" When Tara tries to leave, he stops her, shaking her forcefully. On the verge of assaulting her, Oz begins to change into his wolf form: his jealous rage is part of his animal self, which now comes to the surface. As human Oz disappears, he warns Tara to run, which she does.

Werewolf Oz is captured by the Initiative, which allows the show to advance a dramatic animal rights argument. Initiative scientists conduct medical experiments on Oz. They refuse to stop, even when he reverts to human form. Riley serves as the unlikely voice of animal liberation: "OK, that's enough. Come on, the guy's a student. I know him." But the scientists have classified Oz as a nonhuman animal; they feel entitled to experiment on him even when he's in human form. Defying orders, Riley tries to break Oz out of the Initiative. Riley's mutiny has been a long time coming, but what finally pushes him over the edge is the unethical experiments that the Initiative conducts on Oz. The audience is likely to sympathize with Riley's rebellion against the villainous Initiative; viewers who apply Riley's moral epiphany to real-world ethical debates may conclude that it is unacceptable to torture animals in the name of science.

Four. "Majestic Creature of Legend"

The animal rights politics of *Buffy*'s fourth season are radical enough to be called anarchistic, and the Initiative's commanding officer names them as such. Colonel Macnamara denounces the animal-friendly Scoobies as "anarchists" who are "too backwards for the real world." Any philosophy that recognizes the close affinity between humans and nonhuman animals must seem backwards to the military/scientific complex that Macnamara represents. As Riley and Oz escape from the Initiative with the Scoobies, Macnamara says "You're a dead man, Finn." Riley responds by explicitly embracing the animal rights agenda that Oz has inspired the Scoobies to adopt. "No, sir. I'm an anarchist." Riley's anarchist mutiny enables him to provide a particularly strong statement of *Buffy*'s general ethical thesis. "I was in a totally black and white space," he tells Buffy. "People versus monsters. And it ain't like that."

Riley then connects his ethical breakthrough to the Buffyverse's system of sexual ethics: "Especially when it comes to love." Riley now understands that it is no crime for humans to pursue sexual relationships with nonhumans, as Willow has done with Oz. At the end of "New Moon Rising," Oz leaves Sunnydale again, this time for good. He tells Willow that the one thing that brings out the wolf in him is her. He calls this ironic, but in fact their relationship has always depended upon Willow's connection to Oz's animal aspect. Willow is now free to render her relationship with Tara explicit, which she does immediately after Oz's departure. When Tara tells Willow that she has to be with the person she loves, Willow replies simply, "I am."

Willow doesn't see Oz again until season eight's "Retreat," a five-part comic book story written by Jane Espenson and drawn by Georges Jeanty. Hunted by season eight "Big Bad" Twilight and his allies, the Slayers seek refuge at Oz's new home in Tibet. Here they meet Oz's wife Bayarmaa ("Bay") (8.27). The Scoobies exhibit Western culture's ancient fear that human/animal sex will produce monstrous offspring. When Oz mentions that he and Bay have a baby, everyone looks at a nearby puppy. Oz reassures them. "Yeah. No. See. That's the dog." Oz and Bay explain that Oz has learned to manage his lycanthropy not by trying to tame the wolf, but rather by letting the wolf flow through him without resistance. Oz insists that his spiritual practice works and defends it by contrasting it with something much darker. He tells of an English werewolf called Monroe, a lupine supremacist who "heads a group that thinks like…" Willow finishes for him: "Like Veruca." Oz agrees. "Yeah. They think the wolf is the best part of us." By contrasting Veruca's radical lupine ideology with Oz's spiritual philosophy, Espenson makes the ethical distinctions between the two clear. Veruca pursued the supremacy of the wolf at the expense of the human. Oz, on the other hand, pursues a hybridity which recognizes as legitimate the claims of both wolf and human. Oz works towards the day when wolf and human might live together peacefully. In Tibet, he has made a microcosm of the world he wants to build. He has achieved this through his sexual relationship with Bay, who is herself a werewolf. Their spiritual practice allows the two of them to live together in human form, without losing the wolf aspect that is a fundamental part of their being.

Oz insists that Willow can have what he has. "I'm normal. I'm human. I have a family. And you can too." He's holding the baby through this whole conversation. "It's not true," Willow protests. Oz mistakenly assumes that Willow views her lesbianism as a barrier to having children. "You can adopt, use a donor—," he advises. But what stands in Willow's way is not her queer sexuality, but rather her witchcraft and the responsibility that it brings. "I can't have a baby! Not with what I am! Not with what I have to do." When Willow tries to leave, Oz offers to let her watch the baby. This expression of trust brings tears to her eyes. She takes the baby and visits Buffy. "Buffy, we might have lives," she exults. "For a long time now I've thought I was … I guess a force. Not a person? No life, no babies. But now…" Willow has been greatly troubled by her own partly inhuman nature. But Oz's baby proves that she could be both human and inhuman, without contradiction or conflict.

This is how the story of Willow and Oz ends: with a powerful endorsement of hybridity. Willow and Oz teach us that there is no meaningful distinction between nature and culture, between human and animal. They teach us that humans, animals, and hybrids of both can find joy in one another's arms or paws. They teach us that desire may well flow across the species barrier. And they warn us that to deny such desire categorically is to promote a dangerously restrictive concept of Eros.

"Ridden Hard and Put Away Wet": Dawn and Xander's Inhuman/Human Sexuality

Dawn has always been inhuman. She didn't even exist for *Buffy*'s first four seasons. In season five, a group of monks cast a powerful magic spell to transform a valuable "key" of mystic energy into human form. In order to motivate Buffy to protect the key, the monks used a kind of magical retroactive continuity to turn the key into Buffy's little sister, Dawn Summers. When Buffy confronts one of the monks and demands to know what Dawn is, the dying man assures her that Dawn is "human … now human" ("No Place Like Home" 5.5). But this answer doesn't sit well with Buffy. Despite the feelings that Buffy and her friends have for Dawn, they know that she isn't human and never was. Dawn retains the outward physical form of a teenaged girl who grows into an ordinary young woman, but she never overcomes her mystical origins.

This turns out not to be a problem for Dawn's most important sexual partner, Xander Harris. Xander has a long history of seeking sexual relations with inhumans and superhumans, including a substitute teacher who is actually a giant praying mantis ("Teacher's Pet" 1.4), and a resurrected Incan girl who mummifies men ("Inca Mummy Girl" 2.4). Xander makes one attempt to develop a sexual relationship with a fully human woman, Cordelia (Charisma Carpenter). She dumps him six episodes after they first kiss. In season three, Xander loses his virginity to Faith, whose superhuman Slayer powers derive from demonic energy. Xander's most serious pre–Dawn sexual relationship is with Anya. Anya spent hundreds of years as a vengeance demon; when she begins her sexual relationship with Xander, she is still "newly human and strangely literal" ("Into the Woods" 5.10), and perhaps not entirely human. After Xander and Anya break up, he goes on an ill-fated date with a demon woman who tries to use him as a blood sacrifice to open the Seal of Danthazar ("First Date" 7.14). "It can't just keep happening that demon women find me attractive," he complains. "There's gotta be a reason." By now, Xander is able to marvel at the consistently demonic nature of his partners, though he would still rather blame them than admit the nature of his own desire. As Renee St. Louis argues, Xander rarely takes responsibility for his own sexuality.

Enter Dawn. Xander first begins to take a sexual interest in Dawn in season seven. Dawn thinks that she has been identified as a potential Slayer, and she is acutely disappointed to learn that she is merely ordinary ("Potential" 7.12). In a scene characterized by powerful emotional candor, Xander assures her that she is far from ordinary. Xander presents himself as a human surrounded by superhumans: "A witch. A demon. Hell, I could fit Oz in my shaving kit, but come a full moon, he had a wolfy mojo not to be messed with. Powerful. All of them. And I'm the guy who fixes the windows." Interestingly, Xander is jealous of Oz's animal power here. Compared to Oz, Xander feels like nothing more than a mundane carpenter. Yet Xander's very ordinariness is what lets him recognize that Dawn is exceptional. "I see more than anybody realizes because nobody's watching me. I saw you last night. I see you working here today. You're not special. You're extraordinary." He kisses Dawn on the forehead. While this is a chaste, big brotherly kiss, it also speaks of other possibilities, and foreshadows their future sexual relationship. This is the moment when Xander's feelings for Dawn begin to change from fraternal to sexual. As Dawn grows into a strong, independent, not quite human woman, Xander finds it possible to think of her as a potential romantic and sexual partner.

The Dawn/Xander relationship finally blossoms in the season eight comic books. Throughout season eight, Dawn goes through a series of physical transformations, becoming less human with each one. Xander finds each of Dawn's inhuman forms more attractive than the last. His feelings for her grow as she moves further away from a human "norm" which seems increasingly arbitrary. Dawn begins season eight as a giant, apparently because she had sex with a Thricewise. Georges Jeanty's page layout and panel composition effectively emphasize the sexual nature of Dawn's predicament (Vaughan and Jeanty, "No Future for You" 8.7). On a two-panel page, the first panel is a medium-shot of the Slayers' castle headquarters. Though Dawn isn't shown, she has a word balloon: "This is about sex, isn't it?" The next panel occupies most of the page; this panel focuses on giant Dawn, while Willow, who is about the size of Dawn's hand, floats to the side to provide scale.

Xander is clearly attracted to giant Dawn. Here he experiences the fetishistic desire known as macrophilia. Xander keeps Dawn company while she bathes in a pond (Whedon and Jeanty, "Long Way Home" 8.2). Xander very carefully does not look at Dawn's giant naked body, but a close-up on his face suggests that he wants to. Xander tries to cheer Dawn up by having the wiccan squad super-size her wardrobe (Whedon and Richards, "Anywhere but Here" 8.10). Xander falls into a pile of Dawn's giant undergarments. Action lines around Xander's shocked face show his anxiety, as does his verbal response: "Lord of *Hosts*, I'm in the *frilllly!!!*" From what we know of Xander's history, this kind of anxiety is almost surely a sign of sexual attraction: after desiring the demonic for the last seven years, Xander is understandably afraid of his desire for giant Dawn.

In Joss Whedon's "Time of Your Life" (Whedon and Moline 8.16), Dawn transforms from a giant into a centaur. Centaur-Dawn is the most animal of Dawn's inhuman forms. It is also the most thoroughly eroticized. Dawn first appears as a centaur in a full-page panel by Karl Moline. Topless, her arms crossed over her breasts, she gazes down at the reader to deliver her snarky one-word speech balloon: "Neigh." As Dawn becomes animal, her body is increasingly sexualized, and Xander's desire becomes more explicit. When Dawn complains that her "ass is huge," Xander replies incredulously "Are you kidding? Dawn..." Xander finishes his sentence over a tight reaction shot on Dawn's astonished face: "you really don't know how awesome you look?" The next panel frames Xander's earnest face as he makes his pitch. "You're a frikkin' centaur! Majestic creature of legend! I'm actually jealous." But in fact, he's not jealous so much as he is attracted to Dawn's hybrid horse/human form, and Dawn reciprocates his desire.

Their increasingly obvious mutual attraction generates plenty of Whedonesque sexual awkwardness. Looking away from Xander, Dawn tells him that to escape from attacking demons "you're gonna have to..." and then softly, in small print, "...ride me..." (8.17). Here Dawn invokes the eroticism of the horse/rider relationship. Since Xander will be riding her horse half, Dawn is implicitly authorizing any zoophilic desire that he may feel towards her. This leaves Xander predictably flustered, and Dawn doesn't know how to alleviate his anxiety. They spend a panel quite inarticulate. Xander says, "what?" and Dawn offers only punctuation: "—." The next panel reveals Xander's terror at

Four. "Majestic Creature of Legend" 129

Dawn the centaurette, a powerful female horse/human hybrid with strong sexual agency. Art by Jo Chen. *Buffy the Vampire Slayer* season eight (2008). Dark Horse Comics/Twentieth Century–Fox Film Corporation.

his desire for Dawn's half-horse body. His face shows a panicked expression. "Ah! Ride you! *Aagh!*" Xander looks even more horrified as he actually rides Dawn. To do so, he must come into intimate physical contact with the half of Dawn's body that is pure nonhuman animal. Although he clearly wants to do so, he is also scared of the zoophilic desire that he's experiencing. By now this desire is so powerful that Xander is even starting to read the human parts of Dawn in animal terms. "*You're pulling my hair!*" Dawn complains. "*I'm holding your mane!*" Xander replies. Although centaur-Dawn's hair doesn't differ noticeably from humanoid Dawn's hair, Xander feels like he's holding horsehair. Dawn tries to assert her humanity. "*My mane is my hair!*" she insists. The hallmark of hybrid creatures like centaurs is their ability to blur boundaries. Xander is interacting with Dawn's horse-half, to the dismay of her human half. Neither of them knows where to draw the line between the two, or indeed if any line should be drawn.

They do know, however, that it's getting harder to ignore the sexual nature of Dawn's half-horse, half-human body. After their high-speed escape, Dawn feels like she "was ridden hard and put away wet" (8.18). This is a common saying from horse husbandry (and the word "husbandry" is a decent descriptor of Dawn and Xander's future domestic partnership). The phrase that Dawn uses has always implied sexual intercourse ("ridden hard") and female sexual arousal ("put away wet"). The context makes the sexual nature of this phrase explicit. Dawn's becoming-animal has sexualized her in a powerful way. Jo Chen's stunningly erotic cover painting for this issue (8.18) shows Dawn naked again, breasts covered but not concealed by her hair. Dawn stretches her arms, arching her human back as she lifts her right front hoof. She smiles seductively. This is the first time that Dawn has been portrayed as an active sexual agent. To gain this sexual agency, she had to become animal. The figure of the centaur hasn't been this thoroughly eroticized since John Varley's *Titan* novels (1979–1984). By eroticizing centaur-Dawn, *Buffy* comics authorize Xander's zoophilic desire for her.

Significantly, the first explicitly sexual interaction between Dawn and Xander occurs in Jane Espenson's "Retreat," a story that is largely concerned with Oz's animal sexuality. Part three of "Retreat" is a reprise of the classic Espensode "Storyteller" (7.16). Once again, Andrew takes on his "Masterpiece Theater" persona in order to lay a queer narrative over the action (Espenson and Jeanty 8.28). Readers see the formal beginning of Dawn and Xander's sexual relationship through the queer lens of Andrew's video camera. Dawn has resumed her human form. She takes the initiative, telling Xander there's "a chance. To have a life. For you to go for what you want, Xander." As usual, Andrew doesn't recognize the signifiers of straight desire: "Hmm. A cryptic reference. What does Xander want?" Buffy stumbles upon Dawn and Xander. "What is she looking at?" Andrew wonders. A gay man watches a queer straight woman watching her inhuman sister, and at last the suspense resolves. Dawn and Xander's budding sexual relationship is literally framed as queer: Georges Jeanty draws a half-page panel of Andrew's video frame, which shows Dawn and Xander kissing passionately. Andrew's narrative voice-over deploys the catchphrase of gay icon George Takei: "Oh my."

Buffy emphasizes the non-normative nature of the Dawn/Xander relationship by reading it as intergenerational. When she finally has a chance to talk to Xander about the kiss she saw, she says, "it's fine. Dawn's a grown woman, and you're a disgusting paedophile" (Whedon and Jeanty, "Turbulence" 8.31). Jeanty gives Buffy a big smile, so Xander and readers know she's joking. When Xander protests "paedophile," she tries "cradle robber?" And Xander admits that loving Dawn makes him feel "a tad bit Humbert Humbert." It's unlikely that Xander is more than seven years older than Dawn: he graduated high school at the end of season three, and she was a high school freshman in season seven. But Dawn looks young, and as Xander notes, he has known her since she was little (at least within the memories that the monks created when they made the key into Dawn). So Buffy can locate their sexual relationship in one of the most marginalized zones of Gayle Rubin's outer limits: the intergenerational. Xander observes that Dawn has loved him her whole life. Since the love she has felt for him up until now has been essentially sisterly, their sexual relationship signifies slightly as sibling incest. But since they are not actually siblings, the comics can sanction their sexuality, whereas any desire that Simon Tam might feel for his sister River could never be fulfilled (see Chapter Two). Xander justifies his feelings for Dawn by invoking her inhumanity: "She's grown. And shrunk. She's not the same." Becoming-giant and becoming-small have changed Dawn (as has becoming-centaur). She is clearly Other than human, and it is precisely her Otherness that has sparked Xander's desire. "I'm kind of in love with her," he tells Buffy.

Once she's with Xander, Dawn looks back on her inhuman forms, and what she remembers most is the power that her inhumanity gave her. "Remember when I got powers?" she asks Willow (Melzer and Jeanty 8.32). Willow tries to deny Dawn's animal strength: "You didn't get powers. You became a giant. Then a horse—." "A centaurette," Dawn interrupts. "Girl centaur. There's a difference." Dawn correctly emphasizes that she was a horse/human hybrid rather than a horse, and she notes that she retained her female gender when she changed species. Since the sexually assertive centaur is generally coded male, an eroticized female centaur with strong sexual agency is a subversively feminist figure. Human Dawn recognizes the power of the equine femininity that she enjoyed as a centaurette. "Dawnie, maybe you just miss your own powers," Willow suggests. But Willow's position is inconsistent. Still reeling from her encounter with Oz, Bay, and their baby, Willow tries to affirm the power of animality even as she denies it. Dawn sees the contradiction. "You just said—I didn't *have* powers! Xander doesn't *have* powers." It is Xander who puts it all together, listing Willow, Oz, and Dawn among the Scooby Gang's most powerful inhuman members: "We've got witches, werewolves and centaurs—" (8.34). Again, Dawn interrupts to correct a recurrent misgendering of her equine form: "Centaurettes!" Of all the inhuman forms that she has taken, the one that gave her the greatest sexual power, especially with respect to Xander, was that of the female horse/human hybrid. By becoming a centaurette, she also became a Whedomme.

Events that occur towards the end of season ten emphasize Dawn's inhuman nature and confirm that her relationship with Xander is predicated on her inhumanity. The creation of a new magic seed at the end of season nine erased the sexual feelings that Dawn once had for Xander. As always, Dawn's sexuality is determined by her magical nature here. Late in season ten, Dawn must use her "key" powers to close a mystic portal which threatens to destroy Earth (Gage, Isaacs, and Levens 10.24). But she can only do so from the other side of the portal, which would leave her trapped in a hell dimension. Giles provides a literal *deus ex machina*: "I'm quite confident that, in an entirely magic-based reality, Dawn would have access to her full power. She'd be virtually *godlike*." When the Scoobies enter the hell dimension, Dawn promptly slays the local demon God-king. Xander's one eye gazes adoringly at Dawn as she admits that she "might be feeling a *tad* godlike." If Xander was seduced by Dawn's centaur power, he is absolutely mesmerized by her Goddess power. In fact, he is so smitten with Goddess Dawn that he volunteers to stay with her in the hell dimension when the rest of the Scoobies return home. Dawn tries to refuse; since she can't currently reciprocate Xander's feelings, the power dynamic between them is too imbalanced, and Xander's ability to consent is suspect. But Xander insists. "Friends don't let friends stay in hell alone." He takes her hand as he says this, his gesture undermining the point he's trying to make. Xander's claim of friendship is dubious; he clearly wants them to be lovers again and believes that they will be. Dawn shrugs. "It's dangerous here." Xander's response is persuasive: "Lucky I have a god to protect me." The object of his desire has the power to keep him safe. Finally, Dawn relents. "Thank you for staying with me." She holds his hands as she says this, giving Xander every reason to hope that their romantic and sexual relationship may be rekindled.

As Dawn and Xander traverse the dimensions on their way home, Dawn continues to explore her Goddesslike power, and Xander's submissive love for that power grows. There is a common trope in the masculine fantasy art of artists like Boris Vallejo and Frank Frazetta: the "Conan Pose," which features a helpless, unarmed woman clinging to the leg of the armed, muscular male warrior who towers above her. *Buffy* artist Rebekah Isaacs provides a devastating parody of this pose, by switching the gender configuration that normally obtains in such images (Gage and Isaacs, "Taking Ownership" 10.28). Dawn, armed with a crossbow and her magic powers, stands confidently atop a pile of demon bodies. Xander clings helplessly to her leg, his clothes in tatters, and asks his Goddess to spirit them away. The two are exhausted as they approach the final portal. "Lean on me," says Xander. "And I'll lean on you." This is how they return to Earth: interdependent, arms wrapped around one another. Their sexual relationship is reborn in the crucible of the hell dimensions, their DS dynamic restored by Dawn's acceptance of her Goddess powers and Xander's Goddess worship.

As season twelve opens, readers learn that Dawn and Xander have done the most animal thing they could do: they've had a baby. Dawn may be the Key, but she is also a flesh and blood animal, specifically a mammal. Dawn is comfortable with her mammalian nature, and with Xander's attraction to that nature. Smiling, Dawn nurses baby Joyce without a nursing blanket, while playfully chiding Xander for taking such an interest in the process: "Please stop ogling my boobs while I nurse our baby" (Gage, Whedon, and Jeanty 12.1). Here Xander exhibits a typical straight male breast fetish. On a deeper level, however, he's attracted to Dawn because she gives him access to a purely animal world that would otherwise be closed to him: "They got *so much bigger*! I'm just in awe of the wonders of nature!" Much like Oz and Bay, the Buffyverse's other human/animal parents, Dawn is undeniably part of nature. Dawn's lactation is presented as a power. Xander asks her to stay with Joyce while he goes on a mission. Dawn protests. "Me? Why don't *you* stay with her? If this is some sexist—." But Xander is sidelining her for her strength, not for any perceived weakness. "It's not," he assures her. "I can't feed her, can I?" Dawn has gained her mammalian powers while retaining her Key powers, which are, if anything, stronger than ever now. When the mission goes awry, Xander texts Dawn, who saves the day by opening a portal to bring the Scoobies safely home. Opening portals has become routine for her. It's just something that she does in between feedings. When it's time for the next mission, she makes Xander stay with the baby: "I pumped, there's milk in the fridge." Dawn is in charge, and she can be everything she wants to be: mother, sister, partner, animal, key.

These are the ethical messages that *Buffy* puts forward throughout its twelve seasons. Humans are animals. There is no meaningful distinction between *homo sapiens* and the rest of the animal kingdom, though humans often pretend that there is, for a variety of self-interested reasons. Because humans are not radically distinct from other animals, we have the responsibility to pursue ethical relationships with our non-sapient cousins. This includes rethinking meat eating, as Buffy does in "Doublemeat Palace" (6.12). It includes questioning the ethics of animal experimentation, as Riley does in "New Moon Rising." And it includes recognizing zoophilia as a legitimate form of desire. This is particularly important with respect to those companion animals who already live among us. The fact that our culture celebrates every conceivable intimacy between humans and their companion species *except* sexual intimacy, and roundly condemns that, is a telling inconsistency. It begins to seem as if the prohibition against zoophilia is based on an aesthetic revulsion alone. The Buffyverse's human/animal hybrids show us a better way. Humanoid animals like Oz and Dawn give us a glimpse of an ethical world in which relations between humans and other animals are governed by an ethic of care informed by the triple principle of consent, desire, and trust. In this way, as in so many others, the Buffyverse looks like a utopia when contrasted with our quotidian world.

Five

"The Hammer Is My Penis"

Queer and Heteronormative Sexualities in Dr. Horrible's Sing-Along Blog

Dr. Horrible's Sing-Along Blog is a study in the power of contradiction. It was a web musical that was never broadcast on television, yet it won television's highest honor, a 2009 Emmy award (Joss Whedon's first) for Outstanding Special Class—Short-Format Live-Action Entertainment Program (Pascale 309). The genre-bending supervillain musical *Dr. Horrible* defined the "special class" of which it was taken to be the paramount example. Powerful contradictions drive the show's narrative. The plot seems to be structured around a standard heteronormative love triangle involving the three main characters: aspiring supervillain Dr. Horrible, his nemesis the superhero Captain Hammer, and the object of their mutual desire, an unremarkable young woman named Penny. Yet everything about this notionally straight narrative turns out to be resolutely queer. In ways both subtle and overt, Dr. Horrible and Captain Hammer signify gay masculinity, as does Horrible's sidekick Moist (Simon Helberg). Homosocial and homoerotic relationships between these men are far more important, structurally and psychologically, than their Real or Imaginary sexual relationships with Penny. Strangely for a Whedonverse, the world of *Dr. Horrible* lacks a strong woman character, yet the musical uses this very lack to deliver a powerful feminist message. It does so by showing the violent consequences of the toxic sexualities that early twenty-first-century American masculinities enable.

Dr. Horrible's contradictions arose from the unique circumstances of its creation. In 2007, the Writers Guild of America (WGA) struck the television networks and studios over the residuals that screenwriters were paid (or often not paid) when viewers used then-new digital technology to download or stream TV episodes online (Pascale 290). Joss Whedon and his family participated enthusiastically in the strike (Pascale 293–294). *Dr. Horrible* was born on the picket line. To help him write and produce the show, Joss Whedon enlisted Jed and Zack Whedon, his brothers in both the familial and trade unionist senses of the word, plus Jed's then-fiancée (now wife) Maurissa Tancharoen. To play the part of Penny, Joss Whedon tapped Felicia Day, who had played Potential Slayer Vi in *Buffy* season seven. The role of Captain Hammer went to *Firefly*'s Nathan Fillion. For the title role, Whedon cast Tony-winning actor/singer Neil Patrick Harris, who had performed in a number of Broadway musicals, including queer shows such as *Cabaret*, *Rent*, and *Hedwig and the Angry Inch*. Working outside the studio system gave Whedon total creative freedom.[1] Freed from Hollywood control, *Dr. Horrible* could playfully subvert the tropes of sexual identity and behavior that had dominated American film and television throughout the twentieth century. The show could, and did, deploy a biting critique of contemporary American heterosexuality, while offering a queer aesthetic, queer relationships, and queer sexual practices as alternatives.

Dr. Horrible's queer representations of sexuality are made possible by the show's most radical attribute: its relentless genre hybridity. The musical genre's unions with science fiction have typically produced very queer offspring, such as *The Rocky Horror Picture Show* (Jim Sharman 1975). But *Dr. Horrible* is the product of an even stranger union, between the musical and that peculiar subgenre of science fiction, the superhero story.[2] Joss Whedon emphasized *Dr. Horrible*'s genre hybridity in a letter to his fans that he posted to promote the show, calling it a "unique little epic. A supervillain musical, of which, as we all know, there are far too few" ("Letter from Joss Whedon"). Indeed, there are hardly any, although as David Lavery notes, *Dr. Horrible* is "clearly indebted to Sondheim's *Sweeney Todd* (1979)" (164). *Dr. Horrible*'s genre hybridity reveals strange affinities between the musical and superhero/villain genres. On the surface, both genres are strongly heteronormative. Almost all of their major characters are nominally straight, and the romantic plots of both genres inevitably concern the quest for heterosexual happiness. The action of a musical is driven by the question of *how* Fred and Ginger will get together; the unquestioned assumption that they will do so constitutes the very essence of heteronormativity. Clark Kent's seventy-five-year romance with Lois Lane leads slowly but inexorably to marriage (1996) and reprosexuality, with the birth of their son Jonathan Samuel Kent (2015). Yet the basic formal elements of both genres are recognizably queer. There is something queer about bursting into song at moments of emotional intensity. And there is something equally (though differently) queer about prowling the urban nightscape in fetishistic costumes of leather and latex. Combining the musical and superhero genres produces queerness squared, for this combination permits the creation of characters who don fetish gear to commit or combat crimes *and sing about it*.

The hybrid generic elements of *Dr. Horrible* allow this supervillain musical to develop a queer, anti-homophobic, feminist representational project.

This is particularly evident in the portrayal of Captain Hammer's sexuality. I read Hammer's heteronormative behavior as a manifestation of what the sociologist R.W. Connell calls hegemonic masculinity. This form of masculinity is based upon the dominance of men over women, but also on the subordination of non-normative masculinities to the hegemonic (Connell, *Gender and Power* 183). Dr. Horrible and his secret identity Billy represent masculine identities that are sometimes complicit with Hammer's hegemonic masculinity and sometimes subordinate to it. This complicit/subordinate masculinity shapes Horrible/Billy's ambiguous commitment to heterosexuality. The physically repulsive Moist embodies a failed heterosexual masculinity that can only ever be subordinate to the hegemonic. And the violent interspecies sexuality of the supervillain Bad Horse (Dobber) derives from a masculinity that it is marginalized by his status as a nonhuman animal.

All of these masculine sexualities are haunted by the specter of a queer masculinity which constantly threatens to undermine the feeble foundations of the compulsory heterosexuality upon which they are built. *Dr. Horrible* features intense homosocial and homoerotic relations between men. These male-male relationships perpetually threaten to slide from the homosocial to the homoerotic to, finally, the homosexual. Relations between men in *Dr. Horrible* are not only more satisfying and more meaningful than relations between men and Penny, who lists among her many misfortunes the burden of being the sole representative of her gender in this Bechdel-noncompliant musical. Ultimately, *Dr. Horrible* wonders if heterosexual relationships are even possible in a world ruled by hegemonic masculinity. The failure of Dr. Horrible's Imaginary relationship with Penny and the emptiness of Captain Hammer's Real one point to a crisis of heteronormativity. That crisis bears the promise of a better, queerer world, a world where toxic masculinity has lost its hegemonic status. In this world, men would not be afraid to love men, nor would they be afraid to love the women whom they would finally have learned to regard as people.

"Just Because You Want Her": The Homoerotics of Heterosexual Rivalry in the American Film Musical

Dr. Horrible features all of the major formal elements of the Hollywood film musical. It corresponds precisely to the influential formal model that Rick Altman introduced in *The American Film Musical*. *Dr. Horrible* has a narrative format, the narrative interacts with the musical numbers via various dissolves, and the numbers reverse the traditional hierarchy of image and sound, privileging sound at key climactic moments (Altman, *Film Musical*

102, 109). I would add that the tactical privileging of sound allows *Dr. Horrible* to stage effective encounters with the Lacanian Real. *Dr. Horrible* is shorter than the feature length that Altman takes to be characteristic of the film musical, but Altman finds it "perfectly conceivable" that a musical could miniaturize its segments (*Film Musical* 103), as *Dr. Horrible* does. The characters in a film musical are inevitably a heterosexual romantic couple (Altman, *Film Musical* 103), and here is where *Dr. Horrible* begins to subvert its form. Billy and Penny, its male and female principals, are only ever a potential couple. *Dr. Horrible*'s dual focus narrative features parallelism between the male and female leads (Altman, *Film Musical* 107), particularly when Penny and Billy sing "My Eyes" as a split-screen duet. As in any musical film, the formation of the romantic couple is linked via parallelism to the success of the plot ventures (Altman, *Film Musical* 108). Thus Billy's alter ego Dr. Horrible hopes to use his freeze ray to impress Penny *and* rule the world. But here *Dr. Horrible* reverses a major trope of the musical film (Altman, *Film Musical* 109), for the *failure* of the potential Billy/Penny relationship signals the *success* of the criminal enterprises carried out by Dr. Horrible.

Stacy Wolf argues persuasively that "the ideological project of musical theatre in the mid-twentieth-century United States was to use the heterosexual couple's journey from enemies to lovers to stand in for the unification of problematic differences in American culture" (*Changed* 203). Billy and Penny's incomplete heterosexual journey stands in for the failure of cultural unification (say, between the WGA and the studios). Penny's compassionate quest for social justice proves to be incompatible with Horrible's supervillainy. This aligns *Dr. Horrible* with the "concept musicals" of the 1970s, including queer films like *A Chorus Line* and the early works of Whedon's beloved Sondheim (Griffin 264–265). While the songs of a musical film usually signify the joy and triumph of the couple as they move through courtship (Altman, *Film Musical* 109), *Dr. Horrible*'s songs signify the despair of the failed couple, particularly in "Everything You Ever," the haunting final number that follows Penny's death.

While the surface narrative of *Dr. Horrible* embodies the heterosexual courtship plot that is characteristic of the film musical, beneath the surface *Dr. Horrible* is actually a very queer musical. By casting well-known gay actor Neil Patrick Harris as the male lead, the creators of *Dr. Horrible* sent a strong extra-diegetic signal of the show's queerness. The most important signifier of *Dr. Horrible*'s queerness is the powerful homosocial rivalry between Horrible and Hammer.[3] Altman's more recent work acknowledges that "in addition to the musical's primary *heterosexual* project," the genre features a "carefully targeted *homosocial* project" ("From Homosocial" 25). In a typical musical, at least one member of the straight romantic couple is shown in the company of same-sex friends or military comrades (Altman, "From Homosocial" 25). Dr.

Five. "The Hammer Is My Penis"

Captain Hammer and Doctor Horrible: homosocial, homoerotic BFFs. Hammer gasps with delight as Horrible brandishes tickets to the Broadway musical *Dear Evan Hansen*. Script by Joss Whedon. Art by José Maria Beroy. *Dr. Horrible: Best Friends Forever* (2018). Dark Horse Comics/Timescience Bloodclub.

Horrible spends a great deal of time with his male sidekick (Moist) and his male nemesis (Hammer). The musical film "labours to eradicate homosocial bonds—or at least to keep them from turning into homosexual ties—just as hard as it works to establish durable heterosexual relationships" (Altman, "From Homosocial" 28). Altman argues that this policing of sexuality is, in a sense, "what the musical is all about" (Altman, "From Homosocial" 28). *Dr. Horrible*'s primary heterosexual project fails with Penny's death, yet the homosocial bonds between Horrible and Hammer are by no means eliminated. If anything, these bonds are stronger than ever at the end of the musical. Dr. Horrible's surprise victory sends Captain Hammer to the psychoanalyst, but that only shows how vitally important his homosocial relationship with Horrible is to him. Meanwhile, Horrible's victory in his homosocial competition with Hammer permits his entry into the Evil League of Evil. Penny's death renders this a Pyrrhic victory, but as the groupies sing to Dr. Horrible in the musical's final number, this is everything he always wanted. Joss Whedon's 2018 "Best Friends Forever" comic, which takes place after the musical, depicts Dr. Horrible and Captain Hammer in a very homoerotic friendship. José Maria Beroy's splash page shows Hammer gasping in delight as Horrible brandishes two ill-gotten tickets to the Broadway musical *Dear Evan Hansen*, as if Whedon had tried to devise the gayest possible image for Beroy to draw.

Horrible, Hammer, and Penny offer a particularly strong example of the homoerotic triangulation that Eve Kosofsky Sedgwick describes in *Between Men*. Building on the work of René Girard, Sedgwick argues that "the bond between rivals in an erotic triangle" may be "even stronger ... than anything in the bond between either of the lovers and the beloved" (*Between Men* 21). Alyson Buckman has effectively applied Sedgwick's theory to the Whedonverses' homoerotic triangles, including Angel/Buffy/Spike and others that appear on *Buffy* and *Angel* ("Triangulated Desire"). With respect to *Dr. Horrible*, Buckman argues that Penny functions as "a heterosexual object for the exchange of desire" between Hammer and Horrible ("Say It Was Horrible" ¶ 19). Billy struggles to speak to Penny; even the most basic "audible connection" eludes him. Hammer never sees Penny as anything more than a casual sex partner. Yet the two men's rivalry over Penny is only the latest chapter in a longstanding homosocial competition, documented in the home movie sequence in "Brand New Day." Sedgwick notes that in a rivalry of this kind, "the choice of the beloved is determined in the first place, not by the qualities of the beloved, but by the beloved's already being the choice of the person who has been chosen as a rival" (*Between Men* 21). Hammer has no intrinsic interest in Penny. In fact, his primary reason for having sex with her is to deny Horrible sexual access to her. Hammer makes his motivations painfully explicit when he tells Billy that he's going to give Penny the night of her life "just because you want her. And I get ... what you want."

As Stacy Wolf argues, Sedgwick's theory of erotic triangulation is particularly applicable to musicals, in which the "presumably heterosexual" narrative "places two men in competition for a single woman, and this creates a homoerotic moment, either for the two male characters or for the audience" (*Problem* 152). Expanding on Wolf's theory, I argue that Hammer's seduction of Penny creates a homoerotic moment *both* for the male characters *and* for the audience. The former occurs in the laundromat, when Hammer brags of his impending sexual conquest of Penny. Hammer tells Billy that Penny is "with Captain Hammer now. And these"—here he holds up his fists, which are his phallus, the symbol of his superheroic power—"are not the hammer." He moves briefly out of frame, then, with perfect comedic timing, steps back in and mistakes his phallus for the organ that it symbolizes: "the hammer is my penis." Through his homoerotic relationship with Hammer, Billy/Horrible enters what Bradley Boney, following Lacan, calls the "queer mirror stage": in the realm of the Imaginary, Horrible experiences a queer desire for Hammer's "ideal" male body (Boney 36). Horrible's queer desire manifests textually in his attempts to use his powerful brain to defeat Hammer's mighty masculine body, while queer audience members may enjoy the subtextual sexual tension between the two characters.

Dr. Horrible's narrative creates an important homoerotic moment of opportunity for a queer audience. In his frequently cited essay on the Broadway musical *Place for Us*, D.A. Miller describes the experience of a gay boy living in the 1950s, conducting the "occult ritual" of descending into his parents' basement to listen to original cast albums of Broadway shows, possibly singing along and/or dancing (2–3). Miller associates this basement with the solitude, shame, and secrecy which characterized the gay experience during that period (26). Dr. Horrible's supervillain lair bears a striking resemblance to Miller's basement. The lair is a place of solitude (much like Superman's Fortress, which is named after that attribute). Horrible does share his lair with his sidekick Moist; however, Horrible sings his songs when Moist isn't there. Horrible abruptly halts his rendition of "My Freeze Ray," an "I want" song that would be perfectly at home in the first act of any Disney musical, when Moist returns home. Miller's basement boys labored "under the magical belief that, having lent the score the depth of their own abjection, they might then borrow all its fantastic hope that their solitary condition would end in glory and triumph" (11). This is very much the mood of "My Freeze Ray." Lurking in the abject depths of his solitary lair, Horrible hopes that he can win Penny and rule the world with her, *simply by singing his desires*. "My Freeze Ray" also positions Dr. Horrible as a queer villain, a figure who enacts "trenchant fantasies of empowerment, replacing the shame and stigma of the abject with the defiance and freedom of the outlaw" (Schildcrout 4). Miller's basement boy rehearsed his gay sexuality on an imaginary sing-along stage (14). In the early twenty-first century, this stage becomes Dr. Horrible's Sing-Along Blog. This is where Horrible rehearses the ambiguous straight sexuality that he thinks he wants to share with Penny, and the homoerotic desire which makes him dream of defeating Captain Hammer with his decidedly phallic Freeze Ray. For Miller, the basement boy's performance was powerful enough to make musical theater signify as "a somehow *gay* genre, the only one that mass culture ever produced" (16). In the rubber-gloved hands of Dr. Horrible, this genre signifies as queer more than gay.

"Lacy, Gently Wafting Curtains": The Queer Sexualities and Genders of the Superhero Story

While *Dr. Horrible* is clearly an American musical, it is also clearly a superhero story. The superhero genre is just as queer, in its own way, as the musical. Douglas Wolk observes that "every formal convention of superheroes can be read as something on the continuum between amusingly pervy and genuinely sick: the skintight outfit, the mask, the double life, ... the kid sidekick" etc. (101). I dispute Wolk's use of the word "sick," which pathologizes any sexualities that the observer happens to find disgusting. Apart from this, however, Wolk's analysis is substantially correct. The formal and generic elements of superhero stories evoke a variety of queer and non-normative sexualities. Captain Hammer's skintight uniform t-shirt seems designed to fetishize his hypermasculine physique, while his oversized gauntlet gloves invoke a leather fetish. Dr. Horrible's white welder's gloves suggest that he shares this fetish with his nemesis. The fetish effect is heightened at the end of the musical, when Horrible switches to black gloves and a blood-red lab coat.

Dr. Horrible's sidekick Moist is not noticeably younger than he is, but he depends on his mentor as thoroughly as any kid sidekick. Moist lives with Horrible, which makes their lair into a domestic space just as homosocial as Batman and Robin's Batcave. Since Horrible and Moist spend most of their time together commiserating about their mutual inability to succeed at heterosexual romance, their lair looks like a closet for two men who are too repressed to consider that perhaps heterosexuality isn't really right for them. While Amy Pascale sees Horrible and Moist as "an example of one of the few easy and plausible male friendships in the Whedonverse" (307), I argue that this friendship is enabled by a queer tension between the two men that is always present, yet never acknowledged.

The Horrible/Moist household nicely illustrates Ramzi Fawaz's point that superhero stories celebrate "the production of implicitly queer and non-normative affiliations that exceed ... the bounds of traditional social arrangements such as the nuclear family" (11). The spectacular failure of normative sexual relationships in *Dr. Horrible* opens up a space for such affiliations. The three groupies endorse unspecified strange sexual practices in the musical's Act Three number "So They Say." This reference to mysterious non-normative sexual acts helps the audience imagine Michael Warner's queer planet, just as superhero stories have done since the Second World War (Fawaz 15). But while most superhero stories are told from the viewpoint of a hero who is at least semi-normative, *Dr. Horrible* privileges the viewpoint of a villain who violates norms of gender and sexuality.

Dr. Horrible effectively critiques the superhero genre's model of masculinity, and the normative sexuality which that masculinity underwrites. As Kendra Leonard observes, "constructing and performing masculinity is a near-universal element in traditional superhero comic books and films" (207). Yet Leonard also notes that *Dr. Horrible* "plays up the ambiguities of masculinity as a defining factor" in both the superhero and musical genres (208). The result is a radical critique of masculine sexualities. *Dr. Horrible's* male characters model the major forms of masculine sexuality that are available to early twenty-first-century American men. I argue that the musical reveals the serious ethical and psychological problems inherent in all of these sexualities, and in the relationships between them. I also argue that the musical encourages the construction of healthier, more ethical alternative sexualities.

Captain Hammer models the culturally privileged form of masculinity that R.W. Connell calls *hegemonic*. Hegemonic masculinity subordinates a number of other masculinities, not only that of gay men (Connell, *Masculinities* 78), but also the masculinity of the wimp, the nerd, the dweeb, and the geek (Connell, *Masculinities* 79). Thus, the hegemonically masculine Captain Hammer subordinates Dr. Horrible's wimpy, nerdish masculinity. Connell and Messerschmidt argue that "hegemony works in part through the production of exemplars of masculinity (e.g., professional sports stars), symbols that have authority despite the fact that most men and boys do not fully live up to them" (846). Captain Hammer's exemplary masculinity is an unattainable ideal for Dr. Horrible. Hegemonic masculinity maintains its power in part by incorporating some feminized elements of subordinated gay culture, such as gay fashion (Demetriou 352). This explains Captain Hammer's peculiar fondness for lacy, gently wafting, feminine curtains. His hegemonic masculinity empowers itself by appropriating the queer aesthetic that the curtains represent, yet Hammer's masculinity runs the risk of being consumed from within by the very elements of subordinate masculinity that it has incorporated. Hammer learns this lesson the hard way, when the Death Ray explosion shatters his brittle masculine façade.

While few men actually attain the ideal of hegemonic masculinity, "very large numbers of men are complicit in sustaining the hegemonic model" (Carrigan, Connell, and Lee 592). The major reason that men become complicit with hegemony, Connell says, "is that most men benefit from the subordination of women" which hegemonic masculinity expresses (*Gender and Power* 185). *Complicit* masculinity allows men to realize what Connell calls the "patriarchal dividend"—the benefit of being a man in a society where women are subordinate to men—but without "the tensions or risks of being the front-line troops of patriarchy" (*Masculinities* 79). Dr. Horrible certainly draws the patriarchal dividend. As a straight, white, male professional, Horrible is culturally authorized to compete with other men for money ("It's not about making money, it's about taking money"), power ("the world's a mess, and I just need to rule it"), and especially women (Penny). To the extent that Horrible mimics the masculinity of the hegemonic Hammer, he is complicit with hegemony; to the extent that his mimicry fails, his masculinity remains subordinate to hegemony. Moist offers a clear example of a *subordinate* masculinity. Horrible's henchman is defined by his ability (or disability) to make things soggy. His Moist masculinity can't be hegemonic, or even complicit: it remains subordinate. Connell's final category of masculinity is the *marginalized* masculinity of subordinated social classes or ethnic groups (*Masculinities* 80–81). In *Dr. Horrible*, the supervillain Bad Horse embodies a masculinity that is marginalized by his status as a nonhuman animal.

Penny models what Connell calls "emphasized femininity." I call it *compliant* femininity, to highlight its central feature: this form of femininity is organized around compliance with male dominance and accommodation of male desires (Connell, *Gender and Power* 183). The passive Penny complies with Hammer's dominance and readily accommodates his sexual desire. As Hammer brags, they "totally had sex." Penny's compliance is typical for a female principal in an American musical. As Richard Dyer argues, in a musical, the girl is reconciled to the guy only by capitulating to his definition of her (30).

James Messerschmidt suggests that hegemonic masculinity is constructed not only in relation to compliant femininities and subordinated masculinities, but also in relation to *oppositional* masculinities which explicitly resist and challenge the hegemonic (10). Oppositional masculinities show up in Stonewall Era American musicals like *Mame, A Chorus Line,* and *The Wiz*; these musicals offer gender performances that seem "immune to the sanctions enforcing American masculinity" (Schiavi 88). *Dr. Horrible* updates the musical's oppositional masculinities for the twenty-first century and extends them to the superhero genre. By endorsing a nonspecific queer sexuality organized around strange sexual acts, the male groupie models an oppositional masculinity, while the two female groupies provide an alternative to Penny's compliant femininity.

"I Thought He Was Kind of Cheesy at First": Penny's Compliant Feminine Sexuality

Penny is trapped in a highly heteronormative culture. The only future that she can imagine for herself is one in which she complies with compulsory heterosexuality's prime directive, by establishing a sexual and romantic relationship with a straight man. In her comic book story, a desperately lonely Penny allows a random guy to take her out. Their one and only date reveals their incompatibility: he's obsessed with superheroes, while she's interested in social justice work. Penny tells a sickly pigeon, "I'm done with dating. I'll never be interested in another boy ever again. Not for a second, mark my words" (Zack Whedon, *Horrible Stories* 33). Penny doesn't rule out the possibility of being interested in a girl, but there are no other girls in the excessively masculine world of *Dr. Horrible*, and in any case, she clearly understands dating as an exclusively heterosexual practice. At the laundromat, Billy makes one of his typical inarticulate sounds: "Hmmurmple" (Zack Whedon, *Horrible Stories* 34). Penny immediately seizes on this ambiguous signifier of possible straight masculine desire. In a thought balloon, she wonders "did cute guy just talk to me?" In the final panel of the story, a big pink heart stands between Penny and Billy. It is inscribed with the words "The End," signifying both the end of the story and the end of their potential relationship, which is over before it began.

Penny is the least complex of *Dr. Horrible*'s three major characters, and the one with the least personal agency. As Victoria Willis notes, Penny has no superpowers and "appears to have no power whatsoever" (242). Echoing Buckman, Amy Pascale calls Penny "a one-note 'nice girl' who serves as little more than a prize for which Dr. Horrible and Captain Hammer compete" (306). Joss Whedon's rough draft of the musical originally included a love song called "When You're My Slave" (Joss Whedon et al., *Dr. Horrible: The Book* 9). So Penny began as another of Whedon's meditations on the ethical perils of a sexual slavery mediated by mad science, a category that also includes Warren using the cerebral dampener on Katrina ("Dead Things" *Buffy* 6.13), and Topher programming the dolls for sex work in *Dollhouse*.

Penny's compliant femininity requires her to define herself exclusively in relation to the men around her, to capitulate to the desires of those men without regard to her own desires, and to seek the straight sexual relationships which heteronormativity requires, but which Penny doesn't actually seem to want. Captain Hammer rescues her from the speeding Wonderflonium van, and immediately sings that this rescue was destined to happen. In a heteronormative love story, it is indeed the hero's destiny to save the damsel, while it is her destiny to reward him with sexual favors, as Penny soon does. Yet Penny is not entirely comfortable with this rescuer/rescued relationship. As she sings her gratitude, she wonders about the nature of Hammer's Captaincy. He is, of course, Captain of his Hammer, by which he means his genitals. This Captaincy will certainly require Penny to assume a subordinate position in her impending sexual relationship with him. Penny sings that their prospective love may be lethal. This establishes a structural connection between heterosexual love and death. The musical strengthens this connection via formal parallelism; Captain Hammer simultaneously sings about the same death by love.

"Penny's Song" confirms Penny's status as a prisoner of heteronormativity's fixed expectations and unachievable goals. Felicia Day signals Penny's kinship with the Disney Princesses by wearing Snow White's color scheme: bright blue blouse, red belt, and yellow skirt. Like Snow White, Penny is doomed to live in isolation as she awaits her prince. Indeed, she makes the loneliness that characterizes the Disney model of feminine love explicit when she sings about growing up in a lonesome environment, with an image of love drawn from fairy tales. Throughout the musical, Penny continues to accept heterosexual love as her only option, yet she never quite manages to convince herself that she will find happiness via straight romance. In "So They Say," the things that "they" say are the commonplaces of *Dr. Horrible*'s cultural world. These include the assumption that Penny can and will be happy with Captain Hammer. "They" say that Penny's relationship with Hammer is ideal. But Penny is hardly enthusiastic about the relationship; she merely thinks that Hammer is basically all right. Penny's uncertainty reflects her doubts about her culture's formula for attaining sexual and emotional satisfaction, yet she remains unable to imagine any alternative. When pressed, even heteronormative culture has to admit that straight serial monogamy offers no guarantee of happiness. "They" say that no love story ends happily, and Penny's ending is the opposite of happy. She goes to her grave waiting for her prince to rescue her. Her last words invoke this empty hope: "Captain Hammer will save us." Penny's end represents the failure of the heteronormative, fairy tale sexuality whose horizons she never transcends, and of the compliant femininity which understands this sexuality as a woman's only option.

"Corporate Tool": Captain Hammer's Hegemonically Masculine Sexuality

Sociologist Sharon Bird has shown how male "homosociality contributes to the perpetuation of hegemonic masculinity" by promoting emotional detachment, competitiveness, and the sexual objectification of women (121). The homosocial relationship between Captain Hammer and Dr. Horrible features these three elements in great abundance. Hammer describes Penny as "kind of a quiet, nerdy thing. Not my usual, but nice." His use of the word "thing" turns a humiliating backhanded compliment into an act of objectification. As Bird notes, men often compete with one another for the affections of women and in boasting about their sexual exploits (128). When he meets Billy at the laundromat, Hammer makes a point of telling him that he's going to take "little Penny" back to his place. The diminutive "little" emphasizes Penny's subordinate status. Hammer plans to dazzle Penny with such gadgets as the Hammer Cycle and the Ham-Jet; clearly, he also competes with Horrible in the realm of high-tech consumerism. Hammer concludes with a parodically explicit statement of the straight man's sense of sexual entitlement, letting Billy know that he plans to show Penny the Hammer itself, and making sure that Billy understands what that means: "The hammer is my penis."

Captain Hammer equates his penis with the hammer that symbolizes his superpowers, but it doesn't have to be this way. The most famous hammer in the superhero genre is certainly Thor's Mjolnir. In Jason Aaron and Russell Dauterman's *Thor* comics (2014–2018), Jane Foster wields Mjolnir as the first female Thor. In superhero stories, the hammer may always be a phallus, but it need not be a penis. Captain Hammer, however, can't grasp this distinction. But perhaps he is not entirely to blame for this. As Mary Anne Doane argues, the privilege that Lacan accords the phallus as signifier means that although the phallus may not be the penis, it can't be conceptualized apart from the penis (170)—certainly not by the hegemonic Hammer. For Captain Hammer, penis equals phallus equals weapon. Hammer's hammer is the weaponized tool that this "corporate tool" uses to "nail" Penny. When he assumes that he has the right to do so, Hammer evokes the rape culture that his masculinity sanctions. *Dr. Horrible*'s hammer metaphor also shows how seductive hegemonic male sexuality can be, not only for straight women but also for ostensibly straight men. This is how we can make sense of the almost inexplicable line that Dr. Horrible sings about the encounter between the hammer and the object that it hits in his Act Three victory song "Slipping." Horrible is either expressing a masochistic desire to continue getting beaten up by Hammer, or he is revealing that there is some part of him that wants to be sexually "nailed" by Hammer, or both. Either way, in "Slipping," the homosocial is in grave danger of "slipping" into the homosexual: this is the moment when the American film musical's heterosexual policing function threatens to fail.

Kendra Leonard points out that Hammer's explicit description of his plan to have sex with Penny "sparks Horrible's most emphatic performance of masculinity" (212). In his "I will" song "Brand New Day," Dr. Horrible vows to kill Captain Hammer, and Horrible constructs a Death Ray for this purpose. As Alyson Buckman argues, in its most extreme form, the sexual competition between Horrible and Hammer constitutes a deadly form of misogynistic violence ("Say it was Horrible" ¶ 19). The Death Ray is damaged in the climactic struggle between the two men. When Captain Hammer tries to fire the Ray at Dr. Horrible, it explodes, fatally wounding Penny. As Victoria Willis observes, "Horrible and Hammer kill Penny together" (244). This is the ultimate homosocial expression of a violent, misogynistic masculinity.

It also represents the crisis of that masculinity. Connell observes that hegemonic masculinity reflects and produces the crisis tendencies of the gender order ("A Very Straight Gay" 736). *Dr. Horrible*'s audience has already seen an example of these crisis tendencies in Act One, when a mysterious feminine fissure appears in Hammer's monolithic masculinity. "It's curtains for you, Horrible," Hammer declares. "Lacy, gently wafting curtains." This is Captain Hammer's queerest moment. His sudden, startling interest in the aesthetics of interior design is radically at odds with the hegemonic masculinity that he performs elsewhere. This moment occurs early in the musical's action, just after Hammer's first appearance. Placing this queer moment so early in the narrative makes it much harder for the audience to read Captain Hammer as unproblematically straight. Viewers are led to believe that Hammer's heterosexist masculinity may simply be a performance. Indeed, Hammer may be performing a masculinity whose hegemony requires the subordination of femininities and/or masculinities *with which he might actually identify*. Lurking behind Hammer's lacy, gently wafting curtains, we may find a man every bit as unmasculine as Dr. Horrible—just better at hiding. Hammer's masculine façade finally collapses in Act Three, when he is injured in the Death Ray explosion and experiences pain for the first time. Hammer runs crying from the room, seeking "someone maternal," and ends up sobbing his eyes out on a psychoanalyst's couch. Hammer's hysterical reaction to his injury codes him as feminine. As Don Tresca argues, Hammer's movement from masculine to effeminate, along with Horrible's movement in the opposite direction, is part of the musical's queer subtext ("Skeletons" 37). The Death Ray is more effective than it initially appeared: it kills Penny, it kills Captain Hammer's emotional detachment, and (perhaps most importantly) it kills hegemonic masculinity's claims of monolithic invincibility.

"I Wanna Be an Achiever, Like Bad Horse": Dr. Horrible's Complicit and Subordinate Masculine Sexualities

While both the musical and superhero genres typically represent their protagonists as hegemonically masculine, thus further privileging that already privileged masculinity, *Dr. Horrible* makes a more interesting and subversive representational choice: its protagonist models a complicit masculinity instead. Dr. Horrible aspires to hegemonic masculinity without attaining it.

Horrible seeks money, infamy, and the transformation of society. But really, wealth, power, and reputation are simply the means by which Horrible hopes to gain possession of Penny as a sexual object. Horrible's stark refusal to allow Penny any agency confirms that he is complicit with the subordination of women which makes hegemonic masculinity possible; this refusal also reflects the insecurity of a man who cannot attain that masculinity himself.

In the musical's first song, "My Freeze Ray," Dr. Horrible sings that he can help Penny realize the emotions she fears. He sings these lines not to the real Penny, but to the Imaginary Penny reflected in the mirror of his mind, the Penny with whom he has already formed an intimate relationship. He imagines that Penny must have feelings for him; it's just a matter of being manly enough to make her feel comfortable revealing those feelings. He also dances with the Penny of his mind's eye. The wordless music and physical gestures of this intimate, two-person dance locate it firmly in the Imaginary. Here *Dr. Horrible* uses the formal conventions of the film musical to signal Horrible's desire for straight romance. Horrible wants Penny to be the Ginger Rogers to his Fred Astaire. If this were a typical musical, the male and female principals would dance together at the end, signifying their heterosexual union. In this very atypical musical, they dance together at the beginning, and only in Horrible's mind: he never dances with the real Penny. In real life, Horrible will be busy dancing with Captain Hammer. Their preferred dance is hand-to-hand combat, and the hegemonic Hammer always leads.

Competition with Hammer to possess Penny motivates Horrible throughout the musical. He admits that his "famously successful heist" of the Wonderflonium was "less successful in that I inadvertently introduced my arch-nemesis to the girl of my dreams and now he's taking her out on dates and they're probably gonna French-kiss or something." Horrible is so desperate to possess Penny that he even tells her about his dream of becoming a successful supervillain. Speaking in the persona of his secret identity Billy, Horrible tells Penny, "I wanna be an achiever, like Bad Horse." While this might impress the Imaginary Penny, the actual Penny is far too goodhearted to endorse such aspirations. Shocked, she says, "the Thoroughbred of Sin?" As the fantasy that Billy has used to cover over the gap between the Imaginary and Real Pennies collapses, Billy realizes that he's been trying to pass a counterfeit Penny. He must perform an immediate and hilarious reversal: "I meant Gandhi."

Horrible's victory over Hammer represents the failure not only of hegemonic masculinity, but also of the masculinity that is complicit with hegemony. In the end, Horrible defeats his masculine competitor and gains everything he supposedly ever wanted: power, infamy, and wealth. Yet Penny's death makes his victory hollow. Horrible's voice is heavy with irony as he sings about the attainment of his goals and the completion of his triumph in

"Everything You Ever." His futile pursuit of hegemonic masculinity led him to objectify Penny and use her as a pawn in his sexual competition with Hammer. Now she's dead, which means she's unavailable to him even as an object. He has not won the sexual competition; he and Hammer have both lost. The conclusion of the musical shows the failure of complicit masculinity's pursuit of emotional detachment. Horrible finally achieves his main professional ambition and joins the Evil League of Evil. Dressed in red to symbolize his new status as a successful supervillain, Dr. Horrible promises to dominate the entire planet. He also claims that he will avoid experiencing any emotion as he does so. But then Joss Whedon cuts to a tight shot of Billy in his hoodie, alone in his lair, looking lost, empty, and despondent. It is Billy, not Dr. Horrible, who sings the last part of the line. With that, the musical fades to black. If Dr. Horrible has achieved emotional detachment, Billy clearly has not. The audience is led to believe that Billy will likely spend the rest of his life trying not to feel the pain of Penny's death and failing. In his 2018 comic book appearance, a guilt-ridden Billy wakes himself up from nightmares by forcing the Imaginary Penny of his dreams to ask "why did you kill me?" before she melts into the Real and becomes a Penny-shaped blob of hideous goo (Whedon, Beroy, and Soler).

Although he aspires to, and is often complicit with, hegemonic masculinity, there are several significant ways in which Dr. Horrible's masculinity remains subordinate. The most obvious of these is his physical inferiority to Captain Hammer. The home movie montage that plays in the background during "Brand New Day" reveals the long history of Horrible's subordination to Hammer. We see Hammer beating up Horrible on several different occasions, in several different seasons, once with a tourist taking photos. Hammer pummels Horrible and gives him wedgies. This looks like the kind of playground violence which routinely establishes the hierarchy of hegemonic and subordinate masculinities in American schools. Because of his physical inferiority, Horrible cannot escape the subordinate position of the "wimp" or "sissy."

The other major example of Horrible's subordinate masculinity is his painful inability to negotiate a successful sexual relationship. Horrible (or more precisely, Billy) suffers from extreme social awkwardness. Billy's social anxiety is so severe that he can't even talk to the Imaginary Penny in his head. When he tells the Penny of his fantasies that he loves her hair, she replies, "What?" Billy has just made the most tentative proclamation of his desire, to a woman who exists only in his imagination. Even so, he must immediately walk back this tepid declaration of desire, which he does with great awkwardness, claiming that he loves the air. Billy tries to talk to the actual Penny while operating the Horrible Van Remote, but quickly becomes overwhelmed and retreats into the more comfortable realm of electronically mediated communication: "I'm texting. It's very important or I would stop." Finding it hard to make an emotional connection with Penny, he offers an abstract intellectual discourse: "I'm talking about an overhaul of the system. Putting the power in … different hands." This conversation does nothing to advance his desired relationship with Penny, but it does model an awkward, insincere masculinity which is clearly subordinate to the hegemonic.

"You're Weird": The Queer Sexuality of the Subordinate Sidekick

Moist provides another good example of a subordinate masculinity. Like the disabled superheroes I discussed in Chapter Three, Moist has a "superpower" which is really more of a physical impairment: he makes things soggy, whether he wants to or not. This makes people uncomfortable, and that discomfort disables Moist. Moist understands that his disability forecloses the possibility of professional success, ensuring that he will always remain a mere henchman. "Look at me, man," he complains to Dr. Horrible. "I'm Moist. At my most badass I make people feel like they want to take a shower. I'm not E.L.E. material." Moist's disability also prevents him from achieving sexual success. Moist's comic book backstory shows that before he met Dr. Horrible, he was working hard to construct a viable heterosexuality for himself and failing spectacularly. Speaking to a phone sex worker, Moist narrates over a panel that shows him giving flowers to a rather uninterested young woman. "My love life is…" (Zack Whedon, *Horrible Stories* 17). The next panel shows the intrepid Moist having sex with a different uninterested woman, who gazes at her fingernails, bored and indifferent, as his narration concludes: "…not quite what I'd like it to be." Moist's sex life is bad enough to provoke an existential crisis. "I don't know what my *purpose* is," he complains to the equally bored and indifferent phone sex worker. "You're weird," she concludes, and hangs up on him. Women have sex with Moist only grudgingly, if at all, even when he pays them. And the most desirable women are completely unavailable to him. In the musical, Moist describes how he and Conflict Diamond went on a double date with Bait and Switch. Moist is disappointed with the outcome: "I kinda thought I was supposed to end up with Bait, but…" Moist does become more professionally and sexually successful after Dr. Horrible joins the Evil League of Evil. In the "Best Friends Forever" comic, Moist recruits three attractive henchwomen known, inevitably, as the Towelettes (Whedon, Beroy, and Soler). Yet Moist must compete for the attention and affections of his own henchwomen with another man, the more successful villain (and E.L.E. member) Fake Thomas Jefferson. Moist's masculinity remains subordinate to the hegemonic.

We can't rule out the possibility that Moist may be a closeted gay man. Much like the sexuality of his mentor Dr. Horrible, Moist's sexuality is nominally straight, but signifies as queer in several important respects. Like Horrible, Moist seems to think of himself as straight, but has trouble maintaining an active heterosexuality. Also like Horrible, Moist *does* have a very active homosocial life. Homosociality occupies the space that might otherwise be taken up by heterosexuality in the structure of Moist's interpersonal relations. This manifests most obviously in Moist's relationship with Dr. Horrible, but Horrible is not the only man in Moist's life. A tantalizingly brief scene in "So They Say" demonstrates that Moist has a close relationship with a male villain called the Pink Pummeler (Michael Canaan). The Pummeler is a minor character with no speaking or singing parts, but his name, his costume, and the *mise-en-scène* strongly code him as gay. He wears feminine pink boxing gloves and a pink domino mask. For reasons that are never explained, Moist is in the Pink Pummeler's bedroom, which contains a large collection of adorable stuffed animals. Perhaps Moist has finally realized that while his Moist masculinity will never form the basis for a happy heterosexual life, it might be compatible with a gay or queer sexuality.

Making Men Mares: The Sexual Violence of Bad Horse's Marginalized Masculinity

The supervillain Bad Horse models the marginalized masculinity of a subordinated group. Nonhuman animals are subordinate to humans in contemporary American culture, and indeed throughout Western history (see Chapter Four). Connell suggests that hegemonic masculinity will sometimes, but not always, authorize marginalized masculinity (*Masculinities* 80–81). Hegemony will be most likely to authorize marginalized masculinity when the marginalized advances the agenda of the hegemonic, e.g., when the marginalized contributes to the subordination of non-hegemonic masculinities. Bad Horse speaks, or rather sings, indirectly, through his Chorus. After the fight at the Superhero Memorial Bridge, the Bad Horse Chorus defines Horrible's defeat at the fists of Captain Hammer as humiliating, thus reinforcing the subordinate status of Horrible's masculinity.

The violence that Bad Horse deploys to enforce Horrible's subordination has a specific and disturbing sexual character. Bad Horse threatens to rape Dr. Horrible if Horrible fails to become a successful supervillain. The Chorus sings that if Horrible fails to make Bad Horse happy, Bad Horse will claim Horrible as he would claim a female horse. In order to rape a man, the homophobic, speciesist Bad Horse would have to reimagine that man as a mare. Bad Horse's threat reinforces one of the central assumptions of rape culture: that the active sexual subject is male, and the passive sexual object is female. As Kendra Leonard notes, this threat also positions Horrible "as the weaker, feminized 'bottom' in relation to the presumably more masculine and more successful villains" of the League (210). The threat of rape reinscribes hegemony by suggesting that hegemonically masculine men—or their marginalized equine surrogates—have the right to use subordinate men non-consensually as sexual objects.

Bad Horse's violent masculine sexuality raises the ominous prospect of non-consensual interspecies sex. But while critics accuse real-world zoophiles of disregarding the nonhuman animal's consent (as I discussed in Chapter Four), in this case it is the animal who disregards the human's consent. Jessica Cox argues that horses in general and Bad Horse in particular symbolize a violent "primitive masculinity" (88–89). For the Games of ancient Rome, stallions and other male animals were trained to rape girls and women (Masters 14–15). By evoking this ancient practice, Bad Horse emphasizes the sexual power of the stallion, and shows how easily that power can be harnessed to a violent, abusive purpose. The equine rapist Bad Horse provides another cautionary example of a weaponized penis. This one is even more dangerous than Hammer's hammer, for although Hammer's hegemonic masculinity gives his sexuality a violent dimension, his sexual behavior is, as far as we know, at least formally consensual.

"Geeky Weirdo Perverts": Queer Perversion as Oppositional Sexuality

Although *Dr. Horrible* offers devastating ethical and psychological critiques of the modern forms of masculinity and the sexualities that derive from those masculinities, all is not lost. In Act Three, the musical offers a brief but definite moment of hope. The song "So They Say" features three groupies. These groupies follow first Captain Hammer, then Dr. Horrible: they are not committed to hegemonic, complicit, or subordinate masculinity. One of the groupies is played by Maurissa Tancharoen, who co-wrote the musical along with the Whedon brothers. Casting one of the show's writers as a groupie implies that the groupies have a message that the writers want the audience to hear. The musical's moment of subversion comes when Captain Hammer's hegemonic masculinity reaches its apotheosis. We learn that Hammer has taken the principles of emotional detachment and sexual objectification of women to their logical conclusion: his sexual history consists entirely of one-night stands. Singing about his sexual relationship with Penny, Hammer considers having sex with her more than once, which would be a novel experience for him. He believes that if he has sex with Penny again, he'll get to do strange things with her. At that moment, the three groupies lean into the frame and sing of their willingness to do these strange sexual things. Captain Hammer doesn't really seem to know what these things are; his hegemonic masculinity implies a vanilla sexuality. But the groupies seem genuinely interested in strange sex, which probably includes alternative sexual practices such as BDSM and/or fetishism. This seems particularly plausible given the prevalence of BDSM and fetish sex within real-world science fiction fan communities (Bacon-Smith Chapter 9; see also Newmahr 9). The groupies are clearly presented as members of such a community.

Although Captain Hammer expresses an interest in strange sex in "So They Say," his comic book stories reveal this to be an affectation. In "Captain Hammer: Be Like Me!" Hammer narrates a kind of public service announcement over a panel that shows male and female Goth teens: "You see harmless death nerds…" (Zack Whedon, *Horrible Stories* 12). These Goth kids would be equally at home at a science fiction convention or at the con's after-hours BDSM play party (Bacon-Smith 180–185). "I see future super villains," Hammer concludes over a panel of the same Goths grinning maniacally in front of a dystopian city in flames. Hammer believes that it's his job to discipline young people away from strange sex, towards a wholesome vanilla sexuality. "So you do your part…" he commands, his big gloved hands lingering ominously on the shoulders of a skinny adolescent boy (Zack Whedon, *Horrible Stories* 14). "I'll do mine … and maybe we can put these geeky weirdo perverts in their place." Hammer equates geek culture with non-normative sexuality, in order to reject both.

He also uses the strange things as a kinky means to a vanilla end: although he doesn't really care for them, he will do them if it means he can have more sex. In "Best Friends Forever," he narrates his latest sexual exploits to three kids who look like younger versions of the musical's three groupies (Whedon, Beroy, and Soler). He boasts of having had "spicy" sex with a superwoman called Pepper Spray. Apparently, Pepper lives up to her name, for she gave Captain Hammer swelling and searing pain. Rather than admit the unthinkable—that he might actually enjoy kinky sex—he characterizes the pain as something he had to go through to "close the deal," i.e., to achieve the sexual aim that hegemonic masculinity has assigned him. Later, when the voluptuous Hourglass reveals that she's on her period, he still wants to have sex with her. "It's gross but not a deal-breaker," he declares. His comment reveals his vanilla preferences, his willingness to forgo those preferences to achieve the hegemonic imperative of having sex with as many women as possible, and his transactional view of sexuality, which understands sex acts as "deals" to be closed or broken. His willingness to have sex with a menstruating woman does not indicate an openness to non-normative practices; rather, it is evidence of an instrumental sexuality that sees meaningless sex as an end unto itself.

Five. "The Hammer Is My Penis"

When the musical's groupies endorse strange sex and gleefully volunteer to do it, they offer a radical alternative to the various discredited sexualities that litter *Dr. Horrible*'s landscape. One of James Messerschmidt's major examples of an oppositional masculinity is the masculinity of "freaks" (10). Steve Berg's Groupie #3 models a "freakish" oppositional masculinity. The enthusiasm of Berg's groupie for the strange things suggests that he would be open to radically oppositional sexual practices. These oppositional practices could challenge hegemonically masculine sexuality. Meanwhile, the groupies played by Maurissa Tancharoen and Stacy Shirk suggest that women can gain sexual agency by embracing a strange sexuality, as Whedommes and the real-world dominant women whom they represent have done. Here the strange things serve as a viable alternative to Penny's passive, compliant acceptance of masculine sexual hegemony.

Dr. Horrible mounts an effective resistance to hegemonic masculinity, compliant femininity, and the heteronormative, homophobic sexualities those oppressive gender positions enable. In place of these ethically dubious genders and sexualities, *Dr. Horrible* encourages its audience to imagine a homophilic male sexuality that would not fear the gay desire that flows between Horrible and Hammer. The musical also invites viewers to imagine a female sexuality that would grant Penny the sexual agency that might have let her survive the competition between a hero and a villain who are ultimately the hegemonic and complicit sides of the same toxic masculine coin. This queer supervillain musical dreams of a world that has taken the night back from the sexual violence of Bad Horse, a world where Moist wouldn't be ashamed to pursue a relationship with the Pink Pummeler. The musical gives us only the most tantalizingly brief glimpse of this world, in a single lyric sung by three groupies whose ordinariness allows them to represent mainstream American masculinity and femininity. But the fact that such typical Americans would gleefully volunteer to have strange sex tells us everything we need to know about *Dr. Horrible*'s sexual politics. Its commitment to non-normative sexualities makes *Dr. Horrible* a resolutely queer musical in the tradition of *Rocky Horror*, *Rent*, and *Hedwig and the Angry Inch*. By envisioning these strange sexualities in the superhero milieu, *Dr. Horrible* effectively queers the superhero genre. *Dr. Horrible* thus moves us closer to Michael Warner's queer planet on two seemingly unrelated yet intimately connected fronts. Dr. Horrible doesn't always express himself clearly, especially when it comes to sex. But perhaps what he *meant* to say is "the world's a mess, and we just need to queer it."

Six

"They Want to See Us Punished"

Subverting the Sexual Tropes of the Slasher Film in The Cabin in the Woods

Joss Whedon has called *The Cabin in the Woods* "a very loving hate letter" to horror movies (quoted in Moore). Whedon co-wrote this "letter" with longtime collaborator Drew Goddard, who directed the film. *Cabin* is a loving yet pointed critique of the cycle of American horror films that began with John Carpenter's fantastically successful *Halloween* (1978) and continued into the 1980s with the long-running franchises initiated by *Friday the 13th* (Sean S. Cunningham 1980) and *A Nightmare on Elm Street* (Wes Craven 1984). Film scholars have called these movies "teenie-kill pics" (Robin Wood) or "stalker films" (Vera Dika). I follow the most influential of these scholars, Carol Clover, who calls them "slasher films." The slasher follows a very specific generic formula. A killer stalks a group of teenagers. The killer is almost always male, though his masculinity is flawed in some way (Clover 42, 47). He kills the teens one by one, starting with those who are most sexually active. His last victim, Clover's famous Final Girl, is the least sexualized woman in the group. Her sexual innocence authorizes her to survive the film and escape or capture the killer, who must, however, remain available (or at least imitable) for the inevitable sequels. By punishing teen sexuality and rewarding sexual abstinence, the slasher film perfectly embodied the conservative sexual politics of Reagan era America.

The slasher lends itself to psychoanalytic interpretation. The killer has often suffered some childhood trauma and is often "sexually disturbed" (Clover 28). The very term "slasher" derives from the genre's obsessive fascination with blades, from Michael Myers' kitchen knife to Freddy Krueger's razor glove. Psychoanalytic criticism reads the killer's slashing blades as an evocation of castration anxiety. The killer often stabs his victims to death. As Clover notes, when he thrusts his knife into the body of a young woman, the killer's "phallic purpose" is unmistakable (47).

The slasher is fundamentally a drama of intergenerational conflict in which an older, more powerful man punishes the perceived sexual transgressions of adolescents. In that sense, the slasher is a compulsively repetitive reenactment of the basic psychosexual conflict that psychoanalysis takes to be constitutive of the human family and civilization itself: the Father's prohibition of all sexualities that break his Law. *Cabin* foregrounds the slasher's Oedipal dynamic through the figures of Hadley (Bradley Whitford) and Sitterson (Richard Jenkins), the two middle-aged would-be patriarchs responsible for organizing the doom of the film's young protagonists. Hadley and Sitterson suffer from castration anxiety themselves, and they deploy the slashing, castrating, penetrating violence of *Cabin*'s monsters against the teens. But those teens must earn their doom, for Hadley and Sitterson live by the formal logic of the slasher. "They don't transgress," says Sitterson, "they can't be punished," Hadley finishes.

Psychoanalytic film scholar Robin Wood was the first to recognize the reactionary nature of the slasher's portrayal of teen sexuality. By the mid–1980s, Wood was arguing that the slasher waged a brutal campaign against "liberated female sexuality or the sexual freedom of the young" (123). And this is precisely what has always bothered Joss Whedon about American horror cinema. Buffy was originally intended to be "an homage to all the pretty, frivolous girls who dared to have fun and have sex—like Lynda in *Halloween*" (Pascale 45). Whedon argues that contemporary horror contains "this weird obsession with youth and sex, and at the same time this very puritanical desire to punish it that I think is unseemly and really, really creepy" (Bernstein 42). *Cabin*'s monsters represent this creepy, Puritan anti-sex impulse. They are the Buckners, an undead family of "vaguely religious, backwoods sadomasochists" (Parrish ¶ 10). They embody a repressed, anti-sex sadomasochism, for the slasher film cannot acknowledge the possibility of a healthy, consensual, pro-sex BDSM.

Whedon bemoans the fact that contemporary horror heeds society's dictate to punish young people for doing drugs and having sex (Bernstein 42). *Cabin* is motivated largely by Whedon's desire to critique the campaign against youthful sexuality that the slasher film initiated in the 1980s, just as Nancy Reagan was launching her anti-drug "Just Say No" campaign. At the end of the film, *Cabin*'s Final Girl realizes why her friends are being murdered. "They don't just wanna see us killed," says Dana (Kristen Connolly). "They want to see us *punished*." Her friend Marty (Fran Kranz) asks the obvious question: "punished for what?" The Director (Sigourney Weaver), who has orchestrated their ordeal, responds with a question which is not only an answer but a statement of the film's thesis: "For being young?" Dana's "they" includes the Director, Hadley, Sitterson, their colleagues, the elder gods for whom they all work, and the spectators of the real world, who pay Hollywood hundreds of millions of dollars for the privilege of watching young people like themselves get punished for their youth.

While Whedon speaks out against the modern American horror film in general, his critique applies most directly to the slasher, and he identifies the classic slasher films as the ones against which *Cabin* reacts. "Why do we keep coming back to this formula?" he demands (Bernstein 10). "How many times do ... [the characters] have to start acting like assholes or just *be* assholes? You look at movies like *Halloween* and *Nightmare on Elm Street*..." (Bernstein 11). For Whedon, the tendency of slasher characters to "act like assholes" includes an unrealistic affinity for irresponsible sexual behavior. Here's how Whedon characterizes such behavior: "'I'm an unbelievable asshole and also I'm doing drugs and crime and sex all at the same time, so not only might I die but I deserve to'" (Utichi). This kind of representation promotes a puritan sexual ethics which suggests that the death penalty is a reasonable sanction for sexual behaviors that are well within the mainstream of modern American youth culture. It also makes for unconvincing characterization, and thus constitutes poor filmmaking. Whedon denounces the recent trajectory of the American slasher film, in which the teen protagonists "get more and more expendable and more love is put into the instruments of torture and no love at all is put into dialogue polish" (Bernstein 11). Compelling characterization and sparkling dialogue are, of course, precisely the elements of filmmaking for which Whedon is famous.

Cabin solves the problem of characterization by identifying the fundamental character types of the slasher and developing characters who simultaneously embody, subvert, and transcend those types. "There are five very clear archetypes in the horror genre," Drew Goddard observes (Bernstein 16). There is the Whore, a promiscuous or otherwise sexually transgressive young woman who is inevitably the film's first victim. In *Cabin* this First Girl is Jules (Anna Hutchison). Jules loves sex, has sex as often as possible, and encourages her friends to do so. But Jules is sexually monogamous (with Curt), and she is actually a thoughtful pre-med student whose intelligence has been chemically suppressed. Curt (Chris Hemsworth) is *Cabin*'s First Boy: the Athlete, a muscle-bound jock whom the audience may expect to be an oversexed boor. But Curt is a sensitive sociology major; like Jules, he only exhibits the traits of his archetype under the influence of the drugs the Director's minions feed him. Holden (Jesse Williams) is the Scholar, an intellectual who would typically be coded as sexually inactive. But Holden is just as athletic as Curt, and he has a very active sexuality. Holden is the Middle Boy, who dies after Curt. Marty is the Fool, whose hedonism would normally invite an early death. While the Fool's steady diet of alcohol and/or drugs usually renders him incapable of understanding his doom, the "secret stash" of marijuana that Marty smokes throughout the film inoculates him against the drugs that reduce his friends to their archetypes. Marty survives to the end of the film and takes his place beside Dana as the Final Boy, not despite his hedonism but *because* of it.

Dana is the Virgin, who is destined to die last. As such, she should be sexually innocent, but she is actually the *most* sexually transgressive member of the group, having recently concluded an illicit affair with her married professor.

Cabin occupies a precise sub-genre of the slasher, known variously as the postmodern slasher (Hutchings 192) or metaslasher (Och 195). The prototype of this sub-sub-genre of horror cinema is *Scream* (Wes Craven 1996). The metaslasher is characterized by its awareness of its own status as a slasher film. Its characters understand the situation in which they find themselves (Hutchings 212), and they can comment on the formal elements of the film they inhabit. The metaslasher has the unique ability to embody the slasher's generic conventions even as it critiques them, which makes it perfect for Goddard and Whedon's purposes. Central to the metaslasher's critique of its generic forebears is its challenge to the conservative sexual politics of the classic slasher. The metaslasher is less concerned with the supposed "moral value of virginity," and presents the active sex lives of its young protagonists as normal (Hutchings 214). Thus, *Cabin* only condemns youthful sexuality when the film is explicitly obeying the rules of the slasher genre, and it always critiques itself for doing so.

The defining feature of the metaslasher is its focus on the audience's experience of watching the film's horrific events (Och 198), and on their complicity with these events. *Cabin* locates itself in the metaslasher tradition via a clever and effective formal mechanism. Hadley, Sitterson, and the other technicians constitute a secondary audience that stands between the real-world audience and the film's characters. The real-life audience watches the fictional secondary audience watching the slasher plot. Every element of that plot is mediated via the monitor screens of the technicians. The real audience is thus unable to forget that it *is* an audience. To watch *Cabin* is to become Hadley and Sitterson, which is to become people who are reluctant to acknowledge their complicity in the horrors they create: Goddard based the two men on the nuclear weapons scientists he knew growing up in Los Alamos, New Mexico (Pascale 320). And since Whedon admits that he and Goddard are Hadley and Sitterson (Bernstein 13), *Cabin* acknowledges the moral complicity of the slasher's writers, directors, and producers as well. *Cabin* is perhaps the first film to give a truly complete account of the people who bear the ethical responsibility for cinematic horror.

The twenty-first-century descendant of the slasher is the torture porn film. Critic David Edelstein gave this provocative generic label to a cycle of horror films that includes the franchises inaugurated by *Saw* (James Wan 2004) and *Hostel* (Eli Roth 2005). *Cabin*'s release was delayed three years by MGM's bankruptcy; ironically, the film was eventually distributed by Lionsgate, the same studio that released the *Saw* films (Pascale 372). Edelstein complains that torture porn tortures its audience: "I didn't understand why I had to be tortured, too. I didn't want to identify with the victim *or* the victimizer." Of course, that is precisely *why* the audience has to be tortured: to force the identification with the characters that is one of the most important features of horror spectatorship. The problem with torture porn is that it often fails to achieve the intended identification. Too often these films "allow the viewer to enjoy torture without seeing the source of that enjoyment" (Neroni 72). This certainly cannot be said of *Cabin*.

Whedon intended *Cabin* to be a response to the torture porn sub-genre in general, and a specific reply to *Captivity* (Roland Joffe 2007); he famously petitioned the Motion Picture Association of America to withhold *Captivity*'s rating (Pascale 286). Whedon struggled to understand why "the act of being a free, attractive, self-assertive woman is punishable by torture and death" ("Let's Watch"). For Whedon, the answer was womb envy, the inverse of Freud's much maligned theory of penis envy. In Whedon's view, some men resent women's sexual and reproductive power, and this resentment drives the torture, rape, and murder of women ("Let's Watch"). Whedon can do nothing about the millennia of womb envy that stand behind the slasher genre. But he can throw light on the sadistic pleasure that comes from watching women punished for being women, and young people for being young. He can force audiences to confront their complicity with schemes of punishment whose durability must never be mistaken for ethicality. This is the project of *The Cabin in the Woods*.

"They Don't Transgress, They Can't Be Punished": The Psychoanalytic Interpretation of the American Slasher Film

Psychoanalysis is not coextensive with psychology, and there are certainly psychological approaches to film criticism that do not rely upon psychoanalytic concepts and categories, such as the cognitive approach. However, psychoanalytic criticism is the most relevant approach for interpreting horror cinema, and it is especially useful for analyzing the slasher sub-genre. This is why psychoanalysis has dominated the critical interpretation of the American horror film in general, and the slasher film in particular, since the 1970s. Robin Wood developed the psychoanalytic critical approach in a series of groundbreaking essays, arguing that horror represents the return of the repressed, specifically repressed sexual energy (72). As a Freudian, Wood naturally identifies the family as the "unifying master figure" of American horror (75). The figure of the family includes specific motifs such as the "Terrible Child" and the cannibal (Wood 75). *Cabin* fits Wood's model perfectly. The main monsters in the film's first two acts are the cannibalistic Buckners, whom the technicians describe as a "zombie redneck torture family."

Perhaps the most terrifying Buckner is young Patience, a classic Terrible Child. Patience initiates the film's slasher plot, for it is the Latin incantation that Dana reads from Patience's diary that summons the Buckners. Patience writes in her diary that her "good arm is hacked up and et," which aligns *Cabin* with the cannibal movies of the 1970s. Meanwhile, the Buckners' redneck status invokes another major trope of '70s horror, which Carol Clover calls "Urbanoia." The Buckners are "country people ... beyond the reaches of social law" (Clover 125). As in every redneck horror movie since *The Texas Chain Saw Massacre* (Tobe Hooper 1974), the Buckners come from a world of "tribal law, primitive hygiene, tyrannical patriarchs (or matriarchs), cannibalism, [and] incest" (Clover 136). *Cabin* heavily implies that the Buckners are driven by incestuous desire; Patience writes that her brother Matthew gets a "husband's bulge" from cutting the flesh of his siblings.

Wood argues that American horror took a sharp reactionary turn in the 1980s. While '70s horror had presented *repressed* sexuality as monstrous, '80s horror began to regard sexuality *itself* as monstrous (Wood 171). The older generation of horror creatures had been monsters of the id, famously literalized in the science fiction horror film *Forbidden Planet* (Fred Wilcox 1956). But the creatures of '80s horror were monsters of the superego; their purpose was to punish the sexuality of women and young people (Wood 123). *Cabin* is in intimate dialogue with the '80s slasher film, and it offers a unique solution to the '80s slasher's "sex = death" formula. The Buckners are indeed monstrous superegos, enforcing some ill-defined Puritan moral law. They reject female desire; writing of the sexual arousal her brother derives from torture, Patience says "I do not get like that." The Buckners dutifully punish liberated female sexuality by making Jules their first victim, and they punish all the teens for being young. Wood argues that the "teenie-kill pic" both endorses and punishes the hedonism of its teen protagonists, who are mainly interested in "screwing and smoking dope" (173). This is certainly the strategy of *Cabin*. The film celebrates Marty's prowess with his coffee mug bong, which the heroic stoner wields to fend off the Buckners. But Marty's hedonism is not enough to save him; in the end, all he can do is smoke a joint and await the apocalypse.

In Laura Mulvey's influential psychoanalytic model, the male gaze is motivated by the threat that the female figure presents to the male: the fact that the woman lacks a penis implies a threat of castration (22). Mulvey identifies two possible "avenues of escape" from the castration anxiety that cinema's female figures induce in men: fetishistic scopophilia (pleasure in looking), and sadistic voyeurism (22). The second option is most significant for horror cinema. In horror, as Mulvey argues with respect to Hitchcock's films, "the power to subject another person to the will sadistically or to the gaze voyeuristically is turned onto the woman as the object of both" (24). *Cabin* carefully constructs Hadley and Sitterson as insecure, middle-aged men who are crippled by the castration anxiety that Mulvey describes. In *Cabin*'s very first scene, Hadley complains to Sitterson that even though his girlfriend is not yet pregnant, she is already childproofing their home's drawers and cupboards. The audience's first impression of Hadley is that he is a man who has forfeited all power in order to assume his mandated role within his culture's reprosexual system. Hadley suffers not from a fear of losing his penis, but rather from a broader fear of losing the phallus which is power's master signifier. He plans to pick up some power drills—read, "phalluses"—and "liberate" his cabinets. Here Hadley rebels against the symbolic castration of a fatherhood that he will never attain. But Sitterson is too busy fiddling with his coffee to pay attention to Hadley's doomed revolt: the older technician has already accepted his castration, and now subsists on the meager sensual satisfaction of bureaucracy's favorite drug, caffeine. "Are you even listening to me?" Hadley demands. The frame freezes, and *Cabin* delivers its first "jump scare": the film title appears in large red capital letters, while the audience hears a distorted scream and several notes of eerie "horror movie" music. This suggests that castration anxiety will be among the film's major concerns, as indeed it is. Of *Cabin*'s many monsters, Joss Whedon's favorite is that classic symbol of castration anxiety, the vagina dentata: a ballerina whose face consists entirely of teeth (Pascale 323). Hadley and Sitterson respond to their castration anxiety exactly as Mulvey would predict. They subject Jules and Dana to their sadistic will and to their voyeuristic gaze.

In her 1984 essay "When the Woman Looks," Linda Williams postulated that the horror film contains not just a male gaze, but a radical female gaze that could signify women's sexual power. Williams points out the surprising affinities between horror's monsters and its women: both signify a terrifying sexual difference to their anxious male audience ("Woman Looks" 22). Woman and monster both threaten to take the phallus away from the male viewer. But incredibly, the woman's gaze represents a threat even more horrifying than castration: "the woman's look at the monster offers at least a potentially subversive recognition of the power and potency of a nonphallic sexuality" (Williams, "Woman Looks" 26). This look suggests not just the elimination but the *irrelevance* of phallic sexuality. Williams calls horror "a rare example of a genre that permits the expression of women's sexual potency and desire and that associates this desire with the autonomous act of looking," even if the generic logic of horror means that women must always be punished for this look ("Woman Looks" 34–35). *Cabin* flirts with the possibility of an autonomous female gaze when Dana and Holden are trapped in the Black Room. Dana holds the bare light bulb and uses it to illuminate her gaze. She sees Matthew Buckner's torture tools, and suddenly she understands everything:

Six. "They Want to See Us Punished"

Sitterson (Richard Jenkins), Lin (Amy Acker), and Hadley (Bradley Whitford). Lin's psychoactive drugs ensure that the five teens will play their assigned roles within the formal structure of the slasher film, allowing the middle-aged male technicians to vent their castration anxiety on the teens by punishing them for their drug-induced "transgressions." *The Cabin in the Woods* (2011). Mutant Enemy/Lionsgate.

the horrors of the past, her own status as future victim, and her ability to pick up those monstrous tools and use them to fight her fate.

By far the most influential psychoanalytic interpretation of the American slasher film is Carol Clover's. For Clover, the main generic objective of the slasher film is to kill off sexually transgressive characters (34). An important corollary is that the non-transgressive character may be allowed to survive. This is Clover's Final Girl, the slasher film's female victim-hero. Clover provides a very specific typology of the Final Girl, and *Cabin*'s Dana mostly conforms to this model. The Final Girl "is presented from the outset as the main character" (Clover 39). *Cabin*'s first post-title scene clearly establishes Dana as the film's protagonist. The Final Girl is often a bookworm (Clover 39); in that introductory scene, Curt prohibits Dana from packing the economics textbooks that are the epitome of bookishness. The Final Girl is less sexually active than her friends (Clover 39). That same scene contrasts Dana's vision of the upcoming weekend with her friend's: while Dana hopes to brush up on economic theory, Jules plans to spend the weekend having sex with Curt.

While she may be somewhat sexually active, the Final Girl is at least sexually reluctant (Clover 40). Dana responds cautiously to Holden's sexual advances, and she carefully controls the pace of their sexual interactions.

Most crucially, the Final Girl is masculine. She is "boyish," and often has a masculine or gender-neutral name (Clover 40), such as "Dana" (Parrish ¶ 15). The ostensibly female gender of the Final Girl is compromised by her masculine interests (economics, for example), her sexual reluctance (with someone like Holden), and especially her "active investigating gaze," a gaze that is normally reserved for men, and is usually punished in women (Clover 40). Dana certainly possesses this active gaze and uses it to unearth the vast ancient conspiracy that has led her friends to their deaths. For Clover, the Final Girl offers the slasher an interesting solution to the problem of castration anxiety. Certainly, slashers often resolve the woman's castration by eliminating her (Clover 50), as *Cabin* does with Jules. But the slasher can instead reconstitute the woman as masculine, as it does with Final Girls (Clover 50). This makes possible a radical new form of audience identification. Mulvey's model suggests that the sadistic voyeurism of the young men who are presumed to make up the slasher's audience would lead those men to identify with the monster. But Clover's theory suggests that while the slasher film may *seem* to be "well described by Mulvey's 'sadistic-voyeuristic' gaze" (Clover 8), male viewers can instead develop a masochistic identification with the Final Girl. The Final Girl collapses masculine and feminine categories into a single character "who is anatomically female and ... whose point of view the spectator is unambiguously invited to share" (Clover 61). The male viewer becomes willing and even eager "to throw in his emotional lot, if only temporarily, with not only a woman but a woman in fear and pain" (Clover 61). *Cabin* makes the invitation to sympathize with its Final Girl unusually explicit. Hadley, whose castration anxiety initiates the film, admits that he's actually rooting for Dana; this implies that Dana represents a potential solution to his anxiety. Hadley's admiration is interrupted by the arrival of his "lady," tequila. Yet the audience's sympathies will surely remain with Dana as she fights for her life on the control room's monitor screens, and not with Hadley and his colleagues, who give themselves over to an empty hedonism fueled by alcohol and the mundane classic rock of REO Speedwagon.

Although Clover questions the feminist potential of the Final Girl (53), Linda Williams emphasizes the feminist implications of Clover's theory. Williams understands "horror films' appeal to the emerging sexual identities of its (frequently adolescent) spectators" as sadomasochistic, rather than simply sadistic ("Film Bodies" 7). While "the sadomasochistic teen horror film" may "kill off the sexually active 'bad' girls, allowing only the non-sexual 'good' girls to survive," these good girls become remarkably active and powerful (Williams, "Film Bodies" 8). This gives women in the film's audience an important opportunity for identification. *Contra* Clover, the horror audience does not consist mainly of male adolescents (Short 48). People under the age of 17 made up 45 percent of the audience for the two hugely successful films that initiated the slasher cycle, *Halloween* and *Friday the 13th*—and 55 percent of those under-17s were girls (Nowell 205). The horror audience continues to include a large proportion of women—larger, in fact, than the audiences for other genres, which are often (incorrectly) viewed as more "female friendly" than horror. In 2016, for example, the American horror audience was 49 percent female, with women making up only 47 percent of the overall cinema audience (Lang). For women in *Cabin*'s audience, Dana offers a model of a feminist Final Girl defined not by total sexual abstinence, but rather by "an insistence that sex is conducted on her own terms" (Short 55). She finds Holden attractive and enjoys kissing him (briefly), but she is the one who decides how fast and how far they will go.

Already in 1992, Clover recognized that the ambiguity of the Final Girl's gender meant that the slasher's final character need not necessarily be female. "We may expect horror films of the future to feature Final Boys as well as Final Girls," she predicted (63 note 63). Clover's prediction was accurate. *Cabin* offers a compelling Final Boy: Marty, who survives the Buckners and lives to the film's end. Marty shares a gender-ambiguous name with a classic Final Girl, Marti of *Hell Night* (Tom DeSimone 1981). Like the Final Girl, the Final Boy is typically less sexually experienced than the other protagonists (Elliot-Smith 129). Marty seems to have less sexual experience than his friends, and he certainly has less interest in sex: he is the only member of the group who doesn't at least consider having sex prior to the zombie attack. If the Final Girl is a tomboy, the Final Boy is coded as a sissy (Elliot-Smith 130). Marty explicitly rejects hegemonic masculinity; he denounces Curt's "alpha male bullshit." This aligns him with subordinate and oppositional queer masculinities. Darren Elliot-Smith has recently pointed out that the male audience's cross-gender identification with the Final Girl has strong homoerotic implications: the gay male spectator may identify with the boyish Final Girl who likes boys (but is often afraid to pursue sexual relationships with them) (127). Jack/Judith Halberstam recognizes the radical implications of horror's gender-fluid Final Person. Halberstam argues that the slasher's final character "represents not boyishness or girlishness but monstrous gender, a gender that splatters, rips at the seams, and then is sutured together again as something much messier than male or female" (143).

Halberstam observes that "while women cannot (easily) obtain penises, they can and do pick up chain saws, knives, guns, and ice picks" (156). In other words, penises may be hard to get, but anyone can wield the phallus that is power's signifier. This is what Dana does in the Black Room. She deploys a traditionally masculine sadistic gaze against Matthew Buckner. "You like pain?" she demands as she skewers him with a crowbar. "How's that work for you?" She then penetrates him repeatedly with a knife. This violent penetration of a male zombie by a phallic woman may be read as an assault on the aggressive, patriarchal masculinity that Matthew represents. But Dana's display of phallic power can't save Holden. Indeed, it only foreshadows his death, a mere eight minutes further into the film's run time, when his throat is penetrated by a massive blade. Here the violent penetration of a young man by an older undead man shows that such penetration can also represent a threat to Holden's gentler masculinity. When Holden succumbs to the penetrating blade, Dana learns the limits of phallic sadism, which always leads to destruction. The film's audience learns those limits too, yet they can still take pleasure in the spectacle of a Final Girl who, much like Buffy, wields phallic power against the forces of darkness. Halberstam envisions a "dangerous woman with a chain saw" who channels the "technology of monsters" in order to activate a queer monstrosity, rather than stomping it out (143). Dana ups the ante by deploying the ultimate monster meta-technology: in act three, she pushes the "System Purge" button, releasing all the monsters into the underground facility. This ensures the deaths of Hadley, Sitterson, and the other technicians, opening a space for the queer monstrosity that Dana and Marty share as Final People.

In *Games of Terror* (1990), Vera Dika takes the psychoanalytic interpretation of the slasher in a new direction by showing how the lowered realism of the slasher distances the audience from its extreme violence (23). In *Cabin*, the extreme but quasi-realistic violence of the Buckners gives way to the aggressively unrealistic, over-the-top violence of the third act. Dika's psychoanalytic approach shows that the slasher's representations "effectively mirror ... the psychosexual developmental stage of its young audience," even as the genre's recycled formal elements reveal the superficiality of its representations (25). Thus, *Cabin*'s audience might sympathize with the sexual reluctance that Dana feels following her ill-fated quasi–Oedipal sexual relationship with an older male authority figure (her professor). And that same audience may recognize how absurd it is that Dana occupies the position of the "virginal" Final Girl in the excessively rigorous formal structure of the slasher film. As Jaclyn Parrish notes, Dana's relationship with her professor means that she is actually "guilty of more extensive sexual transgression than the monogamous Jules" (¶ 20), yet Jules is First and Dana is Final. Watching Dana and her friends suffer through *Cabin*'s psychosexual drama may help the film's young viewers figure out how to resolve their own Oedipal conflicts, confront their castration anxiety, and learn safe ways to express their sadomasochistic desires. With any luck, those viewers will grow up to be something better than Hadley and Sitterson, the middle-aged patriarchs whose repressed desires and fears erupt catastrophically out of the earth's depths, ending the world.

"You Have to Be Strong": Cabin's First and Final Girls

The character of Jules allows *Cabin* to critique what is arguably the slasher film's most damaging cliché: the slutty dumb blonde who is inevitably the film's first victim. *Cabin* introduces Jules as an *artificial* blonde: the first thing the audience learns about her is that she has recently dyed her hair. Later, the chemist Wendy Lin (Amy Acker) reveals the significance of this transformation. "Guess how we're slowing down her cognition?" asks Lin. "The hair dye." The male technicians are suitably impressed by this literalization of the slasher cliché. "The dumb blonde," muses Sitterson. "That's artistic." Gerry Canavan notes that *Cabin* uses this device to emphasize the vast difference between the whore trope and the actual character of Jules: "toxic hair dye ... make[s] this monogamous and intelligent college student both sluttier and stupider as required by narrative cliché" (¶ 13). The audience soon learns that the technicians are administering drugs to increase Jules' libido. "Do we pipe it in or do you wanna do it orally?" asks Lin. Sitterson replies, "Ask me that again only slower." The sadistic manipulation of teen sexuality appears to be this middle-aged middle manager's sole source of sexual pleasure.

The chemical manipulation of Jules' sexuality provides an important alibi for her sexual behavior, since it means that she is not responsible for her actions. The film's audience is aware that Jules is under the influence of powerful drugs as they watch her transgress. The friends play "truth or dare," and Marty dares Jules to make out with a taxidermically preserved wolf's head. She does so with great enthusiasm and creativity. Jules makes it clear that she is not just *willing* to kiss the wolf; she *wants* to do it. She concludes the kiss by offering her dead lupine lover a breathless "thank you." This scene represents the zoophilic desire that is common in Whedon's works (see Chapter Four), but also an even more transgressive necrophilic desire.

These transgressions are immediately and severely punished. Curt takes Jules out into the woods, hoping to find some privacy so the two of them can have sex. As Clover notes, the slasher genre "is studded with couples trying to find a place beyond purview of parents and employers where they can have sex, and immediately afterward (or during the act) being killed" (33). Like the slasher film's standard First Girl, Jules does engage in unchaperoned sex. But *Cabin* is careful to emphasize that she does not do so of her own free will. It's cold outside; Jules doesn't want to get naked. The technicians raise the temperature to make her more comfortable. They also release pheromone mists, to ensure that Jules cannot resist Curt's advances. The slasher film may have a powerful generic imperative to punish female sexual agency, but here there is no such agency to punish.

Cabin goes to great lengths to prevent the real-world audience from taking scopophilic pleasure at the sight of Jules' semi-nude body. The male technicians watch Jules strip on their monitors. This is, as Canavan notes, "a self-consciously literal instance of Mulvey's famous male gaze" (¶ 20). Derrick King argues convincingly that "by crosscutting between Jules' nude breasts and Hadley and Sitterson watching, *Cabin* both invites a prurient heterosexual male gaze *and* undermines it" (¶ 14). The film's audience only sees Jules' body on the technicians' monitors. The real-world audience's reaction is mediated by the viewing experience of Hadley and Sitterson. If the technicians can't take pleasure from the spectacle of Jules' nudity, it becomes much harder for the film's audience to do so. And the technicians' male gaze is entirely without pleasure. "Show us the goods," says Sitterson, his voice devoid of desire. When Jules reveals her breasts, the camera immediately cuts back to Hadley in the control room. "Score," he says, with no emotion whatsoever. Hadley is the perfect image of jaded indifference, and this gives the real-world audience an important opportunity to reevaluate his castration anxiety. If the ostensibly heterosexual Hadley is unable to derive any scopophilic pleasure from the sight of a beautiful, naked young woman in the throes of a pheremonally induced arousal which he himself has initiated, then he is, in an important sense, castrated already.

At this point, Jules is viciously killed by the zombie redneck torture family. As Clover observes, in the slasher film, "the murders of women ... are filmed at closer range, in more graphic detail, and at greater length" than the murders of men (35). In a typical slasher, the camera would undoubtedly linger on the beautiful, naked body of the First Girl as the monster tore her to pieces. But *Cabin* is not a typical slasher. Goddard does provide close-ups of Jules' terrified face in the moments prior to her death, and a tight close-up on her eyes as the deadly saw approaches her throat. But then he pulls back to a medium-long shot, as the Buckners prepare to decapitate Jules. The audience doesn't actually see the decapitation at all. Instead, Goddard shows the zombie pulling the saw across Jules' throat, a spurt of her blood, and Curt screaming in the background. Less than ten seconds of screen time elapses between the moment that Jules sees the saw and her death. The scene is also very darkly lit. As Dana Och notes, this darkness "makes the details of Jules' murder and decapitation difficult to see and take pleasure in" (207). Rather than gazing voyeuristically at Jules as she dies a horrible death, *Cabin*'s camera focuses on Sitterson and Hadley. Andrew Patrick Nelson notes that "the emphasis is not on the graphic destruction of Jules' naked body but on the two technicians' *reactions* to it: they stare blankly forward, calmly recite a prayer to the gods, and go about their business" (¶ 18). Their dispassionate reaction denies the film's audience the option of sadistic voyeurism. This illustrates Kristopher Woofter and Jasie Stokes' point that Whedon and Goddard "often undercut the provocative power of spectacle via hypermediated imagery ... that seems intended to place viewers at an emotional remove" (¶ 6). Jerry Metz argues that this scene's critical message doesn't transcend the aestheticization of violence it relies on (¶ 17), but I disagree. By focusing on the sterile environment of the control room and emphasizing the affectless non-response of the technicians, the film radically inverts the aesthetic values which would normally attend the destruction of a slasher film's First Girl.

The ambiguities that surround Dana's gender presentation and sexual desire guarantee her status as a Final Girl. Clover observes that "the scene that reveals the Final Girl in a degree of undress serves to underscore her femaleness" (58 note 57). This scene often occurs towards the end of a film (as in *Alien*), as a way to remind the audience that despite the violent masculine heroics she has just carried out, the Final Girl is at least biologically female. In *Cabin*, however, the underwear scene comes at the beginning of the film. Dana is in her panties when the audience first meets her. Jerry Metz argues that *Cabin* "cannot forget that Dana is cute" (¶ 18), but again I disagree. *Cabin* does establish Dana's cuteness and femininity immediately, but the film does this so that it may slowly render her less cute and less feminine as the narrative progresses. Metz suggests that in this opening scene, Dana "seems self-unaware, innocent of seductive power: boyish, a theoretical 'final girl'" (¶ 18). However, Dana's girlish panties code her as feminine, and she has strong sexual agency here. Jules tries to pin the blame for Dana's recent dating disaster on her unscrupulous professor, but Dana resists this reading. "I knew what I was getting into," she declares. Here Dana insists upon taking responsibility for her sexual choices.

The formal requirements of the slasher film call for the Final Girl to experience a life-or-death struggle which she barely survives; as always, *Cabin* fulfills this requirement while simultaneously subverting it. Dana performs this scene on the dock, but the real-life audience sees it only on the monitors of the control room, and the technicians completely ignore it. Instead of gazing at Dana as she fights for her life, they party hard and congratulate themselves for what they mistakenly believe to be a job well done. This scene is different from Jules' death scene; here the techs do show emotion. But their emotion stems from their erroneous belief that they have accomplished their mission and saved the world; it has nothing to do with voyeuristic pleasure. Again, this forecloses the prospect of sadistic voyeurism on the part of the real-world audience.

Since *Cabin* understands itself as a metaslasher, Dana's supposed sexual innocence is crucial to the film's narrative structure. As Sitterson explains, the virgin's death is optional, as long as she's last (i.e., Final). Although the opening scene establishes quite clearly that Dana is not a virgin, the other characters perceive her as virginal. As Curt leaves the cabin for his ill-fated tryst with Jules, he predicts that Holden will be "busy devirginizing Dana." Shortly thereafter, we see Dana making out with Holden on the couch.

Although Dana is emotionally confused in this scene, she denies her alleged sexual innocence, and emphasizes her sexual experience: "I don't wanna ... I mean I've never ... I don't mean 'never,' but..."

When she encounters the Director at the end of the film, Dana mocks her own alleged virginity: "Me? Virgin?" "We work with what we have," the Director replies drily. This encounter effectively highlights what is different about Dana, for the Director is played by Sigourney Weaver, who famously portrayed the classic Final Girl Ripley in *Alien*. But Dana is a Final Girl for the new millennium, with a stealth sexuality which subtly subverts the sexual innocence of her predecessors. *Cabin* thus culminates in a struggle between two Final Girls. The meaning of the Final Girl trope itself is at stake here. "You have to be strong," the Director tells Dana, meaning that Dana must kill Marty in order to placate the ancient gods and save the world. Confronted with a choice like this, Ripley would have pulled the trigger. Dana makes a different choice and shows a different kind of strength. She chooses to let the world die rather than kill her friend. As Metz notes, "Dana's refusal to be a conventional final girl is so consequential it destroys the planet" (¶ 18). This refusal is motivated by an awareness that the strength of the conventional Final Girl comes at too high a price. Tony Williams points out that the supposedly progressive Final Girl is never entirely victorious at the end of a slasher film; she is often recuperated into the male order (170). The traditional Final Girl may survive, defeat the monster, even save the world. But she does so only by sacrificing her womanhood and her sexuality. As Klaus Rieser says, she is a Final *Girl*, not a Final Woman (379). Dana, on the other hand, is a woman, and she's strong enough to resist an ultimately misogynistic horror culture which permits only a masculine, virginal girl to reach the end of a film's narrative.

"We Are Not Who We Are": Cabin's *First, Middle, and Final Boys*

At first glance, Curt appears to be another horror movie cliché: the heterosexist jock. He calls his friend Holden an egghead, mocks Dana for her supposed virginity, and seems incapable of focusing on any agenda other than having sex with Jules. In short, he seems to embody Whedon's image of the "incredible asshole" who deserves to die. But none of this is his fault, for Curt is really nothing like the hegemonically masculine jock that Wendy Lin's pharmacopeia has created. He's a thoughtful young man "on full academic scholarship," as Marty notes. The disconnect between Curt on drugs and the "real" Curt represents an interesting problem of characterization for *Cabin*. Och argues that "the characters we see have no relationship to the 'real' characters due to chemical manipulation" (206). I argue, however, that there *is* a relationship between drugged Curt and real Curt, just as real-life drug users retain their basic personalities. Though brief, Curt's appearance in the introductory scene at Dana's apartment is sufficient to establish his actual personality. Parrish points out that although Dana is not wearing pants in this scene, Curt doesn't look at her crotch (¶ 19). While Jules suggests that Dana should bring her bikini instead of her economics books (so she can take the bikini off for Holden), Curt suggests a far more intellectual alternative: he recommends a more interesting economics book. Here he treats Dana as an intellectual equal and seems interested in making a mental connection with her, rather than a sexual one.

Curt has established a healthy balance between the sensitivity that American culture codes as feminine and the assertive masculine sexuality that this same culture demands of men. The drugs of Lin's chemistry department upset this delicate balance, reconfiguring Curt as a sexually aggressive alpha male. "Mush, mush!" Curt cries as he pushes Jules out the cabin door, dehumanizing her by speaking to her as one might address a sled dog. "Don't push me around," Jules protests. Her objection is clearly *pro forma*, for she is just as drugged as he is. None of this means, as Och argues, that "with no access to characterization or depth, the investment in psychoanalysis and repression is severed" (206). Lin's drugs are designed to suppress the characters' superegos and liberate their ids. They function as a kind of evil psychoanalysis. While actual psychoanalysis treats neurosis by reducing the demands of the superego for therapeutic purposes (Freud, *Civilization* 108), these drugs suppress the superego so it can be replaced by its monstrous double: the Buckners, whose role is to punish these newly liberated ids. The drugs facilitate what Robin Wood calls the return of the repressed. In that sense, they actually foreground the operation (and failure) of repression.

Curt exhibits a heroism which, though naïve, is noble and potentially inspirational. He rallies his friends and helps them defend themselves against the Buckners. He stages a daring escape attempt, vowing Macarthur-like that he will return to the cabin in the woods, with cops and choppers and large fucking guns, to save his friends and avenge Jules. Mounting his motorbike, Chris Hemsworth's Curt launches himself into the air—incipient Thor! Of course, he crashes into the energy grid which marks the boundary of the cabin environment and plunges to his doom. But his death—unlike the death of the hypersexual jock in a typical slasher—is not meaningless. Curt's death allows Dana to understand the nature of the environment in which she and her friends are trapped. This knowledge will allow her and Marty to descend into the facility to confront the technicians who are manipulating them.

Cabin presents Holden as a young man with healthy sexual appetites; this is important, for it allows the film to show that a man with a strong libido is perfectly capable of controlling his sexual impulses and finding ethical ways to express his sexuality. The other characters understand Holden as a sexual (and sexy) man from the beginning. Jules assumes that he will be the object of Dana's desire before Dana has even met him. Curt introduces Holden to Jules and Dana as the football player with the "best hands on the team." Having positioned Holden as a hegemonically masculine athletic star, however, Curt immediately ascribes to Holden a feminine softness that matches Curt's own: "and he's a sweet guy." Jules, who is already under the influence of the anti-cognitive hair dye, can't resist the obvious sexual allusion. "And he's good with his hands," she says suggestively.

In the famous one-way mirror scene, Holden is suddenly offered the perfect opportunity for sadistic voyeurism. He can secretly watch Dana as she undresses. Here he is the undisputed master of the gaze: if he chooses to, he can take visual pleasure in Dana's naked body, and she need never know. While many men would surely succumb to the temptations of voyeurism here, Holden makes a different choice. After a brief but fierce internal debate, he deliberately abandons his male gaze. He tells Dana about the mirror, and they trade rooms. Dana then watches from the other side as Holden begins to undress. This allows the film to experiment with the autonomous female gaze which Linda Williams links to female desire. However, as Derrick King observes, the film only briefly permits Dana the pleasure and power of the gaze. The camera then pulls back onto Sitterson, who watches on his monitors: the male gaze is reinstated (King ¶ 15).

This scene offers two very different visions of masculinity. The middle-aged patriarch, Sitterson, would deny Dana the power of the gaze, maintaining the male monopoly on looking. Young Holden, however, is an important ally in Dana's struggle to break that monopoly and establish the possibility of an independent female gaze. Not only does *Cabin* suggest that a woman might reasonably seek agency by seizing the power of looking; even more radically, the film suggests that a young man might help her do so, by deliberately denying his own gazing power. Holden seems content to transfer the power of the gaze to the Final Girl. The women who make up almost half of the contemporary horror film's audience may well be grateful for this, and not just because Holden's shirtless, well-muscled torso offers ample opportunities for scopophilia. More importantly, the conclusion of this scene radically reverses the scopic regime that Laura Mulvey once viewed as the very essence of narrative cinema. Not only does *Cabin* show us a woman looking; the film's more radical representational move is to position a man as object of that woman's gaze. *Cabin* emphasizes Holden's to-be-looked-at-ness, a quality that, in Mulvey's model, the structure of cinema reserves for women (Mulvey 26). Gay male spectators may also identify with the active, desiring gaze that Dana directs, however briefly, towards Holden.

Six. "They Want to See Us Punished"

Holden (Jesse Williams, right) can see Dana (Kristen Connolly) in the one-way mirror, but she can't see him. Their positions will soon be reversed, as Holden renounces his male gaze and Dana takes up an active female gaze. *The Cabin in the Woods* (2011). Mutant Enemy/Lionsgate.

Holden's sexual interactions with Dana demonstrate that he understands the importance of consent. Dana makes the supreme understatement that "it's a weird kind of night," and apologizes for her friends' erratic behavior. Holden replies by asking, with the utmost caution, if he would lose points if he told her that he's having a pretty nice time. Here he puts Dana at ease by making explicit the artificial nature of the social situation in which they find themselves: their friends expect that he will try to "earn points" with Dana so he can have sex with her. Dana accepts his gambit. "No, you can tell me that," she says with a shy smile. The next time the audience sees Holden and Dana, they're kissing on the couch. They don't know that Jules has just been killed, but both the real-world and diegetic audiences do: sex leads to death, which leads to sex. Dana pulls away, reluctant to continue. "Hey, nothing you don't want," Holden assures her. Clearly, Holden understands that Dana must give affirmative consent before he goes any further.[1]

Dana smiles, satisfied that Holden respects and values her consent. She is ready to continue kissing him, until Marty, with perfect comic timing, walks by and says, "he's got a husband bulge." By associating Holden's desire for consensual sex with Matthew Buckner's horrific sexual violence,

Whedon and Goddard emphasize the ethical poverty of a slasher genre that conflates the two. Marty's comment suggests that a film genre that condemns *all* expressions of youthful sexuality, even those as responsible as Holden's carefully consensual masculine heterosexuality, must be regarded as ethically bankrupt.

Sitting at the wheel of the RV, Holden tries to formulate escape plans as he and Dana flee the site of Curt's death. "You're missing the point," says Dana. Her active Final Girl's gaze has given her knowledge of their inevitable doom. Holden, the mere Middle Boy in the slasher's formal structure, has no access to this knowledge. Here Goddard and Whedon use the slasher film's unique ability to critique gender stereotypes. "Please, do not go nuts on me, OK, Dana? You're all I've got now," Holden pleads. Even as he tries to perform the traditional role of the male rescuer, Holden basically admits that he needs Dana to rescue *him*. Dana takes a moment to compose herself, then assures him that she's OK, even though she's clearly not. "Good, OK, 'cause I need you calm," says Holden, while the camera gazes at Dana. Holden means well, but when he speaks at Dana from outside the frame and instructs her to be calm, after first asking her not to go nuts, his is the voice of patriarchy disciplining the hysterical woman. The camera switches back to Holden as he says "OK, no matter what happens, we gotta stay cal—." Suddenly Father Buckner's massive scythe thrusts through the back of Holden's neck and out the front of his throat. The symbolism is unsubtle but effective. The dead patriarch thrusts a lethal phallus through the throat of the young man who would have been patriarchy's next generation. Holden's gentler patriarchy is no match for the sexual horror that Father Buckner represents. Buckner once stuffed his wife's belly full of hot coals, in a cruel parody of heteronormative reprosexuality. Now he kills Holden, denying the young man any place in the heterosexual economy.

Cabin's Final Boy is just as sexually reluctant as the typical Final Girl; Marty's sexual apathy contrasts sharply with the sexualities of Holden and Curt, who actively desire Dana and Jules respectively. More importantly, Marty's relative indifference to sex is radically at odds with the slasher genre's assumptions about, and representations of, masculine desire in general. The genre is predicated on the notion of an aggressive male sexuality that produces monsters when repressed and earns young men lethal punishment when given expression. Yet Marty manages to bypass the slasher's sexual economy. He dares Jules to make out with the dead wolf (which he mistakes for a moose), but it's clear that he just wants to see something weird because he's really high. He has little sexual interest in Jules. When Jules tries to give Holden a lap dance, Marty's exquisite sarcasm indicates that he would prefer not to receive such attention: "this is so *classy*."

Curt is actually offended by the sexual indifference that Marty shows

Six. "They Want to See Us Punished"

Jules. Curt's drug-induced hegemonic masculinity requires him to compete with other men for women, even when those other men are unwilling to do so. "Like you wouldn't want a piece of that," Curt insists, pushing Marty to embrace an aggressive masculine sexuality that is alien to him. But Marty won't have it. "Can we not talk about people in *pieces* any more tonight?" he asks. This line serves several important functions. First, it challenges the dehumanizing objectification of young women that is the slasher's stock and trade. Second, it foreshadows the imminent slasher plot, which will begin shortly, with the decapitation of Jules. Third, it suggests that Marty is at least somewhat aware of his status as a character in a metaslasher film, which means that he shares with Dana the Final Person's special knowledge of the diegetic environment in which they operate.

Drug-addled Jules takes Marty's objection as an invitation to direct her seductive power towards him. "Oh! Are you feeling lonely, Marty?" she purrs. But she has badly misjudged his feelings: Marty is alone, not lonely. Jules leans in close to Marty. "Marty and I were sweeties in our freshman hall," she announces to everyone. "We made out *once*," Marty objects. "I never did buy that ring." Marty may once have experienced some low-level desire for Jules, but only enough to motivate a single makeout session, and even this minimal desire has now faded. Jules and Curt's bizarre insistence that Marty conform to the slasher's reactionary stereotype of masculine desire is so unnatural that it allows Marty to break through the illusion and theorize their predicament. When Jules takes a toke off Marty's joint and insists, quite implausibly, that the two of them are still close, Marty announces that he has "a theory about all this." "That's our cue to bail!" Curt declares. Within minutes, Jules will be dead, punished for encouraging Curt to express the same aggressive masculine sexuality that Marty just rejected.

Meanwhile, Marty has not only recognized the supreme artificiality of the slasher's sexual conventions (and by extension, those of American society as a whole). He has also understood the *meaning* of that artificiality. "*We are not who we are*," he realizes after Curt and Jules leave the cabin. Marty now sees that he and his friends are not the character clichés that the slasher genre requires them to be, nor are they the rigid archetypes that Hadley and Sitterson need them to be if they hope to appease the elder gods. They are authentic (though fictional) people, whose humanity has been stripped away by two sadistic narratives: the diegetic narrative of *Cabin*, and the extra-diegetic narrative of the slasher genre, which *Cabin* both embodies and critiques.

Perpetually high, Marty occupies the position of the Fool in the slasher's formal structure. Yet ironically, Marty is the smartest, most capable, and most aware of the three young men who travel to the cabin. This, along with his unique position outside the slasher's sexual economy, means that he alone is able to understand the degree to which he and his friends are being manipulated. Marty uses the language of puppetry to describe this sinister manipulation. "You're not seeing what you don't wanna see," he tells Dana. "Puppeteers." While Jules and Curt are having sex/death and Dana and Holden are making out on the couch, Marty is alone in his bed, reading Winsor McCay's classic early comic strip *Little Nemo in Slumberland*. When he hears voices in his room, Marty takes an explicit stand against the puppeteers. "Enough! What are you saying? Huh? What do you want? You think I'm a puppet, huh? You think I'm a puppet, gonna do a little fucking puppet dance? I'm the boss of my own brain, so give it up!" Strangely, Marty does exactly what the voices suggest, and goes for a walk. Yet this is where his active resistance begins. During the zombie attack, Marty discovers the camera hidden in his bedside lamp. When Judah Buckner attacks him, he defends himself with the coffee mug bong. When Judah drags him off to his apparent death, Marty discovers the entrance to the underground facility. Together with Dana, he eventually engineers the destruction of that facility and the "puppeteers" who run it.

While the survival of a Final Girl would typically signal victory for the good guys, Marty's survival signals the precise opposite. Because he has survived, the elder gods will rise. The Director tells him that if he lives, the world will end. "Maybe that's the way it should be," Marty declares. "If you gotta kill all my friends to survive." Here the Final Boy bravely declares that if the world can only be saved through the fulfillment of the slasher's sex/death equation, then the price is too high. Even better, in its final minutes, *Cabin* boldly manipulates slasher tropes to produce a dramatic critique of heterosexist culture. Marty has violated all expectations about the sexual behavior of a male character in a slasher film. He respects women and treats them as human beings, rather than objects or potential sexual conquests. He does not seek or engage in unauthorized sex, or indeed any sex at all. The film's conclusion suggests that such behavior is radically incompatible with the sexual culture of the slasher film, and with the American culture that the slasher represents. The existence of a straight man who is motivated by something other than sexual desire is intolerable to these cultures. At the end of *Cabin*, the arrival of such a man spells the end of a world which privileges aggressive male sexuality and denies female sexual agency. "Maybe it's time for a change," Marty concludes. This change could include a rejection of male sexual aggression, and an authorization of female sexual power.

Incredibly, *Cabin* offers a happy apocalypse. The end of *Cabin*'s world is also the end of our world, but like Dana and Marty, we are left with the strange impression that this may be a good thing. The destruction of a world founded on patriarchy, heterosexism, and hegemonic masculinity is a productive event. It clears the way for a new world, one in which men and women might share power as equals. In such a world, monsters of the id could roam free, rendered harmless by the absence of repressive superegos. Castration anxiety, Oedipal conflicts, and sexual cruelty might eventually come to be seen as relics of history. Most importantly, this new world would not punish its young people for being young, nor would its artifacts of popular culture portray such unjust punishment. Young people could love one another sexually and otherwise, without fearing that such love must always equal death. To imagine such a world is to dream of utopia, and if the promise of utopia isn't enough to make the thought of apocalypse bearable, it should at least motivate us to challenge a culture which remains stubbornly unwilling to distinguish sex from death.

Seven

"To Bind Me, or Undo Me"

Dominance and Submission in Joss Whedon's Much Ado About Nothing

At the very end of the sixteenth century, William Shakespeare wrote a comedy called *Much Ado About Nothing*. This was, in many ways, Shakespeare's most modern play. It did much to subvert early modern European tropes of gender and sexuality. While Shakespeare wrote many powerful women, *Much Ado*'s Beatrice is perhaps the strongest: a proto-feminist character who consistently and insistently refuses to the accept the constraints that early modern England's patriarchal culture imposed upon women. About four centuries after Shakespeare wrote his play, Joss Whedon wrote and directed a film version of *Much Ado*, set in present-day Southern California. Whedon carefully preserved the feminist themes that he found in Shakespeare's text. Like Shakespeare's play, Whedon's film is very much about women's power. Yet Whedon also managed to expand, enhance, and update *Much Ado*'s representations of female power, not only in his treatment of Beatrice, but also through the less obviously powerful Hero, and the villainous Conrade (a traditionally male character who is female in Whedon's film).

Whedon is almost ideally suited to direct Shakespeare. When the trailer for Whedon's 2013 film declared that "Joss Whedon and Shakespeare are a Match Made in Heaven" (Rabb and Richardson 11), it was exaggerating less than movie trailers typically do. Whedon has a longstanding interest in Shakespeare. He studied Shakespeare as a schoolboy at Winchester in England (Pascale 28). Whedon had already been working on Shakespeare for about a decade when he filmed his production of *Much Ado*. Starting in the fall of 2000, Whedon frequently held Shakespeare readings at his home (Pascale 167). He invited actors with whom he had worked regularly, such as Alexis Denisof, who had previously worked with the Royal Shakespeare Company (Pascale 369). Whedon and his band of players were particularly fond of a reading of *Much Ado* in which Denisof played Benedick to Amy Acker's Beatrice (Pascale 359). Shortly after completing principal photography on *The*

Avengers, Whedon assembled a cast that included Denisof, Acker, and many other Whedonverse regulars, wrote a screenplay based on Shakespeare's play, and filmed *Much Ado*. The film was shot entirely at Whedon's Santa Monica home, a large Mediterranean-style house that had been completely redesigned and renovated by Whedon's then-wife, the architect Kai Cole. This house would not be out of place in Shakespeare's Messina. Whedon's cinematographer Jay Hunter says, "it's almost like Kai designed the house for this movie to be shot in" (quoted in Pascale 367).

Whedon declares that with *Much Ado*, "Shakespeare was deconstructing the romantic comedy while he was inventing it" (*Much Ado: A Film* 18). Whedon has also been known to deconstruct a genre while simultaneously participating in it, as he did with the slasher film in *The Cabin in the Woods* (see Chapter Six). Whedon suggests that Shakespeare's *Much Ado* "completely obliterated the tropes of romantic love, while ultimately championing love itself" (*Much Ado: A Film* 11). Again, this is a very Joss Whedon thing to do. Throughout his career, Whedon has consistently critiqued the outward forms of romantic and sexual love, while upholding love itself as a vital value and a crucial (if sometimes unattainable) goal. Whedon's adaptation of *Much Ado* thus fits perfectly into his broader *oeuvre*. Whedon says that *Much Ado* gave him a chance to explore "the more mature, married love," which he regards as "a much deeper, more adult, and more interesting kind of love [than pre-marital love]" (quoted in Pascale 360).

Shakespeare's play provides a thorough and accurate account of early modern Europe's male-dominated system of kinship and alliance. As Michel Foucault observes, this alliance system structured relations between the sexes throughout Europe until the modern system of sexuality emerged in the eighteenth century (106). Within the aristocratic class that most of *Much Ado*'s characters inhabit, sexual relations were unthinkable outside of the alliance system. This system allowed men to form, maintain, and defend social, economic, and political relationships with other men by using the bodies of women as objects of exchange within the sexual economy. Unsurprisingly, the characters in *Much Ado* generally operate according to the logic of this system, for it's unlikely that a Shakespearean audience could have understood a story that took place outside that system, even if Shakespeare had been able to tell it. Yet Shakespeare also managed to include a proto-feminist critique of this system. By modernizing *Much Ado*, Whedon was able to amplify the feminist themes that were always implicit in Shakespeare's text. Rhonda Wilcox argues that Whedon's modernization of the play creates an important "cognitive counterpoint" effect in the audience, who perceive the differences between Elizabethan England and twenty-first-century Southern California "in a way that forwards one of Whedon's major themes, his awareness of gender inequality" ("Translation" ¶ 14). Building on Wilcox's interpretation,

Rabb and Richardson argue that "Whedon's modernized *Much Ado* shows us that some moral progress has been made since Elizabethan times, while still suggesting that we all have a long way to go" (99). The film's sense that European culture has made some progress, but not nearly enough, is especially strong with respect to the social structures that inform sexual relations.

Whedon remained faithful to Shakespeare's original play, while simultaneously creating a new version of *Much Ado* that is uniquely relevant to present-day American culture in general, and to contemporary concerns about gender and sexuality specifically. To achieve this, he employed two main strategies, one linguistic, one visual. First, he cut substantial amounts of dialogue from the play. Whedon's cuts were strategic. He cut lines that seemed to limit women's power and agency, as well as those that seemed to present the alliance system's male dominance as inevitable. This changed the connotations of the remaining lines, making the women characters more powerful, and the men more willing—even eager—to accept women's power. Second, Whedon employed every visual technique in the film director's tool kit for the same purpose: to create a world full of powerful women, and to show the film's audience that both women and men can find happiness by embracing women's power. Throughout the film, Whedon uses every element of *mise-en-scène* to achieve this, including set design, props, costume, and lighting. Whedon and his cinematographer Jay Hunter use scene composition, shot blocking, and framing to particularly good effect. These techniques drive home the film's visual argument without ever distracting from the brilliance of its language. The words are still Shakespeare's, though there are fewer of them, and their connotations have changed. But the visuals belong entirely to Joss Whedon, his cast and crew. In 1598, *Much Ado About Nothing* was a play by William Shakespeare; in 2013, it was a film by Joss Whedon and company.

These changes allow Whedon's film to focus more on sexual dominance and submission than Shakespeare's play did. The concern for sexual power relations that was already present in the play becomes the main focus in Whedon's film, and the nature of that concern changes. Shakespeare's play understood sexual power primarily in terms of the marriage institution that elite men used to negotiate alliances with other elite men. This institution disregarded women's consent, and did not consider the possibility that women might be unwilling to serve as objects of exchange among men. Shakespeare therefore wrote about sexual power primarily in a male-dominant/female-submissive mode. Though he allowed his male characters to experiment with submission, Shakespeare offered little by way of an alternative to male-dominant marriage. By contrast, Whedon's film emphasizes female dominance and male submission. This is, of course, consistent with the representational strategies that Whedon has pursued throughout his career. As an alternative to the patriarchal marriage institution that he and Shakespeare both criticize,

Whedon offers a very different kind of sexual relationship, one that is based on negotiated female dominance and consensual male submission.

Beatrice and Benedick represent the clearest endorsement of female dominance and male submission in Whedon's film. Beatrice has always lamented women's lack of social and political power, and she has always challenged the male alliance system responsible for that lack. But Amy Acker's Beatrice recognizes more clearly than any other that her sexual power over Benedick offers a possible partial solution to that problem, for this power might allow her to participate in the system of alliance not as an object, but as a subject with her own agency. While Benedick has always succumbed to Beatrice's allure, previous Benedicks have used techniques such as cuckoldry jokes to suggest that their "submission" to Beatrice occurs within the framework of a patriarchal marriage institution which will inevitably reinscribe the relationship as male dominant. But cuckoldry only makes sense in a society where men compete with each other by establishing and exchanging ownership claims over women. In order to imagine a different world, Whedon cut some of Shakespeare's cuckoldry references and changed the connotations of the rest, allowing Benedick to consent actively to Beatrice's dominance. Alexis Denisof performs Benedick as an eagerly submissive man who wants to share power openly with a dominant woman, so that she may operate within the world of men. Whedon's Beatrice/Benedick shows that consensual DS relationships enable a radically egalitarian sharing of power between the dominant and submissive partners, and that these relationships offer the prospect of happiness for those who are brave enough to defy society's constraints and pursue them.

In Shakespeare's *Much Ado*, the submissive Hero confirms women's status as passive objects of exchange in the early modern marital economy. In Whedon's version, Jillian Morgese's Hero emphasizes the quiet strength that Hero's submissive martyrdom requires. More importantly, she shows the ethical limits of such martyrdom. At the end of the film, Hero switches briefly to the dominant role in order to express her righteous innocence. Her accuser (and would-be husband) Claudio (Fran Kranz) must submit to her as he acknowledges her righteousness; this suggests that their future relationship will be more egalitarian, and that this Hero will possess a sexual agency that previous Heroes lacked.

Whedon uses the villain Don John (Sean Maher) as a cautionary example of male dominance run rampant. Shakespeare's text and most productions of the play show Don John exercising a straightforward political dominance over his henchman Conrade; this is an example of the homosocial DS that informs early modern relationships between men. In Whedon's film, Conrade (Riki Lindhome) is Don John's henchwoman and lover. Conrade's blind, unthinking submission to the villainous Don John emphasizes the dangers of a male-dominant/female-submissive sexual relationship that is unconstrained by ethics. Her submission also highlights the vital role that women play in maintaining the patriarchal system of exchange and alliance. Interestingly, Conrade is dominant in her non-sexual political relationships with fellow henchperson Borachio (Spencer Treat Clark) and constables Dogberry (Nathan Fillion) and Verges (Tom Lenk). This shows that Conrade is not entirely submissive, and that she is aware of the possibility of female dominance. Her failure to explore such dominance in her sexual relationship therefore looks like a missed opportunity. It appears that Don John's seductive dominance has prevented Conrade from becoming the Whedomme she might otherwise have been.

"Good Lord, for Alliance!": Women's Sexual Power as a Challenge to Messina's Homosocial Male Alliance System

Shakespeare's *Much Ado* features powerful examples of what Gayle Rubin calls "the traffic in women," and what Eve Kosofsky Sedgwick calls "male homosocial desire" (Rubin, "Traffic"; Sedgwick, *Between Men*). In Shakespeare's fictional Messina, as in his real England and in early modern Europe more broadly, men use women as tools to negotiate alliances with other men. These alliances generally take the form of dominance/submission relationships. In their role as facilitators of male-male DS relationships, women have no significant agency of their own. In her gloss on Claude Lévi-Strauss' theory of kinship systems, Rubin notes that in these systems, men form links with one another by transacting women, "the woman being a conduit of a relationship rather than a partner to it" ("Traffic" 174). Rubin argues that the system prefers a passive female sexuality that responds to the desires of others, i.e., men ("Traffic" 182). I would go further; I believe that the system actually *requires* women to remain sexually passive, because any female sexual agency threatens to undermine the crucial male-male DS relationships by interfering with the exchange of women upon which those relationships are based. This is why Hero's alleged infidelity is so terrifying to Claudio: it threatens the alliance he hopes to make with Hero's father, Leonato. While Lévi-Strauss presents kinship systems as inevitable, and indeed as "the root of romance" (Rubin, "Traffic" 201), Rubin investigates what Lévi-Strauss ignored: the devastating psychological impact that "conscription into systems of kinship" has on individuals, especially women ("Traffic" 188). Operating in Lacanian mode, Rubin interprets the phallus as signifying "the difference between 'exchanger' and 'exchanged,'" i.e., the difference between men and women ("Traffic" 191). In Rubin's model, women can't possess the phallus themselves, but only transmit it to men, which means that the phallus is "an expression of the transmission of male dominance" ("Traffic" 192). This is why Beatrice's insistence that *she* must possess the phallus, which is to say the dominance conventionally reserved for men, is so important.

Sedgwick emphasizes that these kinship systems require the existence of male homosocial desire, by which she means the affective force that informs important social relations between men (*Between Men* 1–2). Sedgwick is especially interested in the homosocial desire she finds in Shakespeare's Sonnets; I argue that such desire is also a powerful force in Shakespearean comedies such as *Much Ado*. With Sedgwick, I argue that Shakespeare presents a kind of "male-male love" that "is set firmly within a structure of institutionalized social relations that are carried out via women: marriage, name, family" (*Between Men* 35). In Shakespeare's works, women are a means to an end, and that end is the establishment of relations between men. Sedgwick argues that in the early Sonnets, "women are merely the vehicles by which men breed more men" (*Between Men* 33). I argue the same with respect to *Much Ado*. This is why Benedick, who otherwise abhors the institution of marriage, justifies it on the grounds that "the world must be peopled" (2.3.197).

Sedgwick concludes that Shakespeare's work contains a nominally heterosexual male desire which takes "the form of a desire to consolidate partnership with authoritative males in and through the bodies of females" (*Between Men* 38).[1] This male desire is structured around homosocial dominance and submission. In *Much Ado*, it manifests in Leonato's tireless efforts to form a partnership with Count Claudio via the body of Leonato's daughter, Hero. Leonato hopes to establish dominance over Claudio by becoming his father in law; at the same time, Leonato wants to confirm his submission to his social superior, the authoritative Don Pedro, by acknowledging that "his grace hath made the match" between Claudio and Hero (2.1.229–230). In a world where nothing is more important than bonds between men, men can enjoy sharing "sexual territory" (i.e., women) with other men, for here they exercise a power over women that all men share, and by doing so, they may grow closer to "more fully entitled males" (Sedgwick, *Between Men* 36–37). This is why Leonato can casually question Hero's paternity when he introduces her to Don Pedro, saying that "her mother hath many times told" Leonato that he is Hero's father (1.1.78). For men of middle rank like Leonato, cuckoldry and uncertain parentage are small prices to pay for the opportunity to build social alliances with entitled men like Don Pedro.

The action in *Much Ado* consists largely of various plots by the men of Messina to build or destroy alliances between men, by facilitating or impeding the exchange of women. When he learns of Claudio's desire for Hero, Benedick immediately invokes the mechanism of exchange, asking if Claudio would buy her (1.1.133). Claudio, who has a dangerously romanticized view of the traffic in women, wonders if the world can "buy such a jewel"

(1.1.134). Benedick knows full well that relations between men and women in early modern Messina are governed by a logic of exchange: "Yea, and a case to put it into" (1.1.135). Benedick reveals the system's contradictions. He sees the heterosexual marriage institution that makes alliances between men possible as a threat to those same alliances. Alexis Denisof is sitting next to an enormous dollhouse when his Benedick imagines that he may never see "a bachelor of three-score again." The dollhouse represents the heterosexual domesticity which threatens to rob Benedick of his comrade Claudio. While Benedick views male-female domesticity as a threat to the comradeship of men, masculine camaraderie can actually thrive on the cultivation of heterosexual relationships. In Whedon's film, when Claudio and Don Pedro see that they have succeeded in their efforts to link Beatrice and Benedick, they perform that iconic twenty-first-century gesture of masculine homosociality: the fist bump. These two manly soldiers have bonded over their matchmaking.

As the highest-ranking man in Messina, it is Don Pedro's prerogative to facilitate the proposed alliance between Claudio and Leonato. Don Pedro therefore offers to woo Hero on Claudio's behalf. The dominant Don Pedro is the man most willing to ignore women's consent and treat them as objects of exchange. He consistently describes courtship with the language of force. He promises to "take [Hero's] hearing prisoner with the force and strong encounter of [his] amorous tale" (1.2.250–251). In Whedon's version, this promise is immediately followed by the sex scene between Don John and Conrade. This codes Don Pedro's plot as unethical by associating it with Don John's evil schemes (which are, ironically, intended to thwart Don Pedro's plan). Don Pedro associates courtship with force again as he works to facilitate an alliance between Benedick and Leonato by gulling Benedick into marrying Beatrice. Don Pedro declares that he would have thought Beatrice's "spirit had been invincible against all assaults of affection" (2.3.102–103). Leonato uses similar language when, in a desperate attempt to excuse Hero's allegedly active sexuality, he suggests that Claudio may have "vanquish'd" her resistance "and made defeat of her virginity" (4.1.41–42). In this world of male alliances, there is no room for female sexual agency, and all heterosexual relationships are understood as male-dominant relations of force.

Leonato has no illusions about the nature of the social and economic exchange that he is trying to negotiate with Claudio. His initial invitation is explicit: "Count, take of me my daughter, and with her my fortunes" (2.1.229). In Whedon's version, Hero must awaken her father from his drunken slumber so he can make the offer: Clark Gregg performs Leonato as a patriarch so comfortable in his role that he can almost literally give his daughter away in his sleep. Claudio is equally happy to view his betrothal as the exchange relationship that it clearly is. Interestingly, however, Claudio views himself as an object of exchange, and perhaps one of lesser value than Hero. "I give away myself for you and dote upon the exchange," he assures her (2.1.233–234). This suggests that Claudio is insecure in his position as a male exchanger of women. Claudio lacks masculine power, as Benedick insinuates later when he calls him "my Lord Lack-beard" (5.1.172).

Claudio's weakness points to significant fissures in Messina's system of male power relations. As Carol Thomas Neely notes, Claudio's passivity ensures that male authority remains "lame and diffused" throughout the play (42). Claudio idealizes women in general, and Hero in particular. But as Neely argues, this idealization is an ineffective defense against Claudio's sexual desire and anxiety (37). And Claudio's unrealistic veneration of women is not just an inadequate treatment for his own sexual insecurities. It also points to a dangerous fear of, and hostility towards, women's sexuality. Valerie Traub argues persuasively that "the flip side of Claudio's romantic idealism is his misogyny, and both stem from a fear of female erotic power" (*Desire and Anxiety* 42). Traub suggests that Claudio represents a strategy of containment which is designed to control female sexuality and restrict women's sexual power ("Jewels, Statues, and Corpses" 132). Claudio's sexual fears flow from a recognition that independent female sexual agency constitutes a serious threat to the male alliance system that he inhabits.

As the proposed union between Claudio and Hero falls apart, Don Pedro's principal concern is how this will impact his relationship with his right-hand man. Don Pedro stands "dishonoured," his dominance and authority in question now that everyone believes he has "gone about To link [his] dear friend [Claudio] to a common stale" (4.1.58–59). But the rules of the early modern alliance system provide an easy solution to this nuptial disaster. Since women are infinitely interchangeable within this system, Claudio need only accept a different woman from Leonato, and all will be well. Leonato invents an imaginary daughter of his brother and offers her to Claudio. He emphasizes that this fictional niece satisfies the requirements of early modern political economy: "she alone is heir to both" Leonato and his brother (5.1.257).

Although Benedick initially views women's sexual power as a threat to the male world he loves, he eventually learns to accept such power, and even cherish it. Thus, Benedick could potentially help restructure the alliance system in a way that would promote women's agency. As Neely argues, the lovesickness that Benedick initially feels towards Beatrice is driven by "anxieties about sexuality and submission" (49). Benedick is understandably afraid to submit to the powerful and terrifying Beatrice. Yet he overcomes this fear by the end of the play. Indeed, his decision to submit to Beatrice marks what is arguably the play's real dramatic climax and establishes the Beatrice/Benedick story as the play's "main" plot. Shakespeare's Benedick (though not Whedon's) closes with a cuckoldry joke: "there is no staff more reverend than one tipped with horn" (5.4.115). Neely suggests that Benedick uses the cuckoldry motif to transform "a potentially humiliating submission in marriage into a proof of [his] power" (56). In the male alliance system, men wield a weaponized female sexuality to cuckold other men, and women are merely instruments of that cuckoldry. Many Shakespearean men, including Claudio, fear women's sexuality for this reason: they know that other men can use it against them. But at the end of *Much Ado*, Benedick discovers that Beatrice's sexual freedom produces not a threat, but a form of sexual power that he finds intoxicating. It makes him into a "giddy thing," and this is his conclusion (5.4.104): he is ready and willing to accept Beatrice's dominance. Tellingly, Whedon cut the cuckoldry line from Benedick's final speech. This dramatically changes the valence of that speech, transforming Benedick from a potential cuckold into a submissive man who has finally made peace with his submissive nature.

Don John's main narrative function is to interfere with the alliance between Claudio and Leonato, by undermining Claudio's proposed marriage to Hero. As a villain who lacks power but seeks it, Don John can make the sexual nature of Messina's alliance system explicit; male characters who hold social power usually don't speak openly about this, for to do so would be to problematize the structure of sexual relations upon which their power depends. In Whedon's film, Don John fondles Conrade under a bedsheet without looking at her as he discusses "the most exquisite Claudio" with Borachio. Claudio is "exquisite" in Don John's eyes not in the sexual sense, but in the sense that by forming an alliance with Leonato, Claudio stands to gain the social power to which Don John aspires. Don John will use his sexual relationship with Conrade to undermine this alliance. This is a very manly thing to do, for to be fully a man in the early modern alliance system required having instrumental use of a woman (Sedgwick, *Between Men* 40). But Don John makes similar instrumental use of Borachio, assuring him that "whatever comes athwart [Claudio's] affection ranges evenly with" Don John's (2.2.5-6). Sean Maher's hand hovers near his heart as he offers Don John's affection to Borachio. This gives the offer a slight homoerotic connotation, but Don John is still operating within the male alliance system, and what he offers to share with Borachio is not sexual pleasure, but the power that men may gain by using women. Borachio understands this, for when Don John asks how he can thwart the marriage, Borachio immediately reveals that he will use a woman, Margaret (Ashley Johnson), as an unwitting pawn. Whedon highlights the exploitative nature of Borachio's scheme by adding a flashback scene that shows Borachio having sex with Margaret while she is in the guise of Hero; Ashley Johnson follows Whedon's stage directions closely in this scene, looking "lost and unhappy" (*Much Ado: A Film* 125).

A comedy requires a happy ending; at the end of *Much Ado*, it appears that Claudio will marry Hero and Benedick will marry Beatrice (after dancing). But before Benedick goes off to dance with Beatrice, he must promise to devise "brave punishments" for Don John (5.4.119–120), the man who tried to destroy the male alliances that these two marriages enable. Shakespeare emphasizes the need to punish those who would subvert the alliance system by making this the last line of the play. Whedon has Denisof say it a few lines earlier, so that the last line in the film is Benedick's advice to Don Pedro and to himself: "get thee a wife." Since this Benedick understands "wife" to mean a dominant woman who represents a far greater challenge to the alliance system than Don John's attempted villainy, this gives the film a very different ending. The film's priority is not to recuperate the alliance system by punishing the villain, but rather to reform the system so that it will admit female social and sexual power.

Although Shakespeare presented the male alliance system as the fundamental aspect of European society that it was in his day, Shakespearean comedy has always understood that female sexual power could represent a serious challenge to that system. As Linda Bamber argues, "in the comedies, the feminine challenges the status quo … through its command of socially subversive forces like sexuality" (29). Shakespearean comedy has no illusions about the constraints that the alliance system places on women's agency. Yet Shakespeare's comedies emphasize the subversive potential of female sexuality in a way that gives the heroines of these plays more agency than women characters typically enjoyed in Elizabethan theater and makes the sexual relationships which these women pursue unusually egalitarian. As Marianne Novy argues, women remain active throughout the action of the comedies, and their relationships develop via mutuality (7). Novy notes that in the comedies, "women's gestures of submission are often balanced by similar gestures from the men" (43). By adding male submission and a corresponding female dominance to the generally male-dominant tradition of Elizabethan theater, Shakespeare's comedies create a potentially egalitarian structure of sexual power relations. As Novy argues, this emphasis on equality is particularly evident in romantic comedies like *Much Ado About Nothing* (22).

On the surface, *Much Ado*'s Hero appears to be a typically passive early modern woman who functions mainly as an object of exchange for men. Yet although Hero seems to be weak and unthinkingly submissive, she possesses a surprising hidden power. In one sense she is, as Harry Berger argues, the "most male-dominated of heroines" (14). But as Lisa Jardine argues, in Shakespeare, the chaste woman falsely accused of sexual misdeeds has a kind of heroic dignity (189). Jardine suggests that "Hero's willing submission to martyrdom" gives her a "halo of female heroism" (189). Hero's submission is active rather than passive, willing rather than coerced. Counter-intuitively, this "Heroic" submission actually represents a kind of female power. To be sure, the patriarchal system of sexual relations regards this power as destructive (Cook 193). The naïve Hero doesn't understand the sexual power she has over men (especially Claudio), so she cannot control that power. And even if she could control it, that would only make her sexual power more dangerous to the male alliance system. Yet if Hero's sexual power were framed not as a dangerous threat to the dominant system of social relations, but rather as a legitimate challenge to a social structure that oppresses women, then the feminist potential of that power could be realized. Shakespeare's sixteenth-century text can't support such a reframing; his play provides no evidence that Hero will learn to wield her sexual power to her advantage, or that her future marriage to Claudio will be anything like egalitarian. However, Whedon's twenty-first-century film is able to frame Hero's power as feminist.

Beatrice's sexual power has always been more obvious than her cousin's, and the feminist potential of that power has been easier to see. Berger suggests that Beatrice "models an enviable alternative" to "Hero's pliant submission" (19). Carol Cook argues that Beatrice participates in Messina's masculine sexual ethos even as she flouts its conventions (190). More precisely, I would say that Beatrice rejects the masculine convention that makes women passive objects of exchange, so that she can become an active subject in the alliance system. Beatrice is wary of the sexual submission that she assumes marriage will require of her (Neely 47). She resists this submission by acting as the "merry 'shrew'" whose tongue resists all efforts at containment (Traub, *Desire and Anxiety* 16). Valerie Traub argues that this resistance enables "a limited form of subjective agency" (*Desire and Anxiety* 18), but I argue that this agency is not as limited as Traub believes. By the end of the play, Beatrice has attained a strong form of agency which enables her participation in a system of power relations that is usually understood as exclusively masculine.

Given Shakespeare's early modern context, it is surprising that his Beatrice can speak openly, explicitly, and even critically about the status of women within the male alliance system. Given Whedon's twenty-first-century context and the overall thematic trajectory of his work, it is equally *un*surprising that his Beatrice delivers a powerful critique of the impact that the male homosocial order has on women. Beatrice is the only character in *Much Ado* who understands how thoroughly this order depends upon the traffic in women. She is thus the only one who can give the system its proper name. "Good Lord for alliance," Beatrice declares as Claudio and Hero profess their mutual affection (2.1.241). Whedon's screenplay adds a comma and an exclamation mark, which emphasizes how the needs of alliance drive every sexual relationship in Messina: "Good Lord, for alliance!" (*Much Ado: A Film* 94). Beatrice excludes herself from the female position in the alliance system: "thus goes every one to the world but I" (2.1.241). She is an active, dominant woman in a system that reserves those traits for men. She concludes by apparently resuming the passive female position she has just rejected: "I may sit in a corner and cry, 'Heigh-ho for a husband'" (2.1.242–243). But the sarcasm dripping from Amy Acker's voice as she delivers this last line makes it clear that her Beatrice is mocking that position.

When Don Pedro offers to get Beatrice a husband, she replies that she would rather have one of his father's getting and asks if he has a brother (2.1.245–246). Beatrice has no interest in participating in the alliance system as a passive woman. If she did, she would maximize her power within the system by aiming high: she would only consider a husband of princely rank. But she would rather participate actively, like a man. While men use women as instruments of alliance, Beatrice uses Benedick as the instrument of her vengeance on Claudio. In Whedon's film, when Claudio asks Benedick to use his wit, Benedick shows his pistol in its holster and says, "it is in my scabbard: shall I draw it?" Denisof's Benedick is willing to wield the phallus against Claudio, but he does so on behalf of Acker's Beatrice, and the phallus is clearly hers. The next time Beatrice and Benedick meet, he is eager to kiss her, but she refuses until he confirms that Claudio undergoes his challenge, at which point she is happy to kiss him. Benedick finally embodies Beatrice's desire: not for mere pleasure or even for love, but for the power to participate in the system of alliance as an equal.

This heroine of Shakespeare's most modern play models a distinctly modern form of female agency: that of the sexually dominant woman. According to Jardine, Beatrice's shrewishness guarantees that her man will be emasculated or cuckolded; the "domineering wife," Jardine argues, "brings shame and humiliation" to her husband (112). But *Much Ado* suggests that Beatrice will be a *dominant* wife rather than a domineering one, and that makes all the difference. Beatrice promises to do nothing more than graciously accept Benedick's willing submission and give him the dominance he clearly craves. As Novy argues, this renders them "capable of a more complex and less asymmetrical love relationship, in which a more complete sharing is possible" (28). When combined with Benedick's male submission, Beatrice's female dominance enables one of the most egalitarian relationships that can be found in Shakespeare, or indeed anywhere in Elizabethan theater. By emphasizing the relationship's consensual DS dynamic, Whedon makes it even more egalitarian.

"Some Steel in Her Eyes": Dominance and Submission in Whedon's Hero/Claudio

It was "very important" to Whedon that his Hero have "real poise of presence and power" (Temple). Whedon acknowledges that he cast relatively unknown actor Jillian Morgese as Hero in part because "there's a strength there" (*Much Ado: A Film* 19). He admits that Morgese's strength is "a kind of strength that you wouldn't notice at first" (*Much Ado: A Film* 22), but that simply means that she's ideal for the part of Hero, whose strength has always been of the subtlest kind. Whedon recognizes that Morgese's Hero is just one of many possible interpretations of the character, but he also insists that she is faithful to Shakespeare's text. "As much as possible I tried to give her character power—it's in the lines if you choose to play them that way. She did," says Whedon (Temple). Under Whedon's direction, Morgese was able to find the Heroic strength that had always been implicit in the source text and make it explicit.

Morgese's Hero shows how a woman can gain strength through submission. We see this when Hero, wrongly accused of infidelity by Claudio, protests her innocence to her father Leonato. Morgese plays the Heroic martyr, declaring forcefully that if Leonato can prove the charges against her, she will forfeit her relationship with him, and even her life: "Refuse me, hate me, torture me to death!" Hero willingly submits to her father's judgment. This act of radical submission is enough to make Leonato doubt Claudio's accusations, and remember his love for his daughter. Whedon's stage directions have "Leonato embrace ... his daughter almost as roughly as he rejected her" (*Much Ado: A Film* 149). Clark Gregg, who had trouble marshaling the cruelty that Leonato is meant to show Hero in this scene (Whedon, *Much Ado: A Film* 19), looks relieved as he holds Morgese's head against his shoulder with his fist.

Whedon reinforces the audience's perception of Hero's strength by making an important change to the play's fifth and final act. Claudio believes that Hero is dead. Leonato requires him to hang an epitaph upon her tomb and sing it to her bones (5.1.251–252). Shakespeare's text for Act 5, Scene 3 calls for Claudio to do this "at the monument of Leonato" (i.e., the family tomb), where Claudio dutifully sings his "solemn hymn" to Hero (5.3.1–11). Whedon replaces Scene 3 with a wordless, candle-lit funeral procession, led by Claudio and Don Pedro. This allows Whedon to add a bit of staging that is crucial to his interpretation of Hero's character. In Whedon's version, Morgese's Hero stands out of sight and watches her own funeral procession. Whedon's stage directions call for her to watch Claudio with "some steel in her eyes, but some sympathy too" (*Much Ado: A Film* 175). Morgese accomplishes this admirably, silently conveying Hero's quiet strength. She draws this strength in part from the powerful Beatrice, who holds her gently during this scene: although they have no formal DS relationship, the submissive Hero can take strength from the dominant Beatrice. Rhonda Wilcox notes that in this scene, Hero and Beatrice stand *above* Claudio and company, where they deploy a female gaze that emphasizes their power and their bond ("Swords"). Fran Kranz's Claudio is "genuinely mournful," as Whedon's script requires (*Much Ado: A*

Film 176). Compassion is evident on Morgese's face as Hero watches Claudio grieve. This scene efficiently establishes Claudio's contrition, and Hero's willingness to forgive him. More importantly, it establishes that Hero has the strength to witness the powerful impact that her "death" has on Claudio, and on the social world of Messina.

Hero's simulated death removes her from Messina's sexual economy and underscores the vital role that she was to have played in establishing an alliance between Claudio and Leonato. Claudio has undertaken to marry Leonato's fictitious niece, but he's hardly enthusiastic about this marital backup plan. The indirect alliance that Claudio might establish with Leonato by marrying his niece would be weaker than the one he could have formed by marrying Hero. The funeral gives Claudio and Don Pedro the opportunity to realize all of this, and to recognize that Hero's "death" has substantially weakened the Messinan alliance system as a whole. This ensures that Claudio and Don Pedro will be relieved and grateful when they learn that Leonato's "niece" is actually the living Hero, whose marriage to Claudio can now be consummated as planned, thus permitting the establishment of a strong, direct alliance between the groom and the father of the bride.

Before that can happen, however, Claudio must acknowledge that he has grievously wronged Hero. Morgese's Hero bears the emotional burden of her own funeral with a quiet dignity, grace, and poise. This gives her the courage and moral authority to confront Claudio. "One Hero died defiled," she declares, "but I do live, and surely as I live, I *am* a maid." Following Whedon's script, Morgese delivers that last phrase in a "steely" voice, to match the steel in her eyes as she watched her funeral (*Much Ado: A Film* 179). She emphasizes the word "am"—"I *am* a maid"—to underscore that she has always behaved ethically, while Claudio has not. Whedon then uses a powerful bit of blocking to show that Claudio recognizes and accepts Hero's power. Morgese is as tall as Kranz (Wilcox, "Swords"); in this scene, she is standing on a step, which makes her half a head taller than him. As Morgese unequivocally proclaims Hero's innocence, Kranz takes her hand and bows his head deeply. Whedon has Jay Hunter shoot over Kranz's shoulder, so the audience sees a look of quiet contemplation on Morgese's face as Hero savors the righteous power she now holds over Claudio.

Here at the end of the film, the characters switch positions in the sexual power structure. Claudio acknowledges that he has wronged Hero and submits to her. Hero briefly takes on the dominant role. Her dominance is born of submission and is enabled by the strength that an authentic submission requires. Whedon made this directorial choice deliberately. "There's a reason she's standing above him and a reason he bows to her at that moment," says Whedon (Temple). This expertly blocked scene equalizes the power relationship between Hero and Claudio, a relationship which has been radi-

The generally submissive Hero (Jillian Morgese) briefly assumes the dominant role in order to confront Claudio (Fran Kranz), declaring "surely as I live, I *am* a maid." *Much Ado About Nothing* (2013). Bellwether Pictures/Lionsgate.

cally unequal for most of the film. Hero may now submit to Claudio in matrimony, but the audience is left with the clear impression that her submission will be consensual and negotiated. Claudio seems to have learned that Hero's submission is provisional and conditional. If he wishes to resume a dominant position in their relationship, he must accept her limits and boundaries. Most urgently, he must *trust* her. Whedon's version of Hero and Claudio's story concludes in a way that shows how a woman may play the female role in the male alliance system while maintaining her dignity, her sexual agency, and her personal power.

"Bid Me Do Any Thing for Thee": Dominance and Submission in Whedon's Beatrice/Benedick

Whedon represents the Beatrice/Benedick relationship as a study in the benefits of consensual female dominance and male submission. To facilitate this representation, Acker and Denisof alter the typical gender presentation of their characters. A scene that feminizes Benedick parallels one in which Beatrice briefly performs masculinity to mock phallic power. This suggests that the characters are going through complementary journeys on the way to their unconventional positions of submission and dominance. The set for the scene where Benedick critiques and rejects marriage is the bedroom of Whedon's daughter Squire, who was about six years old when *Much Ado* was filmed. The film is in black and white, but Whedon's script reveals that this is a "little pink room" (*Much Ado: A Film* 61). Benedick is juxtaposed against Barbie dolls. Benedick enters the closet, literalizing the metaphor of his secret sexuality, i.e., male submission. He comes out of the closet in a frilly hat and declares that he will live a bachelor. His words denote a rejection of marriage, but by surrounding Benedick with signifiers of femininity, Whedon and Denisof radically revise the connotation of those words. Now Benedick's speech signals a rejection not of marriage as such, but rather of the prescribed masculine marital role within the male homosocial alliance system, i.e., the dominant role.

Benedick's feminized gender presentation changes the meaning of his concluding speech in this scene. A translucent ornamental butterfly hovers next to Benedick's face as he declares that if ever he should bear the yoke of marriage, then "in such great letters as they write 'Here is good horse to hire,' let them signify under my sign, 'Here you may see Benedick the married man.'" Denisof whines the last line while miming the cuckold's horns, as if to remind the audience that cuckoldry is a constant threat in competitive, male-dominant marriage (though not, perhaps, in female-dominant marriage). When Denisof's feminized Benedick delivers these lines, they signify his rejection of a patriarchal marriage institution that would force any man, however submissive, to take on the dominant marital role. The feminized Benedick insists upon his right to occupy the submissive marital position conventionally assigned to the wife.

Fortunately for Denisof's Benedick, Acker's Beatrice wants to take on the traditionally masculine dominant role in their budding relationship. In the scene where Beatrice discusses marriage with Leonato, Acker holds up what Whedon's script describes as "various manly masks" as her character prepares for the masquerade (*Much Ado: A Film* 72). As Beatrice discusses the importance of manliness in a potential husband, Acker holds up a mask with a long, phallic nose. This mask resembles one of the masks worn in the Venetian *Carnevale*. There is not too much distance between the early modern Venetian and Messinan cultures, and the Venetian *Carnevale* featured masked balls of the kind that Beatrice is preparing for in this scene, as well as aerialists like the trapeze artists who perform during the film's masquerade scene (Killinger 94–95). The mask in question derives from the *commedia dell'arte*, and it represents *Il Medico della Peste*, the plague doctor (Killinger 95). In early modern Italy, physicians who treated plague victims wore these masks as protection against the miasma that was thought to cause the disease. Contemporary viewers who understand this historical context may read the masks' failure to ward off plague as a more general failure of phallic power. Meanwhile, the presumably larger segment of the audience that doesn't recognize the historical significance of the mask may simply see it as a masculine phallus which can easily be wielded by a dominant woman like Beatrice. Either reading will allow viewers to understand that Acker's Beatrice uses the mask to perform a satirical masculinity, and to mock the phallic pretensions of men. She brandishes the mask as she asserts that she is not the woman for "he that is less than a man," invoking her right to demand a husband who will satisfy her sexually. In Shakespeare's time, this would have connoted the patriarchal culture's investment in female pleasure, which was thought to be necessary for conception to occur (Traub, *Desire and Anxiety* 141). When Acker delivers these lines while wielding the mask-phallus, Beatrice's speech instead connotes women's sexual agency, and a woman's right to seek pleasure for her own sake.

Acker then takes up another, more feminine mask. Placing this sparkly, curved mask on her face, Beatrice says, "Yes, faith; it is my cousin's duty to make curtsy and say 'Father, as it please you.'" Moving the mask to Hero's face, she continues, "But yet for all that, cousin, let him be a handsome fellow, or else make another curtsy and say 'Father, as it please *me*.'" By placing the feminine mask on her own face as she parodies submission to patriarchal authority, then moving it onto Hero's face as she endorses women's rights to pleasure and choice, Acker's Beatrice authorizes an important redefinition of the feminine. She shows Leonato, Hero, and the audience a path away from traditional submissive femininity, towards a modern dominant femininity. Hero wears this same mask to the party, suggesting that she is sympathetic to Beatrice's argument. Beatrice also brings a feminine mask to the party, but doesn't wear it: her confident female dominance needs no disguise.

During the party, Beatrice spends some time mocking Benedick to a group of revelers that includes Benedick in disguise. As she speaks, she casually fends off "the wayward hands of a drunk fellow" (*Much Ado: A Film* 76). The drunken man signifies the male sexual entitlement that is endemic to a social system based on the traffic in women. The dominant Beatrice resists the sexual advances of this entitled fool with such practiced ease that her reflexive resistance doesn't interrupt her discourse at all. She calls Benedick "a very dull fool," and declares that "none but libertines delight in him." But since viewers already suspect that Beatrice delights in Benedick, they may draw the logical conclusion: that Beatrice is herself a libertine. While Whedon's audience may be able to imagine Acker's sexually independent Beatrice taking an interest in the kind of libertinage made infamous by Sade, it is easier to imagine her practicing the safe and consensual sexuality that bears Sade's name, and the conclusion of her speech does make her sound like a (lower case) sadist. She asserts that Benedick "both pleases men and angers them, and then they laugh at him and beat him." Acker's dominant, sadistic Beatrice might enjoy delivering such a beating, while Denisof's submissive, masochistic Benedick might enjoy receiving it.

The negotiations between Beatrice and Benedick culminate in the climactic scene where the two confess their love for one another, and Beatrice bids Benedick avenge her cousin's honor. In the first part of the scene, their communication is very indirect: the two characters speak from the edges of the frame, into mirrors, and to the backs of each other's heads as they discuss what a man might do to right the wrong that has been done to Hero. It is Benedick's *reflection* who declares that he believes Hero has been wronged, and Beatrice's reflection who says "what the man might deserve of me who would right her." Like so many Whedonesque DS relationships, this one begins in the mirror stage of the Lacanian Imaginary. "Is there no way to show such friendship?" asks Benedick's reflection. "A very even way," replies Beatrice's mirror image. Then, turning to face Benedick and the camera, she concludes, "but no such friend." Here Beatrice moves the conversation into the Symbolic as she challenges Benedick to obey her will. Beatrice walks into the next room; Benedick follows. "May a man do it?" he asks, addressing the back of Beatrice's head. Looking away from him, she confirms, "it is a man's office, but not yours." By facing away from Benedick as she states that he cannot fulfill her will, Beatrice issues a double challenge. Her words and her body language combine, urging Benedick to prove her wrong.

Suddenly, Benedick is in the center of the frame, brightly lit with sunlight from the window as he declares, "I do love nothing in the world so well as you." This dramatically highlights the strength of Benedick's desire to submit to Beatrice. Now Beatrice occupies center frame. Staring at Benedick,

The submissive Benedick (Alexis Denisof) "love[s] nothing in the world so well as" the dominant Beatrice (Amy Acker). She loves him "with so much of [her] heart that none is left to protest." *Much Ado About Nothing* (2013). Bellwether Pictures/Lionsgate.

she almost blinks, and the audience sees that she recognizes the truth of his words. Confused, she confesses nothing and denies nothing. "By my sword, Beatrice, thou lovest me!" Benedick swears. But Beatrice warns him, "do not swear, and eat it." Benedick must be sincere in his submission. He must offer his sword, which is to say his power, if and only if he is truly committed to the project of serving Beatrice's will. Benedick protests that he does indeed love her. Whedon and Hunter shoot over Denisof's shoulder, framing Acker's face as she touches his cheeks and declares, with tear-filled eyes, "I love you with so much of my heart that none is left to protest." With admirably convincing passion, Acker and Denisof then implement Whedon's stage direction that "they kiss, fiercely" (*Much Ado: A Film* 154). They are still embracing when Denisof delivers Benedick's declaration of total submission over Acker's shoulder: "Come, bid me do any thing for thee." Benedick is requesting orders from his Mistress.

Beatrice clearly feels herself becoming that Mistress. Acker grabs Denisof's hair as she delivers the ultimate assertion of Beatrice's dominance directly into his ear: "Kill Claudio." These two words test the limits of Benedick's submission. He refuses. And so Beatrice, who has already taken on the conventionally masculine dominant role in this nascent sexual relationship, now expresses her desire to take on a masculine social role in the impending conflict with Claudio. Beatrice boldly asserts her right to intervene in a system of social alliances that her culture views as the exclusive province of men: "O, that I were a man!" Whedon calls this line "one of the most important things Shakespeare ever wrote" (Orr). What Whedon finds extraordinary about this speech is that Shakespeare felt he needed to spell out his critique of gender and sexuality so baldly (Temple). But given how thoroughly the early modern alliance system depended upon men's power over women, perhaps Shakespeare's critique had to be blunt to be effective. To the extent that men still attempt to control women and regulate their sexuality, Shakespeare's critique remains perfectly relevant four centuries later. It is a critique that Whedon has developed throughout his career. Acker's Beatrice summons all her righteous wrath at a patriarchal system of gender and sexuality that denies her the agency to seek her own revenge. She raises her hands as if to clench Claudio's throat, then slams them down and cries out the window, at the very world that so restricts her and Hero and all their sisters, "O God, that I were a man! I would eat his heart in the marketplace." Benedick tries to interrupt, but Beatrice won't have it: "Sweet Hero! She is wronged, she is slandered, she is *undone*."[2]

Beatrice continues her righteous tirade: "A goodly Count! O that I were a man for his sake! Or that I had any friend would be a man for my sake!" Acker smacks Denisof in the chest as she delivers that last line, then points an accusatory finger at him, indicating that *this* Beatrice doesn't need to be a man, so long as she can be a Mistress. But she must be one of the two, or she will die a woman with grieving. The world of men denies her and all women social power, but if she gains sexual power over a man, she can perhaps claim social agency. Resolution flickers across Denisof's face as Benedick makes his decision. He swears "by this hand, I love thee." With barely contained fury, Acker's Beatrice gives him a withering gaze and tells him to "use it for my love some other way than swearing by it." This is a direct order. If followed, it will confirm Beatrice's dominance over Benedick. Benedick pauses only long enough to confirm that Beatrice believes in her soul that Claudio has wronged Hero. Then he accepts Beatrice's offer of dominance. On his knees, Benedick kisses the hand of Beatrice, who is now undeniably his Mistress. As Wilcox observes, Whedon films this interaction in a way that shows Benedick honoring Beatrice's power: Benedick lifts Beatrice's hand as he declares that "by this hand, Claudio shall render me a dear account," and the camera's focus suggests that it is Beatrice's hand that will duel Claudio (Wilcox, "Swords").

Benedick and Beatrice spend the rest of the film confirming that he will now be ruled by her will. When Beatrice asks for which of her good parts Benedick first suffered love for her, Benedick agrees that "suffer love" is "a good epithet! I do suffer love indeed, for I love thee against my will." It makes perfect sense that Benedick would experience love as a kind of masochistic *jouissance*: he would enjoy the suffering. Yet he claims to suffer love against his will. Sedgwick notes that "will" has a variety of sexual connotations in Shakespearean English, including desire, penis, and vagina (*Between Men* 38). The meaning of Shakespeare's line is ambiguous. But when Denisof's explicitly submissive Benedick says it, he appears to mean that he loves Beatrice according to *her* will, which he values more highly than his own. When Benedick entreats the friar "to *bind* me, or undo me; one of them," Denisof strongly emphasizes the second word of the first phrase: "to *bind* me." His delivery indicates that the bondage he seeks is more than that of simple matrimony. Benedick intends to bind himself to Beatrice as her submissive. This explains the urgency of his request. If his powerful need to submit to Beatrice's loving authority goes unmet, he will indeed be undone.

Thankfully, Beatrice experiences the need for dominance that is the complement of Benedick's submissive need. Beatrice has already confirmed, to herself and to the audience (though not yet to Benedick), that she shares his interest in a bondage born of love. After she is gulled by Hero and Ursula (Emma Bates), Beatrice speaks to the Benedick of her mind's eye: "if thou dost love, my kindness shall incite thee To bind our loves up in a holy band." This parallelism allows the audience to read Benedick's later declaration of his desire to be bound as the natural counterpart of Beatrice's dominant desire to make Benedick bind his love to hers.

By the end of the film, Benedick has become so submissive that he can only define his will in terms of the will of others, especially Beatrice, but also

Leonato. He tells Leonato "my will is your good will may stand with ours, this day to be conjoin'd In the state of honourable marriage." Denisof stutters "ma—marriage" in a way that will remind many viewers of the priest in *The Princess Bride* (Rob Reiner 1987), who had similar difficulty pronouncing this powerful word. Benedick's difficulty indicates that he has not yet had enough time to absorb the crucial lesson about marriage that Beatrice has been trying to teach him: that marriage need not serve the interests of the male alliance system, but can instead be reconfigured as an egalitarian institution that may serve the needs of dominant women and submissive men. Benedick is unable to make a formal marriage proposal to Beatrice. When she asks him, "what is your will?" he is literally speechless. He reaches up to loosen the collar of his shirt, and finally answers with a question: "Do not you love me?" This non-response indicates that Benedick is trapped in the dilemma of a submissive man: since his will is to follow *her* will, he can only articulate his by asking her to define hers. But without some explicit statement of his desire to submit to her in marriage, Beatrice can't articulate her will, either. In fact, their mutual wills can't be spoken at all. They can only be written, in the sonnets that Beatrice and Benedick compose to one another, which Claudio and Hero reveal. The dominant and submissive desires that Beatrice and Benedick feel are too powerful for speech; they can only enter the Symbolic via the written word. But no sooner do these desires step tentatively into the Symbolic than they immediately withdraw into the Imaginary: Benedick stops Beatrice's mouth with a kiss.

This Imaginary kiss does not mark the beginning of an unequal marriage, as Carol Neely argues it has done in previous productions of *Much Ado* (56). The film ends with Benedick recommending the joy of submission to Don Pedro. The last lines of the film are Benedick's: "Prince, thou art sad; get thee a wife." He repeats the last line as his newly minted Mistress grabs his necktie and uses it as a leash to lead him onto the dance floor: "Get thee a wife." Neely argues that at the end of Shakespeare's play, "male control is reestablished, and women take their subordinate places in the dance" (57). Whedon's film ends very differently: female control is established, Beatrice takes her dominant place in the dance, and the ancient male-dominant system of sexual relations and social alliances gives way to a modern system of sexual and gender equality.

"To the Death, My Lord": Dominance and Submission in Whedon's Don John/Conrade

Whedon did not focus only on Beatrice and Shakespeare's other female characters; he also made several traditionally male characters into women,

Seven. "To Bind Me, or Undo Me"

casting his sister-in-law Maurissa Tancharoen as Balthasar the singer, and Romy Rosemont as the sexton (Wilcox, "Swords"). Perhaps most significantly, Whedon made Conrade a woman. The decision to cast Riki Lindhome as Conrade was motivated partly by a desire to "get more women in the play," and partly by a desire to "have more sex" in the film (Whedon, *Much Ado: A Film* 27). But this change does not simply add more sex; it adds a specific kind of sex. Conrade is one of the play's antagonists, a minion of Don John. In Whedon's film, the female Conrade is also Don John's lover. This allows for what Whedon calls "villain sex, which is nice and twisted" (Nicholson). This twisted villain sex permits the film to model an unethical form of sexual dominance and submission, one which contrasts sharply with the ethical DS of Beatrice and Benedick. Importantly, the film does this without creating the kind of homophobic representation which would inevitably emerge if Don John had or desired a male lover. In Ronald Eyre's 1971 Stratford production of the play, for example, Richard Pasco performed Don John in a way that suggested the villain's malevolence was motivated by a frustrated sexual desire for Claudio (Wells 169). In 1971, audiences and critics may have been willing to tolerate a production in which the play's main villain provided its only representation of same-gender desire. But Whedon understood that this damaging equation between villainy and homosexuality would not be acceptable in 2013. When Whedon considered presenting Don John as "the evil gay man," he decided "that didn't feel like that would fly" (*Much Ado: A Film* 27).

Whedon gives Conrade and Don John the steamiest sexual relationship in the film. This sexualizes Don John's villainy and extends that villainy to the willing Conrade. Conrade finds her lover's plots and schemes irresistible, a fact which Don John easily exploits. He uses her as a pawn to advance his plots, a minion with benefits. While Beatrice only pushes Benedick to follow her will rather than his own because she knows that's what he wants, Don John never even considers the possibility that he may be pushing Conrade to go against her own will. Indeed, it doesn't seem to occur to him that she may *have* her own independent will. Thus Don John models an unethical male dominance, one that is enabled by Conrade's blind, unthinking female submission. The result is a villainous male-dominant relationship that is quite different from Beatrice and Benedick's consensual female-dominant relationship. Indeed, even the mostly male-dominant relationship that Hero and Claudio finally manage, at great cost, to negotiate looks ethical next to Conrade and Don John. While Hero's deliberate submission actually makes her stronger, Conrade's thoughtless submission only weakens her.

The film's most sexual scene begins with Conrade and Don John in bed together, scheming. Whedon's camera lingers on Riki Lindhome's long legs, moving slowly up her body. Conrade tells her lover that it is impossible for him to take "true root" in an alliance system dominated by his brother Don

Pedro "but by the fair weather" that Don John makes himself. Don John spreads Conrade's legs immediately after she says this, which sexualizes the "fair weather," i.e., Don John's impending attempt to gain power in the alliance system at the expense of his brother. It also confirms the instrumental role that Conrade will play in Don John's scheme to subvert Messina's alliances, which parallels the instrumental role that Hero will play in facilitating those alliances. Don John moves up between Conrade's legs and unbuttons her polka dot dress, kissing her between her breasts. He grabs her breast through her black bra just as he declares himself a "plain-dealing villain," thus making explicit the connection between his alliance-shattering villainy and his sexual relationship with Conrade. He complains that he is only trusted with a muzzle. "If I had my mouth," he swears, pausing to kiss Conrade deeply, "I would bite." Clearly Conrade wants him to bite; she offers him sexual power over her as a means to gain the political power that he lacks. In the short term, Conrade hopes to convert Don John's political impotence into sexual potency. "Can you make no use of your discontent?" she purrs, biting her lower lip seductively.

As Don John prepares to make *all* use of his discontent, Conrade wraps her legs tightly around his lower back and sighs softly, but the couple are interrupted by Borachio. As Borachio reports the intelligence that will enable the villainous plot, Don John slips his hand beneath the bedsheet and begins to pleasure Conrade. While the men conspire, as men do, to gain political power within the alliance system, Don John exercises his sexual power over Conrade. Suddenly Don John stands up, abandoning his lover so he can embark upon his scheme. He bids Borachio "come, come," but Conrade does *not* come, which clearly frustrates her. Nonetheless, she closes the French doors behind Borachio and pledges herself to Don John: "To the death, my lord." She seals this oath with a smile and a long, hard kiss. But the audience sees this kiss only through the thick, wavy glass of the doors, which suggests the ethical weakness of the sexual relationship that the kiss represents. Conrade has committed herself to a scheme she barely understands, for the sake of the political power that Don John seeks but has not yet won. Yet even that potential power is enough to spark her irresistible desire to submit. To satisfy that desire, she must give herself to Don John completely. She cannot truly consent to his dominance, for it is unthinkable that she could say no to him. Untroubled by ethics, Don John is happy to accept her thoughtless submission.

Interestingly, Conrade is dominant with everyone *except* Don John, which suggests that his villainy has transformed a potential Whedomme into a mindlessly compliant servant. Borachio's name is quite similar to the Spanish word for drunk (*borracho*), and he is certainly drunk when he explains his evil scheme to Conrade. Indeed, he admits that he will "utter all" the details of his plot "like a true drunkard." When he calls out, too loudly, for Conrade, she makes it clear that she is unimpressed with this drunken fool: "Here, man. I am at thy elbow." Conrade is smoking a joint in this scene. She hands the joint to Borachio right before she asks him to move forward with his tale. This suggests that she hopes the marijuana may loosen his tongue, as indeed it does. The hit that Borachio takes off Conrade's joint is much too big, however, which sends him into a coughing fit. When he recovers, he describes his scheme so loudly and so explicitly that even the incompetent night watchmen who eavesdrop nearby cannot fail to comprehend his villainy. When the watchmen arrest the conspirators, Conrade immediately tries to dominate them with false submission, much as Black Widow often does. "Masters, masters," Conrade says with a broad smile. She also prudently discards the joint, which has already served its purpose.

During Conrade's interrogation, Verges (Tom Lenk) plays the "bad cop." When he lays his hands on Conrade, she shoves him away; he slams into the wall and lands on the floor. Having effectively established her physical dominance over Verges, Conrade immediately establishes psychological dominance as well. She calls him "coxcomb," a derogatory term for a foppish man who is overly concerned with his appearance. This is certainly ironic, given that Verges wears a cheap, ill-fitting suit and sports an absurd mustache. Coming from a woman, this line reinforces the audience's perception of Conrade's potential dominance by implying a flexible system of gender roles: if a man can be seen as an effeminate coxcomb, then a woman like Conrade can be seen as powerful in conventionally masculine ways. The slap fight between Conrade and Dogberry confirms this reversal of traditional gender norms. Nathan Fillion performs Dogberry as a completely ineffective fighter; Lindhome's performance suggests that Conrade could easily thrash the inept constable. The best that Dogberry can manage is to call Conrade a "naughty varlet." Conrade is not even slightly submissive as she gets up in Dogberry's face and calls him an ass. In fact, she is the most dominant person in the room. Conrade's dominance of Borachio, Verges, and Dogberry implies that her sexual submission to Don John is an aberration.

Thus, Whedon's film subtly subverts the sexual power dynamics of Shakespeare's play, while challenging the male alliance system that stands behind Shakespeare's representations of sexuality. The film reduces Claudio's male dominance while tactically increasing Hero's female dominance, allowing her to submit to Claudio from a position of strength. The centerpiece of the film's argument about sexual power is the Beatrice/Benedick relationship. Here Whedon's *Much Ado* offers unabashed admiration for loving female dominance coupled with consensual male submission. Thus, Beatrice takes her place among the Whedommes, whose stories Joss Whedon has been telling for two decades. Finally, the film offers Conrade and Don John as a model of how *not* to do DS. The film's representations of these three relationships will allow Shakespearean actors, directors, critics, and scholars to see new feminist potential in this canonical comedy. These representations also enable Whedon's audience to leave the art house cinema with a newfound appreciation of consensual, egalitarian sexual DS, or with a renewed recognition of the benefits such DS might bring to those who practice it.

Afterword: Reconsidering Whedonversal Sexualities in the #MeToo Era

Joss Whedon and his wife Kai Cole separated in 2012 and divorced in 2016. In August 2017, the Whedon Studies and fan communities were dismayed to read a blog post in which Cole alleged that over the course of their marriage, Whedon had multiple affairs with actresses, fans, and friends (Cole). Cole claimed that Whedon hid these affairs from her. She said that he made her doubt her own instincts regarding his alleged infidelity, a practice commonly known as "gaslighting." Her gravest accusation, from the perspective of the overlapping feminist and Whedon Studies communities, was that Whedon was guilty of "hypocrisy" for "preaching feminist ideals" while taking away her right to make choices for her own life and body "based on the truth" (Cole). A spokesperson for Whedon released a vague and unsatisfactory response, which claimed that Cole's account contained unspecified "inaccuracies and misrepresentations" (quoted in Cole).

The Whedon Studies community has struggled to come to terms with the Whedon/Cole controversy, which was discussed extensively at the 2018 Slayage conference at the University of North Alabama in Florence. Although there is no consensus regarding the controversy or how scholars ought to respond to it, there is significant support for the following points, and I would like to argue in favor of them. A simple issue of alleged marital infidelity would be a personal matter between Cole and Whedon. There are, however, three issues which demand serious consideration on the part of the Whedon Studies community. If Whedon gaslighted Cole, making her doubt herself when he was, in fact, doing what she accused him of doing, that would constitute psychological and emotional abuse. If it were possible to confirm that Whedon abused Cole in this way—a very large "if"—that would justify a re-evaluation of Whedon's personal relationships with other women.

Second, if Whedon had affairs with his employees, including young actors in the early stages of their careers, that would constitute a serious breach of professional ethics. If it could be confirmed that Whedon had such affairs, that would justify a re-evaluation of his *professional* relationships with women. Again, this is a big "if." No one other than Cole has come forward to accuse Whedon of inappropriate sexual behavior. No one, including Cole, has accused Whedon of rape or sexual assault. Whedon's mentor, Wesleyan film studies professor Jeanine Basinger, argues that "Joss Whedon is not Harvey Weinstein" (quoted in Sides). Nonetheless, the relationship between a television producer and the actors in his employ is undeniably a power relationship. If a producer asked one of the actors working on his show for sex, it is entirely possible that the actor would feel unable to refuse. Active consent would not be possible in such a situation.

The third and most urgent issue is the question of how this controversy affects our understanding of Whedon's claim to be a feminist and, most crucially, our sense of how feminism operates in his works. Whedon would not be the first feminist to have extra-marital affairs, nor would he be the last. I do not believe that marital infidelity, or even ethically dubious workplace sex, should automatically disqualify a person from being a feminist. Whedon's self-professed feminism has always struck me as largely aspirational. It's a vision of what he wants the world to be, and what *he* wants to be, rather than a vision of the world and himself as they are. He has acknowledged, for example, that he understands the motivation of the "terrible objectifying male" (Lavery and Burkhead 58). If Whedon has not always lived up to his own feminist ideals, that does not negate those ideals; it simply shows that all of us, including Whedon, must work harder to realize them.

I also believe that Whedon's work retains its feminist value. As I have argued throughout this book, all of Whedon's works are profoundly collaborative. The works that bear his name are the creative product of numerous writers, actors, cinematographers, editors, costumers, lyricists, comic book artists, and so on. Many of these creators are feminists who have worked hard to put powerful feminist themes and ideas into these works. We would be doing these creators a grave injustice if we were to reclassify their works as anti-feminist because of the alleged actions of the man whose name signifies those works.

Changing public perceptions of Joss Whedon simply remind us that historiography matters. Into every generation of scholars an interpretation is born. We can and should reassess the Whedonverses, and the sexualities they portray, from a contemporary vantage point. A particularly strong case can be made for re-evaluating *Buffy*'s Xander. Over the years, Whedon has discussed Xander's sexuality in ways that now seem, at best, tone deaf. In a 2003 interview, for example, Whedon declared that "Xander got so much goddamn tail" on *Buffy* (Lavery and Burkhead 74). This objectifying comment reduces women to a body part that is characteristic of nonhuman animals: the tail. And there is no sense here of the respect and dignity that Xander would accord Dawn the centaurette, tail and all, when Whedon wrote "Time of Your Life" five years later (Whedon and Moline; see also Chapter Four). Perhaps by 2008, Whedon, and through him Xander, had developed a stronger sense of the dangers of objectification. Yet however sensitive the comic book Xander may have become, the better-known televised Xander undeniably exhibited troubling attitudes towards women.

In an essay that won a well-deserved Mr. Pointy paper award at the 2018 Slayage conference, Renee St. Louis reconsidered the Xander character in the context of the #MeToo movement. St. Louis observed that although *Buffy* usually presents Xander as a sympathetic character, he often exhibits sexist or even misogynistic views. He is often possessive and controlling, and he frequently objectifies women. Yet Xander gets a narrative "pass": his behavior is either excused or blamed on the women around him. Other characters rarely call him out for his sexual misdeeds, so the show seems to condone his actions. A good example is Xander's use of mind control. In the Buffyverse, mind control acts as a surrogate for date rape drugs. When other characters use it, the show roundly condemns them. This is true of both heroes like Willow and villains like Warren (Adam Busch), both of whom use mind control on their intimate partners in season six. Yet when Xander tries to use a spell to make Cordelia love him after she broke up with him, the show treats *him* as the victim ("Bewitched, Bothered and Bewildered" 2.16).

As St. Louis argues, Xander, Whedon, and *Buffy* can be both good *and* bad. I would add that we can, and should, continue to value the positive representations of consensual sexualities, including queer and non-normative ones, that *Buffy* and Whedon's other works provide. At the same time, we must recognize that sexuality in the Whedonverses, as in the real world, is complicated. The Whedonverses endorse many sexualities that are consensual, desired, and beautiful. They also fail to condemn some that are non-consensual, undesirable, and ugly; Whedon and his co-creators must bear responsibility for that. Yet I argue that positive representations of sexualities greatly outweigh negative ones in Whedon's works. For every male character who, like Xander, objectifies women, fails to respect their sexual agency, or disregards the importance of active consent, there are ten who consistently treat women like the human beings they are, cherish their sexual agency, and understand clearly that sex is ethical only when all participants actively consent to it. The televised Xander Harris was a product of the 1990s, and he bore the signs of his times. But today's #MeToo era produces very different men, men like *Firefly*'s Wash, the X-Men's Scott Summers, the Avengers' Bruce Banner, *Cabin in the Woods*' Holden, and *Much Ado*'s Benedick. These men live their sexual lives according to the triple ethical principle of consent, desire, and trust. These men, and the women who love them, will surely determine how Joss Whedon's works shape our culture's understanding of human sexuality.

Chapter Notes

Introduction

1. Buffy was only able to perform the longest lesbian kiss on 1990s American television (in "Restless" 4.22) because the kiss occurred out of frame; the WB network would not actually show a lesbian kiss (Lavery and Burkhead 11). Tanya Cochran points out that this is a problem: this was Willow and Tara's first sexual scene, and in it they seem like straight women cast as lesbians (as indeed Alyson Hannigan and Amber Benson are), performing for a straight male audience (Xander) and for a real-life audience that may include queers, but is likely mostly straight (54).

2. Buffy's relationship with Spike is almost always fully consensual. The one glaring exception is Spike's attempt to rape Buffy in "Seeing Red" (6.19), but that was distinctly out of character for Spike. James Marsters found it extremely difficult to perform the attempted rape scene. He calls it "the hardest day of [his] professional career" (Drew Grant). Yet he also acknowledges that the scene led to important character development for Spike. Marsters argues that "it was essential for Spike to realize he was well short of worthy for Buffy, so that would motivate him to try and get a soul" (Drew Grant). The guilt Spike feels over his rape attempt drives him to regain his soul, atone for his past crimes, and fight by Buffy's side as a trusted ally. When Buffy and Spike eventually resume their sexual relationship in the season ten comics, that relationship is and remains completely consensual.

3. In an important 2016 article, Cael Keegan argues that Willow's "queer melodramatics" resist the "ideal of the 'good gay citizen'" (11)—an ideal that had troubled earlier critics of Willow/Tara. Keegan suggests, counterintuitively but compellingly, that the apocalyptic queer desire that drives Dark Willow's attempt to destroy the world at the end of season six marks Buffy's utopian moment (18–19). This utopian apocalypse culminates in the destruction of Sunnydale at the end of the series, which Keegan views as a representation of Michael Warner's queer planet (Keegan 15). Keegan's view corresponds to mine, for it suggests that the Buffyverse became a much queerer world as Buffy prepared to move into the comic book form.

4. Xander effectively adapts to his visual impairment in the later (comic book) seasons of Buffy. He takes on a leadership role in the Slayer army. His eyepatch allows him to model his leader persona on Nick Fury, the ultimate example of a character who refuses to let his impairment become a disability (Whedon and Jeanty, "Long Way Home").

5. Jenny Alexander contextualizes Buffy's portrayal of sexual dominance by noting that Buffy occupied a specific "late twentieth-century cultural moment" in which it became permissible for a TV show aimed at teens to show women dominating men (¶ 21). In that sense, Buffy arrived at precisely the right time; its message of female dominance could not have been articulated or heard earlier.

6. In his recent study of film noir, Ben Tyrer argues, with Todd McGowan and Slavoj Žižek, for a Lacanian approach to film criticism that engages fully with Lacan's entire body of work (2). While Tyrer sees this approach as an alternative to the now dominant Deleuzianism (22), Agnieska Piotrowska has recently argued that the

two models can coexist (4). After all, Lacan stresses the importance of embodiment, even in the early "mirror stage" essay that formed the basis of much Lacanian film theory in the 1970s (Piotrowska 2, 5). Steven Shaviro, whose 1993 book *The Cinematic Body* challenged psychoanalysis in favor of a Deleuzian theory of affect and embodiment, has more recently argued that the two theories have more in common than either of them has with a cognitivism which (importantly for my purposes) makes it difficult, if not impossible, to ask any questions about desire ("*Cinematic Body* Redux" ¶ 8–9). Since I focus on desire and the other elements of sexuality in this book, I favor Lacanian criticism informed by theories of affect and embodiment, rather than a cognitive approach. My approach is compatible with Laura U. Marks' concept of an embodied "haptic visuality." Marks associates this physical visuality with "intersubjective eroticism" (183), which suggests that haptic visuality may be useful for the analysis of sexuality. She also argues that the haptic form of visuality draws upon the Imaginary erotic relationship between mother and infant (188), which implies that this model of embodied visuality may be productively employed in conjunction with Lacanian criticism.

7. In "The Body" (5.16), *Buffy* uses the traumatic event of Joyce's death to show how the Real can erupt into an Imaginary whose influence is weakened, in this episode, by harsh lighting and the absence of music. This aptly named episode also shows how the Lacanian interpretation of television is compatible with bodily/affect theory.

8. The paradigmatic example of the impossible sexual relationship is Buffy/Angel. This relationship is defined by a desire that literally cannot be fulfilled. The moment that desire gives way to sexual pleasure, Angel loses his soul, which in this context is the *objet petit a* that, by definition, cannot be obtained through sex. A Lacanian might say that Buffy and Angel's relationship "works out" only through the careful prohibition of its consummation.

9. Whedon's comics occupy the golden age of the queer superhero. In 2006, DC Comics introduced a new Batwoman. The woman beneath the cowl was Kate Kane, an out lesbian who had been forced to leave the West Point military academy after refusing to disavow her sexuality. Though Batwoman has been criticized as a heteronormative fantasy of high-femme lesbianism (Howard 79), she did make an important contribution to the mainstreaming of lesbianism in American superhero comics. In 2015, Iceman, a major member of Marvel's X-Men, came out as gay, making what had always been Marvel's queerest superhero comic even queerer.

10. Whedon's interpretation of the X-Men built upon the work of previous creators, including writer Chris Claremont and artist John Byrne, who created the Emma Frost character in 1980. Claremont made Emma a dominant woman with an interest in BDSM; Byrne gave her a fetishistic aesthetic. In *New X-Men* (2001–2004), writer Grant Morrison imagined Emma and Scott Summers having telepathic "mind sex."

11. The X-Men's Kitty Pryde was another Chris Claremont/John Byrne creation from the early 80s. She was a tiny, feisty, teenaged girl with superpowers; in short, she was a prototype for almost every female protagonist that Whedon would go on to create.

12. Don Tresca calls Karolina and Xavin's relationship "lesbian" ("*Runaways*" 137), but this relationship is better understood as transgender. Tresca acknowledges that Xavin has "a very fluid gender identification" ("*Runaways*" 137). But Tresca considers the relationship primarily from Karolina's point of view, arguing that Xavin maintains a female appearance "to sustain a lesbian relationship" with her ("*Runaways*" 137). I argue, however, that Whedon's *Runaways* positions Xavin as a character with an intersex body who identifies as female—in short, a trans woman.

Chapter One

1. I use "dominance/submission" or "DS" to refer to desires and practices that are centrally concerned with the consensual exchange of sexual power. Much of the scholarly literature, particularly from the 1980s and 90s, refers to this sexuality as sadomasochism or SM. More recent literature tends to use the inclusive initialism "BDSM," which incorporates bondage and discipline (BD), dominance and submission (DS), and sadism and masochism (SM). When I use the term BDSM, I am specifically focusing on those aspects of BDSM that include a dominance/submission element.

2. Whedon followed in the footsteps of William Moulton Marston, the renegade psychologist who first recognized that a woman superhero could provide the perfect vehicle to articulate a popular philosophy of female sexual dominance. Marston created Wonder Woman for this purpose. I have argued that Marston's Wonder Woman represented a radical attempt to re-imagine male desire as submissive (Call, *BDSM* Chapter Two). "Give [men] an alluring woman stronger than themselves to submit to and they'll be proud to become her willing slaves!" Marston declared in his pro-comic book manifesto "Why 100,000,000 Americans Read Comics" (43). Wonder Woman was meant to model this female strength; Marston hoped that men would find her alluring and women would find her inspirational. Joss Whedon hoped the same for Buffy, and for his version of Natasha Romanoff. Marston's Wonder Woman occasionally switched to the submissive role, and Whedon's dominant women are equally flexible.

3. Comic book images are usually contained within well defined panels. However, an artist can make an image extend or "bleed" into the gutter (the empty space between panels), or even to the edge of the page. Artists often use this technique to emphasize a particularly important image.

Chapter Two

1. Some *Serenity* comics were written by Joss Whedon and Brett Matthews, a fellow Wesleyan alumnus who had served as Whedon's assistant on *Buffy*, *Angel*, and *Firefly* (Lavery 161). Matthews had scripted the *Firefly* episode "Heart of Gold" (1.12). Joss Whedon's brother Zack Whedon also wrote some *Serenity* comics.

2. Judith Butler emphasizes the extremely positive portrayals of sibling incest that appear throughout modern literature, noting that it "sometimes appears as idyllic" (*Undoing Gender* 159).

3. Simon attempts to explain River's condition by claiming that Alliance scientists "stripped her amygdala" ("Ariel" 1.8). However, it's very unlikely that damage to the amygdala would produce a personality type and behaviors like River's. In the real world, damage to the amygdala can cause Klüver-Bucy syndrome. Symptoms of this syndrome include a dulled sense of emotion, impairments in fear conditioning, and hypersexuality (Daniels 134–135). But River's symptoms are the opposite of those associated with Klüver-Bucy syndrome: she experiences heightened emotions, is often afraid, and doesn't seem to have any interest in having sex (though she is interested in other people's sex lives). Sherry Ginn has plausibly argued that River doesn't present the symptoms of Klüver-Bucy syndrome because Simon rescued her before the Alliance scientists could finish altering her brain (88). In any case, as Bradley Daniels notes, the kind of "fearless, emotionally dulled, hypersexual adolescent girl" that amygdalar damage might actually produce is unlikely to be represented on American network television (136).

Chapter Three

1. Kitty and Peter can literally dissolve into one another. There are precedents for this in late twentieth-century American science fiction. SF author Rudy Rucker imagined a drug called "merge," which permits lovers to dissolve their bodies into intermingled pools of liquid.

2. The final panel in this scene shows Kitty's open hand, as she says that people should take what happiness they can get before it disappears. Interestingly, the Open Hand is also the name of the Breakworld's ruling political party, which suggests that their brand of tyrannical, non-consensual political domination is the very antithesis of happiness.

Chapter Four

1. The vagueness of the category "species" has always haunted modern biology. Darwin himself could conceive of no better way to distinguish a species from a mere variety than to rely upon the opinions of a majority of naturalists, since scientific consensus is often impossible to achieve (71).

Chapter Five

1. *Dr. Horrible*'s principal actors agreed to work for free in exchange for a share of future profits; Whedon carefully avoided becoming the kind of exploitative studio that he and his siblings were fighting against by working with the Writers Guild of America

(WGA) and Screen Actors Guild (SAG) to create fair compensation agreements for the musical (Pascale 300–301).

2. Joss Whedon's fascination with musicals is well known. "Once More, with Feeling," the famous musical episode of *Buffy* (6.7), introduced the now-common practice of transforming a single episode of a television show into a Hollywood-style "book" musical. Whedon's fascination with superhero stories is equally well known. His most obvious paean to the superhero genre is *The Avengers*, and Buffy herself can plausibly be read as a superhero. But *Dr. Horrible* twists the superhero genre, for it is a super*villain* origin story.

3. For Rick Altman, the competition between the American film musical's hero and his villainous rival for the affection of the female lead expresses the ambiguity of the male sexual drive (*Film Musical* 312). *Dr. Horrible* adds an additional layer of ambiguity to this structure, by reversing the usual signification of the terms "hero" and "villain." Audiences will find it hard to admire an egotistical "hero" like Captain Hammer, while viewers are encouraged to sympathize with the villainous but likeable Dr. Horrible (Griffin 329). This locates *Dr. Horrible* within a subgenre of musicals such as Andrew Lloyd Webber's *Phantom of the Opera* and Sondheim's *Sweeney Todd*, which offer their villains sympathy or understanding (Griffin 322).

Chapter Six

1. *Cabin*'s Holden may be a product of the feminist movement to promote affirmative consent and end rape on American college campuses. The foundational text of this movement, *Yes Means Yes: Visions of Female Sexual Power and A World Without Rape* (ed. Jaclyn Friedman and Jessica Valenti), was published in 2008, just a few months before *Cabin* began filming. While the recent allegations of Joss Whedon's former wife Kai Cole have complicated Whedon's relationship with the affirmative consent and #MeToo movements (see Afterword), no one, including Cole, has accused Whedon of non-consensual sexual behavior. It is also important to note the Holden is not only Whedon's character, but also Drew Goddard's.

Chapter Seven

1. While Shakespeare's works contain many male-male relationships that are clearly homosocial and some that may reasonably be read as homoerotic, Eve Kosofsky Sedgwick points out that the sexual context of Elizabethan England is too remote from our own to permit us to determine whether these works represent actual homosexual relationships (*Between Men* 35).

2. Like Scarlett Johannson's Black Widow, Jillian Morgese's Hero knows what it's like to be undone. The heroic Black Widow recovered handily from this undoing, and was stronger for it; Morgese's Hero follows suit.

Bibliography

Aaron, Jason, and Russell Dauterman. *The Mighty Thor.* New York: Marvel Comics, 2014–2018. Print.
Abbott, Stacey. "From Madman in the Basement to Self-Sacrificing Champion: The Multiple Faces of Spike." *European Journal of Cultural Studies* 8.3 (2005): 329–344. *SAGE journals*. Web. 10 November 2018.
Aberdein, Andrew. "The Companions and Socrates: Is Inara a Hetaera?" Wilcox and Cochran 63–75.
Adams, Carol J. "Bestiality: The Unmentioned Abuse." *The Animals' Agenda* 15.6 (November 1995): 29–31. Print.
Adams, Sam. "Age of Ultron's 'Black Widow Problem' Isn't a Problem: It's What the Movie Is About." *CriticWire*. 5 May 2015. Web. 6 June 2015. http://blogs.indiewire.com/criticwire.
Alaniz, José. *Death, Disability, and the Superhero: The Silver Age and Beyond.* Jackson: UP of Mississippi, 2014. *Project Muse*. Web. 10 November 2018.
Aldiss, Brian W. *Trillion Year Spree: The History of Science Fiction.* New York: Avon, 1986. Print.
Alexander, Jenny. "A Vampire is Being Beaten: De Sade Through the Looking Glass in *Buffy* and *Angel*." *Slayage: The Online International Journal of Buffy Studies* 4.3 (December 2004). Web. 10 November 2018.
Altman, Rick. *The American Film Musical.* Bloomington: Indiana UP, 1987. Print.
_____. "From Homosocial to Heterosexual: The Musical's Two Projects." *The Sound of Musicals*. Ed. Steven Cohan. New York: Palgrave Macmillan, 2010. 19–29. Print.
Amy-Chinn, Dee. "Queering the Bitch: Spike, Transgression, and Erotic Empowerment." *European Journal of Cultural Studies* 8.3 (2005): 313–328. *SAGE journals*. Web. 10 November 2018.
_____. "'Tis Pity She's a Whore: Postfeminist Prostitution in Joss Whedon's *Firefly*?" *Feminist Media Studies* 6.2 (2006): 175–189. *Taylor & Francis online*. Web. 10 November 2018.
Anderson-Minshall, Jacob. "The Brains Behind *Husbands*." *The Advocate*. 24 May 2013. Web. 10 November 2018.
Armstrong, Philip, and Laurence Simmons. "Bestiary: An Introduction." *Knowing Animals, Knowing Animals*. Ed. Laurence Simmons and Philip Armstrong. Boston: Brill, 2014. 1–24. *ProQuest Ebook Central*. Web. 10 November 2018.
Bacon-Smith, Camille. *Science Fiction Culture.* Philadelphia: U of Pennsylvania P, 1999. Print.
Bakke, Monika. "The Predicament of Zoopleasures: Human-Nonhuman Libidinal Relations." *Animal Encounters*. Ed. Tom Tyler and Manuela Rossini. Boston: Brill, 2009. 221–242. *ProQuest Ebook Central*. Web. 11 November 2018.

Bamber, Linda. *Comic Women, Tragic Men: A Study of Gender and Genre in Shakespeare*. Stanford: Stanford UP, 1982. Print.

Barker, Meg, Camelia Gupta, and Alessandra Iantaffi. "The Power of Play: The Potentials and Pitfalls in Healing Narratives of BDSM." *Safe, Sane and Consensual: Contemporary Perspectives on Sadomasochism*. Ed. Darren Langdridge and Meg Barker. New York: Palgrave Macmillan, 2007. Print.

Baudry, Jean-Louis. "Ideological Effects of the Basic Cinematographic Apparatus." *Narrative, Apparatus, Ideology*. Ed. Philip Rosen. New York: Columbia UP, 1986. 286–298. Print.

Baumgardner, Jennifer, and Amy Richards. *Manifesta: Young Women, Feminism, and the Future*. New York: Farrar, Straus and Giroux, 2000. Print.

Beeler, Stan. "Outing Lorne: Performance for the Performers." *Reading Angel: The TV Spin-Off with a Soul*. Ed. Stacey Abbott. London: I. B. Tauris, 2005. 88–100. Print.

Beetz, Andrea. "Bestiality/Zoophilia: A Scarcely Investigated Phenomenon Between Crime, Paraphilia, and Love." *Journal of Forensic Psychology Practice* 4.2 (2004): 1–36. *Taylor & Francis online*. Web. 11 November 2018.

Beetz, Andrea M. "Bestiality and Zoophilia: Associations with Violence and Sex Offending." *Bestiality and Zoophilia: Sexual Relations with Animals*. Ed. Andrea M. Beetz and Anthony L. Podberscek. West Lafayette, IN: Purdue UP, 2005. 46–70. Print.

Beirne, Piers. "Rethinking Bestiality: Towards a Concept of Interspecies Sexual Assault." *Companion Animals and Us: Exploring the Relationships Between People and Pets*. Ed. Anthony L. Podberscek, Elizabeth S. Paul, and James A. Serpell. Cambridge: Cambridge UP, 2000. 313–331. Print.

Beirne, Rebecca. "Queering the Slayer-Text: Reading Possibilities in Buffy the Vampire Slayer." *Refractory: A Journal of Entertainment Media* 5 (2004). Web. 11 November 2018.

Berger, Harry, Jr. "Against the Sink-a-Pace: Sexual and Family Politics in Much Ado About Nothing." *New Casebooks: Much Ado About Nothing and The Taming of the Shrew*. Ed. Marion Wynne-Davis. New York: Palgrave, 2001. 13–30. Print.

Bernstein, Abbie. "Into the Woods: Joss Whedon and Drew Goddard on the Making of the Film." *The Cabin in the Woods: The Official Visual Companion*. London: Titan Books, 2012. 8–42. Print.

Bird, Sharon R. "Welcome to the Men's Club: Homosociality and the Maintenance of Hegemonic Masculinity." *Gender and Society* 10.2 (April 1996): 120–132. *JSTOR*. Web. 11 November 2018.

Boggs, Colleen Glenney. "American Bestiality: Sex, Animals, and the Construction of Subjectivity." *Cultural Critique* 76 (Fall 2010): 98–125. *JSTOR*. Web. 11 November 2018.

Boney, Bradley. "The Lavender Brick Road: Paul Bonin-Rodriguez and the Sissy Bo(d)y." *Theatre Journal* 48.1 (March 1996): 35–57. *JSTOR*. Web. 11 November 2018.

Boulware, Taylor. "'I Made Me': Queer Theory, Subjection, and Identity in *Dollhouse*." *Slayage: The Journal of the Whedon Studies Association* 10.1 (Winter 2013). Web. 11 November 2018.

Brame, Gloria G., William D. Brame, and Jon Jacobs. *Different Loving: The World of Sexual Dominance and Submission*. New York: Villard, 1993. Print.

Brioux, Bill. "Firefly series ready for liftoff." *JAM! Television*. 22 July 2002. Web. 21 March 2011. http://jam.canoe.ca/Television/TV_Shows/F/Firefly/2002/07/22/734323.html.

Broverman, Neal. "TV Mastermind Jane Espenson: From *Ellen* to *Buffy* to Evil Queens." *The Advocate*. 27 October 2011. Web. 11 November 2018.

Buckman, Alyson. "'Go ahead! Run away! Say it was Horrible!': *Dr. Horrible's Sing-Along Blog* as Resistant Text." *Slayage: The Journal of the Whedon Studies Association* 8.1 (Spring 2010). Web. 11 November 2018.

_____. "'Much Madness is Divinest Sense': *Firefly*'s 'Big Damn Heroes' and Little Witches." Wilcox and Cochran 41–49.
_____. "Triangulated Desire in *Angel* and *Buffy*." Waggoner 48–92.
Bukatman, Scott. *Matters of Gravity: Special Effects and Supermen in the 20th Century*. Durham: Duke UP, 2003. Print.
Burnett, Tamy. "Anya as Feminist Model of Positive Female Sexuality." Waggoner 117–145.
_____. "'I've Got These Evil Hand Issues': Amputation, Identity, and Agency in *Angel*." 5th Biennial Slayage Conference on the Whedonverses. 12–15 July 2012. University of British Columbia, Vancouver. Lecture.
Burns, Angie. "Passion, Pain and 'bad kissing decisions': Learning about Intimate Relationships from *Buffy* Season Six." *Slayage: The Online International Journal of Buffy Studies* 6.1 (Fall 2006). Web. 10 December 2018.
Burr, Vivien. "Bad Girls Like It Rough (And Good Girls Don't?): Representations of BDSM in *Buffy the Vampire Slayer*." *Phoebe: Gender and Cultural Critiques* 18.1 (2006): 45–57. Print.
Butler, Judith. *Bodies That Matter: On the Discursive Limits of "Sex."* New York: Routledge, 1993. Print.
_____. *Gender Trouble: Feminism and the Subversion of Identity*. New York: Routledge, 1999. Print.
_____. *Undoing Gender*. New York: Routledge, 2004. *ProQuest Ebook Central*. Web. 11 November 2018.
Byers, Michele. "*Buffy the Vampire Slayer*: The Next Generation of Television." *Catching a Wave: Reclaiming Feminism for the 21st Century*. Ed. Rory Dicker and Alison Piepmeier. Boston: Northeastern UP, 2003. 171–187. Print.
Calarco, Matthew. *Zoographies: The Question of the Animal from Heidegger to Derrida*. New York: Columbia UP, 2008. Print.
Califia, Pat. "A Personal View of the History of the Lesbian S/M Community and Movement in San Francisco." *Coming to Power: Writings and Graphics on Lesbian S/M*. Ed. Samois. 2nd ed. Boston: Alyson Publications, 1982. 243–281. Print.
Califia, Patrick. *Speaking Sex to Power: The Politics of Queer Sex*. San Francisco: Cleis Press, 2002. Print.
Call, Lewis. *BDSM in American Science Fiction and Fantasy*. New York: Palgrave Macmillan, 2013. Print.
_____. "Buffy the Post-Anarchist Vampire Slayer." *Post-Anarchism: A Reader*. Ed. Duane Rousselle and Süreyyya Evren. London: Pluto Press, 2011. 183–194. Print.
_____. "'Find What Warmth You Can': Queer Sexualities in *Buffy* Season Eight through Ten Comic Books." *Slayage: The Journal of Whedon Studies* 15.2 (Summer/Fall 2017). Web. 2 December 2018.
Canavan, Gerry. "'Something Nightmares are From': Metacommentary in Joss Whedon's *The Cabin in the Woods*." *Slayage: The Journal of the Whedon Studies Association* 10.2/11.1 (Fall 2013/Winter 2014). Web. 11 November 2018.
Carrigan, Tim, Bob Connell, and John Lee. "Toward a New Sociology of Masculinity." *Theory and Society* 14.5 (September 1985): 551–604. *JSTOR*. Web. 11 November 2018.
Carroll, Noël. "Prospects for Film Theory: A Personal Assessment." *Post-Theory: Reconstructing Film Studies*. Ed. David Bordwell and Noël Carroll. Madison: U Wisconsin P, 1996. 37–70. Print.
Claremont, Chris, and John Byrne. *Uncanny X-Men*. New York: Marvel Comics, 1977–1981. Print.
Clark, Krystal, and Tara Bennett. "How Avengers: Age of Ultron dropped the ball with Black Widow." *Blastr*. 4 May 2015. Web. 6 June 2015. http://www.blastr.com.
Clark, Noelene. "'Avengers: Age of Ultron': Scarlett Johansson on Black Widow's journey." *Los Angeles Times*. 9 May 2015. Web. 6 June 2015. http://herocomplex.latimes.com.

Clover, Carol J. *Men, Women and Chain Saws: Gender in the Modern Horror Film*. Princeton: Princeton UP, 1992. Print.
Cocca, Carolyn. "'First Word "Jail," Second Word "Bait"': Adolescent Sexuality, Feminist Theories, and *Buffy the Vampire Slayer*." *Slayage: The Online International Journal of Buffy Studies* 3.2 (November 2003). Web. 11 November 2018.
Cochran, Tanya. "Complicating the Open Closet: The Visual Rhetoric of *Buffy the Vampire Slayer*'s Sapphic Lovers." *Televising Queer Women: A Reader*. Ed. Rebecca Beirne. New York: Palgrave Macmillan, 2008. 49–63. Print.
Cole, Kai. "Joss Whedon Is a 'Hypocrite Preaching Feminist Ideals,' Ex-Wife Kai Cole Says (Guest Blog)." *The Wrap*. 20 August 2017. Web. 11 November 2018. http://thewrap.com.
Collier, Noelle R., Christine A. Lumadue, and H. Ray Wooten. "*Buffy the Vampire Slayer* and *Xena: Warrior Princess*: Reception of the Texts by a Sample of Lesbian Fans and Web Site Users." *Journal of Homosexuality* 56 (2009): 575–609. *Taylor & Francis online*. Web. 11 November 2018.
Comeford, AmiJo, Ian Klein, and Elizabeth Rambo. "Academics Assemble: A Report on New Scholarship at SC5." *Slayage: The Journal of the Whedon Studies Association* 9.2 (Fall 2012). Web. 11 November 2018.
Connell, R. W. *Gender and Power: Society, the Person and Sexual Politics*. Stanford: Stanford UP, 1987. Print.
_____. *Masculinities*. Second edition. Berkeley: U of California P, 2005. Print.
_____. "A Very Straight Gay: Masculinity, Homosexual Experience, and the Dynamics of Gender." *American Sociological Review* 57.6 (December 1992): 735–751. *JSTOR*. Web. 11 November 2018.
Connell, R. W., and James W. Messerschmidt. "Hegemonic Masculinity: Rethinking the Concept." *Gender and Society* 19.6 (December 2005): 829–859. *JSTOR*. Web. 11 November 2018.
Connolly, Brian. *Domestic Intimacies: Incest and the Liberal Subject in Nineteenth-Century America*. Philadelphia: U of Pennsylvania P, 2014. *Project Muse*. Web. 11 November 2018.
Cook, Carol. "'The Sign and Semblance of Her Honor': Reading Gender Difference in *Much Ado About Nothing*." *PMLA* 101.2 (March 1986): 186–202. *JSTOR*. Web. 11 November 2018.
Cox, Carolyn. "*Age of Ultron* Stars Talk Joss Whedon, Lack of Black Widow Merch, and Female Representation in the MCU." *The Mary Sue*. 6 May 2015. Web. 6 June 2015. http://www.themarysue.com.
Cox, Jessica I. "Lovingly Tweaked: Genre and Gender in Joss Whedon's Dr. Horrible's Sing-Along Blog." M.A. thesis. Colorado State University, 2013. *CSU Theses and Dissertations*. Web. 11 November 2018.
Creed, Barbara. *The Monstrous-Feminine: Film, Feminism, Psychoanalysis*. New York: Routledge, 1993. Print.
_____. "What Do Animals Dream Of? Or King Kong as Darwinian Screen Animal." *Knowing Animals, Knowing Animals*. Ed. Laurence Simmons and Philip Armstrong. Boston: Brill, 2014. 59–78. *ProQuest Ebook Central*. Web. 11 November 2018.
Cross, Patricia A., and Kim Matheson. "Understanding Sadomasochism: An Empirical Examination of Four Perspectives." *Sadomasochism: Powerful Pleasures*. Ed. Peggy J. Kleinplatz and Charles Moser. Binghamton, NY: Haworth Press, 2006. 133–166. Print.
Daniels, Bradley J. "'Stripping' River Tam's Amygdala." *The Psychology of Joss Whedon*. Ed. Joy Davidson. Dallas: BenBella Books, 2007. 131–140. Print.
Darwin, Charles. *The Origin of Species*. 1859. New York: Random House, 1993. Print.
Davidoff, Leonore. *Thicker than Water: Siblings and their Relations, 1780–1920*. Oxford: Oxford UP, 2011. *Oxford Scholarship Online*. Web. 11 November 2018.

Davis, Lennard. *Enforcing Normalcy: Disability, Deafness, and the Body*. London: Verso, 1995. *ACLS Humanities E-book*. Web. 11 November 2018.
Dekkers, Midas. *Dearest Pet: On Bestiality*. New York: Verso, 1994. Print.
Deleuze, Gilles, and Félix Guattari. *A Thousand Plateaus: Capitalism and Schizophrenia*. Trans. Brian Massumi. Minneapolis: U of Minnesota P, 1987. Print.
Demetriou, Demetrakis Z. "Connell's Concept of Hegemonic Masculinity: A Critique." *Theory and Society* 30.3 (2001): 337–361. *JSTOR*. Web. 10 December 2018.
DeRitter, Lillian. "We're Not Men." *Inside Joss Whedon's Dollhouse: from Alpha to Rossum*. Ed. Jane Espenson. Dallas: BenBella Books, 2010. 189–203. Print.
DeRoss, Jennifer. "Not Gay Enough So You'd Notice: Poaching Fuffy." *Slayage: The Journal of Whedon Studies* 16.2 (Summer/Fall 2018). Web. 10 December 2018.
Derrida, Jacques. "The Animal That Therefore I Am (More to Follow)." Trans. David Wills. *Critical Inquiry* 28.2 (Winter 2002): 369–418. *JSTOR*. Web. 11 November 2018.
Dika, Vera. *Games of Terror: Halloween, Friday the 13th, and the Films of the Stalker Cycle*. Cranbury, NJ: Associated University Presses, 1990. Print.
DiPlacidi, Jenny. *Gothic Incest: Gender, Sexuality and Transgression*. Manchester: Manchester UP, 2018. *JSTOR*. Web. 11 November 2018.
Doane, Mary Ann. *Femmes Fatales: Feminism, Film Theory, Psychoanalysis*. New York: Routledge, 1991. Print.
Douglas, Adam. *The Beast Within*. London: Chapmans, 1992. Print.
Driver, Susan. *Queer Girls and Popular Culture: Reading, Resisting, and Creating Media*. New York: Peter Lang, 2007. Print.
Dyer, Richard. *Only Entertainment*. New York: Routledge, 2002. *ProQuest Ebook Central*. Web. 11 November 2018.
Easton, Dossie and Janet W. Hardy. *The New Topping Book*. Eugene, OR: Greenery Press, 2003. Print.
Edelstein, David. "Now Playing at Your Local Multiplex: Torture Porn." *New York*. 28 January 2006. Web. 11 November 2018.
Elliot-Smith, Darren. *Queer Horror Film and Television: Sexuality and Masculinity at the Margins*. London: I. B. Tauris, 2016. *ProQuest Ebook Central*. Web. 11 November 2018.
Epstein, Arthur W. "The Phylogenetics of Fetishism." *Variant Sexuality: Research and Theory*. Ed. Glenn D. Wilson. Baltimore: The Johns Hopkins UP, 1987. 142–149. Print.
Espenson, Jane, and Georges Jeanty. "Retreat." *Buffy the Vampire Slayer: Season Eight*. Milwaukie, OR: Dark Horse Comics, 2009. Print.
Espenson, Jane, Drew Z. Greenberg, and Karl Moline. "Billy the Vampire Slayer." *Buffy the Vampire Slayer: Season Nine*. Milwaukie, OR: Dark Horse Comics, 2012. Print.
Fall, Wendy. "Spike is Forgiven: The Sympathetic Vampire's Resonance with Rape Culture." *Slayage: The Journal of Whedon Studies* 16.2 (Summer/Fall 2018). Web. 10 December 2018.
Fawaz, Ramzi. *The New Mutants: Superheroes and the Radical Imagination of American Comics*. New York: New York UP, 2016. Print.
Firefly: The Official Companion, Volume One. London: Titan Books, 2006. Print.
Firefly: The Official Companion, Volume Two. London: Titan Books, 2007. Print.
Ford, Jessica. "Coming Out of the Broom Closet: Willow's Sexuality and Empowerment in *Buffy*." *Joss Whedon: The Complete Companion*. London: Titan Books, 2012. 94–102. Print.
Foucault, Michel. *The History of Sexuality, Volume I: An Introduction*. Trans. Robert Hurley. 1978. New York: Vintage Books, 1990. Print.
Franich, Darren. "Entertainment Geekly: The Black Widow Conundrum." *Entertainment Weekly*. 1 May 2015. Web. 6 June 2015.
Frankel, Valerie Estelle, ed. *The Comics of Joss Whedon: Critical Essays*. Jefferson, NC: McFarland, 2015. Print.

Freud, Sigmund. *Civilization and Its Discontents*. Trans. James Strachey. 1930. New York: W. W. Norton, 1989. Print.

_____. "The Ego and the Id." 1923. *The Standard Edition of the Complete Psychological Works of Sigmund Freud*. Vol. 19. Trans. and ed. James Strachey. London: Hogarth Press, 1962. Print.

_____. "Fetishism." Trans. Joan Riviere. 1927. *The Standard Edition of the Complete Psychological Works of Sigmund Freud*. Ed. James Strachey. Vol. 21. London: The Hogarth Press, 1962. Print.

_____. *Three Essays on the Theory of Sexuality*. Trans. James Strachey. 1905. New York: Basic Books, 1975. Print.

Friedman, Jaclyn, and Jessica Valenti, eds. *Yes Means Yes: Visions of Female Sexual Power and a World Without Rape*. Berkeley: Seal Press, 2008. Print.

Frost, Karen. "The Long Road to Lesbian Sex & Sensuality on Network TV." *AfterEllen*. February 2016. Web. 11 November 2018. http://www.afterellen.com/tv/474467-long-road-lesbian-sex-sensuality-network-tv.

Gage, Christos, and Rebekah Isaacs. "Day Off (or Harmony in My Head)." *Buffy the Vampire Slayer: Season Ten*. Milwaukie, OR: Dark Horse Comics, 2014. Print.

_____. "Old Demons." *Buffy the Vampire Slayer: Season Ten*. Milwaukie, OR: Dark Horse Comics, 2015. Print.

_____. "Own It." *Buffy the Vampire Slayer: Season Ten*. Milwaukie, OR: Dark Horse Comics, 2016. Print.

_____. "Taking Ownership." *Buffy the Vampire Slayer: Season Ten*. Milwaukie, OR: Dark Horse Comics, 2016. Print.

Gage, Christos, Joss Whedon, and Georges Jeanty. "The Reckoning." *Buffy the Vampire Slayer: Season Twelve*. Milwaukie, OR: Dark Horse Comics, 2018. Print.

Gage, Christos, Nicholas Brendon, and Megan Levens. "Love Dares You." *Buffy the Vampire Slayer: Season Ten*. Milwaukie, OR: Dark Horse Comics, 2015. Print.

Gage, Christos, Nicholas Brendon, and Rebekah Isaacs. "Freaky Giles Day." *Buffy the Vampire Slayer: Season Ten*. Milwaukie, OR: Dark Horse Comics, 2015. Print.

Gage, Christos, Rebekah Isaacs, and Megan Levens. "In Pieces on the Ground." *Buffy the Vampire Slayer: Season Ten*. Milwaukie, OR: Dark Horse Comics, 2015–2016. Print.

Game, Ann. "Riding: Embodying the Centaur." *Body & Society* 7.4 (2001): 1–12. *SAGE journals*. Web. 11 November 2018.

Gamman, Lorraine, and Merja Makinen. *Female Fetishism*. New York: New York UP, 1995. Print.

Garland-Thompson, Rosemarie. "Introduction: From Wonder to Eros—A Genealogy of Freak Discourse in Modernity." *Freakery: Cultural Spectacles of the Extraordinary Body*. Ed. Rosemarie Garland-Thompson. New York: New York UP, 1996. 1–19. Print.

Gerhard, Jane. *Desiring Revolution: Second-Wave Feminism and the Rewriting of American Sexual Thought, 1920 to 1982*. New York: Columbia UP, 2001. Print.

Gerrold, David. "Star Truck." *Finding Serenity: Anti-Heroes, Lost Shepherds and Space Hookers in Joss Whedon's Firefly*. Ed. Jane Espenson. Dallas: BenBella Books, 2004. 183–195. Print.

Ginn, Sherry. *Power and Control in the Television Worlds of Joss Whedon*. Jefferson, NC: McFarland, 2012. Print.

Goddard, Drew, and Georges Jeanty. "Wolves at the Gate." *Buffy the Vampire Slayer: Season Eight*. Milwaukie, OR: Dark Horse Comics, 2007. Print.

Goddard, Drew, dir. *The Cabin in the Woods*. Mutant Enemy / Lionsgate, 2012. DVD.

Gomez, Lisa. "Buffy Is in Bed with a Woman? Problematic and Perfect Gay and Lesbian Representation." Frankel 19–30.

Grant, Barry Keith. *The Hollywood Film Musical*. Malden, MA: Wiley-Blackwell, 2012. Print.

Grant, Drew. "Look Back on 'Buffy': Actor James Marsters on Spike's Worst Moment." *The Observer.* 9 March 2017. Web. 28 June 2019.

Graves, Stephanie. "'You Really Think I'm Pretty?': The Problem of Gender Representation in *The Avengers*." 6th Biennial Slayage Conference on the Whedonverses. California State University, Sacramento. 19–22 June 2014. Lecture.

Greenwood, Steven. "'Life Isn't a Story': Xander, Andrew, and Queer Disavowal in *Buffy the Vampire Slayer*." *Slayage: The Journal of Whedon Studies* 15.2 (Summer/Fall 2017). Web. 11 November 2018.

Griffin, Sean. *Free and Easy? A Defining History of the American Film Musical Genre.* Hoboken, NJ: Wiley Blackwell, 2018. Print.

Grosz, Elizabeth. *Jacques Lacan: A Feminist Introduction.* New York: Routledge, 1990. *ProQuest Ebook Central.* Web. 12 November 2018.

Halberstam, Judith (Jack). *Skin Shows: Gothic Horror and the Technology of Monsters.* Durham: Duke UP, 1995. Print.

Haraway, Donna. "The Companion Species Manifesto: Dogs, People, and Significant Otherness." *Manifestly Haraway.* Minneapolis: U of Minnesota P, 2016. 93–198. *JSTOR.* Web. 12 November 2018.

———. *Simians, Cyborgs, and Women: The Reinvention of Nature.* New York: Routledge, 1991. Print.

Hart, Lynda. *Between the Body and the Flesh: Performing Sadomasochism.* New York: Columbia UP, 1998. Print.

Hawk, Julie. "Hacking the Read-Only File: Collaborative Narrative as Ontological Construction in *Dollhouse*." *Slayage: The Journal of the Whedon Studies Association* 8.2–3 (Summer/Fall 2010). Web. 12 November 2018.

Hawkes, Rebecca. "Joss Whedon: 'I Think of Myself as Ultron.'" *The Telegraph.* 6 June 2015. Web. 28 June 2015.

Heinecken, Dawn. "Fan Readings of Sex and Violence on Buffy the Vampire Slayer." *Slayage: The Online International Journal of Buffy Studies* 3.3–4 (April 2004). Web. 12 November 2018.

Hibbs, Thomas. "*Buffy the Vampire Slayer* as Feminist *Noir*." *Buffy the Vampire Slayer and Philosophy: Fear and Trembling in Sunnydale.* Ed. James B. South. Chicago: Open Court, 2003. 49–60. Print.

Highleyman, Liz. "My Life as a Dom." *The Second Coming: A Leatherdyke Reader.* Ed. Pat Califia and Robin Sweeney. Los Angeles: Alyson Publications, 1996. 77–89. Print.

———. "Playing with Paradox: The Ethics of Erotic Dominance and Submission." *Bitch Goddess: The Spiritual Path of the Dominant Woman.* Ed. Pat Califia and Drew Campbell. San Francisco: Greenery Press, 1997. 153–173. Print.

Holder, Nancy. "I Want Your Sex." *Finding Serenity: Anti-Heroes, Lost Shepherds and Space Hookers in Joss Whedon's Firefly.* Ed. Jane Espenson. Dallas: BenBella Books, 2004. 139–153. Print.

Horkheimer, Max, and Theodor W. Adorno. *Dialectic of Enlightenment.* Trans. John Cumming. 1944. New York: Continuum, 1994. Print.

Howard, Yetta. "Politically Incorrect, Visually Incorrect: *Bitchy Butch*'s Unapologetic Discrepancies in Lesbian Identity and Comic Art." *The Journal of Popular Culture* 45.1 (2012): 79–98. *Wiley Online Library.* Web. 12 November 2018.

Huff, Tanya. "Thanks for the Reenactment, sir." *Finding Serenity: Anti-Heroes, Lost Shepherds and Space Hookers in Joss Whedon's Firefly.* Ed. Jane Espenson. Dallas: BenBella Books, 2004. 105–112. Print.

Huston, Shaun. "Black Widow and the Burden of Being the Female Avenger." *PopMatters.* 20 May 2015. Web. 6 June 2015. http://www.popmatters.com.

Hutchings, Peter. *The Horror Film.* New York: Routledge, 2014. *ProQuest Ebook Central.* Web. 12 November 2018.

Iatropolos, Mary Ellen. "Defining Joss Whedon's Disability Narrative Ethic: The Impairment Arcs of Lindsey McDonald, Bennett Halverson, and Xander Harris." 5th Biennial Slayage Conference on the Whedonverses. 12–15 July 2012. University of British Columbia, Vancouver. Lecture.
Jagose, Annamarie. *Queer Theory: An Introduction*. New York: New York UP, 1996. Print.
Jardine, Lisa. *Still Harping on Daughters: Women and Drama in the Age of Shakespeare*. Brighton, UK: The Harvester Press, 1983. Print.
Johnston, Jacob. *The Art of Marvel's Avengers: Age of Ultron*. New York: Marvel, 2015. Print.
Jowett, Lorna. *Sex and the Slayer: A Gender Studies Primer for the Buffy Fan*. Middletown, CT: Wesleyan UP, 2005. Print.
Kahn, Coppélia. *Man's Estate: Masculine Identity in Shakespeare*. Berkeley: U of California P, 1981. Print.
Kaplan, Louise J. *Female Perversions: The Temptations of Emma Bovary*. New York: Doubleday, 1991. Print.
Karras, Irene. "The Third Wave's Final Girl: Buffy the Vampire Slayer." *Thirdspace: A Journal of Feminist Theory & Culture* 1.2 (2002). Web. 12 November 2018. http://journals.sfu.ca/thirdspace/index.php/journal/article/viewArticle/karras/50.
Kaveney, Roz. *Superheroes! Capes and Crusaders in Comics and Films*. New York: I. B. Tauris, 2008. Print.
_____. "Writing the Vampire Slayer: Interviews with Jane Espenson and Steven S. DeKnight." *Reading the Vampire Slayer: The New, Updated Unofficial Guide to Buffy and Angel*. Ed. Roz Kaveney. New York: I. B. Tauris, 2004. 100–131. Print.
Keegan, Cael M. "Emptying the Future: Queer Melodramatics and Negative Utopia in Buffy the Vampire Slayer." *Queer Studies in Media & Popular Culture* 1.1 (2016): 9–22. Gale Academic OneFile. Web. 12 November 2018.
Killinger, Charles L. *Culture and Customs of Italy*. Westport, CT.: Greenwood Press, 2005. ProQuest Ebook Central. Web. 13 August 2019.
King, Derrick. "The (Bio)political Economy of Bodies, Culture as Commodification, and the Badiouian Event: Reading Political Allegories in The Cabin in the Woods." *Slayage: The Journal of the Whedon Studies Association* 10.2/11.1 (Fall 2013/Winter 2014). Web. 12 November 2018.
Kociemba, David. "Athena's Daughter: Black Widow's Impact Aesthetic." *Marvel's Black Widow from Spy to Superhero: Essays on an Avenger with a Very Specific Skill Set*. Ed. Sherry Ginn. Jefferson, NC: McFarland, 2017. 128–148. Print.
Kociemba, David, and Mary Ellen Iatropoulos. "Separate Worlds or One? Canonicity, Medium and Authorship." Frankel 31–47.
Krafft-Ebing, Richard. *Psychopathia Sexualis*. Trans. Franklin S. Klaf. 1886. New York: Bantam Books, 1969. Print.
Lacan, Jacques. *Écrits: The First Complete Edition in English*. Trans. Bruce Fink. New York: W. W. Norton, 2006. Print.
_____. *Encore: On Feminine Sexuality, The Limits of Love and Knowledge. The Seminar of Jacques Lacan*. Book XX. Trans. Bruce Fink. New York: W. W. Norton, 1999. Print.
_____. *The Ethics of Psychoanalysis. The Seminar of Jacques Lacan*. Book VII. Trans. Dennis Porter. New York: W. W. Norton, 1992. Print.
Lang, Brent. "Horror Movies Make Times Less Scary for Studios." *Variety*. 26 October 2016. Web. 12 November 2018.
Larbalestier, Justine. "The Only Thing Better than Killing a Slayer: Heterosexuality and Sex in Buffy the Vampire Slayer." *Reading the Vampire Slayer: The New, Updated Unofficial Guide to Buffy and Angel*. Ed. Roz Kaveney. New York: I. B. Tauris, 2004. 195–219. Print.
Lavery, David. *Joss Whedon: A Creative Portrait*. London: I. B. Tauris, 2014. Print.

Lavery, David, and Cynthia Burkhead, eds. *Joss Whedon Conversations*. UP of Mississippi, 2011. Print.
Lawrence, Elizabeth Atwood. "The Centaur: Its History and Meaning in Human Culture." *Journal of Popular Culture* 27.4 (March 1994): 57–68. *Wiley Online Library*. Web. 12 November 2018.
Leonard, Kendra Preston. "'The Status is Not Quo': Gender and Performance in *Dr. Horrible's Sing-Along Blog*." *Buffy, Ballads, and Bad Guys Who Sing: Music in the Worlds of Joss Whedon*. Ed. Kendra Preston Leonard. Lanham, MD: Scarecrow Press, 2011. 207–219. *ProQuest Ebook Central*. Web. 12 November 2018.
Liddell, Alex. "Problematic Tropes of Bi Women in the Whedonverses." *Slayage: The Journal of Whedon Studies* 15.2 (Summer/Fall 2017). Web. 12 November 2018.
Lindemann, Danielle J. *Dominatrix: Gender, Eroticism, and Control in the Dungeon*. Chicago: U of Chicago P, 2012. Print.
Linden, Robin Ruth, Darlene R. Pagano, Diana E. H. Russell, and Susan Leigh Starr, eds. *Against Sadomasochism*. San Francisco: Frog in the Well, 1982. Print.
Magill, David. "'I Aim to Misbehave': Masculinities in the 'Verse." Wilcox and Cochran 76–86.
Maines, Rachel P. *The Technology of Orgasm: "Hysteria," the Vibrator, and Women's Sexual Satisfaction*. Baltimore: The Johns Hopkins UP, 1999. Print.
Mangels, Andy. "Lesbian Sex = Death?" *The Advocate*. 20 August 2002. *EBSCOhost*. Web. 25 October 2018.
Marcotte, Amanda. "In Defense of Black Widow in Age of Ultron." *Raw Story*. 11 May 2015. Web. 6 June 2015. http://www.rawstory.com.
Marks, Laura U. *The Skin of the Film: Intercultural Cinema, Embodiment, and the Senses*. Durham: Duke UP, 2000. Print.
Marston, William Moulton. "Why 100,000,000 Americans Read Comics." *The American Scholar* 13 (1944): 35–44. *JSTOR*. Web. 12 November 2018.
Masters, R. E. L. *Forbidden Sexual Behavior and Morality: An Objective Re-Examination of Perverse Sex Practices in Different Cultures*. New York: The Julian Press, 1962. Print.
Mathis, Corey. "Bringing the Pain: An Examination of Marti Noxon's Contributions to *Buffy the Vampire Slayer*." *Slayage: The Journal of Whedon Studies* 11.2/12.1 (Summer 2014). Web. 12 November 2018.
McAvan, Em. "'I Think I'm Kinda Gay': Willow Rosenberg and the Absent/Present Bisexual in *Buffy the Vampire Slayer*." *Slayage: The Online International Journal of Buffy Studies* 6.4 (Summer 2007). Web. 12 November 2018.
McCracken, Allison. "At Stake: Angel's Body, Fantasy Masculinity, and Queer Desire in Teen Television." *Undead TV: Essays on Buffy the Vampire Slayer*. Ed. Elana Levine and Lisa Parks. Durham: Duke UP, 2007. 116–144. Print.
McGee, Masani. "Big Men in Spangly Outfits: Spectacle and Masculinity in Joss Whedon's *The Avengers*." *Slayage: The Journal of Whedon Studies* 11.2/12.1 (Summer 2014). Web. 12 November 2018.
McGowan, Todd. *Real Gaze: Film Theory After Lacan*. New York: State U of New York P, 2007. *ProQuest Ebook Central*. Web. 29 June 2019.
McGowan, Todd, and Sheila Kunkle. "Introduction: Lacanian Psychoanalysis in Film Theory." *Lacan and Contemporary Film*. Ed. Todd McGowan and Sheila Kunkle. New York: Other Press, 2004. xi–xxix. Print.
McRuer, Robert. *Crip Theory: Cultural Signs of Queerness and Disability*. New York: New York UP, 2006. *ProQuest Ebook Central*. Web. 12 November 2018.
_____. "Disabling Sex: Notes for a Crip Theory of Sexuality." *GLQ: A Journal of Lesbian and Gay Studies* 17.1 (2011): 107–117. *Project Muse*. Web. 12 November 2018.
Melzer, Brad, and Georges Jeanty. "Twilight." *Buffy the Vampire Slayer: Season Eight*. Milwaukie, OR: Dark Horse Comics, 2010. Print.

Meredith, Rowan, and Sharon Sutherland. "Dream Queer: Does Fitz Offer Positive Bisexual Representation on Agents of S.H.I.E.L.D.?" *Slayage: The Journal of Whedon Studies* 15.2 (Summer/Fall 2017). Web. 12 November 2018.
Messerschmidt, James. *Nine Lives: Adolescent Masculinities, the Body, and Violence*. Boulder, CO: Westview Press, 2000. Print.
Metz, Christian. *The Imaginary Signifier: Psychoanalysis and the Cinema*. Bloomington: Indiana UP, 1982. Print.
Metz, Jerry. "What's Your Fetish? The Tortured Economics of Horror Simulacra in *The Cabin in the Woods*." *Slayage: The Journal of the Whedon Studies Association* 10.2/11.1 (Fall 2013/Winter 2014). Web. 12 November 2018.
Miletski, Hani. *Understanding Bestiality and Zoophilia*. Bethesda, MD: Hani Miletski, 2002. Print.
Miller, D. A. *Place for Us: Essay on the Broadway Musical*. Cambridge, MA: Harvard UP, 1998. Print.
Mitchell, David T., and Sharon L. Snyder. *Narrative Prosthesis: Disability and the Dependencies of Discourse*. Ann Arbor: U of Michigan P, 2000. Print.
Moore, Trent. "Joss Whedon Explains Why Cabin is Like 'A Very Loving Hate Letter.'" *SyFyWire*. 21 May 2015. Web. 12 November 2018.
Moorman, Jennifer. "'Kinda Gay': Queer Cult Fandom and Willow's (Bi)Sexuality in *Buffy the Vampire Slayer*." *Supernatural Youth: The Rise of the Teen Hero in Literature and Popular Culture*. Ed. Jes Battis. Lanham, MD: Lexington Books, 2011. 102–115. Print.
Morris, Tracy S. "Joss Whedon, Alan Moore and the Whole Horrible Future." Frankel 121–130.
Morrison, Grant, and Frank Quitely. *New X-Men*. New York: Marvel, 2001–2004. Print.
Mukherjea, Ananya. "'It's Like Some Primal, Some Animal Force. .That Used to Be Us': Animality, Humanity, and Moral Careers in the Buffyverse." Wilcox, Cochran, Masson, and Lavery 53–69.
Mulvey, Laura. *Visual and Other Pleasures*. Second edition. New York: Palgrave Macmillan, 2009. Print.
Nadkarni, Samira. "'In My House and Therefore in My Care': Transgressive Mothering, Abuse, and Embodiment." *Joss Whedon's Dollhouse: Confounding Purpose, Confusing Identity*. Ed. Sherry Ginn. Lanham, MD: Rowman and Littlefield, 2014. 98–111. *ProQuest Ebook Central*. Web. 13 August 2019.
Neely, Carol Thomas. *Broken Nuptials in Shakespeare's Plays*. New Haven: Yale UP, 1985. Print.
Nelson, A. P. "*Trick 'R Treat*, *The Cabin in the Woods* and the Defense of Horror's Subcultural Capital." *Slayage: The Journal of the Whedon Studies Association* 10.2/11.1 (Fall 2013/Winter 2014). Web. 12 November 2018.
Neroni, Hilary. *The Subject of Torture: Psychoanalysis and Biopolitics in Television and Film*. New York: Columbia UP, 2015. *ProQuest Ebook Central*. Web. 12 November 2018.
Nicholson, Amy. "As He Likes It: Shakespeare, Comic Books—for Joss Whedon, It's All the Same Thing." *The Village Voice*. 29 May 2013. Web. 12 November 2018.
Norden, Martin F. *The Cinema of Isolation: A History of Physical Disability in the Movies*. New Brunswick, NJ: Rutgers UP, 1994. Print.
Novy, Marianne. *Love's Argument: Gender Relations in Shakespeare*. Chapel Hill: U of North Carolina P, 1984. Print.
Nowell, Richard. *Blood Money: A History of the First Teen Slasher Film Cycle*. New York: Continuum, 2011. *ProQuest Ebook Central*. Web. 12 November 2018.
Och, Dana. "Beyond Surveillance: Questions of the Real in the Neopostmodern Horror Film." *Style and Form in the Hollywood Slasher Film*. Ed. Wickham Clayton. New York: Palgrave Macmillan, 2015. 195–212. *SpringerLink*. Web. 12 November 2018.

Oliver, Michael. *The Politics of Disablement: A Sociological Approach.* New York: St. Martin's Press, 1990. Print.
Orr, Christopher. "Joss Whedon on the 'No Brainer' of Modernizing *Much Ado About Nothing.*" *The Atlantic.* 7 June 2013. Web. 12 November 2018.
Ortmann, David M., and Richard A. Sprott. *Sexual Outsiders: Understanding BDSM Sexualities and Communities.* Lanham, MD: Rowman and Littlefield, 2013. Print.
O'Toole, Corbett Joan. "The View from Below: Developing a Knowledge Base About an Unknown Population." *Sexuality and Disability* 18.3 (2000): 207–224. *SpringerLink.* Web. 12 November 2018.
Parrish, Jaclyn S. "People vs. Humanity: Utilitarianism and Genre Critique in *The Cabin in the Woods.*" *Slayage: The Journal of Whedon Studies* 15.1 (Winter/Spring 2017). Web. 12 November 2018.
Pascale, Amy. *Joss Whedon: The Biography.* Chicago: Chicago Review Press, 2014. Print.
Pender, Patricia. *I'm Buffy and You're History: Buffy the Vampire Slayer and Contemporary Feminism.* London: I. B. Tauris, 2016. Print.
Penny, Laurie. "We Can Be Heroes." *Wired.* September 2019. 50–59. Print.
Peristere, Loni. "Mutant Enemy U." *Serenity Found: More Unauthorized Essays on Joss Whedon's Firefly Universe.* Ed. Jane Espenson. Dallas: BenBella Books, 2007. 117–129. Print.
Piotrowska, Agnieszka. "Introduction." *Embodied Encounters: New Approaches to Psychoanalysis and Cinema.* Ed. Agnieszka Piotrowska. New York: Routledge, 2015. 1–7. Print.
Porter, Heather M. "'They Teach You That in Whore Academy?' A Quantitative Examination of Sex and Sex Workers in Joss Whedon's *Firefly* and *Dollhouse.*" *The Sex is Out of this World: Essays on the Carnal Side of Science Fiction.* Ed. Sherry Ginn and Michael G. Cornelius. Jefferson, NC: McFarland, 2012. 86–101. Print.
Powers, Mistress Lorelei. *The Mistress Manual.* Gardena, CA: Greenery Press, 2000. Print.
Rabb, J. Douglas, and J. Michael Richardson. *Joss Whedon as Shakespearean Moralist: Narrative Ethics of the Bard and the Buffyverse.* Jefferson, NC: McFarland, 2015. Print.
Reyes, Jenna. "Joss Whedon and Mark Ruffalo in Conversation on The Avengers, Shakespeare, and Learning to Work With Insecurity." *Vulture.* 22 April 2016. Web. 12 November 2018. http://vulture.com.
Richardson, Alan. "Rethinking Romantic Incest: Human Universals, Literary Representation, and the Biology of Mind." *New Literary History* 31.3 (Summer 2000): 553–572. *Project Muse.* Web. 12 November 2018.
Rieser, Klaus. "Masculinity and Monstrosity: Characterization and Identification in the Slasher Film." *Men and Masculinities* 3.4 (April 2001): 370–392. *SAGE journals.* Web. 12 November 2018.
Roberson, Chris, and Georges Jeanty. *No Power in the 'Verse.* Milwaukie, OR: Dark Horse Comics, 2016–2017. Print.
Rogers, Adam. "With *The Avengers,* Joss Whedon Masters the Marvel Universe." *Wired.* May 2012. Web. 12 November 2018.
Rosenberg, Alyssa. "The strong feminism behind Black Widow, and why the critiques don't stand up." *Washington Post.* 5 May 2015. Web. 6 June 2015.
Rubin, Gayle. "The Leather Menace: Comments on Politics and S/M." *Coming to Power: Writings and Graphics on Lesbian S/M.* Ed. Samois. 2nd ed. Boston: Alyson Publications, 1982. 192–227. Print.
_____. "Thinking Sex: Notes for a Radical Theory of the Politics of Sexuality." *Pleasure and Danger: Exploring Female Sexuality.* Ed. Carole S. Vance. Boston: Routledge and Kegan Paul, 1984. 267–319. Print.
_____. "The Traffic in Women: Notes on the 'Political Economy' of Sex." *Toward an Anthropology of Women.* New York: Monthly Review Press, 1975. 157–210. Print.

Rubin, Gayle S. "Elegy for the Valley of the Kings: AIDS and the Leather Community in San Francisco, 1981–1996." *In Changing Times: Gay Men and Lesbians Encounter HIV/AIDS.* Ed. Martin P. Levine, Peter M. Nardi, and John H. Gagnon. Chicago: U of Chicago P, 1997. 101–144. Print.

Rucker, Rudy. *The Ware Tetralogy.* Rockville, MD: Prime Books, 2010. Print.

Rudy, Kathy. "LGBTQ … Z?" *Hypatia* 27.3 (Summer 2012): 601–614. *JSTOR.* Web. 12 November 2018.

St. Louis, Renee. "Demon Magnet in the Friend Zone: Reconsidering Xander Harris in the Age of #MeToo." 8th Biennial Slayage Conference on the Whedonverses. University of North Alabama, Florence. 21–24 June 2018. Lecture.

St. Louis, Renee, and Miriam Riggs. "'And Yet': The Limits of *Buffy* Feminism." *Slayage: The Journal of the Whedon Studies Association* 8.1 (Spring 2010). Web. 10 December 2018.

Saxey, Esther. "Staking a Claim: The Series and its Slash Fan-Fiction." *Reading the Vampire Slayer: An Unofficial Companion to Buffy and Angel.* Ed. Roz Kaveney. New York: I. B. Tauris, 2001. Print.

Schiavi, Michael R. "Opening Ancestral Windows: Post-Stonewall Men and Musical Theatre." *New England Theatre Journal* 13 (2002): 77–98. Print.

Schilderout, Jordan. *Murder Most Queer: The Homicidal Homosexual in the American Theater.* Ann Arbor: U of Michigan P, 2014. *JSTOR.* Web. 12 November 2018.

Schultz, Lauren. "'Hot Chicks with Superpowers': The Contested Feminism of Joss Whedon." Wilcox, Cochran, Masson, and Lavery 356–370.

Sedgwick, Eve Kosofsky. *Between Men: English Literature and Male Homosocial Desire.* New York: Columbia UP, 1985. Print.

———. *Tendencies.* Durham: Duke UP, 1993. Print.

Shakespeare, Tom, Kath Gillespie-Sells, and Dominic Davies. *The Sexual Politics of Disability: Untold Desires.* London: Cassell, 1996. Print.

Shakespeare, William. *Much Ado About Nothing.* c. 1598. Ed. F. H. Mares. Cambridge: Cambridge UP, 2003. Print.

Shaviro, Steven. *The Cinematic Body.* Minneapolis: U of Minnesota P, 1993. *JSTOR.* Web. 9 July 2019.

———. "*The Cinematic Body* Redux." *Parallax* 14.1 (February 2008). Web. 19 July 2019. http://www.shaviro.com/Othertexts/Cinematic.pdf.

Shildrick, Margrit. *Dangerous Discourses of Disability, Subjectivity and Sexuality.* New York: Palgrave Macmillan, 2009. *SpringerLink.* Web. 12 November 2018.

Short, Sue. *Misfit Sisters: Screen Horror as Female Rites of Passage.* New York: Palgrave Macmillan, 2007. *SpringerLink.* Web. 12 November 2018.

Sides, Brandon. "Nussbaum Talks TV as TV, the Buffy-Sopranos Problem, and 'Horrible' Artists." *The Wesleyan Argus.* 30 October 2017. Web. 12 November 2018.

Siebers, Tobin. *Disability Theory.* Ann Arbor: U of Michigan P, 2008. Print.

Silverman, Kaja. *The Acoustic Mirror: The Female Voice in Psychoanalysis and Cinema.* Bloomington: Indiana UP, 1988. Print.

———. *Male Subjectivity at the Margins.* New York: Routledge, 1992. Print.

Simula, Brandy L., and J. Sumerau. "The Use of Gender in the Interpretation of BDSM." *Sexualities* 22.3 (2019): 452–477. *SAGE journals.* Web. 13 August 2019.

Singer, Peter. *Animal Liberation.* 1975. New York: HarperCollins, 2009. Print.

———. "Heavy Petting." *Prospect.* April 2001. Web. 12 November 2018.

Slotkin, Richard. *Gunfighter Nation: The Myth of the Frontier in Twentieth-Century America.* Norman: U of Oklahoma P, 1998. Print.

Smith, Angela M. *Hideous Progeny: Disability, Eugenics, and Classic Horror Cinema.* New York: Columbia UP, 2011. Print.

Snyder, Daniel D. "Scarlett Johansson Has the Most Human Moment in 'The Avengers.'" *The Atlantic.* May 2012. Web. 12 Nov. 2012.

Snyder, Sharon L., and David T. Mitchell. "Body Genres: An Anatomy of Disability in Film." *The Problem Body: Projecting Disability on Film*. Ed. Sally Chivers and Nicole Markotic. Columbus: Ohio State UP, 2010. 179–204. Print.

Solvang, Per. "The Amputee Body Desired: Beauty Destabilized? Disability Re-valued?" *Sexuality and Disability* 25 (2007): 51–64. *SpringerLink*. Web. 12 November 2018.

Spaise, Terry. "Necrophilia and SM: The Deviant Side of *Buffy the Vampire Slayer*." *The Journal of Popular Culture* 38.4 (2005): 744–762. *Wiley Online Library*. Web. 12 November 2018.

Stanley, Marni. "*Buffy*'s Season 8, Image and Text." Wilcox, Cochran, Masson, and Lavery 250–267. Print.

Steele, Valerie. *Fetish: Fashion, Sex and Power*. Oxford: Oxford UP, 1996. Print.

Stewart, Sara. "An Open Letter to Joss Whedon from a Disappointed Feminist Fan After Watching 'Age of Ultron.'" *Women and Hollywood*. 30 April 2015. Web. 6 June 2015. http://blogs.indiewire.com/womenandhollywood/.

Stoller, Robert J. *Observing the Erotic Imagination*. New Haven: Yale UP, 1985. Print.

Taylor, Gary W., and Jane M. Ussher. "Making Sense of S&M: A Discourse Analytic Account." *Sexualities* 4.3 (2001): 293–314. *SAGE Journals*. Web. 13 August 2019.

Temple, Emily. "Joss Whedon Praises Shakespeare's Female Characters, Wants to Make a Ballet About a Library." *Flavorwire*. 31 May 2013. Web. 12 November 2018. http://flavorwire.com.

Tharpe, Frazier. "'Avengers' Director Joss Whedon Wants to Make a Star Wars Movie." *Complex*. 20 October 2016. Web. 10 December 2018.

Thompson, Kirrilly. "Theorising Rider-Horse Relations: An Ethnographic Illustration of the Centaur Metaphor in the Spanish Bullfight." *Human-Animal Studies: Theorizing Animals, Re-Thinking Humanimal Relations*. Ed. Nik Taylor and Tania Signal. Boston: Brill, 2011. 221–254. *ProQuest Ebook Central*. Web. 12 November 2018.

Traub, Valerie. *Desire and Anxiety: Circulations of Sexuality in Shakespearean Drama*. New York: Routledge, 1992. Print.

_____. "Jewels, Statues, and Corpses: Containment of Female Erotic Power in Shakespeare's Plays." *Shakespeare and Gender: A History*. Ed. Deborah Barker and Ivo Kamps. London: Verso, 1995. 120–141. Print.

Tresca, Don. "Dancing in the Sky: The Value of Love in *Runaways*." Frankel 133–144.

_____. "Images of Paraphilia in the Whedonverse." Waggoner 146–172.

_____. "Skeletons in the Closet: The Contradictory Views of the Queer in the Works of Joss Whedon." *Queer TV in the 21st Century: Essays on Broadcasting from Taboo to Acceptance*. Ed. Kylo-Patrick R. Hart. Jefferson, NC: McFarland, 2016. *ProQuest Ebook Central*. Web. 10 December 2018.

Tyrer, Ben. *Out of the Past: Lacan and Film Noir*. New York: Palgrave Macmillan, 2016. *SpringerLink*. Web. 28 June 2019.

Udovitch, Mim. "'Buffy the Vampire Slayer': What Makes Buffy Slay?" *Rolling Stone*. 11 May 2000. Web. 12 November 2018.

Utichi, Joe. "A Buffy-Style Kicking for Torture Porn." *The Sunday Times Culture Magazine*. 15 April 2012. Web. 12 November 2018.

Vaughan, Brian K., and Georges Jeanty. "No Future for You." *Buffy the Vampire Slayer: Season Eight*. Milwaukie, OR: Dark Horse Comics, 2007. Print.

Vineyard, Jennifer. "Joss Whedon on Cabin in the Woods, The Avengers, and Nude Blondes." *Vulture*. 16 April 2012. Web. 12 November 2018.

Waggoner, Erin B., ed. *Sexual Rhetoric in the Works of Joss Whedon*. Jefferson, NC: McFarland, 2010. Print.

Warn, Sarah. "How 'Buffy' Changed the World of Lesbians on Television." *AfterEllen*. 6 June 2003. Web. 12 November 2018. https://www.afterellen.com/tv/4539-how-buffy-changed-the-world-of-lesbians-on-television

Warner, Michael. "Introduction: Fear of a Queer Planet." *Social Text* 29 (1991): 3–17. *JSTOR*. Web. 12 November 2018.
Weiss, Margot. "Working at Play: BDSM Sexuality in the San Francisco Bay Area." *Anthropologica* 48.2 (2006): 229–245. *ProQuest*. Web. 12 November 2018.
Wells, Stanley. *Shakespeare, Sex, and Love*. Oxford: Oxford UP, 2010. Print.
Whaley, Katherine E. "'There's Nothing Wrong with my Body': Xander as a Study in Defining Capability of the Disabled Body in *Buffy the Vampire Slayer*." *Slayage: The Journal of the Whedon Studies Association* 12.2/13.1 (Winter 2014/Spring 2015). Web. 12 November 2018.
Whedon, Jed, and Joss Whedon, dir. *Commentary! The Musical*. Mutant Enemy, 2008. DVD.
Whedon, Joss, and Cliff Richards. "Anywhere but Here." *Buffy the Vampire Slayer: Season Eight*. Milwaukie, OR: Dark Horse Comics, 2008.
Whedon, Joss, and Drew Goddard. *The Cabin in the Woods: The Official Visual Companion*. London: Titan Books, 2012. Print.
Whedon, Joss, and Georges Jeanty. "The Long Way Home." *Buffy the Vampire Slayer: Season Eight*. Milwaukie, OR: Dark Horse Comics, 2007. Print.
_____. "Turbulence." *Buffy the Vampire Slayer: Season Eight*. Milwaukie, OR: Dark Horse Comics, 2010. Print.
Whedon, Joss, and John Cassady. *Astonishing X-Men Omnibus*. New York: Marvel, 2011. Print.
Whedon, Joss, and Karl Moline. "Time of Your Life." *Buffy the Vampire Slayer: Season Eight*. Milwaukie, OR: Dark Horse Comics, 2007. Print.
Whedon, Joss, and Michael Ryan. *Runaways: Dead End Kids*. New York: Marvel, 2017. Print.
Whedon, Joss, and Tim Minear, executive producers. *Firefly*. Mutant Enemy / 20th Century Fox Television, 2002–2003. DVD.
Whedon, Joss, Brett Matthews, and Will Conrad. *Serenity: Better Days*. Milwaukie, OR: Dark Horse Comics, 2008. Print.
_____. *Serenity: Those Left Behind*. Milwaukie, OR: Dark Horse Comics, 2005. Print.
Whedon, Joss, David Greenwalt, and Marti Noxon, executive producers. *Buffy the Vampire Slayer*. Mutant Enemy / 20th Century Fox Television, 1997–2003. DVD.
Whedon, Joss, David Greenwalt, Tim Minear, Jeffrey Bell, and David Fury, executive producers. *Angel*. Mutant Enemy / 20th Century Fox Television, 1999–2004. DVD.
Whedon, Joss, David Solomon, and Tim Minear, executive producers. *Dollhouse*. Mutant Enemy / 20th Century Fox Television, 2009–2010. DVD.
Whedon, Joss, dir. *Avengers: Age of Ultron*. Marvel Studios, 2015. DVD.
_____. "Commentary." *Marvel's The Avengers*. Marvel Studios, 2012. DVD.
_____, dir. *Dr. Horrible's Sing-Along Blog*. Mutant Enemy / Timescience Bloodclub, 2008. DVD.
_____. "Joss Talks Astonishing X-Men & Firefly for UGO." *Fireflyfans*. 26 May 2004. Web. 13 November 2018. http://fireflyfans.net.
_____. "Let's Watch a Girl Get Beaten to Death." *Whedonesque*. 19 May 2007. Web. 13 November 2018. http://whedonesque.com.
_____. "Letter from Joss Whedon." *Dr. Horrible's Sing-Along Blog*. N.d. Web. 13 November 2018. http://drhorrible.com.
_____, dir. *Marvel's The Avengers*. Marvel Studios, 2012. DVD.
_____. *Much Ado About Nothing: A Film by Joss Whedon*. London: Titan Books, 2013. Print.
_____, dir. *Much Ado About Nothing*. Bellwether Pictures / Lionsgate, 2013. DVD.
_____. *Serenity: The Official Visual Companion*. London: Titan Books, 2005. Print.
_____, dir. *Serenity*. Universal, 2005. DVD.

Whedon, Joss, Jed Whedon, and Maurissa Tancharoen, executive producers. *Agents of S.H.I.E.L.D.* Mutant Enemy / Marvel, 2013–2019. DVD.
Whedon, Joss, José Maria Beroy, and Sara Soler. "Dr. Horrible: Best Friends Forever." Milwaukie, OR: Dark Horse Comics, 2018. Print.
Whedon, Joss, Maurissa Tancharoen, Jed Whedon, and Zack Whedon, *Dr. Horrible's Sing-Along Blog: The Book*. London: Titan Books, 2010. Print.
Whedon, Zack. *Dr. Horrible and Other Horrible Stories*. Milwaukie, OR: Dark Horse Comics, 2010. Print.
Whedon, Zack, and Georges Jeanty. *Serenity: Leaves on the Wind*. Milwaukie, OR: Dark Horse Comics, 2014. Print.
Wilcox, Rhonda. "'Give Us the Swords': Whedon's Feminism in Shakespeare's *Much Ado*." 6th Biennial Slayage Conference on the Whedonverses. California State University, Sacramento. 19–22 June 2014. Lecture.
_____. "Joss Whedon's Translation of Shakespeare's *Much Ado About Nothing*: Historical Double Consciousness, Reflections, and Frames." *Slayage: The Journal of the Whedon Studies Association* 11.2 / 12.1 (Summer 2014). Web. 13 November 2018.
_____. *Why Buffy Matters: The Art of Buffy the Vampire Slayer*. New York: I. B. Tauris, 2005. Print.
Wilcox, Rhonda V., and Tanya R. Cochran, eds. *Investigating Firefly and Serenity: Science Fiction on the Frontier*. London: I. B. Tauris, 2010. Print.
Wilcox, Rhonda V., Tanya R. Cochran, Cynthea Masson, and David Lavery, eds. *Reading Joss Whedon*. Syracuse, NY: Syracuse UP, 2014. Print.
Wilkerson, Abby L. "Disability, Sex Radicalism, and Political Agency." *NWSA Journal* 14.3 (Fall 2002): 33–57. Project Muse. Web. 13 November 2018.
Williams, Colin J., and Martin S. Weinberg. "Zoophilia in Men: A Study of Sexual Interest in Animals." *Archives of Sexual Behavior* 32.6 (December 2003): 523–535. Springer-Link. Web. 13 November 2018.
Williams, Linda. "Film Bodies: Gender, Genre, and Excess." *Film Quarterly* 44.4 (Summer 1991): 2–13. JSTOR. Web. 13 November 2018.
_____. "When the Woman Looks." *The Dread of Difference: Gender and the Horror Film*. Ed. Barry Keith Grant. Austin: U of Texas P, 1996. 15–34. Print.
Williams, Tony. "Trying to Survive on the Darker Side." *The Dread of Difference: Gender and the Horror Film*. Ed. Barry Keith Grant. Austin: U of Texas P, 1996. 164–180. Print.
Williamson, Milly. "Spike, Sex and Subtext: Intertextual Portrayals of the Sympathetic Vampire on Cult Television." *European Journal of Cultural Studies* 8.3 (2005): 289–311. SAGE journals. Web. 13 November 2018.
Willis, Victoria. "Joining the Evil League of Evil: The Rhetoric of Posthuman Negotiation in *Dr. Horrible's Sing-Along Blog*." Wilcox, Cochran, Masson, and Lavery 237–249.
Wilts, Alissa. "Evil, Skanky, and Kinda Gay: Lesbian Images and Issues." *Buffy Goes Dark: Essays on the Final Two Seasons of Buffy the Vampire Slayer on Television*. Ed. Lynne Y. Edwards, Elizabeth L. Rambo, and James B. South. Jefferson, NC: McFarland, 2009. 41–56. Print.
Woerner, Meredith, and Katharine Trendacosta. "Black Widow: This Is Why We Can't Have Nice Things." *i09*. 5 May 2015. Web. 6 June 2015. http://io9.com.
Wolf, Stacy. *Changed for Good: A Feminist History of the Broadway Musical*. Oxford: Oxford UP, 2011. Oxford Scholarship Online. Web. 13 November 2018.
_____. *A Problem Like Maria: Gender and Sexuality in the American Musical*. Ann Arbor: U of Michigan P, 2002. Print.
Wolfe, Cary. *Animal Rites: American Culture, the Discourse of Species, and Posthumanist Theory*. Chicago: U of Chicago P, 2008. ProQuest Ebook Central. Web. 13 November 2018.

Wolk, Douglas. *Reading Comics: How Graphic Novels Work and What they Mean.* Philadelphia: Da Capo Press, 2007. Print.
Wood, Robin. *Hollywood from Vietnam to Reagan and Beyond.* 1986. New York: Columbia UP, 2003. Print.
Woofter, Kristopher, and Jasie Stokes. "Once More into the *Woods*: An Introduction and Provocation." *Slayage: The Journal of the Whedon Studies Association* 10.2/11.1 (Fall 2013/Winter 2014). Web. 13 November 2018.
Wright, Leigh Adams. "Asian Objects in Space." *Finding Serenity: Anti-Heroes, Lost Shepherds and Space Hookers in Joss Whedon's Firefly.* Ed. Jane Espenson. Dallas: BenBella Books, 2004. 29–35. Print.
Yost, Megan R., and L. E. Hunter. "BDSM Practitioners' Understandings of Their Initial Attraction to BDSM Sexuality: Essentialist and Constructionist Narratives." *Psychology & Sexuality* 3.3 (September 2012): 244–259. *Taylor & Francis online.* Web. 26 June 2019.
Žižek, Slavoj. *Enjoy Your Symptom! Jacques Lacan in Hollywood and Out.* New York: Routledge, 2001.
_____. *The Fright of Real Tears: Krzysztof Kieslowski Between Theory and Post-Theory.* London: British Film Institute, 2001. Print.
_____. *Looking Awry: An Introduction to Jacques Lacan through Popular Culture.* Cambridge, MA: MIT Press, 1993. Print.
Zynda, Lyle. "We're All Just Floating in Space." *Finding Serenity: Anti-Heroes, Lost Shepherds and Space Hookers in Joss Whedon's Firefly.* Ed. Jane Espenson. Dallas: BenBella Books, 2004. 85–95. Print.

Index

Numbers in **_bold italics_** indicate pages with illustrations

Aaron, Jason 147
Abbott, Stacey 48
Aberdein, Andrew 26, 69
abjection 141
able-bodiedness 20, 87, 93, 103, 106–107; compulsory 88–89; temporary 110
ableism 88
abstinence, sexual 86, 156, 165
Academy, Alliance 73–74, 80
Acker, Amy 28, 37, **_163_**, 167, 178–179, 181, 189, 192–194, **_195_**, 196–197
action (of a play) 130, 136, 148, 183, 187
Adams, Carol J. 117
adolescent sexuality 16, 33, 118–119, 157, 164
adoption 126
Adorno, Theodor 22
adult baby play 57
adultery 75
The Advocate 14
aesthetics 14, 33, 78, 136, 143, 148, 169
affairs 34, 159, 203–204
affect 22, 169, 183, 208*n*6, 208*n*7
after care 49
age play 57
agency 9, 15, 17, 19, 26, 29–30, 34–35, 37, 40–41, 55–56, 60, 69, 80, 87, 90–91, 114, 118, 121, **_129_**, 130–131, 145, 149, 155, 167, 169, 172, 176, 180–182, 184–185, 187–189, 192, 194, 197, 205
Agents of S.H.I.E.L.D. 7, 11, 40
AIDS 64
aim, sexual 63, 85, 154; inhibition of 86
Alaniz, José 90
alcohol 158, 164
Aldiss, Brian 73
Alexander, Jenny 20, 207*n*5
Alien 169–170
Alliance 65, 68, 72–74, 76, 79–81, 209*ch*2*n*3
alliance system 179–182, 185–188, 191–193, 199–201
alpha male 165, 171
alter ego 36, 104, 238
alterity 116
Altman, Rick 137–138, 140, 210*n*3

Aluwyn 10, 31, **_32_**, 33
Amazons 65
The American Film Musical 137
amputation 19, 94
amputee 94
Amy (rat) 121
Amy-Chinn, Dee 13, 20, 26–27, 46–47, 69
amygdala 209*ch*2*n*3
analysand 72
anarchism 125
Andrew (Wells) 6, 10–11, 50, 130–131
Angel 10–11, 16–19, 30, 48, 51, 112, 140, 208*n*8
Angel (comic books) 5
Angel (television show) 5, 7, 10–11, 18–20, 140, 209*ch*2*n*1
animal kingdom 133
Animal Liberation 115
Animal Studies 115–117
animal turn 116
animals: demonic 116; domestic 119–120, 122; liberation of 124; nonhuman 112–113, 115–118, 121, 123–125, 130, 137, 144, 152–153, 205; rights of 113, 124–125
antagonist 199
anthropocentrism 112, 115
anxiety 1, 48, 81, 87, 90, 93–94, 96–97, 104–105, 128, 185; castration 26, 35, 78, 85, 156–157, 161–164, 166, 168, 176–177; social 150
Anya 6, 14–15, 18, 40, 49, 127
apathy, sexual 174
apocalypse 49, 121, 161, 177; happy 176
apparatus theory 22
arc reactor 105
architect 179
aristocracy 82, 179
arousal 130, 161, 168
asceticism 64, 85
asexuality 90–91, 93
Ash, Nina 112
ass 128, 201
assholes 158, 170
Astaire, Fred 149
Astonishing X-Men 30, 89, 92–104

Index

Athlete archetype 158
audience 1, 5, 9, 15–18, 20, 22–24, 27–28, 35, 38, 47, 52–53, 58, 62, 64–65, 70, 74, 79, 82, 97–99, 106–109, 112–113, 115, 118, 120, 124, 141, 143, 148, 150, 153, 155, 158–160, 162, 167–169, 173, 179–180, 190–194, 196–197, 199–202, 207*n*1, 210*n*3; horror 162, 164–166; 172
auteurism 3, 11, 14
The Avengers (film) 7, 12, 21, 35, 37, 52–56, 59, 104–105, 179, 210*ch*5*n*2
Avengers (superhero team) 21, 35, 105, 108, 110, 205
Avengers: Age of Ultron 7, 12, 21, 35–37, 39, 44, 53–56, 59, 93, 106–110
Avengers: Endgame 40

babies 57, 71, 77, 86, 120, 125–126, 131, 133
Baccarin, Morena 11, 70
bad cop 201
Bad Horse 137, 144, 148–149, 152–153, 155
Bad Horse Chorus 152
Bagby, Larry 120
Bait and Switch 151
Bakke, Monica 118
Baldwin, Adam 11
ballerinas 107, 162
Balthasar 199
Bamber, Linda 187
bankruptcy 159
Banner, Bruce 7, 11, 20–21, 36–37, 40, 43–44, 52–59, 87, 89, 91, **92**, 93, 104–110, 205; *see also* Hulk
Barbie dolls 193
Barker, Meg-John 44
Barton, Clint 108
Barton, Laura 108
basements 49, 141–142
Basinger, Jeanine 204
Batcave 142
Bates, Emma 197
Batman 142
Batwoman 208*n*9
Baudry, Jean-Louis 22
Baumgardner, Jennifer 15
Bay 112, 125–126, 131, 133
Bayarmaa *see* Bay
BD *see* bondage and discipline
BDSM 5, 7–9, 28, **29**, 38, 41–44, 46–49, 55, 57, 154, 157, 208*n*10, 208*n*1; *see also* bondage and discipline; dominance/submission; sadomasochism
BDSM in American Science Fiction and Fantasy 7
Bea 75, 80
beating 150, 194
Beatrice 2, 7, 37, 178, 181, 183–190, 192–199, **195**, 201
"Beauty and the Beast" trope 37
Bechdel test 137
becoming-animal 116–117, 120, 123, 130
Beeler, Stan 18

Beetz, Andrea 118
Beirne, Piers 117
"Belle Chose" 29
Benedick 2, 7, 37, 178, 181, 183–187, 189, 192–199, **195**, 201, 205
Bennet, Chloe 40
Bennett, Tara 55
Benson, Amber 10, 207*n*1
Berg, Steve 155
Berger, Harry 187–188
Beroy, José Maria **139**, 140
"Best Friends Forever" 140, 151, 154
Bester 81
bestiality 113, 117–118
Better Days 75, 77, 82, 85
Between Men 140
"Bewitched, Bothered and Bewildered" 205
BFFs (best friends forever) **139**
Big Bad 125
bigotry 124
bikini 171
Billy (Dr. Horrible) 137–138, 140–141, 145, 147, 149–150
Billy the Vampire Slayer 10, 31
binary sexuality 13, 18–19
Bird, Sharon 146
bisexuality 5, 10, 18–19, 26–27, 31, 64; erasure of 18, 27, 38
biting 26, 81, 200
Black, Heather 79
Black Room 162, 165
Black Widow 2, 7, 35, **36**, 37–39, 44, **52**, 53–60, 68, 107, 201; *see also* Romanoff, Natasha
bleed (comic book art) 50, 70–71, 209*ch*1*n*3
blindness 19, 100, 102
blocking 37, 180, 191
blondes 6, 85, 167
blood 49, 127, 168
blue 77, 98, 101, 103–104, 146
"The Body" 208*n*7
body language 195
bondage 24, 49, 53, 120, 122, 197, 208*n*1
bondage and discipline 208*n*1; *see also* bondage
Boney, Bradley 141
bong 161, 176
Book, Shepherd Derrial 27, 61, 64, 75, 84–86
bookworm 163
Borachio 182, 186, 200–201
Boreanaz, David 10
bottom 153
bourgeoisie 62, 72
Boyd (Langton) 28
"Brand New Day" 140, 147, 150
bras 122, 200
Breakworld 97–99, 103, 209*ch*3*n*2
breast pump 133
breasts 31, 128, 130, 133, 168, 200
Brendon, Nicholas 50
The Bronze (discussion board) 16
Brooks, Richard 77

Index

brothel 64, 79
brother-hero 62, 73
brothers 11, 62, 73, 75–76, 127, 135, 153, 161, 185, 189, 199–200, 209*ch2n*1
Buckman, Alyson 8, 18, 33, 74, 140, 145, 147
Buckner, Father 174
Buckner, Judah 176
Buckner, Matthew 162, 165, 173
Buckner, Patience 161
Buckner family 157, 161, 165–166, 168, 171
Buffy (Summers) 6, 10–11, 13–18, 20–26, 30–31, **32**, 37, 39–53, 56, 95–96, 98, 112, 119–126, 130–131, 133, 140, 157, 166, 207*n*2, 208*n*8, 209*ch1n*2, 210*ch5n*2
Buffy the Vampire Slayer (comic books) 1–2, 5, 7, 10–11, 30–33, 45, 50–51, 98, 114, 118, 130, 132–133
Buffy the Vampire Slayer (television show) 5–11, 13–20, 23, 27, 30, 35, 39–40, 45, 47–48, 112–114, 118, 120, 123–126, 133, 136, 140, 204–205, 207*n*1, 207*n*3, 207*n*4, 207*n*5, 208*n*7, 209*ch2n*1, 210*ch5n*2
Buffybot 24–25, 45
Buffyverse 5–6, 8, 10, 13–17, 19–20, 26, 31–33, 41, 48–49, 112–114, 116, 118, 123, 125, 133–134, 205, 207*n*3
Bug Room 102
Bukatman, Scott 90
Burnett, Tamy 8, 15–16, 19
Burns, Angie 46
Burr, Vivien 21
Busch, Adam 205
BUST 15
butch 82
Butler, Judith 209*ch2n*2
butterfly 193
Butters, Tara 28
Byrne, John 30, 208*n*10, 208*n*11

Cabaret 136
The Cabin in the Woods 7, 9, 11, 33–35, 156–177, 179, 205, 210*ch6n*1
caffeine 162
cages 99, 120, 122–123
Cain, Cheryl 66
Calcutta, India 105
Califia, Pat/Patrick 12–13, 26
California 16, 178–179
Call, Kate vii, 6
Call, Michelle viii, 6
Call, Rory vii
call girls 64
Call of the Wild 120
Callahan (firearm brand) 78
camaraderie 184
camera 22, 52, 74, 106, 130, 168, 172, 174, 176, 195, 197, 199
camp 18
Canaan, Michael 152
Canavan, Gerry 167–168
cannibalism 160–161

Captain America 12
Captain Hammer 11, 33–34, 135–155, 210*n*3
"Captain Hammer: Be Like Me!" 154
Captivity 160
Cardellini, Linda 108
Caritas 18
Carnevale 193
carpenter 127
Carpenter, Charisma 127
Carpenter, John 156
Carroll, Noël 22
Cassady, John 30, 91–93, **95**, 96–98, 100, ***101***, 102–103
castration 19, 25–26, 43, 85, 103, 161–162, 164; anxiety *see* anxiety, castration
Caulfield, Emma 15
celibacy 27, 61, 64, 84–86
centaurette ***129***, 131–132, 205
centaurs 2, 10, 17, 112–115, 128–132, 205
chainsaws 165–166
characterization 90, 158, 170–171
Charmed Circle 12, 38, 69
Chase, Cordelia 127, 205
Chen, Jo ***129***, 130
child abuse 28
childhood 63, 76, 156
A Chorus Line 138, 144
Christianity 115
The Cinematic Body 208*n*6
cinematography 180, 204
circus 100, 105
civilization 74–75, 157
Claremont, Chris 30, 102, 208*n*10, 208*n*11
Clark, Krystal 55
Clark, Spencer Treat 182
Clarke, Melinda 68
Claudio 12, 38, 181–192, 196–199, 201
cliché 18, 31, 167, 170, 175
close-up 50, 96, 99, 106, 128, 168
closet 3, 6, 10, 48, 54, 142, 152, 193
Clover, Carol J. 34, 156, 161, 163–165, 167–169
Cocca, Carolyn 16
Cochran, Tanya 207*n*1
coffee 161–162, 176
cognitivism 22–23, 160, 208*n*6
Cole, Kai 14, 179, 203–204, 210*ch6n*1
collar 51
Collier, Noelle R. 9
colorblindness 101
Colossus 30, 97; *see also* Rasputin, Peter
comedy 7, 178, 186–187, 202; romantic 179
Comics Code Authority 95
coming out 6, 18, 48, 108, 110, 124
comma 188
commedia dell'arte 193
commercial break 121
companion species 115, 122, 134
"Companion Species Manifesto" 115
Companions 26–27, 61–62, 69–70, 85
compassion 112–113, 138, 191
Conan Pose 132

Index

conception 194
Conflict Diamond 151
Connell, R.W. 33, 137, 143–144, 148, 152
Connolly, Kristen 34, 157, **173**
conquest, sexual 141, 176
Conrad, Will 68, 77, 82, 85
Conrade 38, 178, 181–182, 184, 186, 198–201
consent 5, 9, 12–13, 17, 21, 24–25, 28, 38, 46–47, 58, 61, 80, 117–118, 132, 134, 153, 173, 180–181, 184, 206; active 204–205; affirmative 173, 210ch6n1; age of 72; nonverbal 113
consumerism 147
Cook, Carol 188
Cordelia (Chase) 127, 205
costumes 136, 152, 180, 204
Coulson, Phil 53
Councillor 69
courtship 79, 138, 184
cousins 194–195
Cox, Jessica 153
coxcomb 201
cradle robber 131
Craven, Wes 156, 159
Crazy Ivan maneuver 81
credits 28, 122
Creed, Barbara 22, 26, 118
crime 34, 76, 82, 125, 136, 158, 207n1
crip theory 88–89
crowbar 166
cuckoldry 181, 183, 185–186, 189, 193
Cunningham, Sean S. 156
cure narrative 100
Curt 34, 158, 163, 165, 167–172, 174–176
curtains 142–143, 148
Cyclops 89; *see also* Summers, Scott

Daisy 40
damsel in distress 36, 55–56, 145
Dana 34–35, 157–166, 169–176, **173**
dancing 46, 141, 149, 174, 176, 187, 198
Daniel, Rod 114
Daniels, Bradley 209ch2n3
Dark Horse Comics 61
Darwin, Charles 209ch4n1
dating 2, 16, 19, 30, 119, 124, 127, 145, 149, 151, 169
daughters 14, 76, 183–185, 190, 192
Dauterman, Russell 147
Davies, Dominic 108
Davis, Lennard 91
Dawn (Summers) 2, 10–11, 14, 17, 19, 25, **32**, 33, 50, 112–118, 126–134, **129**, 205
Day, Felicia 33, 136, 146
"Days of Future Past" 30
DC Comics 208n9
Dead-Evil Lesbian Cliché 18
Dear Evan Hansen **139**, 140
death drive 54, 58
Death Ray 143, 147–148
decapitation 168, 175
deconstruction 116

dehumanization 119, 171, 175
Dekkers, Midas 118
De Knight, Steven S. 47
Deleuze, Gilles 116–117
Delpy, Julie 107
demon 10, 18, 31, **32**, 45, 50, 116–117, 127–128, 132–133; vengeance 127
Denisof, Alexis 178–179, 181, 184, 187, 189, 192–198, **195**
Depner, Kurt 6
DeRitter, Lillian 29
DeRoss, Jennifer 31
Derrida, Jacques 115–116
de Sade, Donatien Alphonse François, Marquis 25, 66, 194
DeSimone, Tom 165
desire 5, 9, 12–13, 21–29, 31, 33, 38, 42–43, 46, 48, 50, 54–56, 58, 61, 63–64, 67, 69–71, 124, 127–128, 132, 134–135, 140–141, 144–145, 147, 150, 161–162, 166–169, 172–176, 182–183, 185, 189, 195, 197–200, 208n6, 208n8, 208n1, 209ch1n2; incestuous 5, 27, 56, 61–63, 72–76, 79–85, 88, 91, 94, 97, 99, 106–107, 110, 131, 161; intergenerational 5, 16, 33; queer 141–142, 155, 207n3; same-gender 82; straight 120, 130, 145, 149; zoophilic 10, 17, 113–118, 126, 128, 130, 167
deus ex machina 132
devotee, amputation 94
diagnosis 63, 105
dialogue 6, 30, 37, 52, 102, 109, 158, 180
diegesis 138, 173, 175
difference, sexual 108, 162
Dika, Vera 156, 166
DiPlacidi, Jenny 73–74
the Director 157–158, 170, 176
disability 5, 8–9, 19–20, 30, 38, 41, 44, 54, 87–111; emotional 91; invisible 107; management of 20, 30, 91, 105–107, 110; physical 91; temporary 106
Disability Studies 37
disability theory 19, 87–89, 93
disabled sexuality 5, 8–9, 19–20, 30, 38, 41, 87–111
discipline 21, 37, 39, 57–58, 77, 89, **101**, 103–104, 106, 154, 174; *see also* bondage and discipline
disguise 122, 194
Disney 141, 146; princesses 146
dissolves 137
diversity, sexual 14, 38, 64, 81, 88
Doane, Mary Ann 22, 147
Dobber 137
Dr. Horrible 33–34, 135, 137–138, **139**, 140–153, 155
Dr. Horrible's Sing-Along Blog (comic books) 7, 11, 140, 145, 151, 154
Dr. Horrible's Sing-Along Blog (musical) 7, 9, 11, 33–34, 135–155
Dogberry 182, 201
dogs 115, 119, 122, 125, 171

Dollhouse 2, 5, 7, 10–11, 14, 19, 26–29, 33, 40, 145
dollhouse 184
domestication 120, 122
domesticity 17, 71, 76, 108, 120, 130, 142, 184
dominance: female 12, 20–21, 24, 35–36, 39–62, 68, 77, 180–182, 186–187, 189, 191–192, 194, 196–197, 201, 207*n*5, 209*ch*1*n*2; male 20, 38, 47, 61, 70, 137, 144, 180–181, 183, 199–201; professional 28–29, 41–42, 68; *see also* BDSM; dominance/dominance; dominance/submission
dominance/dominance 68–71
dominance/submission 6, 10, 20, 39–60, 65–68, 100, 178–202, 208*n*1; *see also* BDSM
dominatrix 28, **29**, 68, 121; *see also* dominance, female; dominance, professional
Don John 38, 181–182, 184, 186–187, 198–201
Don Pedro 183–185, 187, 189–191, 198
doormat 67
"Doppelgängland" 121
Dos Santos, Dan **83**, 84
"Doublemeat Palace" 133
Downey, Robert, Jr. **92**
Dracula 10, 98
drills 162
Driver, Susan 17
drugs 157–158, 162–163, 167, 170–171, 175, 205, 209*ch*3*n*1
drunkards 194, 200–201
DS *see* dominance/submission
dual focus 138
duel 197
duet 138
Dushku, Eliza 15, **29**
dweeb 143
Dyer, Richard 144
dystopia 154

Early, Jubal 77, 83–84
Earth 98–99, 132–133
Echo 7, 28, **29**, 40
economics 15, 163–164, 171, 179, 184–185
economy, sexual 19, 174–175, 179, 191
Edelstein, David 159
egghead 170
ego 54
ego-formation 43–44, 58
Ejiofor, Chiwetel 74
Electra complex 82, 96
Elliot-Smith, Darren 165
emasculation 189
embodiment 93–94, 208*n*6
Emma (Washburne) 71, 76, 86
Emmy award 135
"End of Days" 15, 49
engines 11, 81–84
England 178–179, 182, 210*ch*7*n*1
English, Shakespearean 197
Enlightenment 115
entitlement, sexual 147, 194

Epstein, Arthur 78
erections 79
erogenous zones 88
Espensode 130
Espenson, Jane 11, 14, 29, 45, 82, 125, 130
essentialism 119
ethics 2–3, 5, 9, 11–12, 17, 20–21, 25, 28–30, 33, 38, 47–48, 56, 59, 61, 64, 67, 69–70, 80, 100, 112–113, 115–118, 123–125, 133–134, 143, 145, 153, 155, 158–160, 172, 174, 182, 184, 191, 199–200, 204–206
eugenics 92–93, 100, 108–110
Europa and the Bull 118
Europe 118, 178–179, 182, 187
Evans, Chris 12
Eve 19
"Everything You Ever" 138, 150
Evil League of Evil 140, 150–151
exclamation mark 188
exogamy 63, 76
experimentation: animal 117, 133; medical 124; sexual 88
eyepatch 207*n*4
Eyre, Ronald 199

fade to black 123, 150
Fain, Sarah 28
fairy tales 77, 146
Faith 15, 18, 46, 49, 127
Fake Thomas Jefferson 151
Fall, Wendy 20, 48
family 33, 72–75, 112, 126, 135, 143, 157, 160–161, 183, 190
fan communities 2, 154, 203
fan fiction 16, 45
fans 3, 6
fantasy 75, 82, 141, 208*n*9
farmhouse 55, 108–109
fashion 15, 143
Faszekas, Michele 28
fathers 21, 43, 50, 55–57, 73, 82, 96, 157, 162, 174, 182–184, 189–190, 194; of the bride 191; in law 183
Fawaz, Ramzi 142
femininity 15, 27, 33, 42–43, 53, 69, 82, 114, 131, 143, 148, 152, 155, 164, 169, 171–172, 187, 193–194; compliant 33, 144–146, 155; emphasized 144
feminism 9, 11–14, 20, 22, 25, 28, 35, 37, 41–43, 54, 109–110, 114, 131, 135–136, 164–165, 178–179, 188, 202–204, 210*ch*6*n*1; cultural 13; girlie 6, 15, 35, 42; radical 15, 31; second wave 15; third wave 15, 35
femme 18, 208*n*9
fetishism 5, 8–9, 11–12, 24, 27, 38, 63–64, 78, 81, 94, 101, 107, 116, 136, 142, 154, 161, 208*n*10; breast 133; female 27, 61, 80–82; firearm 61, 63, 78–80, 85; machine 61, 63, 81–84, **83**; male 26–27, 43, 61, 81
Fillion, Nathan 11, 33, 61, 136, 182, 201
Final Boy 34–35, 158, 165, 174, 176

Index

Final Girl 34, 156–157, 163–166, 169–170, 172, 174, 176
Final Person 165, 175
Final Woman 170
Finn, Riley *see* Riley (Finn)
Firefly (comic books) 7, 11, 61–86
Firefly (television show) 7, 11, 15, 26–27, 39–40, 61–86, 136, 205, 209*ch2n*1
First Boy 158
fist bump 184
flashbacks 20, 73, 81, 107–108, 186
Fool archetype 158, 175
football 172
fop 201
Forbidden Planet 161
foreplay 83
foreshadowing 53, 68, 127, 166, 175
Fortress of Solitude 141
Foster, Jane 147
Foucault, Michel 72, 117, 179
Fowler, Gene, Jr. 114
framing 30, 37, 46, 52, 59, 70, 74, 109, 121, 128, 131, 141, 154, 162, 174, 180, 195–196, 207*n*1
Franich, Darren 58
Frankenstein 73
Frazetta, Frank 132
freak show 74, 105
freaks 100, 105, 155
freeze frame 162
freeze ray 138, 141–142, 149
Freud, Sigmund 16, 22–23, 63, 76, 78, 80, 86, 160; *see also* psychoanalysis
friar 197
Friday the 13th 156, 165
friendship 36, 50, 132, 140, 142, 195
Frohard-Dourlent, Hélène 8
Frost, Emma 11, 20, 30, 40, 89, 99–104, ***101***, 208*n*10
funeral 190–191
Fury, Nick 106, 110, 207*n*4

Gage, Christos 50
Games of ancient Rome 153
Games of Terror 166
Gamman, Lorraine 80–81
Gandhi, Mahatma 149
gaslighting 14, 123, 203
gay 5–6, 10–11, 14, 18–19, 31, 33, 50, 64, 100, 120, 130–131, 135, 138, 140–143, 152, 155, 165, 172, 199, 207*n*3, 208*n*9
gaze 25, 46, 58; active 164, 172, 174; female 35, 162, 172, 190; male 25, 35, 74, 94, 161–162, 165, 168, 172, ***173***
geek 143, 153–154
Gellar, Sarah Michelle 14
gender 5–8, 10–11, 13–14, 17, 22, 36, 41–43, 53–54, 64, 82, 88, 114, 119, 131–133, 137, 142–145, 148, 155, 164–165, 178–180; binary 18, 29, 47; fluidity 165, 208*n*12; identity 29, 31; monstrous 165; presentation 31, 42, 82, 169, 192–193, 196, 198–199, 201; stereotypes 174

Gender Studies 15
genital sexuality 63
genitals 63, 146
genre 7, 34–36, 79, 87, 90, 92, 120, 135–138, 142–144, 147–148, 155–160, 162, 165–167, 174–175, 179, 210*ch5n*2; *see also* horror (genre); science fiction; Western (genre)
Gentlemen 23, 31, 56
Gerrold, David 81
giant 127–128, 131
Giles, Rupert ***32***, 33, 50, 119, 132
Gillespie-Sells, Kath 108
Ginn, Sherry 209*ch2n*3
Girard, René 140
girl power 15
Gjokaj, Enver 29
Glass, Ron 64
Glau, Summer 19, 63
Glory 25
gloves 142, 152, 154, 156
Goddard, Drew 11, 34, 156, 158–159, 168, 174, 210*ch6n*1
Goddess 132–133
gods, elder 35, 157, 168, 170, 175–176
Gomez, Lisa 31
"Gone" 98
"good man with a gun" trope 79–80
Goth 154
Gothic 27, 61–63, 72–76
"Graduation Day, Part 1" 121
Graves, Stephanie 7, 35
grease 83–84
Greece 69, 114
Green, Seth 10, 112
Gregg, Clark 53, 184, 190
Grey, Jean 30, 100, 102
grief 197
Griffin, Dax 81
groom 191
groupies 140, 143–144, 153–155
Guattari, Felix 116–117
gulling 184
Gunfighter Nation 79
guns 11, 27, 61, 63, 78–80, 165, 171
gutter (comic books) 209*ch1n*3

Hadley 35, 157, 159, 162, ***163***, 164, 166, 168, 175
hair 2, 101, 122–123, 130, 150, 196; dye 167, 172
Halberstam, Jack/Judith 165–166
Hallett, Andy 18
Halloween 156–158, 165
Halverson, Bennett 19
Ham-Jet 147
Hammer Cycle 147
hammers 135, 141, 147, 153
hands 19, 31, 47, 59, 77, 104, 107, 123, 132, 142, 151, 154, 172, 194, 196, 201
Hannigan, Alyson 10, 207*n*1
"happy ending" (sex work) 96
Haraway, Donna 115–116

Index

Harmony 52
Harris, Neil Patrick 33, 136, 138
Harris, Xander *see* Xander (Harris)
Hart, Lynda 12
Hawk, Julie 29
Hawkeye 36, 106; *see also* Barton, Clint
Heart of Gold (brothel) 64, 80
"Heart of Gold" (episode) 68, 70, 78–79, 209*ch*2*n*1
Heaven 24, 45–46, 178
hedonism 35, 158, 161, 164
Hedwig and the Angry Inch 136, 155
Helberg, Simon 135
Helen 79
hell dimension 132
Hell Night 165
Hemsworth, Chris 34, 59, 158, 171
henchman 144, 151, 181
henchperson 182
henchwoman 151, 181
Hendricks, Christina 68
Hero 37–38, 178, 181, 183–191, **192**, 194–200, 210*ch*7*n*2
"Hero of Canton" 79
hetaeras 69
heteroflexibility 31
heteronormativity 1–3, 5, 10, 13, 20, 33–34, 37–38, 73, 87–88, 100, 124, 135–137, 145–146, 155, 174, 208*n*9
heterosexism 176
heterosexuality 10, 12–14, 18–19, 34, 41, 69, 79, 89, 94, 120, 136–138, 140–142, 147, 149, 151–152, 168, 174, 184; compulsory 88, 137, 145–146
Hiddleston, Tom 36, 53
Highleyman, Liz 13, 41–42
hill folk 74–75
historiography 204
Hitchcock, Alfred 161
Holden 34, 158, 162, 164–166, 169–174, **173**, 176, 205, 210*ch*6*n*1
Holder, Nancy 67–68
Hollywood, California 91, 105, 136–137, 157, 210*ch*5*n*2
holster 189
homo sapiens 133
homoeroticism 10–11, 18, 33–34, 135, 137, **139**, 140–142, 165, 186, 210*ch*7*n*1
homophobia 10, 14, 38, 120, 136, 152, 155, 199
homosexuality 12, 19, 34, 100, 137, 140, 147, 199, 210*ch*7*n*1; *see also* gay
homosociality 34, 135, 137–138, **139**, 140, 142, 146–148, 152, 181–184, 188, 193, 210*ch*7*n*1
honesty 62, 69–70
Hooper, Tobe 161
Horkheimer, Max 22
horns, cuckold's 193
Horrible Van Remote 150
horror (genre) 7, 26, 34–35, 37, 92, 118, 120, 156–165, 170, 172
horsehair 130

horses 2, 112, 114, 128, **129**, 130–132, 137, 144, 148–149, 152–153, 155, 193
Hostel 159
Hourglass 154
Hulk 7, 21, 36–37, 39–40, 44, 53–60, 87, 89, 91, 104–110; *see also* Banner, Bruce
humanities 116
Humbert, Humbert 131
Hunter, Jay 179–180, 191, 196
hurt/comfort fiction 45
husbandry, animal 130
husbands 1–2, 27, 61, 66–68, 77, 181, 189, 193–194
husband's bulge 161, 173
"Hush" 23, 31, 56, 96
Huston, Shaun 54
Hutchison, Anna 34, 158
hybrid 2, 6, 17, 112–116, 126, 128, **129**, 130–134
hyena 119–120
hygiene 161
hymn 190
hypersexuality 171, 209*ch*2*n*3
hysteria 83, 148, 174

"I Want" song 141
I Was a Teenage Werewolf 114
"I Will" song 147
Iatropoulos, Mary Ellen 1–3, 19, 29–30
Iceman 208*n*9
id 58–59, 161, 176
idealization 14, 64, 72–73, 185
identification 91, 160, 164–165
identity: gender 29, 31; secret 137, 149; sexual 12–13, 81, 117–118, 136
identity politics 13
ideology 41, 125, 138
imaginary 21–23, 26, 43–51, 55–58, 96, 103, 135, 137, 141, 149–150, 195, 198, 208*n*6, 208*n*7
imago 43–44, 54
impairment 11, 19–20, 30, **32**, 87–89, 91–93, 96–97, 99–111, 151, 207*n*4, 209*ch*2*n*3; chronic 106; mobility 106; narrative 90; reproductive 37, 107–108; temporary 106
impotence 200
Inara (Serra) 11, 26–27, 40, 61–62, 64, 68–70, **71**, 75, 86
Inca 127
incest 5, 56, 72, 161; narrative 27, 61, 72–76; sibling 27, 61–63, 72–76, 131, 209*ch*2*n*2; taboo 75–76; *see also* desire, incestuous
infantilization 57, 90, 93
infidelity 14, 120, 182, 190, 203–204
initiative 26, 124–125
innocence, sexual 34, 91, 93, 156, 169–170
intangibility 89, 93–94, **95**, 97–99
intercourse, sexual 130
intergenerational sexuality 5, 9, 16–17, 33, 38, 131
interracial sex 49
interrogation 53, 65, 201
intersex 208*n*12

234 Index

interspecies sex 113, 117–118, 137, 153; *see also* bestiality; zoophilia
intimacy 49, 66, 75, 88, 97, 134
Isaacs, Rebekah *32*, 50, 132
isolation 91, 105–106, 110, 146

Jardine, Lisa 187, 189
Jayne (Cobb) 11, 27, 61, 63–64, 67, 75, 78–80, 85–86
"Jaynestown" 75, 79
jealousy 11, 62, 68–70, 86, 120, 122, 124, 127–128
Jeanty, Georges 70, *71*, 77, 86, 125, 128, 131
"Jeckyll and Hyde" trope 108
Jenkins, Richard 35, *163*
Jew 99
jock 158, 170–171
Joffe, Roland 160
Johansson, Scarlett 12, *36*, *52*, 56, 106, 109
Johnson, Ashley 186
joints (marijuana) 161, 175, 201
jouissance 23, 25–26, 48, 66, 75, 85, 197
Jowett, Lorna 8, 17
Joyce (Harris) 133
Jules 34, 158, 161–176
jump scare 162
"Just Say No" 157

Kane, Christian 19
Kane, Kate 208n9
Kaplan, Louise 82
Karolina 31, 208n12
Karras, Irene 15
Katrina 145
Kaylee (Frye) 11, 27, 61, 63–64, 74, 76–78, 80–86, *83*
Keegan, Cael 207n3
Kennedy (Slayer) 10, 18
Kent, Clark 136
Kent, Jonathan Samuel 136
Key 25, *32*, 112, 126, 131–133; *see also* Dawn (Summers)
Kiki 29
King, Derrick 168, 172
Kingston University 7
kinship 72, 179, 182–183
Kirby, Jack 90
kiss 23, 44, 46, 50–51, 56, 58, 96–97, 121, 123, 127, 131, 167, 189, 196, 198, 200; French 149; lesbian 9–10, 207n1
Klüver-Bucy syndrome 209ch2n3
knives 156, 165–166
Kociemba, David 11, 29–30, 36–37
Kranz, Fran 11, 34, 38, 157, 181, 190–191, *192*
Krueger, Freddy 156
Kruun, Powerlord 103–104
Kunkle, Sheila 23

lab coat 142
Lacan, Jacques 21–26, 41, 43–45, 48, 51, 54–55, 58, 60, 63–64, 68–69, 75, 85, 91, 138, 141, 147, 182, 195, 207n6, 208n7, 208n8; *see also* psychoanalysis
Lachman, Dichen 28
lack 23–24
lactation 133
lair 141–142, 150
Lane, Lois 136
language 3, 21, 47, 49, 55, 58, 85, 96, 102–103, 115–117, 124, 176, 180, 184
lap dance 174
Larbalestier, Justine 49
Larry 120, 123
Lassek, Lisa 67
latex 136
Latin 161
laundromat 141, 145, 147
Lavery, David 11, 136
Law of the Father 56–60, 157
leash 198
leather 28, 46, 136, 142
Leaves on the Wind 27, 62, 70, *71*, 79–80, *83*, 84
Leda and the Swan 118
Lee, Stan 90
legs 132–133, 199–200
Leia (Organa), Princess 73
Lenk, Tom 10, 182, 201
Leonard, Kendra Preston 33, 143, 147, 153
Leonato 182–186, 190–194, 198
lesbianism 5, 9–10, 13–14, 17–18, 24, 31, 49, 64, 124, 126, 207n1, 208n9, 208n12; lipstick 18
Levens, Megan 50
Lévi-Strauss, Claude 182
LGBTQ+ 3, 8, 10–11, 88
libertines 194
libido 167, 171
lifestyle DS 66–67
lighting 30, 47, 103, 162, 168, 180, 190, 195, 208n7
Limon, Iyari 10
Lin, Wendy *163*, 167, 170–171
Lincoln 40
Lindemann, Danielle J. 42, 44
Lindhome, Riki 38, 181, 199, 201
Lionsgate 159
"little death" (orgasm) 103
Little Nemo in Slumberland 176
Loki 36, 53, 55, 59
London, Jack 120
loneliness 145–146, 175
long shot 168
Lorne 18
Los Alamos, New Mexico 159
"Love Dares You" 50
love triangle 135
loyalty 112, 119, 122
Luchkov 52–53, 55
lullaby 21, 37, 53, 55–60, 106, 110
lycanthropy 118–120, 122, 125
Lynda (Van der Klok) 157

MacArthur, General Douglas 171
Macnamara, Colonel 125
macrophilia 128
Madame B 107
Magill, David 66
Magneto 100
Maher, Sean 38, 72, 181, 186
maid (virgin) 191–192
Makinen, Merja 80–81
making out 167, 169, 174–176
Mame 144
mammal 133
mane 130
Manhattan Project 100
Manifesta 15
mare 152
Margaret 186
marijuana 35, 158, 201
Marks, Laura U. 208*n*6
marriage 12, 34, 62, 64, 66–67, 72, 74–76, 112, 136, 159, 179–181, 183–184, 186–188, 191–193, 198, 203
Marsters, James 10, 207*n*2
Marston, William Moulton 209*ch*1*n*2
Marti (*Hell Night*) 165
Martin, Laura 96, 102–103
Marty 11, 34, 157–158, 161, 165–167, 170–171, 173–176
martyrdom 181
Marvel Studios 35
Marvel's The Avengers see *The Avengers* (film)
masculinity 11–12, 15, 29, 33–34, 37, 42–43, 82, 118, 132, 135, 137, 141–145, 155–156, 164–166, 170–172, 174–175, 184–185, 188, 192–196, 201; complicit 33, 137, 144, 148–150; hegemonic 11, 33, 42–43, 137, 143–144, 146–155, 165, 170, 172, 175–176; marginalized 137, 144, 152–153; oppositional 43, 144, 155; primitive 153; queer 34, 135, 137, 152; subordinate 33, 137, 144, 148, 150–151; toxic 34, 137, 155
masks 142, 152, 193–194
masochism 23, 25, 43, 49, 75, 85, 116, 147, 164, 194, 197, 208*n*1; *see also* BDSM; sadomasochism
masquerade 82, 193
Masterpiece Theater 130
masturbation 27, 78, 85, 97
Mathis, Cori 45
matriarchy 161
Matthews, Brett 79, 209*ch*2*n*1
May, Melinda 7, 40
McAvan, Em 18
McCay, Winsor 176
McCoy, Hank 104
McCracken, Allison 20
McDonald, Lindsey 19
McGee, Masani 53, 105
McGowan, Todd 23–25, 207*n*6
McRuer, Robert 88–90
meat 117, 133
mechanic 61, 63, 80–84

medical model (disability theory) 89
Il Medico della Peste 193
Mediterranean 179
Men, Women, and Chainsaws 34
menstruation 119, 154
Meredith, Rowan 27
Messerschmidt, James 143–144, 155
Messina, Sicily 179, 182–188, 191, 193, 200
metaphysics 112–113, 115, 123
metaslasher film 159
#MeToo 3, 203–206, 210*ch*6*n*1
Metz, Christian 22
Metz, Jerry 168–170
MGM (Metro-Goldwyn-Mayer) 159
Middle Boy 158, 174
Miletski, Hani 118
military/scientific complex 125
Miller, D.A. 141–142
mind control 36, 205
minions 158, 199
minorities, sexual 8, 12–14, 38, 88, 117
Miranda (planet) 74
mirror, one-way 172, **173**
mirror stage 23, 43, 45–46, 51, 58, 91, 195, 208*n*6; queer 141
mise-en-scène 37, 52, 66, 152, 180
misgendering 132
misogyny 11, 93, 147–148, 170, 185, 205
missionary position 98, 107
Mr. Pointy award 3, 6–7, 19, 205
Mistress 49, 57, 121, 196–198
Mitchell, David T. 90–92
Mitchell, Luke 40
Mjolnir 147
Moist 135, 137, 140–142, 144, 151–152, 155
Moline, Karl 128
Mollen, Jenny 112
money 70, 144, 149
monitors 159, 164, 168, 172
monogamy 10, 12, 27, 61, 69–70, 158, 166–167; serial 146
Monroe 125
monsters 35, 45, 48, 53, 56, 58, 92–93, 104, 109, 124–125, 157, 160–162, 164, 166, 168, 170, 174; of the id 161, 176
monstrosity, queer 166
moon 77, 120, 122, 127
moose 174
morality 12, 19, 64, 86, 112, 124, 159, 161, 180, 191
Morgese, Jillian 37–38, 181, 190–191, **192**, 210*ch*7*n*2
Morrison, Grant 102, 208*n*10
Moss, Paige 112
mother-penis 78
mothers 14–15, 21, 43–44, 55, 57, 73, 78, 86, 120, 133, 183, 208*n*6
Motion Picture Association of America 160
motorbike 171
mounts 114
Much Ado About Nothing (film) 7, 11, 35, 37, 178–202

Much Ado About Nothing (play) 37, 178–189, 198–199
Mudders 79
Mukherjea, Ananya 17, 113
Mulvey, Laura 22, 25–26, 43, 161–162, 164, 168, 172
mummy 127
musical 5, 45–46, 135–155, 209*ch*5*n*1; "book" 210*ch*5*n*2; concept 138; film 7, 33–34, 137–141, 147, 149, 210*n*3; theater 33, 37, 136, 138–142
mutants 89–93, 97, 99–100, 102, 104
mutiny 124–125
muzzle 200
"My Eyes" 138
"My Freeze Ray" 141, 149
Myers, Michael 156

Nadkarni, Samira 28
Name-of-the-Father 43–44, 55–57
Nandi 68, 70
narcissism 69
Nazi party 100
necktie 198
necrophilia 167
Neely, Carol Thomas 185–186, 198
negotiation 3, 19, 46, 66, 69, 71, 79, 87, 96–98, 119, 150, 180–182, 184, 192, 194, 199
Nelson, Andrew Patrick 168
nerd 143, 147, 154
network television, American 9–10, 16, 18, 30, 49, 62, 123, 135, 209*ch*2*n*3
neuroses 171
New Mexico State University 6
"New Moon Rising" 14, 123, 125, 134
New Right 12
New X-Men 208*n*10
Newmahr, Staci 42
nieces 185, 191
A Nightmare on Elm Street 156, 158
nineteenth century 72–73, 78, 83, 100
Niska, Adlai 66–67
No Power in the 'Verse 86
nonphallic sexuality 162
non-reproductive sexuality 20, 37, 54, 89, 93, 108–109, 116
Norden, Martin 91
Novy, Marianne 187, 189
Noxon, Marti 11, 14, 45, 47, 122–123
nudity 2, 70, 83–84, 86, 97–98, 104, 122–123, 128, 130, 167–168, 172
nursing 133

oath 200
object: fetish 26, 63, 78–81; sexual 13, 63, 149, 153
objectification 31, 35, 146–147, 150, 153, 175, 204–205
"Objects in Space" 77, 83–85
objet petit a 24–25, 48, 75, 208*n*8
Och, Dana 168, 170–171

Oedipal complex 43–44, 55, 57–58, 157, 166, 177
Olivia **32**, 33
Olsen, Elizabeth 107
"Once More with Feeling" 6, 26, 45, 210*ch*5*n*2
one-night stands 153
ontology 112
Open Hand party 209*ch*3*n*2
the Operative 74
Oppenheimer, Dr. J. Robert 100
Ord 98
orgasm 81, 83, 88, 96–98, 103
Ortmann, David 57
the Other 25, 55
"Our Mrs. Reynolds" 65–66, 75, 78–79, 86
"Out of Gas" 81
Outer Limits 12–13, 17, 38, 54, 64, 131
Oz (werewolf) 10, 17, 112–127, 130–134

packs 112, 116
paedophilia 131
page layout 30, 128
pain 24, 99, 121, 148, 150, 154, 164, 166
panels (comic books) 2, 50, 70, **71**, 84, 86, 97–98, 100, 102–103, 128, 131, 145, 151, 154, 209*ch*1*n*3, 209*ch*3*n*2; composition of 30, 128; full-width 70, 96, 98, 103; vertical 104
panties 85, 169
parallelism 138, 146, 192, 197, 200
Parrish, Jaclyn 34, 166, 171
part objects 26
Pascale, Amy 142, 145
Pasco, Richard 199
paternity 183
pathology 44, 142
patriarchal dividend 144
patriarchy 13, 22, 35, 41–42, 52, 60, 62, 73–74, 93, 109–110, 144, 157, 161, 166, 172, 174, 176, 178, 180–184, 188, 193–196
Paul (Ballard) 29
Pender, Patricia 8, 15
penetration 29, 37, 88, 97, 107, 157, 166
Penikett, Tahmoh 29
penis 78, 135, 141, 147, 153, 161–162, 165, 197
penis envy 160
Penny 33–34, 135–155
"Penny's Song" 146
Pepper Spray 154
performance 35–36, 69, 86, 88, 105, 142, 144, 147–148, 201
Peristere, Loni 78
perversions 24, 64, 72, 153–154
phallic woman 166
phallus 24, 41, 78, 80, 141, 147, 162, 165, 174, 182–183, 189, 194
Phantom of the Opera 210*n*3
pharmacopeia 170
phasing 89, 93–99, **95**
pheromones 167–168
phone sex 151
picket line 135

Index

Pink Pummeler 152, 155
Piotrowska, Agnieska 207n6
pistols 80, 189
Place for Us 141
plague doctor 193
play (BDSM) 43, 55; party 154
play-slavery 7, 28–29
pleasure 2–3, 12–13, 15, 25, 35, 52, 61, 66, 85–86, 88, 160–161, 166–169, 172, 186, 189, 194, 200, 208n8
pluralism, sexual 9, 12–13, 38, 61, 64, 83–84, 89
political economy 185
politics, sexual 13, 34, 36, 64, 117, 155–156, 159
polyamory 51, 70
polymorphous perversity 16, 61, 63, 72, 76–77
popular culture 1, 5, 20, 22, 87, 90, 93, 177
pornography 13
Porter, Heather M. 64
Post-Theory 22
posthumanism 113, 115
postmodernism 6, 115, 159
potency, sexual 114, 162, 200
power exchange 39, 58, 114
Powers, Mistress Lorelei 57
prayer 168
praying mantis 127
pregnancy 6, 75, 77, 108, 162
presence 189
princes 146, 189, 198
The Princess Bride 198
privacy 105, 167
promiscuity 12, 158
props 37, 180
prosthesis 89–91, 101, 105; narrative 90, 103
prostitution 13, 28, 69; *see also* sex work
protagonists 148, 157–159, 161, 163, 165, 208n11
Pryde, Kitty 11, 20, 30, 89–99, **95**, 101, 104, 107, 110, 208n11, 209ch3n1, 209ch3n2
psychoanalysis 21–25, 43, 63, 72, 76, 78, 85, 140, 148, 156–157, 160–166, 171, 208n6; evil 171; *see also* Freud, Sigmund; Lacan, Jacques
psychology 9, 22, 34, 37, 39, 55, 70, 72, 76, 91, 102, 104, 135, 143, 153, 160, 182, 201, 203
puberty 114
public service announcement 154
puppeteers 176
puppets 176
Puritan 157–158, 161

queer 3, 5–6, 8–14, 17–18, 20, 24, 29–31, 34, 38, 48, 64, 88–89, 100, 108, 120, 123, 126, 130–131, 135–138, 141–144, 148, 151–155, 165, 166, 205, 207n1, 207n3, 208n9
queer straight *see* straight queer
queer theory 13

Rabb, J. Douglas 180
Rao, Dr. Kavita 100
rape 28, 47–49, 84, 152–153, 160, 204, 207n2, 210ch6n1; date 205; statutory 16

rape culture 20, 48, 147, 152–153
Rasputin, Peter 11, 20, 30, 89, 93–99, **95**, 104, 107, 209ch3n1; *see also* Colossus
rationality 56, 113, 115
reaction-formation 76
Reagan, Nancy 157
Reagan, Ronald 156
Real 21–26, 43–50, 55–58, 96, 103, 121, 135, 137–138, 149, 150, 208n7
realism 9, 31, 87, 166
red 47, 89, 101–104, 121, 142, 146, 150, 162
Red Room 107
redhead 101
rednecks 161, 168
Reiner, Rob 198
reluctance, sexual 34, 36, 119, 164, 166, 173–174
Renner, Jeremy 36
Rent 136, 155
REO Speedwagon 164
repression 22, 72, 74, 91, 142, 157, 160–161, 166, 171, 174, 176
reprosexuality 12, 54–55, 63, 76, 89, 109, 136, 162, 174
residuals 135
"Rest in Peace" 26, 45–46
"Restless" 56, 207n1
"Retreat" 125, 130
retroactive continuity 126
return of the repressed 160, 171
Reynolds, Malcolm 27, 61–63, 66–70, **71**, 74, 79–82, 84, 86
Richards, Amy 15
Richardson, Alan 72
Richardson, J. Michael 180
riders 114, 128
Rieser, Klaus 170
Riggs, Miriam 14, 119
Riley (Finn) 23, 26, 56, 96, 123–125, 133
Ripley, Lieutenant Ellen 170
River (Tam) 27, 61, 63, 72–78, 80, 84, 86, 131, 209ch2n3
Roberson, Chris 86
Robin 142
The Rocky Horror Picture Show 136, 155
Rogers, Ginger 149
roleplaying 57
Romanoff, Natasha 11–12, 20–21, 35–37, 40, 43–44, **52**, 54–59, 87, 89, 91, 93, 104–110, 209ch1n2; *see also* Black Widow
Romantic literature 72–73, 75–76
Rome 153
Rosemont, Romy 199
Rosenberg, Alyssa 56
Rosenberg, Willow *see* Willow (Rosenberg)
Roth, Eli 159
Rotten Tomatoes 35, 37
Royal Shakespeare Company 178
Rubin, Gayle 12–13, 17, 38, 54, 64, 69, 89, 131, 182
ruby quartz visor 91, 100–101, 104

238 Index

Rucker, Rudy 209*ch*3*n*1
Ruffalo, Mark 56, **92**
Runaways 5, 10, 31, 208*n*12
Russo, Anthony 12, 40
Russo, Joe 12, 40

Sacramento State University 7
sadism 25–26, 36, 66, 160–169, 172, 175, 194, 208*ch*1*n*1; *see also* sadomasochism
sadomasochism 12–13, 25, 157, 164, 166, 208*ch*1*n*1; *see also* masochism; sadism
"Safe" 73–74, 81, 86
safeword 47
Saffron 68, 86
Saint Francis of Assisi 86
St. Louis, Renee 14, 119, 127, 205
Santa Monica, California 179
sapience 133
Satsu 11, 31, 98
Saunders, Dr. 28
Saw 159
Saxey, Esther 16
scabbard 189
Scarlett Witch 107
scene composition 37, 180
Scholar archetype 158
Schultz, Lauren 14, 28
science fiction 2, 68, 72–73, 136, 154, 161; convention 154
science, mad 93, 145
Scoobies 10, 49, 51, 119–120, 125, 132
scopophilia 26, 35, 161, 167–168, 172
Scream 159
screams 159, 162, 168
Screen Actor's Guild 209*ch*5*n*1
screen animal 118
screenplay 179, 188
screenwriters 5, 135
scythe 174
Seal of Danthazar 127
secret identity 137, 149
Sedgwick, Eve Kosofsky 14, 33, 140–141, 182–183, 197, 210*ch*7*n*1
seduction 38, 121, 123, 130, 132, 141, 147, 169, 175, 182, 200
"Seeing Red" 47–48, 207*n*2
sensuality 63, 76–77, 81
Serenity (comic books) 61, 68, **71**, 75, 79, 82, **83**, 209*ch*2*n*1
Serenity (film) 61–63, 74, 83
Serenity (ship) 27, 39, 61, 63–64, 67, 70, 74, 76–78, 81–84, 86
set design 37, 180
Sex and the Slayer 8
sex/death equation 176
sex radicals 12–13, 64
sex scenes 9, 18, 47, 184
sex therapy 88, 97
sex toys 83
sex trafficking 28
sex wars 12–13

sex work 5, 8–9, 11, 26–28, 38, 62, 69–70, 96, 145; *see also* prostitution
sexism 133, 205
sexton 199
sexual cultures 9–10, 14, 38, 64, 76, 84, 86–89, 176
Sexual Rhetoric in the Works of Joss Whedon 8
Shadow Men 41
Shakespeare, Tom 108
Shakespeare, William 7, 37, 178–190, 194, 196–198, 201–202, 210*ch*7*n*1
shame 2, 57, 69, 88, 103–104, 141, 155, 189
Shan Yu 66
Shane 79
Sharman, Jim 136
Shaviro, Steven 208*n*6
Shepherds (preachers) 86
Shildrick, Margrit 91, 93
"Shindig" 11, 82
shippers 45
Shirk, Stacy 155
shrew 188–189
siblings 27, 61–63, 72–76, 131, 161, 209*ch*2*n*2, 209*ch*5*n*1
sidekicks 135, 140–142, 151
Siebers, Tobin 87–89
Sierra 28
silhouette 102–103
Silverman, Kaja 22, 26, 43
Simon (Tam) 27, 61–62, 72–77, 81–84, 86, 131, 209*ch*2*n*3
Simula, Brandy L. 42
sin 85, 149
Singer, Bryan 91–92
Singer, Peter 113, 115, 117
sissy 150, 165
sisters 61–63, 72–75, 107, 112, 126, 131, 133, 196; in law 199
Sitterson 35, 157, 159, 162, **163**, 166–169, 172
sixteenth century 178, 188
Skolimowski, Jerzy 52
Skrulls 31
Skywalker, Luke 73
slap fight 201
slash fiction 45
slasher films 9, 34–35, 156–177, 179; postmodern 159
slavery, sexual 145
Slayage (conference) 7, 19, 203, 205
Slayage (journal) 6, 8
Slayers 10, 15, 24, 31, **32**, 41, 45, 50, 125, 127–128, 207*n*4; potential 127, 136; Primal 41, 56
"Slipping" 147
Slotkin, Richard 79–80
slut 167
Smith, Angela 92
Smith, Mere 28
Snow White 146
Snyder, Daniel 53
Snyder, Sharon L. 90–92
"So They Say" 146, 153

Index 239

social justice 138, 145
social model (disability theory) 19, 87, 92
sociology 33, 42, 146, 158
Sokovia 110
"Something to Sing About" 46
Sondheim, Stephen 136, 138, 210*ch*5*n*3
sonnets 183, 198
souls 16, 20–21, 40, 48–51, 115, 197, 207*n*2, 208*n*8
sound 26, 47, 137–138, 145
Southwest Popular/American Culture Association 1, 7
Spaise, Terry 44
species 113–118, 122, 126, 131, 134, 209*ch*4*n*1
speciesism 115, 152
spectatorship 22, 157, 160, 164–165, 172; *see also* audience
speech 23, 56, 75, 113, 117, 198
sperm donor 126
Spike 6, 10–11, 13, 18–26, **32**, 39–40, 43–52, 56, 140, 207*n*2
splash page 140
split screen 138
sports 143
Sprott, Richard 57
Spuffy 45
"A Spy in the House of Love" 28
stage 141–142, 186, 190, 196
Staite, Jewel 11
stale 185
stalker films 156; *see also* slasher films
stallions 114, 153
Stanton, Harry Dean 105
Star Wars 73
Stark, Tony **92**, 93, 105
Stark Tower 107
stash, secret 158
Stearns, Lee 15
steel 93, 95, 98, 107, 189–191
Steele, Valerie 78
Steeves, George 79
stereotypes 10, 70, 80, 87, 89, 91–92, 95, 105, 107, 119, 121, 124, 174–175
sterility 20, 37, 54, 93, 109
stigma 12, 16, 94, 103, 110, 117–118, 141
Stokes, Jasie 168
Stonewall 13, 144
Story, Karl **71**
"Storyteller" 6, 11, 130
straight 6, 10, 18–20, 27, 120, 130–131, 133, 135–136, 138, 142, 144–149, 152, 176, 207*n*1
straight queer 6, 14, 64
strange sex 143–144
Stratford, England 199
strawberry 81
Strickland (firearm brand) 80
strike (labor) 33, 135
structuralism 115
studio system 136
sublimation 85
submission 28, 39–40; female 33, 37–38, 49, 66–68, 107, 123, 180–182, 187–188, 190–192, 194, 199–201; male 20–21, 24–25, 30, 35–37, 42–62, 65–68, 100, 103, 107, 114, 132, 180–181, 183, 185–187, 189, 192–194, 196–198, 201, 209*ch*1*n*2; *see also* BDSM; dominance/submission
subtext 10, 16, 18, 27, 61, 74, 141, 148
suicide 3, 103
Sumerau, J. 42
Summers, Buffy *see* Buffy (Summers)
Summers, Dawn *see* Dawn (Summers)
Summers, Joyce 208*n*7
Summers, Scott 11, 20, 30, 39–40, 89–91, 99–105, **101**, 107, 108, 110, 205, 208*n*10
Sun Tzu 66
Sunnydale, California 56, 123, 125, 207*n*3
sunset 56, 123
superego 44, 54, 57–59, 161, 171, 176; cultural 22; maternal 55
Superhero Memorial Bridge 152
superheroes 7, 11, 20, 30, 33–37, 39–40, 58, 87–111, 135–136, 141–145, 147–148, 151, 155, 208*n*9, 209*ch*1*n*2, 210*ch*5*n*2
Superman 141
supervillains 33, 135–138, 141, 144, 149–150, 152, 155, 210*ch*5*n*2
Sutherland, Sharon 27
Sweeney Todd 136, 210*ch*5*n*3
switch (BDSM) 46–47, 49–50, 53, 68, 121, 123, 181, 191, 209*ch*1*n*2
sword 196
Symbolic 21, 23–26, 43–50, 55–58, 96, 103, 121, 198
sympathy 190, 210*ch*5*n*3
System Purge button 166

taboos 44, 75, 113
Takei, George 131
"Taking Ownership" 51, 133
Tam, River *see* River (Tam)
Tam, Simon *see* Simon (Tam)
Tancharoen, Maurissa 11, 153, 155, 199
Tara (Maclay) 10, 17–19, 25, 31, 48, 122–125, 207*n*1, 297*n*3
taxidermy 167
technicians 35, 159, 161–163, 166–169, 171
"techno marvel" trope 91
Teen Wolf 114
"teen wolf" trope 118–119, 121, 124
teenagers 30, 35, 126, 156, 208*n*11
teenie-kill pics 156, 161; *see also* slasher films
telepathy 30, 89, 96, 99–104, 208*n*10
tequila 164
"Terrible Child" trope 160–161
territory, sexual 183
The Texas Chain Saw Massacre 161
texting 151
theater 33, 142, 187, 189
Thompson, Sarah 19
Thor 59, 147, 171
Thor: Ragnarok 59–60

240 Index

Thoroughbred of Sin 149; *see also* Bad Horse
thought balloons 30, 145
A Thousand Plateaus 116
Thricewise 128
Tibet 125
"Time of Your Life" 2, 128, 205
Titan 2, 130
tolerance, sexual 13, 18, 64, 75, 78
tomb 190
tomboy 165
tongues 49, 188
Tony award 136
tools 78, **83**, 84, 162–163; corporate 146–147
Topher 11, 19, 145
Torres, Gina **65**, 67
torture 25, 48, 52, 66, 80, 103, 124, 158–162, 168, 190
torture porn 159–160
Towelettes 151
Trachtenberg, Michelle 112
traffic in women 182–183, 188, 194
Trans-Exclusive Radical Feminist (TERF) 31
transgender erasure 38
transgender sexuality 5, 10, 26, 29, 31, 208*n*12
transgender woman 31, 208*n*12
transgression 34, 157–160, 163, 166–167
transplants 19
transsexuals 64
Traub, Valerie 185, 188
trauma 23, 26, 44–49, 76, 108, 156, 208*n*7
Trendacosta, Katharine 57
Tresca, Don 8, 14, 16–17, 148, 208*n*12
triangulation, homoerotic 140–141
tropes 33, 36–37, 56, 118–120, 132, 136, 138, 156, 161, 167, 170, 176, 178–179
trust 9, 12–13, 21, 28–29, 38–39, 49, 58, 60, 66, 100, 106, 126, 134, 192, 200, 206, 207*n*2
truth or dare 167
Tudyk, Alan 62
twentieth century 13, 72–73, 78, 83, 100, 108, 114–117, 136, 138, 207*n*5, 209ch3*n*1
twenty-first century 23, 41–42, 72, 90, 135, 142–144, 159, 179, 184, 188
Twilight (villain) 125
Tyrer, Ben 207*n*6

Ultron 56, 58, 93, 107, 110
unconscious 96
underwear 169; *see also* panties
unionism 136
University of British Columbia 19
University of North Alabama 7, 203
Urbanoia 161
Ursula 197
utilitarianism 117
utopia 26, 39, 134, 177, 207*n*3

vagina dentata 162
Vallejo, Boris 132
vampires 18, 32, 37, 51, 121, 124
Vancouver, British Columbia 19

vanilla 46, 55, 58, 154
Varley, John 2, 130
vengeance 127, 189
Venice, Italy 193
Vera (gun) 61, 78–80, 86
Verges 182, 201
the 'verse 63, 68–69, 72, 75, 77
Veruca 112, 122–123, 125
Vi 136
vibrators 82–83
victim-hero 163; *see also* Final Girl
Victor 29
villain sex 199
Virgin archetype 159
virginity 121, 127, 159, 166, 169–170, 184
"Visual Pleasure and Narrative Cinema" 25
visuality, haptic 208*n*6
voice 25
voice-over 30, 82, 103–104, 131
von Frankenstein, Elizabeth 73
von Frankenstein, Viktor 73, 92–93
von Krafft-Ebing, Richard 78, 80
voyeurism 26, 161–162, 164, 168–169, 172

Waggoner, Erin B. 8
Waititi, Taika 59
Walsh, Professor Maggie 26
Wan, James 159
"War Stories" 27, 66–69, 78
Warner, Michael 13, 143, 155, 207*n*3
Warren (Mears) 145, 205
warrior woman 65–67
Wash (Hoban Washburne) 27, 39, 61–64, 67–68, 77–79, 81, 85–86, 205
Washburne, Hoban *see* Wash
Washburne, Zoë *see* Zoë (Washburne)
watchmen 201
WB network 207*n*1
weapons, nuclear 159
Weaver, Sigourney 157, 170
Web, World Wide 135
Webber, Andrew Lloyd 210*n*3
wedgies 150
Weinberg, Martin S. 117
Weinstein, Harvey 204
Wen, Ming-Na 40
werewolves 10–11, 17, 112–125
Wesleyan University 8, 15, 79, 204, 209ch2*n*1
West, American 72
West Point 208*n*9
Western (genre) 26, 61, 79–80
Whaley, Katherine 19
Whedon, Jed 11, 135–136
Whedon, Squire 192
Whedon, Zack 11, 27, 62, 70–71, 135, 209ch2*n*1
Whedon Studies 2–3, 7–8, 11, 20, 203
Whedommes 7, 21, 27, 30, 33, 35, 38, 39–60, 62, 65, 106, 132, 155, 182, 200–201
Whedonverses 1–3, 5, 7–14, 19–22, 24, 28–29, 31, 38–40, 47, 61–62, 69–70, 121, 135, 142, 179, 204–205

Index

wheelchairs 91, 102
"When You're My Slave" 145
White, Barry 121
Whitford, Bradley 35, 157, **163**
Whore archetype 158, 167
whorehouse *see* brothel
"Why 100,000,000 Americans Read Comics" 209*ch*1*n*2
Wicca 122, 128
Wilcox, Fred 161
Wilcox, Rhonda 37, 47, 49, 179, 190, 197
"Wild at Heart" 122
Wilkerson, Abby 88
William (Pratt) 51
Williams, Colin J. 117
Williams, Jesse 34, 158, **173**
Williams, Linda 162, 164, 172
Williams, Tony 170
Williamson, Milly 45
Willis, Victoria 145, 148
Willow (Rosenberg) 9–10, 14, 17–19, 26, 31, **32**, 45, 49–51, 99, 114–115, 118–126, 128, 131–132, 207*n*1, 207*n*3
Wilts, Alissa 18
wimp 143, 150
Winchester College 178
The Winter Solider 12
Witchcraft 122
witches 32, 107, 115, 118, 121–122, 126–127, 132
wives 6, 11, 14, 61, 66–67, 108, 125, 136, 174, 179, 187, 189, 193, 198, 203, 210*ch*6*n*1
The Wiz 144
Woerner, Meredith 57
Wolf, Stacy 138, 141
Wolfe, Cary 116
Wolfram and Hart 19
Wolk, Douglas 142
wolves 112, 114–115, 118–120, 122–127, 167, 174

womb envy 93, 160
Wonder Woman 65, 209*ch*1*n*2
Wonderflonium 145, 149
Wood, Robin (film scholar) 156–157, 160–161, 171
Wood, Robin (vampire hunter) 49
Woodside, D.B. 49
Woofter, Kristopher 168
word balloons 128
working class 82, 105
workplace sex 204
World War II 143
wrench **83**, 84
Wright, Leigh Adams 65
Writer's Guild of America 33, 135, 209*ch*5*n*1

X-Men (comic books) 7, 30, 89–104, 208*n*10
X-Men (film) 91–92
X-Men (superhero team) 40, 89–90, 93, 97, 99, 102–105, 205, 208*n*9, 208*n*10
X-Men 2 (film) 91–92
Xander (Harris) 2, 10–11, 17–19, **32**, 33, 40, 49–50, 114–115, 118–121, 123, 126–133, 204–205, 207*n*1, 207*n*4
Xavier, Professor Charles 91, 102, 104
Xavin 31, 208*n*12

Yes Means Yes 210*ch*6*n*1

Zeus 118
Žižek, Slavoj 22–26, 55, 207*n*6
Zoë (Washburne) 7, 27, 39, 61–68, **65**, 71, 75–82, 85–86
zombies 161, 165–166, 168, 176
zoophilia 2, 5, 10, 17, 112–134, 153, 167
zoosexuality 115, 118
Zynda, Lyle 76

www.ingramcontent.com/pod-product-compliance
Ingram Content Group UK Ltd.
Pitfield, Milton Keynes, MK11 3LW, UK
UKHW041939140426
5217IPUK00014B/561